Oxford
Puzzle Solver

Edited by
Catherine Soanes
with
Bernadette Mohan

This book has been printed digitally and produced in a standard specification in order to ensure its continuing availability

OXFORD
UNIVERSITY PRESS

Great Clarendon Street, Oxford OX2 6DP

Oxford University Press is a department of the University of Oxford. It furthers the University's objective of excellence in research, scholarship, and education by publishing worldwide in

Oxford New York

Auckland Cape Town Dar es Salaam Hong Kong Karachi Kuala Lumpur Madrid Melbourne Mexico City Nairobi New Delhi Shanghai Taipei Toronto

With offices in

Argentina Austria Brazil Chile Czech Republic France Greece Guatemala Hungary Italy Japan South Korea Poland Portugal Singapore Switzerland Thailand Turkey Ukraine Vietnam

Oxford is a registered trade mark of Oxford University Press in the UK and in certain other countries

Published in the United States by Oxford University Press Inc., New York

Reprinted 2009

ISBN 978-0-19-280712-0

Contents

Foreword

This brand-new edition of the *Oxford Puzzle Solver* will be invaluable for all those who like to amuse themselves and exercise their minds doing word games, puzzles, quizzes, and quick crosswords. Based on data from the Oxford Dictionaries Department and the world's largest language research programme, it consists of over 300 themed lists, covering everything from titles of well-known films and musicals and kinds of pasta and cheese to characters from popular fiction and names of famous football clubs, as well as all the more obvious lists of famous people, places, and all things animal, vegetable or mineral.

All this material has been selected and edited with the needs of the typical solver (or for that matter the setter) of popular word puzzles in mind. To make it as user-friendly as possible, the *Oxford Puzzle Solver* has organized its entries into fourteen main subject categories (for example, Famous People, Food and Drink, Science and Technology). Each of these main sections contains a number of thematic sections (such as Actors, Architects, and Presidents of the USA), which appear in alphabetical order. Each of these thematic sections is in turn broken down into subsections: in general, single-word items are listed first, by word length and then alphabetically, then multi-word items by the number of words in the item and in alphabetical order. Single-word entries are from 2 to 13 letters long, while multi-word items are from 2 to 6 words long, and up to 26 letters in all.

So if you are on the track of, for example, the actor Robert De Niro, you should first look at the main 'Famous People' section, and within that section, under 'A' for 'Actors'; as his surname is a two-word one, you would then need to go to the 'multiple word' section and you will find him listed after Daniel Day-Lewis. There are two further ways to help you find your way around the book: the list of contents at the front provides a list of all the thematic sections in page order, while the handy index at the end of the book lists all sections, sub-sections, and helpful pointers towards sections in alphabetical order.

Taken with its companion title, the *Oxford Crossword Dictionary*, the *Oxford Puzzle Solver* should provide all the information you need to solve a wide range of popular puzzles, crosswords, and other word games. The *Oxford Puzzle Solver* might also serve as a work of reference to settle the odd factual argument, as it gives you extra information such as the dates and nationalities of famous people, the capitals of countries and states, and the dates of wars and battles.

Hugh Stephenson
Crossword Editor
The Guardian

Animals, plants, and farming

Amphibians

1 WORD

axolotl
bullfrog
frog
newt
salamander
toad

2 WORDS

cane toad
fire salamander
flying frog
horned toad
marsh frog
natterjack toad
tree frog

Birds

1 WORD

2 LETTERS

ou

3 LETTERS

auk
emu
hen
jay
moa
owl
tit
tui

4 LETTERS

chat
coot
crow
dodo
dove
duck
gull
hawk
ibis
kagu
kite
kiwi
knot
lark
loon
nene
rail
rhea
rook
ruff
shag
skua
smew
swan
teal
tern
wren

5 LETTERS

booby
crake
crane
diver
eagle
egret
finch
goose
grebe
heron
hobby
macaw
noddy
ouzel
owlet
pipit
quail
raven
robin
scaup
serin
snipe
stork
swift
twite

6 LETTERS

avocet
barbet
bulbul
canary
chough
condor
coucal
cuckoo
curlew
darter
dipper
dunlin

falcon
fulmar
gannet
godwit
grouse
hoopoe
jabiru
jacana
kakapo
lanner
linnet
magpie
martin
merlin
motmot
oriole
osprey
parrot
peewee
peewit
petrel
pigeon
plover
puffin
roller
scoter
shrike
siskin
takahe
thrush
toucan
trogon
turkey
whydah
wigeon
willet

7 LETTERS

antbird
babbler
bittern
bunting
bustard
buzzard
catbird
chicken
cowbird
dunnock
fantail
flicker
gadwall
goshawk
grackle
harrier
hoatzin
jacamar
jackdaw
kestrel
lapwing
mallard
manakin
moorhen
oilbird
ortolan
ostrich
peacock
peafowl
pelican
penguin
pintail
pochard
quetzal
redhead
redpoll
redwing
rosella
seagull
seriema
skimmer
skylark
sparrow
sunbird
swallow
tanager
titlark
vulture
wagtail
warbler
waxbill
waxwing
wrybill
wryneck

8 LETTERS

bellbird
blackcap
bluebird
bobolink
caracara
cardinal
cockatoo
curassow
dabchick
dotterel
flamingo
garganey
grosbeak
hawfinch
hornbill
kingbird
lorikeet
lovebird
lyrebird
megapode
moorcock
moorfowl
nightjar
notornis
nuthatch
ovenbird
oxpecker
parakeet
pheasant
redshank
redstart
ringdove
ringneck
screamer
shelduck
shoebill
shoveler
starling
swiftlet
titmouse
tragopan
wheatear
whimbrel
whinchat
whipbird
whistler
woodchat
woodcock
woodlark

9 LETTERS

albatross
blackbird
bowerbird
brambling
broadbill
bullfinch
cassowary
chaffinch
chickadee
cockatiel
cormorant
corncrake
crossbill
fieldfare
firecrest
francolin
friarbird
frogmouth
gallinule
goldcrest
goldeneye
goldfinch
goosander
guillemot
gyrfalcon
kittiwake
merganser
mousebird
nighthawk
partridge
phalarope
ptarmigan
razorbill
sandpiper
sapsucker
snakebird
spoonbill
stonechat
turnstone

10 LETTERS

budgerigar
canvasback
chiffchaff
flycatcher
greenfinch
greenshank
guineafowl
honeyeater
honeyguide
kingfisher
kookaburra
meadowlark
nutcracker
roadrunner
saddleback
sanderling
shearwater
sheathbill
sunbittern
tailorbird
tropicbird
wattlebird
woodpecker

11 LETTERS

gnatcatcher
hummingbird
lammergeier
mockingbird
nightingale
sparrowhawk
treecreeper
wallcreeper
whitethroat

12 LETTERS

capercaillie
flowerpecker
honeycreeper
umbrellabird
whippoorwill
yellowhammer

13 LETTERS

oystercatcher

2 WORDS

adjutant bird
Arctic tern
bald eagle
barnacle goose
barn owl
bateleur eagle
bee-eater
Bewick's swan
black swan
blue tit
brent goose
brown owl
brush turkey
butcher-bird
Canada goose
carrion crow
coal tit
collared dove
cuckoo-shrike
demoiselle crane
diamond bird
eagle owl
eider duck
emperor penguin
frigate bird
golden eagle
golden plover
great auk
great tit
green woodpecker
greylag goose
griffon vulture
harlequin duck
harpy eagle
Hawaiian goose
hawk owl
hedge sparrow
hen harrier
herring gull
hooded crow
hoot owl
horned owl
house martin
house sparrow
king penguin
laughing jackass
little grebe
little owl
mandarin duck
marabou stork
marsh harrier
mistle thrush

mourning dove
Muscovy duck
mute swan
mutton bird
mynah bird
night heron
peregrine falcon
pilot bird
red kite
reed bunting
reed warbler
rhinoceros bird
rifle bird
ring ouzel
rock dove
ruddy duck
sand martin
scops owl
screech owl
scrub turkey
sea eagle
secretary bird
snow bunting
snow goose
snowy owl
song thrush
stock dove
stone curlew
storm petrel
tawny owl
turkey vulture
turtle dove
tyrant flycatcher
water rail
weaver bird
whooping crane
willow warbler
wood duck
wood pigeon

3 WORDS

bird of paradise
great crested grebe
long-tailed tit

Breeds and types of sheep

1 WORD

Afrikander
aoudad
argali
bharal
bighorn
blackface
broadtail
caracul
Cheviot
Cotswold
Dartmoor
Hebridean
Herdwick
Jacob
karakul
Kent
Leicester
Merino
mouflon
Orkney
Radnor
Rambouillet
Shetland
Soay
Southdown
Suffolk
Swaledale
Teeswater
Texel
Wensleydale

2 WORDS

Barbary sheep
Border Leicester
Clun Forest
Dorset Down
Dorset Horn
Kerry Hill
Romney Marsh
Rough Fell
Scottish Blackface
Welsh mountain

Breeds of cattle

1 WORD

Ayrshire
Charolais
Devon
Durham
Friesian
Galloway
Guernsey
Hereford
Highland
Holstein
Jersey
Kerry
Kyloe

Limousin
longhorn
Mongolian
Shetland
shorthorn

2 WORDS

Aberdeen Angus
South Devon
Texas longhorn
Welsh Black
West Highland

Butterflies and moths

1 WORD

3 LETTERS

pug

4 LETTERS

blue

5 LETTERS

argus
brown
comma
eggar
heath
owlet
swift

6 LETTERS

apollo
burnet
copper
dagger
ermine
lackey
lappet
morpho

7 LETTERS

bagworm
drinker
emerald
emperor
monarch
noctuid
pyralid
ringlet
satyrid
skipper
sulphur
tortrix

8 LETTERS

birdwing
cecropia
cinnabar
geometer
grayling
hawkmoth
milkweed
vapourer

9 LETTERS

brimstone
clearwing
geometrid
nymphalid
prominent
underwing

10 LETTERS

fritillary
gatekeeper
hairstreak
papilionid

11 LETTERS

swallowtail

13 LETTERS

tortoiseshell

2 WORDS

Adonis blue
angle shades
atlas moth
buff-tip
burnished brass
cabbage moth
cabbage white
Camberwell beauty
chalkhill blue
clothes moth
clouded yellow
codling moth
codlin moth
common heath
goat moth
gypsy moth
io moth
leopard moth
lobster moth
luna moth
magpie moth
marbled white
meadow brown
Mother Shipton
mourning cloak
oak eggar
old lady
painted lady
peacock butterfly
peppered moth
plume moth
purple emperor
puss moth

red admiral
silk moth
silver Y
speckled wood
tiger moth
tussock moth
wall brown
wax moth
white admiral
white spot
winter moth
yellow-tail

3 WORDS

death's head hawkmoth
merveille du jour
swallow-tailed moth

Cat breeds

1 WORD

Abyssinian
angora
Birman
Burmese
chinchilla
longhair
Persian
Rex
shorthair
Siamese
Sphynx
tabby
tortoiseshell

2 WORDS

Burmese cat
Maine coon
Manx cat
marmalade cat
Turkish Van

Collective names for animals

3 LETTERS

cry (hounds)
mob (kangaroos)
pod (seals)

4 LETTERS

band (gorillas)
bask (crocodiles)
bevy (roe deer, quails, larks, pheasants)
bury (rabbits)
down (hares)
herd (cattle, elephants)
hive (bees)
knot (toads)
leap (leopards)
pack (hounds, grouse)
safe (ducks)
span (mules)
stud (mares)
trip (goats)
turn (turtles)
yoke (oxen)
zeal (zebras)

5 LETTERS

bloat (hippopotami)
brood (chickens)
charm (finches)
cloud (gnats)
covey (partridges)
crash (rhinoceros)
drove (bullocks)
flock (sheep)
hover (trout)
pride (lions)
shoal (fish)
siege (herons)
skein (geese in flight)
skulk (foxes)
sloth (bears)
stare (owls)
swarm (bees, flies)
troop (baboons)
watch (nightingales)

6 LETTERS

flight (birds)

gaggle (geese)
kennel (dogs)
kindle (kittens)
labour (moles)
litter (kittens, pigs)
murder (crows)
muster (peacocks, penguins)
parade (elephants)
school (whales, dolphins, porpoises)
string (horses)
tiding (magpies)

7 LETTERS

descent (woodpeckers)
rookery (rooks)
turmoil (porpoises)

8 LETTERS

busyness (ferrets)

9 LETTERS

bellowing (bullfinches)
obstinacy (buffalo)

10 LETTERS

exaltation (larks)
parliament (owls)
shrewdness (apes)
unkindness (ravens)

11 LETTERS

murmuration (starlings)
pandemonium (parrots)

Crustaceans

1 WORD

barnacle
crab
crawfish
crayfish
crevette
krill
langouste
langoustine
lobster
prawn
sandhopper
shrimp
woodlouse

2 WORDS

acorn barnacle
edible crab
fairy shrimp
fiddler crab
fish louse
freshwater crayfish
ghost crab
goose barnacle
hermit crab
horseshoe crab
king crab
king prawn
land crab
mitten crab
Norway lobster
opossum shrimp
spider crab
spiny lobster
tiger prawn

Dinosaurs

1 WORD

allosaurus
ankylosaur
apatosaurus
brachiosaurus
brontosaurus
carnosaur
coelurosaur
deinonychus
diplodocus
dromaeosaur
hadrosaur
iguanodon
megalosaurus
pliosaur
protoceratops
pteranodon
pterodactyl
raptor
saurischian

sauropod
seismosaurus
stegosaur
theropod
triceratops
tyrannosaur
tyrannosaurus
velociraptor

3 WORDS

duck-billed dinosaur

Dog breeds

1 WORD

4 LETTERS

chow
peke
puli

5 LETTERS

boxer
corgi
hound
husky
spitz

6 LETTERS

beagle
borzoi
collie
kelpie
poodle
setter

7 LETTERS

bouvier
bulldog
griffon
harrier
mastiff
pointer
redbone
sheltie
spaniel
terrier
whippet

8 LETTERS

Alsatian
cockapoo
foxhound
malamute
papillon
Pekinese
sheepdog

9 LETTERS

chihuahua
coonhound
dachshund
Dalmatian
deerhound
greyhound
retriever
schnauzer
staghound
wolfhound

10 LETTERS

bloodhound
Clydesdale
Pomeranian
Rottweiler
schipperke
Weimaraner

11 LETTERS

labradoodle

12 LETTERS

Newfoundland

13 LETTERS

affenpinscher

2 WORDS

Afghan hound
Airedale terrier
basset hound
bearded collie
Bedlington terrier
bichon frise
Blenheim spaniel
Border collie
Border terrier
bull mastiff
bull terrier
cairn terrier
carriage dog
Clumber spaniel
cocker spaniel
Dandie Dinmont
Dobermann pinscher
elk hound
English setter
English springer
fox terrier
French bulldog
German shepherd
golden retriever
Gordon setter
Great Dane
Irish setter
Irish terrier

Irish wolfhound
Kerry blue
Labrador retriever
Lakeland terrier
Maltese dog
Maltese terrier
Manchester terrier
Norfolk terrier
otter dog
pug dog
red setter
Rhodesian ridgeback
Scottie dog
Scottish terrier
Sealyham terrier
Shar Pei
Shetland sheepdog
shih-tzu
Skye terrier
springer spaniel
St Bernard
Welsh corgi
Welsh hound
Welsh springer
Welsh terrier
Yorkshire terrier

3 WORDS

black and tan
Jack Russell terrier
King Charles spaniel
Old English sheepdog
pit bull terrier
Staffordshire bull terrier
West Highland terrier

Farm workers

1 WORD

4 LETTERS

hind
peon
serf

6 LETTERS

cowboy
cowman
gaucho
grieve
milker
oxherd
pigman
reaper
ringer

7 LETTERS

cowgirl
cowherd
cowpoke
gleaner
herdboy
peasant

8 LETTERS

dairyman
farmhand
goatherd
haymaker
jackaroo
milkmaid
musterer
outrider
ranchero
shedhand
sheepman
shepherd
stockman
thresher
vintager
wrangler

9 LETTERS

cattleman
dairymaid
harvester
ploughman
swineherd

11 LETTERS

shepherdess

2 WORDS

field hand
grape-picker
hop-picker
land girl
station hand

Farming, types of

1 WORD

agribusiness
agriculture
agroforestry
apiculture
aquaculture
arboriculture
biodynamics
crofting
dairying
floriculture
forestry
horticulture
hydroponics
mariculture
monoculture
orcharding
pisciculture
polyculture
pomiculture
sericulture
sharecropping
silviculture
smallholding
viniculture
viticulture

2 WORDS

agro-industry
animal husbandry
arable farming
battery farming
dairy farming
extensive farming
factory farming
fish farming
intensive farming
livestock farming
market gardening
organic farming
share farming
strip cropping
subsistence farming

Fish

1 WORD

3 LETTERS

bib
cod
dab
eel
ide
ray

4 LETTERS

bass
carp
chub
cusk
dace
dory
goby
hake
hoki
huss
ling
mako
orfe
pike
rudd
scad
scat
scup
shad
sole
tope
tuna

5 LETTERS

bleak
bream
brill
charr
coley
fluke
guppy
loach
manta
molly
perch
porgy
roach
ruffe
saury
shark
skate
smelt
snook
sprat
tench
tetra
trout
tunny
wahoo
witch

6 LETTERS

barbel
beluga
blenny

bonito
bowfin
burbot
darter
dorado
gunnel
marlin
minnow
mullet
plaice
salmon
sucker
turbot
weever
whaler
wrasse
zander

7 LETTERS

alewife
anchovy
batfish
bluefin
boxfish
candiru
capelin
catfish
chimera
crappie
dogfish
eelpout
garfish
garpike
gourami
grouper
grunion
gudgeon
gurnard
haddock
halibut
herring
hogfish
houting
icefish
jewfish
lamprey
lingcod
mudfish
oarfish
oilfish
piranha
pollack
pollock
pomfret
pompano
redfish
sardine
sawfish
sculpin
sevruga
skipper
snapper
spurdog
sterlet
sunfish
tilapia
vendace
walleye
whiting

8 LETTERS

albacore
arapaima
bandfish
billfish
blowfish
bluefish
boarfish
bonefish
brisling
bullhead
coalfish
filefish
flatfish
flathead
flounder
frogfish
goatfish
goldfish
grayling
halfbeak
kingfish
lungfish
mackerel
monkfish
moonfish
pickerel
pilchard
pipefish
rockling
sailfish
sandfish
sparling
stingray
sturgeon
tarwhine
thresher
toadfish
trevally
weakfish

9 LETTERS

amberjack
angelfish
argentine
barracuda
blackfish
clingfish
clownfish
globefish
goosefish
grenadier
killifish
megamouth
mudminnow
pikeperch
pilotfish
porbeagle
snipefish
spearfish
stargazer
stonefish
swordfish
swordtail
thornback
threadfin
trunkfish
whitebait
whitefish
wobbegong
yellowfin

10 LETTERS

anglerfish

archerfish
barracouta
barramundi
bitterling
bonnethead
butterfish
candlefish
coelacanth
damselfish
dragonfish
guitarfish
hammerhead
lumpsucker
mudskipper
needlefish
paddlefish
parrotfish
rabbitfish
ribbonfish
sheepshead
shovelhead
silverside
yellowtail

11 LETTERS

balloonfish
hatchetfish
lanternfish
muskellunge
stickleback
surgeonfish
triggerfish

12 LETTERS

scorpionfish

13 LETTERS

leatherjacket

2 WORDS

allis shad
anemone fish
angel shark
basking shark
blue shark
brown trout
butterfly fish
butterfly ray
carpet shark
chum salmon
climbing perch
conger eel
crucian carp
devil ray
Dover sole
eagle ray
electric eel
electric ray
fighting fish
flying fish
flying gurnard
grey mullet
gulper eel
horse mackerel
humpback salmon
John Dory
koi carp
labyrinth fish
lake trout
lemon sole
moray eel
nurse hound
nurse shark
porcupine fish
puffer fish
rainbow trout
red mullet
red snapper
rock bass
salmon trout
sand eel
sand shark
sea bass
sea bream
sea horse
sea perch
sea robin
sea trout
shark-sucker
skipjack tuna
smooth hound
snake mackerel
sockeye salmon
tiger shark
whale shark
wolf fish

3 WORDS

great white shark

Flower parts

3 LETTERS

lip

4 LETTERS

cyme
spur

5 LETTERS

calyx
glume
lemma
ovary
ovule
palea
petal
sepal
spike
style
tepal
torus
umbel
whorl

6 LETTERS

anther
carpel
catkin
corymb
floret
pistil
pollen
raceme
rachis
spadix
spathe
stamen
stigma
tassel

7 LETTERS

corolla
nectary
panicle
pedicel

8 LETTERS

filament
nucellus
peduncle
perianth
placenta
spikelet

9 LETTERS

capitulum

10 LETTERS

receptacle

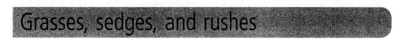

Grasses, sedges, and rushes

1 WORD

3 LETTERS

fog
oat
rye

4 LETTERS

bent
corn
milo
reed
rice
rush

5 LETTERS

brome
carex
chufa
durra
maize
sedge
spelt
wheat

6 LETTERS

bamboo
barley
darnel
fescue
melick
millet

7 LETTERS

bulrush
esparto
foxtail
papyrus
sorghum
timothy

8 LETTERS

dogstail
ryegrass
spartina
spinifex
woodrush

9 LETTERS

bluegrass
cocksfoot
cordgrass
deergrass

2 WORDS

buffalo grass
bunch grass
canary grass
cat's-tail
cheat grass
cotton grass
couch grass
elephant grass
hair grass
lemon grass
marram grass
oat grass
pampas grass
pearl millet
quaking grass
quitch grass
reed mace
sugar cane
tussock grass
twitch grass
umbrella plant
vernal grass
wild oat
wild rice
wire grass
Yorkshire fog

Homes for animals

anthill (ant)
apiary (bee)
aquarium (fish)
aviary (bird)
beehive (bee)
burrow (rabbit)
byre (cow)
coop (poultry)
den (bear, fox, lion)
dovecote (dove)
drey (squirrel)
earth (fox)
eyrie (eagle)
fold (sheep, livestock)
form (hare)
hole (badger, rat)
holt (otter)
kennel (dog)
lodge (beaver)
nest (bird, hornet, mouse, rat, snake, wasp)
pen (pig, sheep)
sett (badger)
stable (horse)
sty (pig)
vespiary (wasp)
warren (rabbit)

Horse and pony breeds

1 WORD

Appaloosa
Arab
barb
Clydesdale
Connemara
Falabella
Haflinger
Hanoverian
hunter
Lipizzaner
mustang
percheron
Shetland
Shire
thoroughbred
trotter

2 WORDS

Cleveland bay
Connemara pony
Dales pony
Dartmoor pony
Exmoor pony
Fell pony
Highland pony
polo pony
Quarter Horse
Shetland pony
shire horse
Suffolk punch

3 WORDS

New Forest pony
Welsh mountain pony

Insects and worms

1 WORD

3 LETTERS

ant
bee
fly

4 LETTERS

flea
gnat
moth
wasp

5 LETTERS

aphid
borer
fluke
leech
louse
midge

6 LETTERS

bedbug
beetle
botfly
chafer
cicada
darter
earwig
gadfly

hawker
hornet
locust
mantis
mayfly
sawfly
sawyer
scarab
thrips
weevil

7 LETTERS

annelid
blowfly
chigger
cricket
cutworm
filaria
firefly
lugworm
sandfly
termite

8 LETTERS

alderfly
blackfly
bookworm
flatworm
greenfly
honeybee
hookworm
horsefly
housefly
hoverfly
lacewing
ladybird
mealworm
mosquito
nematode
stonefly
tapeworm
toxocara
whitefly
wireworm
woodwasp
woodworm

9 LETTERS

anopheles
bloodworm
booklouse
bumblebee
butterfly
cockroach
damselfly
dragonfly
earthworm
roundworm
whirligig

10 LETTERS

bluebottle
cankerworm
cockchafer
froghopper
leafhopper
phylloxera
silverfish
spittlebug
springtail
threadworm
thunderbug
thunderfly
treehopper

11 LETTERS

grasshopper
greenbottle

12 LETTERS

groundhopper

13 LETTERS

leatherjacket

2 WORDS

amazon ant
ambrosia beetle
animated stick
ant lion
army ant
army worm
assassin bug
bark beetle
bee fly
black ant
black beetle
blister beetle
body louse
boll weevil
bombardier beetle
bulldog ant
burying beetle
bush cricket
caddis fly
carpenter ant
carpenter bee
carpet beetle
carrion beetle
chalcid wasp
chinch bug
click beetle
cluster fly
Colorado beetle
crab louse
crane fly
cuckoo bee
cuckoo wasp
digger wasp
diving beetle
driver ant
drone fly
dung beetle
dung fly
fire ant
flea beetle
flesh fly
fruit fly
furniture beetle
gall midge
gall wasp
glow-worm
goliath beetle
head louse
Hercules beetle
Hessian fly
honey ant
jewel beetle
June bug
lantern fly

leaf beetle
leafcutter ant
leafcutter bee
leaf insect
leaf miner
longhorn beetle
louse fly
mason bee
May bug
meal beetle
mealy bug
mining bee
oil beetle
pharaoh ant
plant hopper
plant louse
pond skater
praying mantis
rhinoceros beetle
robber fly
rove beetle
scale insect
scorpion fly
screw worm
sexton beetle
soldier beetle
stable fly
stag beetle
stick insect
stink bug
tsetse fly
velvet ant
warble fly
water beetle
water boatman
water measurer
water scorpion
white ant
witchetty grub

3 WORDS

daddy-long-legs
death-watch beetle
devil's coach-horse

Male and female animals

antelope (buck; doe)
badger (boar; sow)
bear (boar; sow)
bird (cock; hen)
buffalo (bull; cow)
cat (tom; queen)
cattle (bull; cow)
chicken (cock; hen)
deer (stag; doe)
dog (dog; bitch)
donkey (jackass; jenny)
duck (drake; duck)
elephant (bull; cow)
ferret (jack; gill)
fish (cock; hen)
fox (dog; vixen)
goat (billy goat; nanny)
goose (gander; goose)
hare (buck; doe)
horse (stallion; mare)
kangaroo (buck; doe)
leopard (leopard; leopardess)
lion (lion; lioness)
lobster (cock; hen)
otter (dog; bitch)
peafowl (peacock; peahen)
pheasant (cock; hen)
pig (boar; sow)
rabbit (buck; doe)
seal (bull; cow)
sheep (ram; ewe)
swan (cob; pen)
tiger (tiger; tigress)
weasel (boar; cow)
whale (bull; cow)
wolf (dog; bitch)
zebra (stallion; mare)

Mammals

1 WORD

2 LETTERS

ox

3 LETTERS

ape
ass
bat
cat
cow
dog
elk
fox
gnu
hog
kob
pig
rat
roe
yak

4 LETTERS

bear
boar
deer
gaur
goat
hare
ibex
kudu
lion
lynx
mink
mole
mule
orca
oryx
pika
puma
saki
seal
titi
topi
vole
zebu

5 LETTERS

bison
camel
chimp
civet
coati
coypu
dingo
drill
eland
gayal
hippo
horse
hyena
hyrax
lemur
liger
llama
loris
minke
moose
mouse
okapi
otter
ounce
panda
potto
rhino
sable
sheep
shrew
skunk
sloth
stoat
tapir
tiger
tigon
whale
zebra

6 LETTERS

alpaca
angora
baboon
badger
beaver
beluga
bobcat
bonobo
colugo
cougar
coyote
donkey
dugong
duiker
ermine
fennec
ferret
galago
gelada
gerbil
gibbon
gopher
guenon
impala
jackal
jaguar
langur
margay
marten
monkey
ocelot
onager
possum
rabbit
rhebok
rodent
serval
teledu
walrus
wapiti
weasel
wisent

7 LETTERS

aurochs
buffalo
caracal
caribou
chamois
cheetah
colobus
dolphin
echidna
gazelle
gemsbok
giraffe
gorilla
grampus
grizzly
guanaco
hamster
leopard
macaque
manatee
meerkat
muntjac
narwhal
noctule
opossum
panther
peccary
polecat
raccoon
rorqual
siamang
tamarin
tarsier
warthog
wildcat

8 LETTERS

aardvark
anteater
antelope
babirusa
bushbaby
hedgehog
kinkajou
mandrill
mangabey
marmoset
mongoose
pangolin
platypus
porpoise
reindeer
squirrel
talapoin

9 LETTERS

armadillo
dromedary
hamadryas
marsupial
porcupine
razorback
springbok
waterbuck
wolverine

10 LETTERS

chimpanzee
chinchilla
hartebeest
jaguarundi
rhinoceros
wildebeest

11 LETTERS

douroucouli
pipistrelle

2 WORDS

agile gibbon
baleen whale
Barbary ape
beaked whale
black bear
blue whale
bottlenose dolphin
bottlenose whale
bowhead whale
brown bear
brown hare
capuchin monkey
chacma baboon
common seal
Diana monkey
elephant seal
fallow deer
fin whale
flying fox
fur seal
giant panda
goat-antelope
grey seal
grivet monkey
grizzly bear
hanuman langur
harp seal
honey bear
hooded seal
howler monkey
humpback whale
killer whale
Kodiak bear
laughing hyena
leaf monkey
leopard seal
minke whale
monk seal
mountain goat
mountain lion
musk deer
musk ox
orang-utan
owl monkey
patas monkey
pilot whale
pine marten
polar bear
proboscis monkey
red deer
red panda
rhesus monkey
right whale
Risso's dolphin
river dolphin
roe deer
royal antelope
sea cow
sea elephant
sea lion
sei whale

sloth bear
snow leopard
spectacled bear
sperm whale
spider monkey
spiny anteater
squirrel monkey
sun bear
toothed whale
vampire bat
vervet monkey
water buffalo
whalebone whale
white whale
wild boar

3 WORDS

duck-billed platypus

Marsupials

1 WORD

antechinus
bandicoot
bettong
bilby
brushtail
cuscus
dasyure
dibbler
dunnart
glider
kangaroo
koala
mulgara
numbat
opossum
pademelon
phalanger
planigale
possum
potoroo
quokka
quoll
ringtail
thylacine
wallaby
wallaroo
wombat
yapok

2 WORDS

brushtail possum
flying phalanger
rat kangaroo
Tasmanian devil
Tasmanian tiger

Mushrooms, toadstools, and other fungi

1 WORD

agaric
armillaria
blewit
blusher
boletus
cep
champignon
chanterelle
earthstar
ergot
grisette
morel
mousseron
polypore
porcini
portobello
puffball
reishi
russula
shiitake
sickener
stinkhorn
tartufo
truffle

2 WORDS

amethyst deceiver
beefsteak fungus
bird's-nest
black bulgar
bracket fungus
button mushroom
death cap
destroying angel
fairies' bonnets
field mushroom
fly agaric
giant puffball
honey fungus

horse mushroom
ink cap
Jew's ear
liberty cap
oyster mushroom
panther cap
parasol mushroom
penny bun
straw mushroom
white truffle

3 WORDS

dead man's fingers
horn of plenty
shaggy ink cap

Parts of a horse

1 WORD

4 LETTERS

dock
frog
heel
hock
hoof
knee
loin
mane
poll
ribs
tail

5 LETTERS

cheek
chest
crest
croup
elbow
ergot
flank
shank

6 LETTERS

gaskin
gullet
sheath
stifle
tendon

7 LETTERS

coronet
fetlock
forearm
pastern
withers

8 LETTERS

chestnut
feathers
forelock
shoulder
windpipe

12 LETTERS

hindquarters

2 WORDS

cannon bone
coffin bone
navicular bone
splint bone

Parts of a leaf

1 WORD

apex
axil
blade
chloroplast
epidermis
footstalk
midrib
nervure
petiole
pinna
pinnule
rachis
rib
sinus
stalk
stipule
stoma
stomata
vein

2 WORDS

palisade layer

Parts of a plant

1 WORD

bark
bract
flower
fruit
leaf
phloem
root
stem
stoma
xylem

2 WORDS

guard cell
lateral root
root cap
root hair
tap root
vascular bundle

Plants and shrubs

1 WORD

3 LETTERS

hop
may

4 LETTERS

aloe
dill
dock
flax
hebe
hoya
iris
ixia
lily
mint
moly
pink
rape
rose

5 LETTERS

agave
aster
avens
broom
bugle
daisy
elder
furze
gorse
holly
hosta
kudzu
lilac
lotus
lupin
oxlip
pansy
peony
phlox
poppy
sedum
stock
tansy
tulip
vetch
yucca

6 LETTERS

abelia
acacia
akebia
arabis
arnica
azalea
balsam
betony
borage
bryony
burnet
cactus
chives
cholla
cicely
cistus
clover
crocus
dahlia
daphne
datura
kalmia
kerria
lovage
mallow
mimosa
myrtle
nettle
orchid
orpine
peyote
privet
protea
salvia
scilla
sorrel
spurge
squill
teasel

thrift
violet
yarrow
zinnia

7 LETTERS

aconite
alkanet
alyssum
anchusa
anemone
arbutus
astilbe
banksia
begonia
bistort
boneset
bramble
buckeye
bugbane
bugloss
bulrush
burdock
campion
catmint
champak
chervil
chicory
choisya
clarkia
comfrey
cowslip
dittany
dogbane
figwort
freesia
fuchsia
gazania
gentian
gerbera
gladdon
godetia
hawkbit
heather
hemlock
hogweed
honesty
jasmine
jonquil
kingcup
lobelia
mahonia
mayweed
milfoil
mullein
nemesia
nigella
opuntia
parsley
petunia
primula
ragweed
ragwort
rampion
ramsons
spignel
spiraea
spurrey
thistle
trefoil
verbena
vervain

8 LETTERS

abutilon
acanthus
agrimony
amaranth
angelica
asphodel
aubretia
barberry
bedstraw
bergamot
bilberry
bindweed
bluebell
buddleia
calamint
camellia
camomile
cattleya
centaury
charlock
cinchona
clematis
crowfoot
cyclamen
daffodil
dianthus
dropwort
duckweed
feverfew
fleabane
foxglove
fumitory
gardenia
geranium
gloxinia
harebell
hawkweed
hawthorn
hepatica
heuchera
hibiscus
hyacinth
japonica
knapweed
laburnum
larkspur
lavatera
lavender
lungwort
magnolia
mandrake
marigold
milkwort
oleander
plantain
plumbago
primrose
sainfoin
samphire
sandwort
scabious
shamrock
skullcap
snowdrop
soapwort
sowbread
starwort
toadflax
trillium
tuberose

turnsole
valerian
veronica
viburnum
wisteria
woodruff
wormwood

9 LETTERS

allamanda
amaryllis
anthurium
aquilegia
astrantia
baneberry
bearberry
butterbur
buttercup
calendula
campanula
candytuft
carnation
ceanothus
celandine
chaffweed
chickweed
cockscomb
coltsfoot
columbine
coreopsis
corydalis
crosswort
dandelion
echinacea
edelweiss
eglantine
eucryphia
eyebright
firethorn
forsythia
gladiolus
groundsel
hellebore
hollyhock
hydrangea
jacaranda
juneberry
kalanchoe
knotgrass
marshwort
mayflower
mistletoe
monkshood
moschatel
narcissus
nicotiana
paulownia
penstemon
pimpernel
pyrethrum
safflower
saxifrage
snowflake
speedwell
spikenard
stonecrop
sunflower
tormentil
twayblade
wolfsbane

10 LETTERS

agapanthus
arrowgrass
aspidistra
barrenwort
belladonna
bellflower
blackthorn
butterwort
chinaberry
chionodoxa
chokeberry
cinquefoil
cloudberry
coneflower
corncockle
cornflower
cottonweed
cranesbill
delphinium
frangipani
fraxinella
fritillary
gaillardia
goldilocks
gypsophila
hawksbeard
heartsease
helianthus
heliotrope
marguerite
mignonette
montbretia
moonflower
motherwort
nasturtium
nightshade
pennyroyal
peppermint
periwinkle
poinsettia
polyanthus
potentilla
pulsatilla
pyracantha
restharrow
snapdragon
soldanella
sowthistle
spiderwort
stitchwort
storksbill
sweetbriar
wallflower
willowherb

11 LETTERS

calceolaria
convolvulus
cotoneaster
gillyflower
globeflower
helleborine
honeysuckle
loosestrife
meadowsweet
pelargonium
schizanthus
strawflower
wintergreen
wintersweet

12 LETTERS

alstroemeria
cuckooflower
helianthemum
rhododendron
salpiglossis
tradescantia

13 LETTERS

bougainvillea
chrysanthemum
streptocarpus

2 WORDS

Aaron's rod
African daisy
African violet
angel's trumpet
arum lily
autumn crocus
baby's breath
bachelor's buttons
bear's breech
bleeding heart
bog asphodel
bog rosemary
busy Lizzie
butterfly bush
cabbage rose
California poppy
canary creeper
canna lily
Canterbury bell
Cape primrose
Cherokee rose
Chinese lantern
Christmas cactus
Christmas rose
clove pink
cow parsley
creeping Jenny
crown imperial
cuckoo pint
damask rose
deadly nightshade
desert rose
dog rose
dog's mercury
dog violet
Dutchman's breeches
evening primrose
globe thistle
goat's beard
golden rod
grape hyacinth
guelder rose
hemp agrimony
herb Christopher
herb Paris
herb Robert
Hottentot fig
hound's tongue
ice plant
Jacob's ladder
Kaffir lily
kidney vetch
lady's mantle
lady's slipper
lady's smock
lady's tresses
lemon balm
leopard lily
London pride
madonna lily
marsh marigold
meadow rue
meadow saffron
Michaelmas daisy
mock orange
monkey flower
morning glory
musk rose
oyster plant
Parma violet
pasque flower
passion flower
pheasant's eye
pitcher plant
prickly pear
prickly poppy
ragged robin
rock rose
rosebay willowherb
saffron crocus
scarlet pimpernel
sea holly
sheep's-bit
shrimp plant
Solomon's seal
spider flower
spider plant
sweet cicely
sweet pea
sweet rocket
sweet william
tea rose
thorn apple
tiger lily
Transvaal daisy
traveller's joy
Venus flytrap
viper's bugloss
water lily
water violet
winter jasmine
witch hazel
wood anemone
wood avens
wood sorrel
woody nightshade
yellow rattle
yerba buena

3 WORDS

bird's-foot trefoil
black-eyed Susan
crown of thorns
devil's bit scabious
forget-me-not
grass of Parnassus
lords and ladies
love-lies-bleeding
marvel of Peru
night-scented stock
old man's beard
ox-eye daisy
red-hot poker
rose of Sharon
snow-in-summer
star of Bethlehem

St John's wort

4 WORDS

bird of paradise flower
glory-of-the-snow
Jack-by-the-hedge
lily of the valley
love-in-a-mist

Poisonous plants and fungi

1 WORD

aconite
baneberry
belladonna
buttercup
cowbane
foxglove
hellebore
hemlock
henbane
laburnum
manchineel
mezereon
monkshood
oleander
privet
sickener
stavesacre
upas
wolfsbane

2 WORDS

black bryony
deadly nightshade
death cap
desert rose
destroying angel
dog's mercury
fly agaric
fool's parsley
greater celandine
Indian poke
lucky bean
meadow saffron
naked boys
naked ladies
panther cap
poison ivy
spurge laurel
thorn apple
water dropwort
water hemlock
white snakeroot

Reptiles

1 WORD

3 LETTERS

asp
boa

5 LETTERS

adder
agama
anole
cobra
gecko
krait
mamba
racer
skink
snake
tokay
viper

6 LETTERS

caiman
cooter
dugite
iguana
lizard
moloch
mugger
python

slider
taipan
turtle

7 LETTERS

axolotl
gharial
tuatara

8 LETTERS

anaconda
basilisk
colubrid
keelback
matamata
padloper
rinkhals
terrapin
tortoise

9 LETTERS

alligator
blindworm
boomslang
chameleon
coachwhip
crocodile
galliwasp
hamadryad
hawksbill

10 LETTERS

bushmaster
copperhead
sidewinder

11 LETTERS

constrictor
cottonmouth
diamondback
leatherback
rattlesnake

2 WORDS

alligator lizard
bearded dragon
black mamba
blind snake
boa constrictor
box turtle
bull snake
coral snake
corn snake
death adder
diamondback terrapin
Egyptian cobra
flying lizard
frilled lizard
Gaboon viper
garter snake
giant tortoise
Gila monster
glass lizard
grass snake
green snake
green turtle
hognose snake
horned toad
indigo snake
king cobra
Komodo dragon
loggerhead turtle
marine iguana
monitor lizard
pit viper
puff adder
rat snake
reticulated python
sea snake
slow-worm
smooth snake
snapping turtle
spitting cobra
tiger snake
water moccasin
water snake
whip snake
worm lizard

3 WORDS

fer de lance

Rodents

1 WORD

3 LETTERS

rat

4 LETTERS

cavy
jird
paca
vole

5 LETTERS

coypu
hutia
mouse

6 LETTERS

agouti
beaver
gerbil
gopher
jerboa
marmot

7 LETTERS

acouchi
hamster
lemming
meerkat
muskrat

souslik
woodrat

8 LETTERS

capybara
chipmunk
dormouse
pacarana
squirrel
viscacha

9 LETTERS

chickaree
groundhog
porcupine
woodchuck

10 LETTERS

chinchilla

2 WORDS

bank vole
black rat
brown rat
cane rat
deer mouse
desert rat
field mouse
field vole
flying squirrel
grey squirrel
ground squirrel
guinea pig
harvest mouse
house mouse
kangaroo mouse
kangaroo rat
mole rat
mountain beaver
Norway rat
pocket gopher
prairie dog
red squirrel
ship rat
water rat
water vole
white mouse
wood mouse

Shellfish and other molluscs

1 WORD

4 LETTERS

clam
paua
slug

5 LETTERS

conch
drill
drupe
gaper
mitre
murex
olive
ormer
snail
squid
whelk

6 LETTERS

chiton
cockle
cowrie
helmet
limpet
mussel
nerite
oyster
quahog
teredo
triton
volute
winkle

7 LETTERS

abalone
bivalve
geoduck
octopus
piddock
scallop

8 LETTERS

argonaut
nautilus
pteropod
shipworm

9 LETTERS

gastropod
shellfish

10 LETTERS

cephalopod
cuttlefish
nudibranch
periwinkle
wentletrap

2 WORDS

angel wings
auger shell
bubble shell
cone shell
dog whelk
dove shell
duck mussel
edible snail
giant clam
harp shell

jewel box
lamp shell
paper nautilus
pearl oyster
ramshorn snail
razor shell
sea butterfly
sea hare
sea slug
softshell clam
swan mussel
tooth shell
top shell
turret shell
tusk shell
wedge shell

Spiders and other arachnids

1 WORD

chigger
harvestman
jigger
mite
redback
scorpion
spider
tarantula
tick
varroa

2 WORDS

black widow
camel spider
crab spider
false scorpion
harvest mite
itch mite
money spider
raft spider
spider mite
sun spider
trapdoor spider
water scorpion
whip scorpion
wind scorpion
wolf spider

3 WORDS

bird-eating spider
funnel-web spider
red spider mite

Trees and shrubs

1 WORD

3 LETTERS

ash
box
elm
fig
fir
koa
may
oak
tea
yew

4 LETTERS

acer
cola
gean
ilex
kola
lime
mako
maté
neem
nipa
palm
pear
pine
plum
poui
rimu
shea
teak

5 LETTERS

ackee
alder
anise
apple
aspen
balsa
beech
birch
broom
cacao
carob
cedar
ceiba
clove
ebony
elder
ficus
genip
gorse

guava
hazel
holly
iroko
kapok
larch
lemon
lilac
mango
maple
olive
osier
piñon
plane
ramin
rowan
savin
senna
Sitka
sumac
thuja
yucca

6 LETTERS

acacia
alerce
almond
azalea
bamboo
banyan
baobab
cashew
cassia
cherry
citron
coffee
cornel
croton
damson
deodar
fustic
ginkgo
hinoki
jojoba
jujube
kalmia
laurel
linden
locust
loquat
lychee
mammee
mastic
medlar
mimosa
myrtle
nutmeg
obeche
padauk
papaya
pawpaw
peepul
pomelo
poplar
privet
protea
quince
redbud
sallow
sapele
spruce
storax
tupelo
walnut
wattle
willow
yaupon

7 LETTERS

ambatch
annatto
apricot
arbutus
avocado
banksia
bluegum
buckeye
bullace
cajuput
cascara
cassava
catalpa
champak
criollo
cypress
damiana
dogwood
filbert
fuchsia
guayule
hickory
jasmine
juniper
kumquat
lantana
logwood
madroño
palmyra
quassia
redwood
robinia
sequoia
soursop
spindle
yohimbe

8 LETTERS

albizzia
allspice
angelica
basswood
beefwood
bergamot
calabash
camellia
cecropia
chestnut
cinchona
cinnamon
coolibah
euonymus
genipapo
guaiacum
hawthorn
hornbeam
ironbark
ironwood
japonica
laburnum
loblolly
magnolia
mahogany
mandarin
mangrove

mesquite
mulberry
ocotillo
oleaster
opopanax
pandanus
rambutan
rosewood
sycamore
tamarind
tamarisk
viburnum

9 LETTERS

ailanthus
araucaria
buckthorn
butternut
candlenut
carambola
casuarina
cherimoya
firethorn
forastero
greengage
hydrangea
jacaranda
jackfruit
leylandii
macadamia
mirabelle
myrobalan
nectarine
paloverde
paperbark
paulownia
persimmon
pistachio
poinciana
ponderosa
roseapple
sapodilla
sassafras
satinwood
soapberry
stinkwood
tangerine
terebinth

tulipwood
whitebeam

10 LETTERS

afrormosia
blackthorn
breadfruit
chinaberry
chinquapin
coromandel
cottonwood
eucalyptus
flamboyant
frangipani
grapefruit
macrocarpa
manchineel
mangosteen
sandalwood
schefflera

11 LETTERS

bottlebrush
candleberry
chaulmoogra
cryptomeria
honeysuckle
liquidambar
pomegranate

12 LETTERS

rhododendron
wellingtonia

2 WORDS

balsam fir
bay tree
bodh tree
bog oak
bo tree
bottle tree
box elder
bristlecone pine
bur oak
camphor tree
candelabra tree

cherry laurel
cherry plum
choke cherry
coconut palm
copper beech
coral tree
cork oak
crab apple
crack willow
curry leaf
custard apple
dawn redwood
divi-divi
Douglas fir
dove tree
dragon tree
false acacia
fever tree
flame tree
gum tree
handkerchief tree
hemlock fir
holly oak
holm oak
honey locust
horse chestnut
Huon pine
jack pine
Joshua tree
Judas tree
kermes oak
lacquer tree
Leyland cypress
live oak
lodgepole pine
Lombardy poplar
London plane
maidenhair tree
mammee sapote
manna ash
maritime pine
monkey puzzle
mountain ash
Norway spruce
nux vomica
pagoda tree
paper mulberry
pedunculate oak

pitch pine
pussy willow
rain tree
red cedar
royal palm
rubber plant
rubber tree
sausage tree
Scots pine
sea grape
service tree
silver birch
slippery elm
smoke tree
star anise
stone pine
strawberry tree
sugar maple
sweet chestnut
sweet gum
tallow tree
tea tree
trembling poplar
tulip tree
turkey oak
umbrella tree
wayfaring tree
weeping willow
witch hazel
wych elm
ylang-ylang

3 WORDS

coco de mer
silk-cotton tree
tree of heaven

Young animals

calf (antelope; buffalo; camel; cattle; elephant; elk; giraffe; rhinoceros; seal; whale)
chick (chicken; hawk; pheasant)
cub (badger; bear; fox; leopard; lion; tiger; walrus; wolf)
colt (horse)
cygnet (swan)
duckling (duck)
eaglet (eagle)
elver (eel)
eyas (hawk)
fawn (caribou; deer)
filly (horse)
foal (horse; zebra)
fry (fish)
gosling (goose)
joey (kangaroo; wallaby; possum)
kid (goat; roe deer)
kit (beaver; ferret; fox; mink; weasel)
kitten (cat; cougar; rabbit; skunk)
lamb (sheep)
leveret (hare)
owlet (owl)
parr (salmon)
peachick (peafowl)
pickerel (pike)
piglet (pig)
pup (dog; rat; seal; wolf)
puppy (coyote; dog)
smolt (salmon)
squab (pigeon)
tadpole (frog; toad)
whelp (dog; wolf)

Arts, crafts, and entertainment

Acting roles

1 WORD

4 LETTERS

dame
hero
lead
star

5 LETTERS

cameo
extra
Punch
super

6 LETTERS

chorus
costar
double
guiser
mummer
stager

7 LETTERS

actress
farceur
hambone
heroine
ingénue
Pierrot
starlet
trouper
villain

8 LETTERS

antihero
comedian
figurant
juvenile
prologue
showgirl
stuntman

9 LETTERS

harlequin
Pantaloon
principal
soubrette
tragedian
underpart

10 LETTERS

comedienne
stuntwoman
understudy

11 LETTERS

antiheroine
protagonist
tragedienne

13 LETTERS

supernumerary

2 WORDS

actor-director
actor-manager
bit part
body double
character actor
character part
comic actor
comic relief
film actor
film star
ham actor
leading lady
leading man
leading woman
love interest
matinee idol
pantomime horse
principal boy
principal girl
spear carrier
stage actor
stage performer
stage player
stock character
stunt double
title role
walking gentleman
walking lady
walk-on

Architectural terms and styles

1 WORD

3 LETTERS

rib

4 LETTERS

boss
cove
cusp
dado
dome

5 LETTERS

ancon
atlas
Doric
flute
gable
groin
Ionic
porch
quoin
Roman
Saxon
truss
Tudor
vault

6 LETTERS

abacus
column
coping
corbel
coving
cupola
facade
fascia
frieze
Gothic
lierne
lintel
loggia
Norman
pillar
plinth
rococo
scroll
stucco
Tuscan
volute

7 LETTERS

baroque
Bauhaus
beading
capital
cornice
Grecian
Islamic
lantern
lunette
mansard
Moorish
mullion
obelisk
portico
Regency
respond
sedilia
tambour
tracery
transom
trefoil
Usonian

8 LETTERS

buttress
capstone
caryatid
colonial
cresting
entresol
epistyle
extrados
gargoyle
Georgian
intrados
Jacobean
keystone
medieval
Moresque
moulding
pediment
pilaster
spandrel
springer
tympanum
vaulting
vignette

9 LETTERS

brutalist
Byzantine
campanile
cartouche
classical
colonnade
composite
dripstone
Edwardian
embrasure
hexastyle
hypostyle
inglenook
mannerist
mezzanine
modernist
Palladian
peristyle
scuncheon

10 LETTERS

architrave
clerestory
Corinthian
Romanesque
saddleback
tetrastyle
vernacular

11 LETTERS

Elizabethan

entablature
entablement
Renaissance

12 LETTERS

fenestration
frontispiece
neoclassical
quattrocento
transitional

13 LETTERS

Perpendicular
postmodernist

2 WORDS

Art Deco
Art Nouveau
Beaux Arts
dog-tooth
Early English
fan vault
flying buttress
half-timbered
hammer beam
neo-Gothic
onion dome
pent roof
Queen Anne
rope-moulding
tie beam

Art schools, styles, and movements

1 WORD

baroque
classicism
constructivism
cubism
Dada
expressionism
fauvism
futurism
Impressionism
Jugendstil
Mannerism
minimalism
modernism
naturalism
Nazarenes
neoclassicism
neoplasticism
photorealism
postmodernism
Purism
realism
rococo
romanticism
suprematism
surrealism
symbolism
tenebrism

2 WORDS

abstract expressionism
Aesthetic Movement
Art Deco
art nouveau
avant-garde
Beaux Arts
Blaue Reiter
Bloomsbury Group
conceptual art
De Stijl
Florentine school
Grand Manner
magic realism
metaphysical painting
naive art
neo-Impressionism
neo-realism
Neue Sachlichkeit
op art
performance art
pop art
post-Impressionism
Pre-Raphaelitism
primitive art
Renaissance art
socialist realism
social realism
ukiyo-e

3 WORDS

Arts and Crafts
Group of Seven
plein-air painting
Sturm und Drang

Art techniques and media

1 WORD

5 LETTERS

batik
Conté

6 LETTERS

fresco
mosaic
pastel

7 LETTERS

collage
drawing
etching
montage
tachism
woodcut

8 LETTERS

aquatint
ceramics
frottage
intaglio
marbling
painting
tapestry

9 LETTERS

cloisonné
encaustic
engraving
marquetry
metalwork
mezzotint
sculpture
sketching

10 LETTERS

cartooning
enamelling

11 LETTERS

airbrushing
calligraphy
divisionism
lithography
photography
watercolour

12 LETTERS

photogravure
photomontage

2 WORDS

acrylic painting
action painting
brass rubbing
colour print
colour wash
engineering drawing
finger-painting
lino cut
oil painting
screen printing
stained glass
technical drawing
trompe l'oeil
wood carving
wood engraving

3 WORDS

silk-screen printing

Art terms

1 WORD

4 LETTERS

icon
nude

5 LETTERS

gesso
glaze
mural
pietà
secco
tondo

6 LETTERS

enamel
fresco
primer

7 LETTERS

acrylic
diorama
diptych
écorché
gouache
impasto
paysage
tempera
vanitas

8 LETTERS

emulsion
kakemono
nativity
nocturne
panorama
portrait
predella
seascape
skyscape
triptych

9 LETTERS

aquarelle
capriccio
cityscape
distemper
encaustic
grisaille
grotesque
landscape
miniature
polyptych
roofscape
scumbling
snowscape
townscape

10 LETTERS

altarpiece
cloudscape
dreamscape
polychromy
riverscape
waterscape

11 LETTERS

chiaroscuro
crucifixion
divisionism
pointillism
watercolour

12 LETTERS

annunciation

2 WORDS

acrylic painting
action painting
cave painting
colour wash
conversation piece
Ecce Homo
fête galante
genre painting
half-length
miniature painting
mural painting
oil painting
old master
still life
sumi-e
trompe l'oeil
wall painting

3 WORDS

colour-field painting

Ballet steps and positions

1 WORD

arabesque
assemblé
ballon
battement
batterie
bourrée
brisé
cabriole
chassé
développé
écarté
elevation
enchaînement
entrechat
fouetté
frappé
glissade
glissé
jeté
pirouette
plié
relevé
sauté

2 WORDS

pointe work

3 WORDS

pas de chat
pas de deux
port de bras
rond de jambe

Carpets and rugs

1 WORD

Axminster
broadloom
carpet
dhurrie
drugget
flokati
hearthrug
kaross
Kidderminster
kilim
numdah
Persian
rug
runner
shagpile
sheepskin
Turkish
Turkoman
twist
Wilton

2 WORDS

Brussels carpet
ingrain carpet
prayer mat
rag rug
Savonnerie carpet
scatter rug
tiger-skin

Dances and types of dancing

1 WORD

3 LETTERS

bop
jig

4 LETTERS

jive
jota
mosh
reel

5 LETTERS

ceroc
conga
disco
fling
galop
limbo
mambo
polka
ronde
rumba
salsa

samba
shake
skank
stomp
strut
tango
twist
waltz

6 LETTERS

ballet
bolero
boogie
Boston
cancan
cumbia
minuet
shimmy

7 LETTERS

beguine
carioca
farruca
foxtrot
gavotte
hoedown
lambada
mazurka
shuffle

8 LETTERS

ballroom
boogaloo
cakewalk
fandango
flamenco
hornpipe
moonwalk
vogueing

9 LETTERS

cotillion
ecossaise
jitterbug
moonstomp
polonaise
quadrille
quickstep
roundelay

10 LETTERS

charleston

2 WORDS

barn dance
belly dance
body popping
bossa nova
break-dancing
cha-cha
circle dance
clog dance
Cossack dance
country dance
eightsome reel
fan dance
folk dance
formation dancing
Gay Gordons
Highland fling
hokey-cokey
hula-hula
Irish jig
Irish reel
jazz dance
Lambeth Walk
line dancing
maypole dance
morris dance
old-time
one-step
paso doble
pas seul
Paul Jones
rain dance
robotic dancing
round dance
slam dance
snake dance
square dance
sun dance
sword dance
tap dance
turkey trot
twosome reel
two-step
war dance

3 WORDS

cha-cha-cha
do-si-do
pas de deux
rock and roll

Entertainers

1 WORD

2 LETTERS

DJ
MC

5 LETTERS

actor
clown
comic
emcee
mimic

6 LETTERS

busker
dancer
deejay
jester
player
rapper
singer

7 LETTERS

acrobat
chorine
commère
compère
diseuse
gleeman
juggler
masquer
redcoat
selecta
showman
toaster
tumbler

8 LETTERS

comedian
conjuror
jongleur
magician
minstrel
musician
rhapsode
selector
stripper
stuntman

9 LETTERS

aerialist
gladiator
harlequin
hypnotist
mixmaster
puppeteer
raconteur
strongman

10 LETTERS

comedienne
raconteuse
ringmaster
stuntwoman
unicyclist

11 LETTERS

bullfighter
equilibrist
funambulist
illusionist
storyteller

12 LETTERS

escapologist
impersonator
vaudevillian

13 LETTERS

contortionist
impressionist
ventriloquist

2 WORDS

chorus girl
circus artist
disc jockey
drag artist
drum major
drum majorette
escape artist
exotic dancer
female impersonator
fire-eater
lap dancer
lion tamer
mime artist
mind-reader
organ grinder
pole dancer
snake charmer
striptease artist
sword-swallower
tightrope walker
trapeze artist
wire-walker

3 WORDS

go-go dancer
one-man band
stand-up comedian

4 WORDS

song-and-dance act

Film and TV programme, types of

1 WORD

4 LETTERS

epic
noir
romp
soap
toon

5 LETTERS

anime
caper
flick
nasty
promo
short
spoof
trail
weepy

6 LETTERS

biopic
horror
kidult
remake
repeat
romcom
sequel
series
sitcom
talkie
vérité

7 LETTERS

cartoon
feature
musical
prequel
preview
romance
slasher
trailer
western

8 LETTERS

actioner
docusoap
newsreel
policier
roadshow
showreel
telefilm
teleplay
telethon
thriller

9 LETTERS

docudrama
threequel

10 LETTERS

miniseries
telenovela

11 LETTERS

blockbuster

12 LETTERS

mockumentary
swashbuckler

2 WORDS

B-movie
buddy movie
chat show
chick flick
cinéma-vérité
costume drama
director's cut
film noir
game show
home movie
horse opera
neo-realism
peep show
phone-in
quiz show
reality TV
re-release
road movie
situation comedy
skin flick
snuff movie
soap opera
spaghetti western
supporting film
talking picture
teen movie
tie-in

Film titles

1 WORD

3 LETTERS

Hud
Ran

4 LETTERS

Babe
Heat
Jaws
Léon
MASH
Troy

5 LETTERS

Alien
Birds
Fargo
Ghost
Laura
Piano
Rocky
Seven
Shrek
Sting
Yentl

6 LETTERS

Aliens
Amélie
Batman
Becket
Brazil
Festen
Gandhi
Grease
Harvey
Matrix
Patton
Psycho
Tarzan

7 LETTERS

Amadeus
Aviator
Cabaret
Charade
Hustler
Network
Pianist
Platoon
Rebecca
Scrooge
Shining
Titanic
Tootsie
Vertigo
Yojimbo

8 LETTERS

Amarcord
Clueless
Dogville
Exorcist
Fugitive
Godzilla
Graduate
Papillon
Rashomon
Scarface
Sideways

9 LETTERS

Chinatown
Gladiator
Godfather
Kagemusha
Manhattan
Ninotchka
Nosferatu
Notorious
Producers
Searchers
Spartacus

10 LETTERS

Braveheart
Casablanca
Goodfellas
Metropolis
Stagecoach
Terminator
Unforgiven

11 LETTERS

Deliverance
Incredibles
Intolerance

12 LETTERS

Conversation
Fitzcarraldo
Frankenstein
Ghostbusters
Untouchables

13 LETTERS

Trainspotting

2 WORDS

African Queen
American Beauty
American Pie
Annie Hall
Apocalypse Now
Austin Powers
Barry Lyndon
Battleship Potemkin
Before Sunrise
Before Sunset
Being There
Ben-Hur
Bicycle Thieves
Big Lebowski
Big Sleep
Black Narcissus
Blade Runner
Blazing Saddles
Brief Encounter
Christmas Story
Cinema Paradiso

Citizen Kane
Clockwork Orange
Crocodile Dundee
Das Boot
Deer Hunter
Die Hard
Doctor Zhivago
Donnie Darko
Double Indemnity
Dr Strangelove
Duck Soup
Ed Wood
Elephant Man
Fatal Attraction
Fight Club
Finding Nemo
Forrest Gump
French Connection
Full Monty
Gold Rush
Great Dictator
Great Escape
Great Expectations
Green Mile
Groundhog Day
Henry V
High Noon
Home Alone
Howard's End
Independence Day
Italian Job
Jurassic Park
Kill Bill
Killing Fields
King Kong
LA Confidential
Lady Vanishes
La Strada
Les Diaboliques
Lion King
Lost Weekend
Love Story
Magnificent Ambersons
Maltese Falcon
Manchurian Candidate
Mary Poppins
Midnight Cowboy
Miller's Crossing
Mission Impossible
Modern Times
Mrs Doubtfire
Muriel's Wedding
Mystic River
Notting Hill
Ocean's Eleven
Oliver Twist
Ordinary People
Phantom Menace
Philadelphia Story
Pretty Woman
Pulp Fiction
Quiet Man
Quo Vadis
Raging Bull
Rain Man
Rear Window
Red River
Red Shoes
Reservoir Dogs
Right Stuff
Rio Bravo
Roman Holiday
Rosemary's Baby
Schindler's List
Seven Samurai
Seventh Seal
Shawshank Redemption
Sixth Sense
Snow White
Spider-Man
Star Wars
Strictly Ballroom
Sunset Boulevard
Taxi Driver
Thin Man
Third Man
Top Gun
Top Hat
Toy Story
Twelve Monkeys
Two Towers
Usual Suspects
Vera Drake
Wayne's World
White Heat
Wild Bunch

Wild Strawberries
Young Frankenstein

3 WORDS

All About Eve
Beverly Hills Cop
Blair Witch Project
Bonnie and Clyde
Bride of Frankenstein
Bridget Jones's Diary
Bringing Up Baby
City of God
Cool Hand Luke
Crimes and Misdemeanors
Dances with Wolves
Days of Heaven
Dog Day Afternoon
Dumb and Dumber
Empire Strikes Back
Fanny and Alexander
Full Metal Jacket
Goodbye Mr Chips
Grapes of Wrath
Heat and Dust
His Girl Friday
In Cold Blood
Inherit the Wind
Jean de Florette
Kramer vs Kramer
La Dolce Vita
La Grande Illusion
Last Picture Show
Lawrence of Arabia
Life is Beautiful
Life of Brian
Lion in Winter
Lost in Translation
Manon des Sources
Men in Black
Million Dollar Baby
My Darling Clementine
My Fair Lady
North by Northwest
Oh Mr Porter
On Golden Pond
On the Waterfront
Ox-Bow Incident
Règle du Jeu
Saturday Night Fever
Saving Private Ryan
Sleepless in Seattle
Sound of Music
Stand by Me
Streetcar Named Desire
Terms of Endearment
Thirty Nine Steps
Three Colours Red
Throne of Blood
Touch of Evil
Trouble in Paradise
Twelve Angry Men
Wages of Fear
Wings of Desire
Wizard of Oz

4 WORDS

Adventures of Robin Hood
Aguirre Wrath of God
All about my Mother
All the President's Men
Anatomy of a Murder
Arsenic and Old Lace
Attack of the Clones
Au revoir les Enfants
Back to the Future
Beauty and the Beast
Birth of a Nation
Cabinet of Dr Caligari
Crouching Tiger Hidden Dragon
Fellowship of the Ring
Gone with the Wind
Hannah and her Sisters
It Happened One Night
It's a Wonderful Life
Kind Hearts and Coronets
Le Jour se Lève
Les Enfants du Paradis
Lord of the Rings
Man for All Seasons
Mutiny on the Bounty
Night at the Opera
Night of the Hunter

Officer and a Gentleman
Of Mice and Men
Passion of the Christ
Pirates of the Caribbean
Planet of the Apes
Raise the Red Lantern
Return of the Jedi
Return of the King
Revenge of the Sith
Rocky Horror Picture Show
Shadow of a Doubt
Silence of the Lambs
Singin' in the Rain
Some Like it Hot
Strangers on a Train
Sweet Smell of Success
Tale of Two Cities
Tarzan of the Apes
This Is Spinal Tap
To Kill a Mockingbird
2001: A Space Odyssey
When Harry Met Sally

5 WORDS

Bridge on the River Kwai
Charlie and the Chocolate Factory
Day the Earth Stood Still
For a Few Dollars More
Four Weddings and a Funeral
How Green Was My Valley
Man who Shot Liberty Valance
Man who Would Be King
Matter of Life and Death
Mr Deeds Goes to Town
Raiders of the Lost Ark
To Have and Have Not
Treasure of the Sierra Madre
Who's Afraid of Virginia Woolf?

6 WORDS

All Quiet on the Western Front
Bridget Jones: The Edge of Reason
In the Heat of the Night
Life and Death of Colonel Blimp
Monty Python and the Holy Grail
Once Upon a Time in America
One Flew Over the Cuckoo's Nest
Snow White and the Seven Dwarfs

Furniture, types and styles of

1 WORD

3 LETTERS

bed
cot
pew

4 LETTERS

crib
desk
sofa

5 LETTERS

bench
berth
chair
chest
couch
divan
futon
press
stall
stool
table

6 LETTERS

buffet
bureau
canapé
carver
closet
cradle
daybed
Empire
larder
locker
lowboy
mirror
pallet
pantry
pouffe
rocker
settee
settle
Shaker

teapoy
throne
tuffet

7 LETTERS

armoire
Bauhaus
cabinet
charpoy
commode
dresser
hammock
lectern
lounger
Regency
sleeper
tallboy
whatnot

8 LETTERS

armchair
bassinet
bedstead
cellaret
credenza
cupboard
duchesse
recliner
Sheraton
tabouret
wardrobe
waterbed

9 LETTERS

couchette
davenport
deckchair
faldstool
footstool
palliasse
sideboard

10 LETTERS

canterbury
chiffonier
escritoire
nightstand
secretaire

11 LETTERS

Biedermeier
Chippendale
Hepplewhite

12 LETTERS

chesterfield
Scandinavian

2 WORDS

bar stool
bedside table
billiard table
bunk bed
camp bed
card table
chaise longue
cheval glass
coffee table
console table
credence table
dining chair
dressing table
dumb waiter
easy chair
feather bed
four-poster
gateleg table
half-tester
high chair
hope chest
kneehole desk
ladder-back
loo table
Louis Quatorze
Louis Quinze
love seat
Morris chair
music stool
night table
partners' desk
piecrust table
pier glass
pier table
Queen Anne
refectory table
rocking chair
sea chest
side chair
sofa bed
studio couch
swivel chair
tea table
trestle table
truckle bed
trundle bed
tub chair
vanity table
Welsh dresser
Windsor chair
wing chair
writing desk

3 WORDS

chest of drawers
drop-leaf table
roll-top desk

Musical directions

1 WORD

2 LETTERS

DC
DS
ff
mf
mp
pp
sf

3 LETTERS

bis
dim.
rit.
sfz
ten.

4 LETTERS

arco
fine
meno
poco
rall.

5 LETTERS

assai
cresc.
dolce
forte
largo
lento
mezzo
molto
mosso
piano
tacet
tanto
tempo
tutti

6 LETTERS

adagio
arioso
legato
presto
sempre
tenuto
troppo
vivace

7 LETTERS

agitato
allegro
amoroso
andante
animato
calando
furioso
marcato
stretto

8 LETTERS

maestoso
moderato
parlando
ritenuto
semplice
spiccato
staccato

9 LETTERS

andantino
cantabile
crescendo
glissando
larghetto
obbligato
pizzicato
sforzando
smorzando
sostenuto

10 LETTERS

allargando
allegretto
diminuendo
espressivo
fortissimo
pianissimo
portamento
ritardando
scherzando
stringendo
tremolando

11 LETTERS

accelerando
capriccioso
decrescendo
prestissimo
rallentando

2 WORDS

a cappella
ad lib
ad libitum
a tempo
con amore
con brio
con moto
con sordino
da capo
dal segno
forte piano
meno mosso
mezza voce
mezzo forte
mezzo piano
più mosso
sotto voce
una corda

3 WORDS

ma non troppo

Musical forms and genres

1 WORD

3 LETTERS

air
AOR
bop
dub
duo
emo
jit
MOR
pop
rag
rai
rap
ska

4 LETTERS

aria
duet
fado
folk
funk
glee
Goth
hymn
jazz
jive
juju
Lied
mass
punk
raga
rave
rock
soca
solo
song
soul
trio
zouk

5 LETTERS

bebop
blues
canon
carol
catch
chant
crunk
dirge
disco
ditty
étude
fugue
grime
gumbo
house
indie
kwela
march
mento
motet
nonet
octet
opera
psalm
ragga
rondo
round
salsa
scena
study
suite
swing

6 LETTERS

anthem
aubade
ballad
ballet
chorus
cumbia
finale
fugato
fusion
garage
gospel
grunge
jingle
jungle
kwaito
lament
medley
monody
Motown
parang
reggae
septet
sextet
shanty
sonata
techno
Tejano
thrash
trance
zydeco

7 LETTERS

ambient
baroque
bhangra
Britpop
calypso
canzone
chanson
chorale
country
descant
electro
Europop
fanfare
fantasy
gradual
introit
klezmer
lullaby
musette
partita
passion
pibroch
prelude

qawwali
quartet
quintet
ragtime
refrain
requiem
reverie
romance
scherzo
setting
skiffle
soukous
toccata

8 LETTERS

berceuse
canticle
Cantopop
cavatina
chaconne
concerto
coronach
courante
entr'acte
fantasia
flamenco
flourish
madrigal
mariachi
merengue
movement
nocturne
operetta
oratorio
overture
pastoral
postlude
rhapsody
ricercar
serenade
serenata
sinfonia
sonatina
symphony
terzetto
threnody

9 LETTERS

bagatelle
barcarole
bluegrass
breakbeat
cabaletta
capriccio
crossover
dancehall
Dixieland
impromptu
interlude
Krautrock
plainsong
roundelay
Singspiel
spiritual
variation
voluntary

10 LETTERS

barbershop
canzonetta
concertino
humoresque
intermezzo
ragamuffin
recitative
ritornello
rockabilly
rocksteady

11 LETTERS

barrelhouse
electronica
passacaglia
psychedelic
sinfonietta

2 WORDS

acid house
acid jazz
acid rock
alt.country
boogie-woogie
chamber music
choral music
classical music
comic opera
concerto grosso
cool jazz
country rock
dead march
death metal
doo-wop
drinking song
easy listening
free jazz
glam rock
go-go
grand opera
heavy metal
heavy rock
hip hop
honky-tonk
jazz funk
light opera
modern jazz
moto perpetuo
musique concrète
New Age
New Romantic
new wave
opera buffa
opera seria
part-song
pop music
popular music
progressive rock
signature tune
sinfonia concertante
song cycle
symphonic poem
talking blues
Tex-Mex
tone poem
trad jazz
trip hop
two-step
UK garage
world music

3 WORDS

country and western
drum and bass
rhythm and blues
rock and roll

Musical instruments

1 WORD

3 LETTERS

oud

4 LETTERS

bell
drum
erhu
fife
gong
harp
horn
kora
koto
lute
lyre
oboe
pipe
tuba
viol

5 LETTERS

banjo
bongo
bugle
cello
dobro
flute
gamba
kazoo
organ
piano
rebec
sarod
shawm
sitar
tabla
tabor
viola

6 LETTERS

bongos
citole
claves
cornet
cuatro
cymbal
fiddle
guitar
maraca
rattle
shaker
spinet
violin
zither

7 LETTERS

althorn
balafon
bandora
bandura
bassoon
bodhrán
celesta
cittern
clarion
clavier
cowbell
crotale
gittern
goombay
helicon
mandola
ocarina
pianola
piccolo
sackbut
samisen
santoor
sarangi
saxhorn
serpent
sistrum
tambour
theorbo
timpani
trumpet
ukelele
ukulele
vihuela
violone
whistle

8 LETTERS

archlute
autoharp
bagpipes
bombarde
bouzouki
carillon
castanet
charango
cimbalom
clarinet
clarsach
cornetto
dulcimer

handbell
mandolin
melodeon
melodica
psaltery
recorder
tamboura
timbales
triangle
trombone
virginal

9 LETTERS

accordion
alpenhorn
balalaika
bombardon
dulcitone
euphonium
flageolet
harmonica
harmonium
krummhorn
mellotron
saxophone
virginals
washboard
Wurlitzer
xylophone

10 LETTERS

chitarrone
clavichord
contrabass
didgeridoo
flugelhorn
fortepiano
kettledrum
pianoforte
sousaphone
stylophone
tambourine
tamburitza
vibraphone

11 LETTERS

harpsichord
heckelphone
synthesizer
violoncello
wobbleboard

12 LETTERS

glockenspiel
sarrusophone

13 LETTERS

contrabassoon

2 WORDS

acoustic guitar
aeolian harp
American organ
barrel organ
bass drum
basset horn
bass guitar
bass viol
Celtic harp
chamber organ
chime bar
cinema organ
conga drum
cor anglais
double bass
electric guitar
electric organ
electronic organ
fipple flute
French horn
grand piano
Hammond organ
Hawaiian guitar
hi-hat
hurdy-gurdy
Jew's harp
kick drum
mouth organ
oboe d'amore
ondes martenot
piano accordion
piano organ
pipe organ
player-piano
portative organ
post horn
reed organ
reed pipe
side drum
sleigh bell
slide guitar
slide trombone
snare drum
Spanish guitar
steel drum
string bass
tam-tam
tassa drum
temple block
tenor drum
thumb piano
tin whistle
tom-tom
triple harp
tubular bell
upright piano
viola d'amore
Wagner tuba
Welsh harp
wood block

3 WORDS

pedal steel guitar
viola da gamba

Musicals

1 WORD

Annie
Brigadoon
Cabaret
Camelot
Carousel
Cats
Chess
Chicago
Evita
Follies
Godspell
Grease
Hair
Mame
Oklahoma
Oliver!

2 WORDS

Boy Friend
Chorus Line
42nd Street
Hello Dolly
Les Misérables
Miss Saigon
Show Boat
South Pacific
Starlight Express
Student Prince
Sweeney Todd

3 WORDS

Guys and Dolls
Jesus Christ Superstar
King and I
Kiss Me Kate
Little Night Music
My Fair Lady
No No Nanette
Paint Your Wagon
Rocky Horror Show
Sound of Music
West Side Story
Wizard of Oz

4 WORDS

Annie Get Your Gun
Fiddler on the Roof
La Cage aux Folles
Little Shop of Horrors
Me and My Girl
Phantom of the Opera

Musicians

5 LETTERS

piper

6 LETTERS

harper
lutist
lyrist
oboist
saxist
vibist

7 LETTERS

bassist
cellist
drummer
fiddler
harpist
pianist
violist

8 LETTERS

banjoist
flautist
lutenist
organist

9 LETTERS

cornetist
cymbalist
guitarist
timpanist
trumpeter
violinist

10 LETTERS

bassoonist
trombonist

11 LETTERS

keyboardist
mandolinist
saxophonist
xylophonist

12 LETTERS

accordionist
clarinettist
tambourinist
vibraphonist

13 LETTERS

percussionist

Operas and operettas

1 WORD

4 LETTERS

Aida
Lulu

5 LETTERS

Faust
Lakmé
Manon
Norma
Orfeo
Tosca

6 LETTERS

Alcina
Carmen
Ernani
Mikado
Oberon
Otello
Rienzi
Salome
Semele
Xerxes

7 LETTERS

Alceste
Candide
Elektra
Fidelio
Macbeth
Nabucco
Thespis
Trojans
Werther
Wozzeck

8 LETTERS

Falstaff
Idomeneo
Iolanthe
Parsifal
Patience
Sorcerer
Turandot

9 LETTERS

Lohengrin
Rigoletto
Ruddigore
Siegfried

10 LETTERS

Gondoliers
Semiramide
Tannhäuser

2 WORDS

Albert Herring
Bartered Bride
Beggar's Opera
Billy Budd
Boris Godunov
Cavalleria Rusticana
Das Rheingold
Der Freischütz
Der Rosenkavalier
Die Fledermaus
Die Meistersinger
Die Walküre
Don Carlos
Don Giovanni
Don Pasquale
Eugene Onegin
Flying Dutchman
Golden Cockerel
Grand Duke
HMS Pinafore
Il Seraglio
Il Trovatore
I Pagliacci
I Puritani
Knot Garden
La Bohème
La Cenerentola
La Gioconda
La Sonnambula
La Traviata
L'Elisir d'amore
Les Huguenots
Lucrezia Borgia
Madam Butterfly
Magic Flute
Manon Lescaut
Merry Widow
Noye's Fludde

Oedipus Rex
Pearl Fishers
Peter Grimes
Prince Igor
Princess Ida
Rake's Progress
Simon Boccanegra
Thieving Magpie
Threepenny Opera
William Tell

3 WORDS

Ariadne auf Naxos
Ballo in Maschera
Barber of Seville
Cosí fan tutte
Cunning Little Vixen
Damnation of Faust
Death in Venice
Dido and Aeneas
Duke Bluebeard's Castle
Force of Destiny
Hansel and Gretel
L'Incoronazione di Poppea
L'Italiana in Algeri
Lucia di Lammermoor
Marriage of Figaro
Mask of Orpheus
Midsummer Night's Dream
Orpheus and Eurydice
Pelléas et Mélisande
Pirates of Penzance
Porgy and Bess
Samson et Dalila
Tales of Hoffman
Trial by Jury
Tristan and Isolde

4 WORDS

Daughter of the Regiment
Die Frau ohne Schatten
La Clemenza di Tito
Lady Macbeth of Mtsensk
Love for Three Oranges
Merry Wives of Windsor
Orpheus in the Underworld
Ring of the Nibelung
Turn of the Screw
Village Romeo and Juliet
Yeomen of the Guard

5 WORDS

Amahl and the Night Visitors
Girl of the Golden West

Orchestral instruments

1 WORD

bassoon
celesta
cello
clarinet
contrabassoon
cymbal
flute
glockenspiel
harp
kettledrum
oboe
piccolo
timpani
triangle
trombone
trumpet
tuba
viola
violin

2 WORDS

bass clarinet
bass drum
basset horn
bass tuba
cor anglais
double bass
French horn
oboe d'amore
side drum

snare drum
tam-tam
tubular bells
viola d'amore
Wagner tuba

Parts of a church

1 WORD

3 LETTERS

pew

4 LETTERS

apse
dome
font
loft
nave

5 LETTERS

aisle
choir
crypt
spire
stall
tower
vault

6 LETTERS

aumbry
belfry
chapel
chevet
flèche
parvis
pulpit
squint
vestry

7 LETTERS

chancel
chantry
gallery
piscina
sedilia
steeple
tribune

8 LETTERS

buttress
ciborium
crossing
sacristy
transept
traverse

9 LETTERS

baptistry
sanctuary
vestibule

10 LETTERS

ambulatory
antechapel
baptistery
clerestory
fenestella
presbytery
retrochoir
tabernacle

12 LETTERS

confessional

2 WORDS

choir stall
flying buttress
high altar
Lady chapel
organ loft
rood screen

Parts of a theatre

1 WORD

aisle
apron
auditorium
backstage
balcony
boards
box
bridge
catwalk
circle
coulisse
curtain
cyclorama

flies
footlights
foyer
gallery
gods
loge
mezzanine
orchestra
pit
proscenium
set
stage
stalls
upstage
velarium
wings

2 WORDS

apron stage
box office
dress circle
dressing room
drop cloth
drop curtain
fire curtain
green room
house lights
lighting gallery
orchestra pit
orchestra stalls
prompt box
proscenium arch
proscenium stage
revolving stage
safety curtain
scene dock
stage door
tableau curtains
thrust stage
upper circle

3 WORDS

front of house

Pottery and porcelain, types of

1 WORD

Arita
celadon
champlevé
cloisonné
Coalport
creamware
delft
Doulton
earthenware
faience
graniteware
Imari
ironstone
jasper
jasperware
lustreware
maiolica
majolica
Meissen
Ming
Minton
queensware
raku
Sèvres
slipware
Spode
stoneware
terracotta
Wedgwood
Worcester

2 WORDS

biscuit ware
bisque ware
bone china
Chelsea ware
Clarice Cliff
Crown Derby
Dresden china
famille jaune
famille noire
famille rose
famille verte
Iznik ware
Parian ware
Royal Worcester
Samian ware
Satsuma ware
Staffordshire ware
terra sigillata

3 WORDS

black-figure ware
Capo di Monte
red-figure ware

Sewing and knitting terms

1 WORD

3 LETTERS

rib

4 LETTERS

dart
purl
tack
tuck

5 LETTERS

plain
pleat

6 LETTERS

facing

7 LETTERS

basting
binding
cutwork
darning
mitring
ribbing
ruching
tacking
tufting

8 LETTERS

appliqué
couching
pleating
quilting
ruffling
shirring
smocking
tapestry

9 LETTERS

blackwork
faggoting
gathering
hemstitch
patchwork
topstitch
whitework

10 LETTERS

backstitch
crocheting
embroidery
oversewing
overstitch
scalloping
whipstitch

11 LETTERS

needlepoint
overcasting
overlocking

2 WORDS

bar tack
blanket stitch
blind stitch
buttonhole stitch
cable stitch
chain stitch
cross stitch
drawn work
feather stitch
fine-drawing
French knot
garter stitch
gros point
herringbone stitch
ladder stitch
lock stitch
loop stitch
moss stitch
petit point
running stitch
saddle stitch
satin stitch
shadow stitch
slip stitch
stab stitch
stay stitch
stem stitch
stocking stitch
Swiss darning
tent stitch

3 WORDS

lazy daisy stitch

Singers and singing voices

1 WORD

alto
balladeer
baritone
bass
castrato
choirboy
choirgirl
chorister
coloratura
countertenor
crooner
diva
falsetto

gleeman
Heldentenor
jongleur
Meistersinger
mezzo
minstrel
soloist
soprano
spinto
tenor
treble
troubadour

2 WORDS

basso profundo
folk singer
mezzo-soprano
opera singer
pop singer
pop star
prima donna

Television programmes

1 WORD

2 LETTERS

ER

4 LETTERS

Bill
Fame
Lost
MASH
Taxi

5 LETTERS

Angel
Bread
Kojak
Roots
Saint

6 LETTERS

Batman
Cheers
Dallas
Minder
Monkey
Office
TISWAS

7 LETTERS

Bagpuss
Bonanza
Columbo
Cracker
Dragnet
Dynasty
Frazier
Friends
Goodies
Jackass
Lovejoy
Muppets
Poldark
Rainbow
Rawhide
Sweeney
Taggart
Waltons
Wombles

8 LETTERS

Avengers
Baywatch
Bergerac
Casualty
Clangers
Fugitive
Ironside
Munsters
Panorama
Popstars
Porridge
Prisoner
Roseanne
Seinfeld
Simpsons
Sopranos
Stingray
Trumpton

9 LETTERS

Bewitched
Brookside
Catweazle
Countdown
Emmerdale
Heartbeat
Hollyoaks
Jackanory
Osbournes

10 LETTERS

Blackadder
Crossroads
Eastenders
Mastermind
Neighbours
Persuaders
Quatermass
Woodentops

11 LETTERS

Crackerjack
Dangermouse

Flintstones
Teletubbies

12 LETTERS

Thunderbirds

2 WORDS

Absolutely Fabulous
Addams Family
Allo Allo
Ally McBeal
American Idol
Andy Pandy
A-Team
Bad Girls
Basil Brush
Battlestar Galactica
Big Brother
Blake's Seven
Blankety Blank
Blind Date
Blue Peter
Brady Bunch
Brideshead Revisited
Camberwick Green
Candid Camera
Changing Rooms
Charlie's Angels
Cold Feet
Coronation Street
Cosby Show
Dad's Army
Dawson's Creek
Desperate Housewives
Diff'rent Strokes
Doctor Kildare
Doctor Who
Faking It
Fast Show
Father Ted
Fawlty Towers
Footballers' Wives
Forsyte Saga
General Hospital
Generation Game
Good Life
Grange Hill
Happy Days
High Chaparral
Holby City
I Claudius
Inspector Morse
Knight Rider
Knots Landing
LA Law
Likely Lads
Little Britain
Lone Ranger
Magic Roundabout
Magnum, PI
Miami Vice
Mission: Impossible
Mr Benn
Muppet Show
NYPD Blue
Onedin Line
Partridge Family
Peak Practice
Perry Mason
Play School
Pop Idol
Postman Pat
Prime Suspect
Railway Children
Red Dwarf
Rising Damp
Rockford Files
Royle Family
Scooby Doo
Sesame Street
Singing Detective
South Park
Star Trek
St Elsewhere
That's Life
Twilight Zone
Twin Peaks
Two Ronnies
Up Pompeii
Upstairs Downstairs
Wacky Races
Weakest Link
West Wing
Wife Swap

Worzel Gummidge
X Factor
X-Files
Yes Minister
Young Ones
Z Cars

3 WORDS

Auf Wiedersehen Pet
Band of Brothers
Bob the Builder
Cagney and Lacey
Dalziel and Pascoe
Dukes of Hazzard
Edge of Darkness
Hancock's Half Hour
Hawaii Five-O
Hi-de-hi
Hill Street Blues
Home and Away
I Love Lucy
Jerry Springer Show
Jim'll Fix It
Keeping up Appearances
Law and Order
Lost in Space
Man from UNCLE
Men Behaving Badly
Morecambe and Wise
Mork and Mindy
Muffin the Mule
Murder She Wrote
On the Buses
Open All Hours
Pennies from Heaven
Phil Silvers Show
Pinky and Perky
Queer as Folk
Rab C. Nesbitt
Ready Steady Go
Roobarb and Custard
Saturday Night Live
Starsky and Hutch
Steptoe and Son
Strictly Come Dancing
Terry and June
Tom and Jerry
Touch of Frost
Van der Valk
Vicar of Dibley
Wheel of Fortune
Will and Grace

4 WORDS

Are You Being Served
Beavis and Butt-head
Boys from the Blackstuff
Buffy the Vampire Slayer
Darling Buds of May
Dixon of Dock Green
Hammer House of Horror
Match of the Day
Monty Python's Flying Circus
Only Fools and Horses
Prisoner Cell Block H
Randall and Hopkirk Deceased
Sex and the City
Six Million Dollar Man
Tales of the Unexpected
This is your Life
Thomas the Tank Engine
Top of the Pops
What Not To Wear

5 WORDS

All Creatures Great and Small
It Ain't Half Hot Mum
Last of the Summer Wine
Little House on the Prairie
One Foot in the Grave
Till Death Us Do Part

6 WORDS

That was the Week that Was
Who Wants to be a Millionaire

Tonic sol-fa notes

doh
ray
mi
fah
soh
lah
te

Clothes and fabrics

Clothes

1 WORD

2 LETTERS

gi

3 LETTERS

bib
boa
bra
hat
mac
obi
tee
tie
top
tux

4 LETTERS

bags
belt
body
boot
cape
coat
cope
cowl
gown
haik
hose
kilt
mask
maxi
midi
mini
mink
mitt
muff
robe
ruff
sari
sash
shoe
sock
suit
toga
tutu
veil
vest
wrap

5 LETTERS

apron
ascot
burka
burqa
chaps
choli
cords
dhoti
dress
ducks
fichu
frock
gilet
glove
hoody
jeans
jibba
kecks
kurta
loden
loons
lungi
pants
parka
pinny
Puffa
scarf
shawl
shrug
skirt
slops
smock
stock
stole
trews
tunic

6 LETTERS

achkan
anorak
basque
bikini
blazer
blouse
bodice
bolero
braces
breeks
burkha
chador
chinos
coatee
cravat
denims
dirndl
djibba
dolman

domino
duster
flares
fleece
hoodie
jacket
jerkin
jersey
jilbab
jumper
kaftan
kagoul
kameez
kimono
kirtle
kuccha
lehnga
mantle
mitten
muumuu
peplum
poncho
raglan
salwar
sandal
sarape
sarong
serape
shorts
skivvy
slacks
tabard
tights
tippet
trunks
tuxedo
tweeds
ulster
woolly
yukata

7 LETTERS

baggies
bandeau
Barbour
blouson
burnous
bustier
cagoule
catsuit
chemise
chlamys
cutaway
dashiki
doublet
foulard
gymslip
hosiery
jellaba
joggers
lehenga
leotard
maillot
manteau
mantlet
muffler
overall
pakamac
pallium
pelisse
pyjamas
shalwar
surcoat
surtout
sweater
topcoat
twinset
yashmak

8 LETTERS

ballgown
bandanna
bloomers
bodysuit
breeches
bumsters
Burberry
cardigan
culottes
djellaba
dustcoat
flannels
guernsey
hipsters
jodhpurs
jumpsuit
knickers
leathers
leggings
lingerie
mantilla
oilskins
overcoat
peignoir
pinafore
plastron
pullover
raincoat
slipover
stocking
sundress
swimsuit
tailcoat
trousers
woollens

9 LETTERS

bedjacket
cheongsam
churidars
corduroys
crinoline
dungarees
gabardine
gaberdine
greatcoat
guayabera
housecoat
loincloth
macintosh
maxidress
minidress
miniskirt
nor'wester
overdress
overshirt
overskirt
polonaise
rainproof
redingote
sheepskin
tracksuit
waistcoat

10 LETTERS

chaparajos
cummerbund
drainpipes
fustanella
lederhosen
macfarlane
mackintosh
nightdress
nightshirt
overblouse
pantaloons
salopettes
sweatpants
sweatshirt
turtleneck
undershirt
underskirt
waterproof

11 LETTERS

clamdiggers
neckerchief
windbreaker
windcheater

12 LETTERS

lumberjacket
overtrousers
shirtwaister

2 WORDS

Afghan coat
aloha shirt
ballet skirt
bathing costume
bathing suit
bathing trunks
bell-bottoms
Bermuda shorts
biker jacket
board shorts
body stocking
body warmer
bolo tie
bomber jacket
bootlace tie
bow tie
bush jacket
capri pants
car coat
cargo pants
carpenter trousers
cigarette pants
coat dress
cocktail dress
combat trousers
crew neck
crop top
cut-offs
cycling shorts
denim jacket
dicky bow
dinner gown
dinner jacket
divided skirt
donkey jacket
dress coat
dressing gown
dress shirt
duffel coat
Eton jacket
evening gown
evening shirt
flak jacket
flying jacket
frock coat
fur coat
grandad shirt
grass skirt
hacking jacket
hair shirt
halter neck
harem pants
hip-huggers
hobble skirt
hot pants
hula skirt
hunting jacket
jogging pants
kipper tie
knee breeches
leather jacket
leg warmers
lumberjack shirt
mandarin jacket
Mao jacket
maternity dress
matinee coat
mess jacket
middy blouse
morning coat
Nehru jacket
Norfolk jacket
opera cloak
Oxford bags
palazzo pants
pea coat
pea jacket
pedal pushers
pencil skirt
pilot jacket
pinafore dress
pleated skrit
plus fours
polo neck
polo shirt
Puffa jacket
puffball skirt
reefer jacket
riding breeches
riding jacket
roll-neck
sack coat
sack dress
safari jacket
sailor suit
Sam Browne
sheath dress
shell suit
shift dress
shirt dress
shooting coat
shooting jacket
short trousers
skinny-rib
ski pants
slip dress
sloppy joe
smoking jacket
sports coat
sports shirt

stirrup pants
string tie
swimming costume
swing coat
tank top
tea gown
tennis skirt
tent dress
toreador pants
trench coat
trouser suit
T-shirt
tube dress
V-neck
waxed jacket
wedding dress

3 WORDS

rah-rah skirt

Clothing worn by priests, monks, etc.

1 WORD

alb
amice
biretta
cassock
chasuble
cope
cotta
cowl
dalmatic
frock
habit
hood
mitre
pallium
rochet
scapular
skullcap
soutane
stole
surplice
tallith
tippet
tunicle
wimple
yarmulke
zucchetto

2 WORDS

clerical collar
dog collar
Geneva bands
shovel hat

Fabrics and fibres

1 WORD

3 LETTERS

net
rep

4 LETTERS

ciré
coir
cord
drab
felt
flax
gimp
hemp
ikat
jean
jute
kemp
lace
lamé
lawn
leno
lint
silk
slub
wool

5 LETTERS

bafta
baize
chino
crêpe
cupro
denim
drill
flock
gauze
kapok
khadi
khaki
kikoi
linen
lisle
loden
Lurex
Lycra
moiré
mungo
nylon
oakum

Orlon
piqué
plaid
plush
ramie
rayon
satin
serge
sheer
sisal
suede
surah
terry
toile
tulle
tweed
twill
voile

6 LETTERS

alpaca
angora
bouclé
burlap
calico
canvas
chintz
cloqué
cotton
crépon
crewel
Dacron
damask
devoré
dimity
Dralon
duffel
dupion
faille
fleece
frieze
jersey
kersey
madras
melton
merino
mohair
moreen
muslin
pongee
poplin
raffia
sateen
saxony
shoddy
tricot
Velcro
velour
velvet
vicuña
wincey

7 LETTERS

acetate
acrylic
batiste
brocade
buckram
cambric
challis
cheviot
chiffon
doeskin
fishnet
flannel
foulard
fustian
gingham
grogram
guipure
hessian
holland
hopsack
jaconet
matting
nankeen
oilskin
organza
ottoman
paisley
percale
ripstop
sacking
Spandex
tabaret
taffeta
tatting
ticking
tiffany
torchon
tussore
viscose
Viyella
webbing
worsted

8 LETTERS

asbestos
barathea
bobbinet
cashmere
chambray
chenille
corduroy
cretonne
dungaree
elastane
gossamer
jacquard
marocain
moleskin
moquette
nainsook
oilcloth
organdie
pashmina
sarsenet
tapestry
tarlatan
Terylene
waxcloth
whipcord

9 LETTERS

astrakhan
barkcloth
bombazine
Crimplene
crinoline
gaberdine
georgette
grenadine
grosgrain
haircloth

horsehair
huckaback
lambswool
micromesh
organzine
petersham
polyester
sackcloth
sailcloth
satinette
shahtoosh
sharkskin
stockinet
swansdown
tarpaulin
towelling
velveteen

10 LETTERS

blanketing
broadcloth
candlewick
chinchilla
grasscloth
kerseymere
microfibre
mousseline
needlecord
polycotton
seersucker
tattersall
winceyette

11 LETTERS

cheesecloth
flannelette
herringbone
leatherette
marquisette

12 LETTERS

leathercloth
Valenciennes

2 WORDS

Bedford cord
bobbin lace
Botany wool
butter muslin
camel hair
cavalry twill
Chantilly lace
coconut matting
crushed velvet
Donegal tweed
duchesse lace
duchesse satin
Gore-tex
gros point
Harris tweed
Honiton lace
Kendal Green
Lincoln green
linsey-woolsey
Nottingham lace
panne velvet
pillow lace
pilot cloth
plush velvet
point lace
Shetland wool
spun silk
wild silk

3 WORDS

crêpe de Chine
peau-de-soie
sea-island cotton
toile de Jouy

Footwear

1 WORD

3 LETTERS

dap

4 LETTERS

clog
mule
pump
shoe
zori

5 LETTERS

Derby
sabot
thong
wader
wedge

6 LETTERS

bootee
brogan
brogue
buskin
galosh
gillie
loafer
mukluk
Oxford
patten
sandal

7 LETTERS

chappal
ghillie
gumboot
slipper
sneaker
trainer

8 LETTERS

balmoral

huarache
jackboot
moccasin
napoleon
overboot
overshoe
platform
plimsoll
snowshoe
stiletto

9 LETTERS

slingback

10 LETTERS

espadrille

2 WORDS

ankle boot
ballet shoe
beetle-crusher
bovver boot
brothel creeper
carpet slipper
Chelsea boot
court shoe
cowboy boot
Cuban heel
deck shoe
desert boot
Dr Martens
elevator shoe
flip-flop
half-boot
Hessian boot
high heels
high-low
high-top
hobnail boot
jelly shoe
kitten heel
lace-up
Mary Jane
moon boot
peep-toe
penny loafer
saddle shoe
slip-on
snow boot
step-in
tap shoe
tennis shoe
top boot
track shoe
Turkish slipper
walking boot
wellington boot
winkle-picker

Hats and other headgear

1 WORD

3 LETTERS

cap
fez
taj
tam

4 LETTERS

coif
cowl
hood
kepi
topi
veil

5 LETTERS

beret
busby
crown
derby
hijab
mitre
snood
tammy
tiara
toque

6 LETTERS

beanie
boater
bonnet
bowler
calash
cloche
diadem
fedora
helmet
panama
topper
trilby
turban
wimple
wreath

7 LETTERS

bandeau
biretta
chaplet
circlet
coronet
garland
hairnet
headtie
homburg
leghorn
pillbox
Stetson

8 LETTERS

balmoral
bearskin
earmuffs

hairband
headband
keffiyeh
mantilla
nightcap
skullcap
sombrero
tarboosh
tricorne

9 LETTERS

balaclava
glengarry
headscarf
sou'wester
wideawake
zucchetto

11 LETTERS

deerstalker

2 WORDS

Alice band
baseball cap
beaver hat
bobble hat
bowler hat
cloth cap
cocked hat
coolie hat
crash helmet
Dolly Varden
dunce's cap
Dutch cap
flat cap
gibus hat
hard hat
high hat
jester's cap
jockey cap
Juliet cap
mob cap
mortar board
opera hat
peaked cap
picture hat
pixie hat
poke bonnet
sailor hat
slouch hat
stocking cap
stovepipe hat
sun bonnet
sun hat
sun helmet
top hat
triple crown

3 WORDS

pork-pie hat
snap-brim hat
tam-o'-shanter
ten-gallon hat

Jewellery

1 WORD

3 LETTERS

pin

4 LETTERS

band
clip
pavé
ring
stud
torc

5 LETTERS

beads
cameo
chain
tiara

6 LETTERS

amulet
anklet
armlet
bangle
brooch
choker
diadem
hatpin
locket
strand
tiepin

7 LETTERS

circlet
earring
manilla
necklet
pendant
sleeper

8 LETTERS

barrette
bracelet
marquise
necklace
stickpin
wristlet

9 LETTERS

hairslide
medallion
wristband

2 WORDS

charm bracelet
cuff link
ear stud
engagement ring
eternity ring
friendship bracelet
nose ring
nose stud
scarf ring
signet ring
slave bangle
slave bracelet
toe ring
wedding ring

Underwear

1 WORD

3 LETTERS

bra

4 LETTERS

body
slip
vest

5 LETTERS

choli
combs
jocks
kecks
pants
shift
stays
tanga
teddy
thong

6 LETTERS

bodice
boxers
briefs
corset
garter
girdle
nylons
shorts
string
tights
waspie

7 LETTERS

chemise
drawers
panties
spencer

8 LETTERS

bloomers
camisole
chuddies
frillies
knickers
scanties
thermals
trolleys
trollies

9 LETTERS

brassiere
crinoline
jockstrap
pantyhose
petticoat
undervest

10 LETTERS

corselette
suspenders
underpants
undershirt

11 LETTERS

farthingale
pantalettes
undershorts

12 LETTERS

camiknickers
combinations

2 WORDS

bikini briefs
body stocking
boxer shorts
Directoire drawers
foundation garment
French knickers
G-string
hold-ups
jockey shorts
liberty bodice
long johns
panty girdle
posing pouch
roll-on
string vest
suspender belt
Y-fronts

Famous people

Actors

1 WORD

3 LETTERS

Bow (Clara; 1905–65; American)
Day (Doris; b. 1924; American)
Lee (Bruce; 1940–73; American)
Lee (Christopher; b. 1922; English)

4 LETTERS

Alda (Alan; b. 1936; American)
Cage (Nicholas; b. 1964; American)
Chan (Jackie; b. 1954; Hong Kong)
Cook (Peter; 1937–95; English)
Dean (James; 1931–55; American)
Depp (Johnny; b. 1963; American)
Diaz (Cameron; b. 1972; American)
Ford (Harrison; b. 1942; American)
Gere (Richard; b. 1949; American)
Gish (Lillian; 1893–1993; American)
Hawn (Goldie; b. 1945; American)
Holm (Ian; b. 1931; English)
Hope (Bob; 1903–2003; American)
Hurt (John; b. 1940; English)
Hurt (William; b. 1950; American)
Kaye (Danny; 1913–87; American)
Kean (Edmund; 1787–1833; English)
Kerr (Deborah; b. 1921; Scottish)
Peck (Gregory; 1916–2003; American)
Pitt (Brad; b. 1963; American)
Reed (Oliver; 1938–99; English)
Roth (Tim; b. 1961; American)
Ryan (Meg; b. 1963; American)
Tati (Jacques; 1908–82; French)
West (Mae; 1892–1980; American)
Wood (Elijah; b. 1981; American)
Wood (Natalie; 1938–81; American)

5 LETTERS

Allen (Woody; b. 1935; American)
Bates (Alan; 1934–2003; English)
Berry (Halle; b. 1968; American)
Bloom (Claire; b. 1931; English)
Bloom (Orlando; b. 1977; English)
Boyer (Charles; 1897–1978; French)
Caine (Michael; b. 1933; English)
Chase (Chevy; b. 1943; American)
Clift (Montgomery; 1920–66; American)
Close (Glenn; b. 1947; American)
Crowe (Russell; b. 1964; New Zealand)
Dafoe (Willem; b. 1955; American)
Davis (Bette; 1908–89; American)
Delon (Alain; b. 1935; French)
Dench (Judi; b. 1934; English)
Evans (Edith; 1888–1976; English)
Flynn (Errol; 1909–59; American, b. in Australia)
Fonda (Bridget; b. 1964; American)
Fonda (Henry; 1905–82; American)
Fonda (Jane; b. 1937; American)
Gable (Clark; 1901–60; American)
Garbo (Greta; 1905–90; American, b. in Sweden)
Grant (Cary; 1904–86; American, b. in Britain)
Grant (Hugh; b. 1960; English)
Hanks (Tom; b. 1956; American)
Hardy (Oliver; 1892–1957; American)
Hauer (Rutger; b. 1944; Dutch)
Irons (Jeremy; b. 1948; English)
Jason (David; b. 1940; English)
Jolie (Angelina; b. 1975; American)
Kelly (Gene; 1912–96; American)
Kelly (Grace; 1929–82; American)

Kline (Kevin; b. 1947; American)
Lange (Jessica; b. 1947; American)
Leigh (Vivien; 1913–67; British, b. in India)
Lloyd (Marie; 1870–1922; English)
Lopez (Jennifer; b. 1970, American)
Loren (Sophia; b. 1934; Italian)
Lorre (Peter; 1904–64; American, b. in Hungary)
Mason (James; 1909–84; English)
Mills (John; 1908–2005; English)
Moore (Demi; b. 1962; American)
Moore (Dudley; 1935–2002; English)
Moore (Roger; b. 1927; English)
Neill (Sam; b. 1948; New Zealand)
Niven (David; 1910–83; English)
O'Neal (Ryan; b. 1941; American)
Price (Vincent; 1911–93; American)
Quaid (Dennis; b. 1955; American)
Quinn (Anthony; 1915–2001; American, b. in Mexico)
Reeve (Christopher; 1952–2004; American)
Ryder (Winona; b. 1971; American)
Scott (George C.; 1927–1999; American)
Sheen (Martin; b. 1940; American)
Smith (Maggie; b. 1934; English)
Smith (Will; b. 1969; American)
Stamp (Terence; b. 1939; English)
Stone (Sharon; b. 1958; American)
Terry (Ellen; 1847–1928; English)
Tracy (Spencer; 1900–67; American)
Tutin (Dorothy; 1930–2001; English)
Wayne (John; 1907–79; American)

6 LETTERS

Adjani (Isabelle; b. 1955; French)
Bacall (Lauren; b. 1924; American)
Bardot (Brigitte; b. 1934; French)
Beatty (Warren; b. 1937; American)
Bogart (Humphrey; 1899–1957; American)
Brando (Marlon; 1924–2004; American)
Brooks (Mel; b. 1926; American)
Burton (Richard; 1925–84; Welsh)
Cagney (James; 1899–1986; American)
Callow (Simon; b. 1945; English)
Chaney (Lon; 1883–1930; American)
Cibber (Colley; 1671–1757; English)
Cleese (John; b. 1939; English)
Cooper (Gary; 1901–61; American)
Crosby (Bing; 1904–77; American)
Cruise (Tom; b. 1962; American)
Curtis (Jamie Lee; b. 1958; American)
Curtis (Tony; b. 1925; American)
Cusack (Cyril; 1910–93; Irish, b. in South Africa)
Cusack (Sinead; b. 1948; Irish)
Dalton (Timothy; b. 1946; Welsh)
Farrow (Mia; b. 1945; American)
Fields (W. C.; 1880–1946; American)
Finlay (Frank; b. 1926; English)
Finney (Albert; b. 1936; English)
Foster (Jodie; b. 1962; American)
Gambon (Michael; b. 1940; Irish)
Gibson (Mel; b. 1956; Australian, b. in America)
Harlow (Jean; 1911–37; American)
Heston (Charlton; b. 1923; American)
Hopper (Dennis; b. 1936; American)
Howard (Leslie; 1893–1943; English)
Howard (Trevor; 1916–88; English)
Hudson (Rock; 1925–85; American)
Huston (Angelica; b. 1952; American)
Irving (Henry; 1838–1905; English)
Jacobi (Derek; b. 1938; English)
Kapoor (Raj; 1924–88; Indian)
Keaton (Buster; 1895–1966; American)
Keaton (Diane; b. 1946; American)
Keaton (Michael; b. 1951; American)
Keitel (Harvey; b. 1939; American)
Kemble (Fanny; 1809–93; English)
Kemble (Peter; 1757–1823; English)
Kidman (Nicole; b. 1967; Australian, b. in Hawaii)
Kinski (Klaus; 1926–91; Polish)
Kinski (Nastassja; b. 1960; Polish, b. in Germany)
Lamarr (Hedy; 1913–2000; American, b. in Austria)
Laurel (Stan; 1890–1965; English)
Lemmon (Jack; b. 1925; American)
Lugosi (Bela; 1884–1956; American, b. in Hungary)
Martin (Steve; b. 1945; American)
McEwan (Geraldine; b. 1932; English)
Midler (Bette; b. 1945; American)
Mirren (Helen; b. 1945; English)
Monroe (Marilyn; 1926–62; American)

Moreau (Jeanne; b. 1928; French)
Murphy (Eddie; b. 1961; American)
Murray (Bill; b. 1950; American)
Neeson (Liam; b. 1952; Irish)
Newman (Paul; b. 1925; American)
Noiret (Philippe; b. 1930; French)
Oldman (Gary; b. 1958; English)
O'Toole (Peter; b. 1932; British, b. in Ireland)
Pacino (Al; b. 1939; American)
Porter (Eric; 1928–95; English)
Reeves (Keanu; b. 1965; American, b. in Lebanon)
Rogers (Ginger; 1911–95; American)
Rooney (Mickey; b. 1920; American)
Rourke (Mickey; b. 1956; American)
Sinden (Donald; b. 1923; English)
Slater (Christian; b. 1931; American)
Streep (Meryl; b. 1949; American)
Suzman (Janet; b. 1939; South African)
Taylor (Elizabeth; b. 1932; American, b. in Britain)
Temple (Shirley; b. 1928; American)
Turner (Kathleen; b. 1954; American)
Walken (Christopher; b. 1943; American)
Weaver (Sigourney; b. 1949; American)
Welles (Orson; 1915–85; American, also a director)
Willis (Bruce; b. 1955; American, b. in Germany)
Wolfit (Donald; 1902–68; English)

7 LETTERS

Andress (Ursula; b. 1936; Swiss)
Andrews (Julie; b. 1935; English)
Astaire (Fred; 1899–1987; American)
Auteuil (Daniel; b. 1950; French, b. in Algeria)
Aykroyd (Dan; b. 1952; American)
Bergman (Ingrid; 1915–82; Swedish)
Bogarde (Dirk; 1921–99; British, of Dutch descent)
Branagh (Kenneth; b. 1960; English)
Bridges (Jeff; b. 1949; American)
Bridges (Lloyd; 1913–98; American)
Bronson (Charles; 1920–2003; American)
Bullock (Sandra; b. 1966; American)
Burbage (Richard; c.1567–1619; English)
Carlyle (Robert; b. 1961; Scottish)
Chaplin (Charlie; 1889–1977; English)
Clooney (George; b. 1961; American)
Colbert (Claudette; 1903–96; French)
Collins (Joan; b. 1933; English)
Connery (Sean; b. 1930; Scottish)
Costner (Kevin; b. 1955; American)
Cushing (Peter; 1913–94; English)
Deneuve (Catherine; b. 1943; French)
Douglas (Kirk; b. 1916; American)
Douglas (Michael; b. 1944; American)
Dunaway (Faye; b. 1941; American)
Elliott (Denholm; 1922–92; English)
Fiennes (Ralph; b. 1962; English)
Gardner (Ava; 1922–90; American)
Garland (Judy; 1922–69; American)
Garrick (David; 1717–79; English)
Gielgud (John; 1904–2000; English)
Goodman (John; b. 1953; American)
Granger (Stewart; 1913–93; English)
Hackman (Gene; b. 1931; American)
Hepburn (Audrey; 1929–93; American, b. in Belgium)
Hepburn (Katharine; 1909–2003; American)
Hoffman (Dustin; b. 1937; American)
Hopkins (Anthony; b. 1937; Welsh)
Hordern (Michael; 1911–95; English)
Hoskins (Bob; b. 1942; English)
Jackson (Glenda; b. 1936; English)
Johnson (Celia; 1908–82; English)
Karloff (Boris; 1887–1969; English)
Langtry (Lillie; 1853–1929; English)
Matthau (Walter; 1920–2000; American)
McQueen (Steve; 1930–80; American)
Mitchum (Robert; 1917–97; American)
Montand (Yves; 1921–91; Italian)
Nielsen (Leslie; b. 1926; Canadian)
Olivier (Laurence; 1907–89; English)
Paltrow (Gwyneth; b. 1972; American)
Poitier (Sidney; b. 1924; American)
Redford (Robert; b. 1936; American)
Robards (Jason; 1922–2000; American)
Robbins (Tim; b. 1958; American)
Roberts (Julia; b. 1967; American)
Robeson (Paul; 1898–1976; American)
Russell (Jane; b. 1921; American)
Sellers (Peter; 1925–80; English)
Siddons (Sarah; 1755–1831; English)
Steiger (Rod; 1925–2002; American)
Stewart (James; 1908–97; American)

Swanson (Gloria; 1899–1983; American)
Ustinov (Peter; 1921–2004; British, of Russian descent)
Winslet (Kate; b. 1975; English)

8 LETTERS

Arquette (Rosanna; b. 1959; American)
Ashcroft (Peggy; 1907–91; English)
Bancroft (Anne; 1931–2005; American)
Banderas (Antonio; b. 1960; Spanish)
Bankhead (Tallulah; 1903–68; American)
Basinger (Kim; b. 1953; American)
Belmondo (Jean-Paul; b. 1933; French)
Campbell (Mrs Patrick; 1865–1940; English)
Christie (Julie; b. 1940, British, b. in India)
Crawford (Joan; 1908–77; American)
DiCaprio (Leonardo; b. 1974; American)
Dietrich (Marlene; 1901–92; American, b. in Germany)
Dreyfuss (Richard; b. 1947; American)
Eastwood (Clint; b. 1930; American, also a director)
Goldberg (Whoopi; b. 1949; American)
Goldblum (Jeff; b. 1952; American)
Grenfell (Joyce; 1910–79; English)
Griffith (Melanie; b. 1957; American)
Guinness (Alec; 1914–2000; English)
Hayworth (Rita; 1918–87; American)
Kingsley (Ben; b. 1943; English)
Laughton (Charles; 1899–1962; American, b. in Britain)
Lawrence (Gertrude; 1898–1952; English)
Maclaine (Shirley; b. 1934; American)
McKellen (Ian; b. 1939; English)
Mercouri (Melina; 1925–94; Greek)
Minnelli (Liza; b. 1946; American)
Pfeiffer (Michelle; b. 1957; American)
Pickford (Mary; 1893–1979; American, b. in Canada)
Rampling (Charlotte; b. 1946; English)
Redgrave (Michael; 1908–85; English)
Redgrave (Vanessa; b. 1937; English)
Robinson (Edward G.; 1893–1972; American, b. in Romania)
Sarandon (Susan; b. 1946; American)
Scofield (Paul; b. 1922; English)
Stallone (Sylvester; b. 1946; American)
Stanwyck (Barbara; 1907–90; American)
Steadman (Alison; b. 1946; English)
Thompson (Emma; b. 1959; English)
Travolta (John; b. 1954; American)
Turturro (John; b. 1957; American)
Williams (Robin; b. 1952; American)

9 LETTERS

Barrymore (Ethel; 1879–1959; American)
Barrymore (Lionel; 1878–1954; American)
Bernhardt (Sarah; 1844–1923; French)
Betterton (Thomas; 1635–1710; English)
Chevalier (Maurice; 1888–1972; French)
Courtenay (Tom; b. 1937; English)
Depardieu (Gérard; b. 1948; French)
Fairbanks (Douglas; 1909–2000)
Hawthorne (Nigel; 1929–2001; English)
Lancaster (Burt; 1913–94; American)
Lapotaire (Jane; b. 1944; English)
MacDowell (Andie; b. 1958; American)
MacGregor (Ewan; b. 1971; Scottish)
Mansfield (Jayne; 1933–67; American)
Nicholson (Jack; b. 1937; American)
Plowright (Joan; b. 1929; English)
Streisand (Barbra; b. 1942; American)
Thorndike (Sybil; 1882–1976; English)
Valentino (Rudolf; 1895–1926; American)
Zellweger (Renée; b. 1969; American)

10 LETTERS

Richardson (Ralph; 1902–83; English)
Rutherford (Margaret; 1892–1972; English)
Sutherland (Donald; b. 1934; American)
Washington (Denzel; b. 1954; American)

11 LETTERS

Mastroianni (Marcello; 1924–96; Italian)
Weissmuller (Johnny; 1904–84; American)

12 LETTERS

Attenborough (Richard; b. 1923; English)
Stanislavsky (Konstantin; 1863–1938; Russian)

2 WORDS

Bonham-Carter (Helena; b. 1966; English)

Day-Lewis (Daniel; b. 1958; English)
De Niro (Robert; b. 1943; American)
Von Sydow (Max; b. 1929; Swedish)
Zeta-Jones (Catherine; b. 1969; Welsh)

Architects

1 WORD

3 LETTERS

Pei (I. M.; b. 1917; American, b. in China)

4 LETTERS

Adam (Robert; 1728–92; Scottish)
Kent (William; c.1685–1748; English)
Nash (John; 1752–1835; English)
Wren (Christopher; 1632–1723; English)

5 LETTERS

Aalto (Alvar; 1898–1976; Finnish)
Barry (Charles; 1795–1860; English)
Costa (Lúcio; 1902–1998; Brazilian)
Gaudí (Antonio; 1853–1926; Spanish)
Gibbs (James; 1682–1754; Scottish)
Horta (Victor; 1861–1947; Belgian)
Jones (Inigo; 1573–1652; English)
Nervi (Pier Luigi; 1891–1979; Italian)
Piano (Renzo; b. 1937; Italian)
Pugin (Augustus; 1812–52; English)
Scott (George Gilbert; 1811–78; English)
Scott (Giles Gilbert; 1880–1960; English)
Soane (John; 1753–1837; English)
Speer (Albert; 1905–81; German)
Tange (Kenzo; 1913–2005; Japanese)
Terry (Quinlan; b. 1937; English)
Wyatt (James; 1746–1813; English)

6 LETTERS

Casson (Hugh; 1910–99; English)
Foster (Norman; b. 1935; English)
Rogers (Richard; b. 1933; English)
Spence (Basil; 1907–76; Scottish)
Wright (Frank Lloyd; 1869–1959; American)

7 LETTERS

Alberti (Leon Battista; 1404–72; Italian)
Behrens (Peter; 1868–1940; German)
Bernini (Gian Lorenzo; 1598–1680; Italian)
Gropius (Walter; 1883–1969; German)
Ictinus (5th century BC; Greek)
Imhotep (fl. 27th century BC; Egyptian)
Lutyens (Edwin; 1869–1944; English)
Mansart (François; 1598–1666; French)
Venturi (Robert; b. 1925; American)
Vignola (Giacomo da; 1507–73; Italian)

8 LETTERS

Bramante (Donato; 1444–1514; Italian)
Chambers (William; 1723–96; Scottish)
Jacobsen (Arne; 1902–71; Danish)
Niemeyer (Oscar; b. 1907; Brazilian)
Palladio (Andrea; 1508–80; Italian)
Stirling (James; 1926–92; Scottish)
Vanbrugh (John; 1664–1726; English)
Yamasaki (Minoru; 1912–86; American)

9 LETTERS

Borromini (Francesco; 1599–1667; Italian)
Hawksmoor (Nicholas; 1661–1736; English)
Sansovino (Jacopo; 1486–1570; Italian)
Vitruvius (1st century BC; Roman)

10 LETTERS

Mackintosh (Charles Rennie; 1868–1928; Scottish)
Waterhouse (Alfred; 1830–1905; English)

11 LETTERS

Butterfield (William; 1814–1900; English)
Callicrates (5th century BC; Greek)

12 LETTERS

Brunelleschi (Filippo; 1377–1446; Italian)

2 WORDS

Le Corbusier (1887–1965; French)

3 WORDS

van de Velde (Henri; 1863–1957; Belgian)

4 WORDS

Mies van der Rohe (Ludwig; 1886–1969; German)

Artists and sculptors

1 WORD

3 LETTERS

Arp (Jean; 1887–1966; French)
Dix (Otto; 1891–1969; German)

4 LETTERS

Bell (Vanessa; 1879–1961; English)
Dadd (Richard; 1819–87; English)
Dali (Salvador; 1904–89; Spanish)
Dufy (Raoul; 1877–1953; French)
Gabo (Naum; 1890–1977; American, b. in Russia)
Gill (Eric; 1882–1940; English)
Goes (Hugo van der; c.1440–82; Flemish)
Goya (Francisco; 1746–1828; Spanish)
Gris (Juan; 1887–1927; Spanish)
Hals (Frans; c.1580–1666; Dutch)
Hunt (Holman; 1827–1910; English)
John (Augustus; 1878–1961; English)
John (Gwen; 1876–1939; Welsh)
Klee (Paul; 1879–1940; Swiss)
Lely (Peter; 1618–80; Dutch)
Long (Richard; b. 1945; English)
Miró (Joan; 1893–1983; Spanish)
Nash (Paul; 1889–1946; English)
Opie (John; 1761–1807; English)
Rosa (Salvator; 1615–73; Italian)
West (Benjamin; 1738–1820; American)

5 LETTERS

Andre (Carl; b. 1935; American)
Appel (Karel; b. 1921; Dutch)
Bacon (Francis; 1909–92; Irish)
Bakst (Léon; 1866–1924; Russian)
Beuys (Joseph; 1921–86; German)
Blake (William; 1757–1827; English)
Bosch (Hieronymus; c.1450–c.1516; Dutch)
Brown (Ford Madox; 1821–93; English)
Burra (Edward; 1905–76; English)
Corot (Camille; 1796–1875; French)
Crome (John; 1768–1821; English)
David (Jacques-Louis; 1748–1825; French)
Degas (Edgar; 1834–1917; French)
Denis (Maurice; 1870–1943; French)
Dürer (Albrecht; 1471–1528; German)
Ensor (James; 1860–1949; Belgian)
Ernst (Max; 1891–1976; German)
Freud (Lucian; b. 1922; English)
Frink (Elisabeth; 1930–93; English)
Frith (William; 1819–1909; English)
Gorky (Arshile; 1904–48; American, b. in Turkey)
Grant (Duncan; 1885–1978; Scottish)
Grosz (George; 1893–1959; German)
Henri (Robert; 1865–1929; American)
Heron (Patrick; 1920–99; English)
Hirst (Damien; b. 1965; English)
Johns (Jasper; b. 1930; American)
Kitaj (R. B.; b. 1932; American)
Klein (Yves; 1928–62; French)
Klimt (Gustav; 1862–1918; Austrian)
Léger (Fernand; 1881–1955; French)
Lippi (Filippino; c.1457–1504; Italian)
Lippi (Fra Filippo; c.1406–69; Italian)
Lotto (Lorenzo; c.1480–1556; Italian)

Lowry (L. S.; 1887–1976; English)
Macke (August; 1887–1914; German)
Manet (Edouard; 1832–83; French)
Monet (Claude; 1840–1926; French)
Moore (Henry; 1898–1986; English)
Moses (Grandma; 1860–1961; American)
Mucha (Alphonse; 1860–1939; Czech)
Munch (Edvard; 1863–1944; Norwegian)
Myron (c.480–440 BC; Greek)
Nolan (Sidney; 1917–93; Australian)
Nolde (Emil; 1867–1956; German)
Piper (John; 1903–92; English)
Redon (Odilon; 1840–1916; French)
Riley (Bridget; b. 1931; English)
Rodin (Auguste; 1840–1917; French)
Sarto (Andrea del; 1486–1531; Italian)
Steer (Philip Wilson; 1860–1942; English)
Watts (George; 1817–1904; English)

6 LETTERS

Albers (Josef; 1888–1976; American, b. in Germany)
Bewick (Thomas; 1753–1828; English)
Boudin (Eugene; 1824–98; French)
Braque (Georges; 1882–1963; French)
Buffet (Bernard; 1928–99; French)
Butler (Reginald; 1913–81; English)
Calder (Alexander; 1898–1976; American)
Canova (Antonio; 1757–1822; Italian)
Cotman (John; 1782–1842; English)
Derain (André; 1880–1954; French)
Duccio (c.1255–c.1320; Italian)
Eakins (Thomas; 1844–1916; American)
Escher (M. C.; 1898–1972; Dutch)
Fuseli (Henry; 1741–1825; British, b. in Switzerland)
Giotto (c.1267–1337; Italian)
Greuze (Jean-Baptiste; 1725–1805; French)
Hopper (Edward; 1882–1967; American)
Ingres (Jean Auguste Dominique; 1780–1867; French)
Kiefer (Anselm; b. 1945; German)
Lebrun (Charles; 1619–90; French)
Mabuse (Jan; c.1478–c.1533; Flemish)
Masson (André; 1896–1987; French)
Millet (Jean; 1814–75; French)
Newman (Barnett; 1905–70; American)
Ostade (Adriaen van; 1610–85; Dutch)
Palmer (Samuel; 1805–81; English)
Pisano (Andrea; c.1290–1348; Italian)
Pisano (Nicola; c.1220–78; Italian)
Ramsay (Allan; 1713–84; Scottish)
Renoir (Auguste; 1841–1919; French)
Ribera (José; c.1591–1652; Spanish)
Rivera (Diego; 1886–1957; Mexican)
Romney (George; 1734–1802; English)
Rothko (Mark; 1903–70; American, b. in Latvia)
Rubens (Peter Paul; 1577–1640; Flemish)
Seurat (Georges; 1859–91; French)
Signac (Paul; 1863–1935; French)
Sisley (Alfred; 1839–99; French)
Stella (Frank; b. 1936; American)
Stubbs (George; 1724–1806; English)
Tanguy (Yves; 1900–55; French)
Titian (c.1488–1576; Italian)
Turner (Joseph Mallord William; 1775–1851; English)
Vasari (Giorgio; 1511–74; Italian)
Warhol (Andy; c.1928–87; American)
Weyden (Rogier van der; c.1400–64; Flemish)
Wilkie (David; 1785–1841; Scottish)
Zeuxis (5th century BC; Greek)

7 LETTERS

Allston (Washington; 1779–1843; American)
Apelles (4th century BC; Greek)
Bellini (Gentile; c.1429–1507; Italian)
Bellini (Giovanni; c.1430–1516; Italian)
Bellini (Jacopo; c.1400–70; Italian)
Bernini (Gian Lorenzo; 1598–1680; Italian)
Bonnard (Pierre; 1867–1947; French)
Boucher (François; 1703–70; French)
Brouwer (Adriaen; c.1605–38; Flemish)
Bruegel (Jan; 1568–1623; Flemish)
Bruegel (Pieter; 1525–69)
Cassatt (Mary; 1844–1926; American)
Cellini (Benvenuto; 1500–71; Italian)
Cézanne (Paul; 1839–1906; French)
Chagall (Marc; 1887–1985; French, b. in Russia)
Chirico (Giorgio de; 1888–1978; Italian, b. in Greece)
Christo (Christo Javacheff; b. 1935; Bulgarian)
Courbet (Gustave; 1819–77; French)
Cranach (Lucas; 1472–1553; German)

Daumier (Honoré; 1808–78; French)
Duchamp (Marcel; 1887–1968; American, b. in France)
Epstein (Jacob; 1880–1959; British, b. in America)
Exekias (6th century BC; Athenian)
Flaxman (John; 1755–1826; English)
Gauguin (Paul; 1848–1903; French)
Gibbons (Grinling; 1648–1721; British, b. in the Netherlands)
Gormley (Anthony; b. 1950; English)
Hobbema (Meindert; 1638–1709; Dutch)
Hockney (David; b. 1937; English)
Hogarth (William; 1697–1764; English)
Hokusai (Katsushika; 1760–1849; Japanese)
Holbein (Hans; 1497–1543)
Matisse (Henri; 1869–1954; French)
Millais (John Everett; 1829–96; English)
Morisot (Berthe; 1841–95; French)
Murillo (Bartolomé; c.1618–82; Spanish)
O'Keeffe (Georgia; 1887–1986; American)
Orcagna (Andrea; c.1308–68; Italian)
Pasmore (Victor; 1908–98; English)
Pevsner (Antoine; 1886–1962; French, b. in Russia)
Phidias (c.490–c.417 BC; Athenian)
Picasso (Pablo; 1881–1973; Spanish)
Pollock (Jackson; 1912–56; American)
Poussin (Nicolas; 1594–1665; French)
Rackham (Arthur; 1867–1939; English)
Raeburn (Henry; 1756–1823; Scottish)
Raphael (1483–1520; Italian)
Rouault (Georges; 1871–1958; French)
Sargent (John Singer; 1856–1925; American)
Schiele (Egon; 1890–1918; Austrian)
Sickert (Walter; 1860–1942; English)
Soutine (Chaim; 1893–1943; French)
Spencer (Stanley; 1891–1959; English)
Teniers (David; 1610–90; Flemish)
Tiepolo (Giovanni Battista; 1696–1770; Italian)
Uccello (Paolo; 1397–1475; Italian)
Utamaro (Kitagawa; 1753–1806; Japanese)
Utrillo (Maurice; 1883–1955; French)
Valadon (Suzanne; 1867–1938; French)
Vermeer (Jan; 1632–75; Dutch)
Watteau (Antoine; 1684–1721; French)
Zoffany (Johann; c.1733–1810; German)

8 LETTERS

Angelico (Fra; c.1400–55; Italian)
Annigoni (Pietro; 1910–88; Italian)
Beckmann (Max; 1884–1950; German)
Brancusi (Constantin; 1876–1957; Romanian)
Bronzino (Agnolo; 1503–72; Italian)
Carracci (Annibale; 1560–1609; Italian)
Daubigny (Charles François; 1817–78; French)
Delaunay (Robert; 1885–1941; French)
Dubuffet (Jean; 1901–85; French)
Ghiberti (Lorenzo; 1378–1455; Italian)
Hepworth (Barbara; 1903–75; English)
Hitchens (Ivon; 1893–1979; English)
Kirchner (Ernst; 1880–1938; German)
Landseer (Edwin; 1802–73; English)
Lawrence (Thomas; 1769–1830; English)
Leighton (Frederick; 1830–96; English)
Lipchitz (Jacques; 1891–1973; French, b. in Lithuania)
Lysippus (4th century BC; Greek)
Magritte (René; 1898–1967; Belgian)
Malevich (Kazimir; 1878–1935; Russian)
Mantegna (Andrea; 1431–1506; Italian)
Masaccio (1401–28; Italian)
Mondrian (Piet; 1872–1944; Dutch)
Montagna (Bartolommeo; c.1450–1523; Italian)
Paolozzi (Eduardo; 1924–2005; Scottish)
Piranesi (Giovanni; 1720–78; Italian)
Pissarro (Camille; 1830–1903; French)
Pontormo (Jacopo da; 1494–1557; Italian)
Reynolds (Joshua; 1723–92; English)
Rossetti (Dante Gabriel; 1828–82; English)
Rousseau (Henri; 1844–1910; French)
Ruisdael (Jacob van; c.1628–82; Dutch)
Schnabel (Julian; b. 1951; American)
Tinguely (Jean; 1925–91; Swiss)
Vasarely (Viktor; 1908–97; French, b. in Hungary)
Veronese (Paolo; c.1528–88; Italian)
Vlaminck (Maurice de; 1876–1958; French)
Vuillard (Edouard; 1868–1940; French)

Whistler (James; 1834–1903; American)
Zurbarán (Francisco de; 1598–1664; Spanish)

9 LETTERS

Altdorfer (Albrecht; c.1485–1538; German)
Bartholdi (Auguste; 1834–1904; French)
Beardsley (Aubrey; 1872–98; English)
Canaletto (Antonio Canale; 1697–1768; Italian)
Carpaccio (Vittore; c.1455–1525; Italian)
Constable (John; 1776–1837; English)
Correggio (Antonio Allegri da; c.1494–1534; Italian)
Delacroix (Eugène; 1798–1863; French)
Donatello (c.1386–1466; Italian)
Fragonard (Jean-Honoré; 1732–1806; French)
Friedrich (Caspar; 1774–1840; German)
Géricault (Théodore; 1791–1824; French)
Giorgione (c.1478–1510; Italian)
Greenaway (Kate; 1846–1901; English)
Grünewald (Mathias; c.1460–1528; German)
Hiroshige (Ando Tokitaro; 1797–1858; Japanese)
Kandinsky (Wassily; 1866–1944; Russian)
Kauffmann (Angelica; 1740–1807; Swiss)
Kokoschka (Oskar; 1886–1980; Austrian)
Nicholson (Ben; 1894–1982; English)
Rembrandt (Harmensz van Rijn) (1606–69; Dutch)
Sansovino (Jacopo Tatti; 1486–1570; Italian)
Velázquez (Diego; 1599–1660; Spanish)
Whiteread (Rachel; b. 1963; English)

10 LETTERS

Archipenko (Aleksandr; 1887–1964; American, b. in Russia)
Botticelli (Sandro; 1445–1510; Italian)
Caravaggio (Michelangelo Merisi da; 1573–1610; Italian)
Carrington (Dora; 1893–1932; English)
Cruikshank (George; 1792–1878; English)
Giacometti (Alberto; 1901–66; Swiss)
Michelozzo (1396–1472; Italian)
Modigliani (Amedeo; 1884–1920; Italian)
Pollaiuolo (Piero; 1443–96; Italian)
Polyclitus (5th century BC; Greek)
Praxiteles (mid-4th century BC; Greek)
Rowlandson (Thomas; 1756–1827; English)
Schwitters (Kurt; 1887–1948; German)
Signorelli (Luca; c.1441–1523; Italian)
Sutherland (Graham; 1903–80; English)
Tintoretto (1518–94; Italian)

11 LETTERS

Bartolommeo (Fra; c.1472–1517; Italian)
Ghirlandaio (Domenico; c.1448–94; Italian)

12 LETTERS

Gainsborough (Thomas; 1727–88; English)
Lichtenstein (Roy; 1923–97; American)
Michelangelo (Michelangelo Buonarroti; 1475–1564; Italian)
Parmigianino (1503–40; Italian)
Rauschenberg (Robert; b. 1925; American)
Winterhalter (Franz; 1806–73; German)

2 WORDS

Alma-Tadema (Laurence; 1836–1912; British, b. in the Netherlands)
Burne-Jones (Edward; 1833–98; English)
Claude Lorraine (Claude Gellée; 1600–82; French)
de Hooch (Pieter; c.1629–c.1684; Dutch)
de Kooning (Willem; 1904–97; American)
della Quercia (Jacopo; c.1374–1438; Italian)
della Robbia (Luca; 1400–82; Italian)
El Greco (1541–1614; Spanish, b. in Crete)
Fantin-Latour (Henri; 1836–1904; French)
Gaudier-Brzeska (Henri; 1891–1915; French)
La Tour (Georges de; 1593–1652; French)
Moholy-Nagy (László; 1895–1946; American, b. in Hungary)
Toulouse-Lautrec (Henri de; 1864–1901; French)
Van Dyck (Anthony; 1599–1641; Flemish)

Van Eyck (Jan; c.1370–1441; Flemish)
Van Gogh (Vincent; 1853–90; Dutch)
Vigée-Lebrun (Élisabeth; 1755–1842; French)

3 WORDS

Gentile da Fabriano (c.1370–1427; Italian)
Leonardo da Vinci (1452–1519; Italian)
Lucas van Leyden (c.1494–1533; Dutch)
Piero della Francesca (1416–92; Italian)

Composers

1 WORD

3 LETTERS

Bax (Arnold; 1883–1953; English)

4 LETTERS

Arne (Thomas; 1710–78; English)
Bach (Johann Sebastian; 1685–1750; German)
Berg (Alban; 1885–1935; Austrian)
Byrd (William; 1543–1623; English)
Cage (John; 1912–92; American)
Ives (Charles; 1874–1954; American)
Kern (Jerome; 1885–1945; American)
Orff (Carl; 1895–1982; German)
Pärt (Arvo; b. 1935; Estonian)
Wolf (Hugo; 1860–1903; Austrian)

5 LETTERS

Auric (Georges; 1899–1983; French)
Berio (Luciano; 1925–2003; Italian)
Bizet (Georges; 1838–75; French)
Bliss (Arthur; 1891–1975; English)
Boyce (William; 1711–79; English)
Durey (Louis; 1888–1979; French)
Elgar (Edward; 1857–1934; English)
Falla (Manuel de; 1876–1946; Spanish)
Fauré (Gabriel; 1845–1924; French)
Field (John; 1782–1837; Irish)
Glass (Philip; b. 1937; American)
Gluck (Christoph Willibald von; 1714–87; German)
Grieg (Edvard; 1843–1907; Norwegian)
Haydn (Franz Joseph; 1732–1809; Austrian)
Henze (Hans Werner; b. 1926; German)
Holst (Gustav; 1874–1934; English)
Lehár (Franz; 1870–1948; Hungarian)
Liszt (Franz; 1811–86; Hungarian)
Lully (Jean-Baptiste; 1632–87; French, b. in Italy)
Nyman (Michael; b. 1944; English)
Parry (Hubert; 1848–1918; English)
Ravel (Maurice; 1875–1937; French)
Reich (Steve; b. 1936; American)
Satie (Erik; 1866–1925; French)
Sousa (John; 1854–1932; American)
Verdi (Giuseppe; 1813–1901; Italian)
Weber (Carl Maria von; 1786–1826; German)
Weill (Kurt; 1900–50; German)

6 LETTERS

Arnold (Malcolm; b. 1921; English)
Barber (Samuel; 1910–81; American)
Bartók (Béla; 1881–1945; Hungarian)
Boulez (Pierre; b. 1925; French)
Brahms (Johannes; 1833–97; German)
Busoni (Ferruccio; 1866–1924; Italian)
Carter (Elliott; b. 1908; American)
Chopin (Frédéric; 1810–49; Polish)
Czerny (Karl; 1791–1857; Austrian)
Davies (Peter Maxwell; b. 1934; English)
Delius (Frederick; 1862–1934; English)
Dvořák (Antonín; 1841–1904; Czech)
Franck (César; 1822–90; French, b. in Belgium)
Glinka (Mikhail; 1804–57; Russian)
Gounod (Charles; 1818–93; French)
Handel (George Frederick; 1685–1759; German)
Kodály (Zoltán; 1882–1967; Hungarian)
Lassus (Orlande de; c.1532–94; Flemish)

Ligeti (György; b. 1923; Hungarian)
Mahler (Gustav; 1860–1911; Austrian)
Mozart (Wolfgang Amadeus; 1756–91; Austrian)
Tallis (Thomas; c.1505–85; English)
Varèse (Edgar; 1883–1965; American, b. in France)
Wagner (Richard; 1813–83; German)
Walton (William; 1902–83; English)
Webern (Anton von; 1883–1945; Austrian)

7 LETTERS

Allegri (Gregorio; 1582–1652; Italian)
Babbitt (Milton; b. 1916; American)
Bellini (Vincenzo; 1801–35; Italian)
Bennett (Richard Rodney; b. 1936; English)
Berlioz (Hector; 1803–69; French)
Borodin (Aleksandr; 1833–87; Russian)
Britten (Benjamin; 1913–76; English)
Campion (Thomas; 1567–1620; English)
Copland (Aaron; 1900–90; American)
Corelli (Arcangelo; 1653–1713; Italian)
Debussy (Claude; 1862–1918; French)
Delibes (Léo; 1836–91; French)
Gibbons (Orlando; 1583–1625; English)
Górecki (Henryk; b. 1933; Polish)
Janáček (Leos; 1854–1928; Czech)
Knussen (Oliver; b. 1953; Scottish)
Lambert (Constant; 1905–51; English)
Lutyens (Elisabeth; 1906–83; English)
Milhaud (Darius; 1892–1974; French)
Nielsen (Carl; 1865–1931; Danish)
Poulenc (Francis; 1899–1963; French)
Puccini (Giacomo; 1858–1924; Italian)
Purcell (Henry; 1659–95; English)
Rodgers (Richard; 1902–79; American)
Rodrigo (Joaquín; 1901–99; Spanish)
Romberg (Sigmund; 1887–1951; Hungarian)
Rossini (Gioacchino; 1792–1868; Italian)
Salieri (Antonio; 1750–1825; Italian)
Smetana (Bedrich; 1824–84; Czech)
Strauss (Johann; 1804–49; Austrian)
Strauss (Johann; 1825–99; Austrian)
Strauss (Richard; 1864–1949; German)
Tavener (John; b. 1944; English)
Tippett (Michael; 1905–98; English)
Vivaldi (Antonio; 1678–1741; Italian)
Xenakis (Iannis; 1922–2001; French)

8 LETTERS

Albinoni (Tomaso; 1671–1751; Italian)
Berkeley (Lennox; 1903–89; English)
Bruckner (Anton; 1824–96; Austrian)
Couperin (François; 1668–1733; French)
Gershwin (George; 1898–1937; American)
Grainger (Percy; 1882–1961; American, b. in Australia)
Honegger (Arthur; 1892–1955; French)
Mascagni (Pietro; 1863–1945; Italian)
Massenet (Jules; 1842–1912; French)
Messiaen (Olivier; 1908–92; French)
Paganini (Niccolò; 1782–1840; Italian)
Respighi (Ottorino; 1879–1936; Italian)
Schubert (Franz; 1797–1828; Austrian)
Schumann (Robert; 1810–56; German)
Scriabin (Aleksandr; 1872–1915; Russian)
Sibelius (Jean; 1865–1957; Finnish)
Sondheim (Stephen; b. 1930; American)
Stanford (Charles; 1852–1924; British, b. in Ireland)
Sullivan (Arthur; 1842–1900; English)
Taverner (John; c.1490–1545; English)
Telemann (Georg Philipp; 1681–1767; German)

9 LETTERS

Beethoven (Ludwig van; 1770–1827; German)
Bernstein (Leonard; 1918–90; American)
Boulanger (Nadia; 1887–1979; French)
Buxtehude (Dietrich; c.1637–1707; Danish)
Cherubini (Luigi; 1760–1842; Italian)
Donizetti (Gaetano; 1797–1848; Italian)
Hindemith (Paul; 1895–1963; German)
Meyerbeer (Giacomo; 1791–1864; German)
Offenbach (Jacques; 1819–80; German)
Pachelbel (Johann; 1653–1706; German)
Prokofiev (Sergei; 1891–1953; Russian)
Scarlatti (Alessandro; 1660–1725; Italian)
Scarlatti (Domenico; 1685–1757; Italian)
Schnittke (Alfred; 1934–98; Russian, of German descent)

10 LETTERS

Birtwistle (Harrison; b. 1934; English)
Boccherini (Luigi; 1743–1805; Italian)

Monteverdi (Claudio; 1567–1643; Italian)
Mussorgsky (Modest; 1839–81; Russian)
Palestrina (Giovanni Pierluigi da; c.1525–94; Italian)
Penderecki (Krzysztof; b. 1933; Polish)
Rubinstein (Anton; 1829–94; Russian)
Schoenberg (Arnold; 1874–1951; American, b. in Austria)
Stravinsky (Igor; 1882–1971; Russian)

11 LETTERS

Humperdinck (Engelbert; 1854–1921; German)
Leoncavallo (Ruggiero; 1857–1919; Italian)
Lutosławski (Witold; 1913–94; Polish)
Mendelssohn (Felix; 1809–47; German)
Rachmaninov (Sergei; 1873–1943; Russian)
Stockhausen (Karlheinz; b. 1928; German)
Tailleferre (Germaine; 1892–1983; French)
Tchaikovsky (Pyotr; 1840–93; Russian)

12 LETTERS

Dallapiccola (Luigi; 1904–75; Italian)
Khachaturian (Aram; 1903–78; Soviet)
Shostakovich (Dmitri; 1906–75; Russian)

2 WORDS

Lloyd Webber (Andrew; b. 1948; English)
Rimsky-Korsakov (Nikolai; 1844–1908; Russian)
Saint-Saëns (Camille; 1835–1921; French)
Vaughan Williams (Ralph; 1872–1958; English)
Villa-Lobos (Heitor; 1887–1959; Brazilian)

Criminals

1 WORD

Blunt (Anthony; 1907–83; British)
Brady (Ian; b. 1938; Irish)
Bundy (Ted; 1946–89; American)
Burgess (Guy; 1911–63; British)
Burke (William; 1792–1829; Irish)
Capone (Al; 1899–1947; American)
Crippen (Doctor; 1862–1910; British, b. in America)
Dahmer (Jeffrey; 1960–94; American)
Fawkes (Guy; 1570–1606; English)
Fuchs (Klaus; 1911–88; British, b. in Germany)
Genovese (Vito; 1897–1969; American)
Giancana (Sam; 1908–75; American)
Gotti (John; 1940–2002; American)
Hare (William; ?1792–1859; Irish)
Hindley (Myra; 1942–2002; British)
James (Jesse; 1847–82; American)
Kelly (Ned; 1855–80; Australian)
Kray (Reggie; 1933–2000; English)
Kray (Ronnie; 1933–1995; English)
Maclean (Donald; 1913–83; British)
Manson (Charles; b. 1934; American)
Nilsen (Dennis; b. 1945; English)
Oswald (Lee Harvey; 1939–63; American)
Philby (Kim; 1912–88; British)
Shipman (Harold; 1946–2004; English)
Siegel (Bugsy; 1906–47; American)
Sutcliffe (Peter; b. 1946; English)
Turpin (Dick; 1706–39; English)
West (Rose; b. 1953; English)
West (Fred; 1941–95; English)

2 WORDS

Lucky Luciano (1896–1962; Italian)
Mata Hari (1876–1917; Dutch)

3 WORDS

Billy the Kid (William Bonney; 1859–81; American)
Jack the Ripper (19th century)

Dancers

1 WORD

Ashton (Frederick; 1904–88; English)
Astaire (Fred; 1899–1987; American)
Baker (Josephine; 1906–75; American)
Balanchine (George; 1904–83; American, b. in Russia)
Baryshnikov (Mikhail; b. 1948; American, b. in Latvia)
Bussell (Darcey; b. 1969; English)
Cunningham (Merce; b. 1919; American)
Dolin (Anton; 1904–83; English)
Duncan (Isadora; 1878–1927; American)
Fonteyn (Margot; 1919–91; English)
Graham (Martha; 1893–1991; American)
Guillem (Sophie; b. 1965; French)
Helpmann (Robert; 1909–86; Australian)
Kelly (Gene; 1912–96; American)
Laban (Rudolf von; 1879–1958; Hungarian)
Markova (Alicia; 1910–2004; English)
Massine (Léonide; 1895–1979; French, b. in Russia)
Nijinsky (Vaslav; 1890–1950; Russian)
Nureyev (Rudolf; 1939–93; Austrian, b. in Russia)
Pavlova (Anna; 1881–1931; Russian)
Rambert (Marie; 1888–1982; British, b. in Poland)
Robbins (Jerome; 1918–98; American)
Rogers (Ginger; 1911–95; American)
Seymour (Lynn; b. 1939; Canadian)
Shearer (Moira; b. 1926; Scottish)
Ulanova (Galina; 1910–98; Russian)

2 WORDS

de Valois (Ninette; 1898–2001; Irish)

Dramatists

2 LETTERS

Fo (Dario; b. 1926; Italian)

3 LETTERS

Fry (Christopher; 1907–2005; English)
Kyd (Thomas; 1558–94; English)

4 LETTERS

Bolt (Robert; 1924–95; English)
Bond (Edward; b. 1934; English)
Ford (John; c.1586–c.1640; English)
Gray (Simon; b. 1936; English)
Hare (David; b. 1947; English)
Rowe (Nicholas; 1674–1718; English)
Shaw (George Bernard; 1856–1950; Irish)
Vega (Lope de; 1562–1635; Spanish)

5 LETTERS

Albee (Edward; b. 1928; American)
Behan (Brendan; 1923–64; Irish)
Betti (Ugo; 1892–1953; Italian)
Capek (Karel; 1890–1938; Czech)
Frayn (Michael; b. 1933; English)
Genet (Jean; 1910–86; French)
Gorky (Maxim; 1868–1936; Russian)
Havel (Václav; b. 1936; Czech)
Ibsen (Henrik; 1828–1906; Norwegian)
Jarry (Alfred; 1873–1907; French)
Lorca (Federico García; 1898–1936; Spanish)
Mamet (David; b. 1947; American)
Odets (Clifford; 1906–63; American)
Orton (Joe; 1933–67; English)
Otway (Thomas; 1652–85; English)
Simon (Neil; b. 1927; American)
Synge (J. M.; 1871–1909; Irish)
Wilde (Oscar; 1854–1900; Irish)

6 LETTERS

Barrie (J. M.; 1860–1937; Scottish)
Brecht (Bertolt; 1898–1956; German)
Coward (Noel; 1899–1973; English)
Dekker (Thomas; c.1570–1632; English)
Fugard (Athol; b. 1932; South African)
Goethe (Johann Wolfgang von; 1749–1832; German)
Jonson (Ben; 1572–1637; English)
Miller (Arthur; 1915–2005; American)
Musset (Alfred de; 1810–57; French)
O'Casey (Sean; 1880–1964; Irish)
O'Neill (Eugene; 1888–1953; American)
Pinero (Arthur Wing; 1855–1934; English)
Pinter (Harold; b. 1930; English)
Potter (Dennis; 1935–94; English)
Racine (Jean; 1639–99; French)
Rowley (William; c.1585–1626; English)
Seneca (Lucius Annaeus; c.4 BC–AD 65; Roman)
Storey (David; b. 1933; English)
Wesker (Arnold; b. 1932; English)
Wilder (Thornton; 1897–1975; American)

7 LETTERS

Anouilh (Jean; 1910–87; French)
Beckett (Samuel; 1906–89; Irish)
Bennett (Alan; b. 1934; English)
Chekhov (Anton; 1860–1904; Russian)
Cocteau (Jean; 1889–1963; French)
Farquar (George; 1678–1707; Irish)
Feydeau (Georges; 1862–1921; French)
Hellman (Lillian; 1907–84; American)
Ionesco (Eugène; 1912–94; French, b. in Romania)
Lessing (Gotthold; 1729–81; German)
Marlowe (Christopher; 1564–93; English)
Molière (Jean-Baptiste Poquelin; 1622–73; French)
Osborne (John; 1929–94; English)
Plautus (c.259–184 BC; Roman)
Pushkin (Aleksandr; 1799–1837; Russian)
Rostand (Edmond; 1868–1918; French)
Soyinka (Wole; b. 1934; Nigerian)
Terence (c.185–159 BC; Roman)
Vicente (Gil; c.1465–c.1536; Portuguese)
Webster (John; c.1580–c.1625; English)

8 LETTERS

Beaumont (Francis; 1584–1616; English)
Congreve (William; 1670–1729; English)
Fletcher (John; 1579–1625; English)
Menander (c.342–c.292 BC; Greek)
Rattigan (Terence; 1911–77; English)
Schiller (Friedrich von; 1759–1805; German)
Sheridan (Richard Brinsley; 1751–1816; Irish)
Stoppard (Tom; b. 1937; British, b. in Czechoslovakia)
Tourneur (Cyril; c.1576–1626; English)
Vanbrugh (John; 1664–1726; English)
Wedekind (Frank; 1864–1918; German)
Williams (Tennessee; 1911–83; American)

9 LETTERS

Aeschylus (c.525–c.456 BC; Greek)
Ayckbourn (Alan; b. 1939; English)
Churchill (Caryl; b. 1938; English)
Corneille (Pierre; 1606–84; French)
Euripides (c.480–406 BC; Greek)
Goldsmith (Oliver; 1728–74; Irish)
Hauptmann (Gerhart; 1862–1946; German)
Massinger (Philip; 1583–1640; English)
Middleton (Thomas; c.1570–1627; English)
Poliakoff (Stephen; b. 1952; English)
Sophocles (c.496–406 BC; Greek)
Wycherley (William; c.1640–1716; English)

10 LETTERS

Pirandello (Luigi; 1867–1936; Italian)
Strindberg (August; 1849–1912; Swedish)

11 LETTERS

Maeterlinck (Comte Maurice; 1862–1949; Belgian)
Shakespeare (William; 1564–1616; English)

12 LETTERS

Aristophanes (c.450–c.385 BC; Greek)
Beaumarchais (Pierre-Augustin Caron de; 1732–99; French)

Economists, historians, and philosophers

1 WORD

4 LETTERS

Ayer (A. J.; 1910–89; English philosopher)
Bede (the Venerable Bede; c.673–735; English historian)
Hume (David; 1711–76; Scottish philosopher, economist, and historian)
Kant (Immanuel; 1724–1804; German philosopher)
Livy (59 BC–17 AD; Roman historian)
Marx (Karl; 1818–83; German economist and philosopher)
Mill (John Stuart; 1806–73; English economist and philosopher)
Ryle (Gilbert; 1900–76; English philosopher)
Vico (Giambattista; 1668–1744; Italian philosopher)
Webb (Beatrice; 1858–1943; English historian and economist)
Webb (Sidney; 1859–1947; English historian and economist)
Weil (Simone; 1909–43; French philosopher)
Zeno (of Citium; c.335–c.263 BC; Greek philosopher)

5 LETTERS

Arrow (Kenneth; b. 1921; American economist)
Bacon (Francis; 1561–1626; English philosopher)
Bacon (Roger; c.1214–94; English philosopher)
Comte (Auguste; 1798–1857; French philosopher)
Frege (Gottlob; 1848–1925; German philosopher)
Hayek (Friedrich August von; 1899–1992; Austrian economist)
Hegel (Georg; 1770–1831; German philosopher)
Hicks (John Richard; 1904–1989; English economist)
James (William; 1842–1910; American philosopher)
Lacan (Jacques; 1901–81; French philosopher)
Locke (John; 1632–1704; English philosopher)
Moore (G. E.; 1873–1958; English philosopher)
Plato (c.429–c.347 BC; Greek philosopher)
Smith (Adam; 1723–90; Scottish economist)
Weber (Max; 1864–1920; German economist)

6 LETTERS

Adorno (Theodor; 1903–69; German philosopher)
Arendt (Hannah; 1906–75; American philosopher, b. in Germany)
Berlin (Isaiah; 1909–97; British philosopher, b. in Latvia)
Carnap (Rudolf; 1891–1970; American philosopher)
Engels (Friedrich; 1820–95; German philosopher)
Fichte (Johann; 1762–1814; German philosopher)
Frisch (Ragnar; 1895–1973; Norwegian economist)
Gibbon (Edward; 1737–94; English historian)
Hobbes (Thomas; 1588–1679; English philosopher)
Irving (David; b. 1938; English historian)
Keynes (John Maynard; 1883–1946; English economist)
Littré (Émile; 1801–81; French philosopher)
Lukács (György; 1885–1971; Hungarian philosopher)
Pareto (Vilfredo; 1848–1923; Italian economist)
Pascal (Blaise; 1623–62; French philosopher)
Peirce (Charles; 1839–1914; American philosopher)
Popper (Karl; 1902–94; British philosopher, b. in Austria)
Sartre (Jean-Paul; 1905–80; French philosopher)
Schama (Simon; b. 1945; English historian)
Stubbs (William; 1825–1901; English historian)
Taylor (A. J. P.; 1906–90; English historian)
Veblen (Thorstein; 1857–1929; American economist)

Walras (M. E. Léon; 1834–1910; French economist)

7 LETTERS

Aquinas (St Thomas; 1225–74; Italian philosopher)
Bagehot (Walter; 1826–77; English economist)
Barthes (Roland; 1915–80; French philosopher)
Bentham (Jeremy; 1748–1832; English philosopher)
Carlyle (Thomas; 1795–1881; Scottish historian)
Chomsky (Noam; b. 1928; American philosopher)
Derrida (Jacques; 1930–2004; French philosopher)
Diderot (Denis; 1713–84; French philosopher)
Emerson (Ralph Waldo; 1803–82, American philosopher)
Husserl (Edmund; 1859–1938; German philosopher)
Leacock (Stephen Butler; 1869–1949; Canadian economist)
Leibniz (Gottfried; 1646–1716; German philosopher)
Lyotard (Jean-François; 1924–98; French philosopher)
Malthus (Thomas; 1766–1834; English economist)
Marcuse (Herbert; 1898–1979; American philosopher, b. in Germany)
Mommsen (Theodor; 1817–1903; German historian)
Needham (Joseph; 1900–95; English historian)
Nennius (9th century AD; Welsh historian)
Ricardo (David; 1772–1823; English economist)
Russell (Bertrand; 1872–1970; British philosopher)
Sallust (c.86–c.34 BC; Roman historian)
Schlick (Moritz; 1882–1936; German philosopher)
Spinoza (Baruch; 1632–77; Dutch philosopher)
Steiner (Rudolf; 1861–1925; Austrian philosopher)
Tacitus (Cornelius; c.55–c.120 AD; Roman historian)
Toynbee (Arnold; 1852–83; English economist)
Toynbee (Arnold; 1889–1975; English historian)

8 LETTERS

Avicenna (980–1037; Persian philosopher)
Beauvoir (Simone de; 1908–86; French philosopher)
Berkeley (George; 1685–1753; Irish philosopher)
Diogenes (c.400–c.325 BC; Greek philosopher)
Epicurus (341–270 BC; Greek philosopher)
Foucault (Michel; 1926–84; French philosopher)
Friedman (Milton; b. 1912; American economist)
Huizinga (Johan; 1872–1945; Dutch historian)
Macaulay (Thomas; 1800–59; English historian)
Proudhon (Pierre Joseph; 1809–65; French philosopher)
Rousseau (Jean Jacques; 1712–78; French philosopher)
Schlegel (Friedrich von; 1772–1829; German philosopher)
Socrates (c.469–399 BC; Greek philosopher)
Xenophon (c.430–c.354 BC; Greek historian)

9 LETTERS

Althusser (Louis; 1919–90; French philosopher)
Aristotle (384–322 BC; Greek philosopher)
Beveridge (William; 1879–1963; British economist)
Clarendon (Earl of; 1609–74; English historian)
Confucius (c.551–479 BC; Chinese philosopher)
Descartes (René; 1596–1650; French philosopher)
Galbraith (John Kenneth; b. 1908; American economist)
Heidegger (Martin; 1889–1976; German philosopher)
Herodotus (c.484–c.425 BC; Greek historian)

Lamartine (Alphonse de; 1790–1869; French historian)
Nietzsche (Friedrich; 1844–1900; German philosopher)
Suetonius (c.69–c.140 AD; Roman historian)
Tinbergen (Jan; 1903–94; Dutch economist)
Trevelyan (G. M.; 1876–1972; English historian)

10 LETTERS

Democritus (c.460–370 BC; Greek philosopher)
Empedocles (c.493–433 BC; Greek philosopher)
Heraclitus (c.500 BC; Greek philosopher)
Horkheimer (Max; 1895–1973; German philosopher)
Pythagoras (c.560–480 BC; Greek philosopher)
Schumacher (E. F.; 1911–77; German economist)
Swedenborg (Emanuel; 1688–1772; Swedish philosopher)
Thucydides (c.455–c.400 BC; Greek historian)

11 LETTERS

Kierkegaard (Søren; 1813–55; Danish philosopher)

12 LETTERS

Schopenhauer (Arthur; 1788–1860; German philosopher)
Theophrastus (c.370–287 BC; Greek philosopher)
Wittgenstein (Ludwig; 1889–1951; British philosopher)

2 WORDS

Lao-tzu (6th century BC; Chinese philosopher)
Saint-Simon (Claude-Henri de Rouvroy, Comte de; 1760–1825; French philosopher)
Trevor-Roper (Hugh; 1914–2003; English historian)

3 WORDS

Cato the Elder (234–149 BC; Roman historian)
Gregory of Tours (c.540–94; French historian)
Ortega y Gasset (José; 1883–1955; Spanish philosopher)
Teilhard de Chardin (1881–1955; French philosopher)
William of Malmesbury (c.1090–c.1143; English historian)
William of Occam (c.1285–1349; English philosopher)
Zeno of Citium (c.335–c.263 BC; Greek philosopher)

Explorers, aviators, and astronauts

1 WORD

4 LETTERS

Byrd (Richard; 1888–1957; American)
Cook (Captain James; 1728–79; English)
Dias (Bartolomeu; c.1450–1500; Portuguese)
Eyre (Edward John; 1815–1901; Australian, b. in Britain)
Park (Mungo; 1771–1806; Scottish)
Ross (James; 1800–62; Scottish)
Ross (John; 1777–1856; Scottish)

5 LETTERS

Banks (Joseph; 1743–1820; English)
Boone (Daniel; c.1734–1820; American)
Brown (Arthur Whitten; 1886–1948; Scottish)
Bruce (James; 1730–94; Scottish)

Burke (Robert O'Hara; 1820–61; Irish)
Cabot (John; c.1450–c.1498; Italian)
Clark (William; 1770–1838; American)
Drake (Francis; c.1540–96; English)
Fuchs (Vivian; 1908–99; English)
Glenn (John; b. 1921; American)
Lewis (Meriwether; 1774–1809; American)
Peary (Robert; 1856–1920; American)
Scott (Robert; 1868–1912; English)
Speke (John Hanning; 1827–64; English)
Sturt (Charles; 1795–1869; English)
Wills (William John; 1834–61; English)

6 LETTERS

Alcock (John; 1892–1919; English)
Aldrin (Buzz; b. 1930; American)
Baffin (William; c.1584–1622; English)
Balboa (Vasco Núñez de; 1475–1519; Spanish)
Batten (Jean; 1909–82; New Zealand)
Bering (Vitus; 1681–1741; Danish)
Burton (Richard; 1821–90; English)
Cortés (Hernando; 1485–1547; Spanish)
Diemen (Anthony van; 1593–1645; Dutch)
Hudson (Henry; c.1565–1611; English)
Hughes (Howard; 1905–76; American)
Nansen (Fridtjof; 1861–1930; Norwegian)
Selous (Frederick Courteney; 1851–1917; English)
Tasman (Abel; 1603–c.1659; Dutch)
Wright (Orville; 1871–1948; American)
Wright (Wilbur; 1867–1912; American)
Yeager (Chuck; b. 1923; American)

7 LETTERS

Barents (Willem; d. 1597; Dutch)
Blériot (Louis; 1872–1936; French)
Cartier (Jacques; 1491–1557; French)
Cochran (Jacqueline; 1910–80; American)
Curtiss (Glenn; 1878–1930; American)
Dampier (William; 1652–1715; English)
Earhart (Amelia; 1898–1937; American)
Fiennes (Ranulph; b. 1944; English)
Frémont (John; 1813–90; American)
Gagarin (Yuri; 1934–68; Russian)
Gilbert (Humphrey; c.1539–83; English)
Hillary (Edmund; b. 1919; New Zealand)
Johnson (Amy; 1903–41; English)
Pizarro (Francisco; c.1478–1541; Spanish)
Raleigh (Walter; c.1552–1618; English)
Selkirk (Alexander; 1676–1721; Scottish)
Stanley (Henry Morton; 1841–1904; Welsh)

8 LETTERS

Amundsen (Roald; 1872–1928; Norwegian)
Columbus (Christopher; 1451–1506; Spanish, b. in Italy)
Cousteau (Jacques; 1910–97; French)
Ericsson (Leif; 11th century; Norse)
Flinders (Matthew; 1774–1814; English)
Humboldt (Alexander von; 1769–1859; German)
Magellan (Ferdinand; c.1480–1521; Portuguese)
McKinlay (John; 1819–72; Australian, b. in Scotland)
Thesiger (Wilfred; 1910–2003; English)
Vespucci (Amerigo; 1451–1512; Italian)

9 LETTERS

Armstrong (Neil; b. 1930; American)
Champlain (Samuel de; 1567–1635; French)
Ellsworth (Lincoln; 1880–1951; American)
Frobisher (Martin; c.1535–94; English)
Lindbergh (Charles; 1902–74; American)
Mackenzie (Alexander; 1764–1820; Scottish)
Marquette (Jacques; 1637–75; French)
Vancouver (George; 1757–98; English)

10 LETTERS

Shackleton (Ernest; 1874–1922; British, b. in Ireland)
Tereshkova (Valentina; b. 1937; Russian)

11 LETTERS

Livingstone (David; 1813–73; Scottish)

12 LETTERS

Bougainville (Louis Antoine de; 1729–1811; French)

2 WORDS

da Gama (Vasco; c.1469–1524; Portuguese)
Marco Polo (c.1254–c.1324; Italian)
Tenzing Norgay (1914–86; Sherpa)

3 WORDS

Eric the Red (c.940–c.1010; Norse)
Ponce de León (Juan; c.1460–1521; Spanish)
Van der Post (Laurens; 1906–96; South African)

Fashion designers

1 WORD

4 LETTERS

Dior (Christian; 1905–57; French)
Erté (1892–1990; French)
Lang (Helmut; b. 1956; Austrian)
Muir (Jean; 1933–95; English)

5 LETTERS

Amies (Hardy; 1909–2003; English)
Blass (Bill; 1922–2002; American)
Clark (Ossie; 1944–96; English)
Freud (Bella; b. 1961; English)
Karan (Donna; b. 1948; American)
Kenzo (b. 1940; Japanese)
Klein (Calvin; b. 1942; American)
Ozbek (Rifat; b. 1955; Turkish)
Patou (Jean; 1880–1936; French)
Pucci (Emilio; 1914–93; Italian)
Quant (Mary; b. 1934; English)
Reger (Janet; 1935–2005; English)
Smith (Paul; b. 1946; English)

6 LETTERS

Armani (Giorgio; b. 1936; Italian)
Cardin (Pierre; b. 1922; French)
Chanel (Coco; 1883–1971; French)
Conran (Jasper; b. 1959; English)
Lanvin (Jeanne; 1867–1946; French)
Lauren (Ralph; b. 1939; American)
Miyake (Issey; b. 1939; Japanese)
Mugler (Thierry; b. 1948; French)
Rhodes (Zandra; b. 1940; English)
Rykiel (Sonia; b. 1930; French)
Ungaro (Emmanuel; b. 1933; French)

7 LETTERS

Balmain (Pierre; 1914–82; French)
Cerruti (Nino; b. 1930; Italian)
Halston (1932–90; American)
Hamnett (Katharine; b. 1952; English)
Lacroix (Christian; b. 1951; French)
Laroche (Guy; 1923–89; French)
McQueen (Alexander; b. 1969; English)
Missoni (Ottavio; b. 1921; Italian, b. in Yugoslavia)
Montana (Claude; b. 1949; French)
Versace (Gianni; 1946–97; Italian)

8 LETTERS

Cacharel (Jean; b. 1932; French)
Fiorucci (Elio; b. 1935; Italian)
Galliano (John; b. 1960; English)
Gaultier (Jean-Paul; b. 1952; French)
Givenchy (Hubert de; b. 1927; French)
Hartnell (Norman; 1901–78; English)
Moschino (Franco; 1950–94; Italian)
Oldfield (Bruce; b. 1950; English)
Westwood (Vivienne; b. 1941; English)
Yamamoto (Yohji; b. 1943; Japanese)

9 LETTERS

Courrèges (André; b. 1923; French)
Lagerfeld (Karl-Otto; b. 1938; German)
Valentino (b. 1933; Italian)

10 LETTERS

Balenciaga (Cristóbal; 1895–1972; Spanish)

12 LETTERS

Schiaparelli (Elsa; 1896–1973; French, b. in Italy)

2 WORDS

Saint Laurent (Yves; b. 1936; French)

3 WORDS

De la Renta (Oscar; b. 1932; Dominican)

Film directors

1 WORD

3 LETTERS

Lee (Ang; b. 1954; Taiwanese)
Lee (Spike; b. 1957; American)
Ray (Satyajit; 1921–92; Indian)
Woo (John; b. 1946; Chinese)

4 LETTERS

Coen (Ethan; b. 1958; American)
Coen (Joel; b. 1955; American)
Ford (John; 1895–1973; American)
Hill (George Roy; 1922–2002; American)
Lang (Fritz; 1890–1976; Austrian)
Lean (David; 1908–91; English)
Reed (Carol; 1906–76; English)
Roeg (Nicholas; b. 1928; English)
Tati (Jacques; 1908–82; French)
Vigo (Jean; 1905–34; French)
Weir (Peter; b. 1944; Australian)

5 LETTERS

Allen (Woody; b. 1935; American)
Capra (Frank; 1897–1991; American)
Carné (Marcel; 1906–96; French)
Clair (René; 1898–1981; French)
Cukor (George; 1899–1983; American)
Demme (Jonathan; b. 1944; American)
Gance (Abel; 1889–1981; French)
Hawks (Howard; 1896–1977; American)
Ivory (James; b. 1928; American)
Kazan (Elia; 1909–2003; American)
Korda (Alexander; 1893–1956; British)
Leigh (Mike; b. 1943; English)
Leone (Sergio; 1921–89; Italian)
Loach (Ken; b. 1936; English)
Lucas (George; b. 1944; American)
Lumet (Sydney; b. 1924; American)
Lynch (David; b. 1946; American)
Malle (Louis; 1932–95; French)
Raimi (Sam; b. 1959; American)
Scott (Ridley; b. 1939; English)
Scott (Tony; b. 1944; English)
Stone (Oliver; b. 1946; American)
Vadim (Roger; 1928–2000; French)
Vidor (King; 1894–1982; American)
Wajda (Andrzej; b. 1929; Polish)
Wyler (William; 1902–81; German)

6 LETTERS

Altman (Robert; b. 1925; American)
Beatty (Warren; b. 1937; American)
Besson (Luc; b. 1959; French)
Brooks (Mel; b. 1926; American)
Buñuel (Luis; 1900–83; Spanish)
Burton (Tim; b. 1958; American)
Craven (Wes; b. 1939; American)
Curtiz (Michael; 1888–1962; Hungarian)
Forman (Milos; b. 1932; American)
Gibson (Mel; b. 1956; Australian)
Godard (Jean-Luc; b. 1930; French)
Herzog (Werner; b. 1942; German)
Huston (John; 1906–87; American)
Jarman (Derek; 1942–94; English)
Jordan (Neil; b. 1950; Irish)
Kitano (Takeshi; b. 1948; Japanese)
Murnau (F. W.; 1888–1931; German)
Pagnol (Marcel; 1895–1974; French)

Pakula (Alan; 1928–98; American)
Parker (Alan; b. 1944; English)
Powell (Michael; 1905–90; English)
Reiner (Rob; b. 1945; American)
Renoir (Jean; 1894–1979; French)
Rohmer (Eric; b. 1920; French)
Welles (Orson; 1915–85; American)
Wilder (Billy; 1906–2002; American)

7 LETTERS

Bergman (Ingmar; b. 1918; Swedish)
Boorman (John; b. 1933; English)
Branagh (Kenneth; b. 1960; English)
Bresson (Robert; 1907–99; French)
Cameron (James; b. 1954; Canadian)
Campion (Jane; b. 1954; New Zealand)
Chabrol (Claude; b. 1930; French)
Chaplin (Charlie; 1889–1977; English)
Cocteau (Jean; 1889–1963; French)
Coppola (Francis Ford; b. 1939; American)
Fellini (Federico; 1920–93; Italian)
Gilliam (Terry; b. 1940; American)
Jackson (Peter; b. 1961; New Zealand)
Jewison (Norman; b. 1926; Canadian)
Kubrick (Stanley; 1928–99; American)
Pollack (Sydney; b. 1934; American)
Resnais (Alain; b. 1922; French)
Ritchie (Guy; b. 1968; English)
Russell (Ken; b. 1927; English)
Wenders (Wim; b. 1945; German)

8 LETTERS

Anderson (Lindsay; 1923–94; English)
Berkeley (Busby; 1895–1976; American)
Boulting (John; 1913–85; English)
Boulting (Roy; 1913–2001; English)
Crichton (Charles; 1910–99; English)
Eastwood (Clint; b. 1930; American)
Farrelly (Bobby; b. 1958; American)
Farrelly (Peter; b. 1956; American)
Grierson (John; 1898–1972; Scottish)
Griffith (D. W.; 1875–1948; American)
Kurosawa (Akira; 1910–98; Japanese)
Levinson (Barry; b. 1942; American)
Minnelli (Vincente; 1910–86; American)
Pasolini (Pier Paolo; 1922–75; Italian)
Polanski (Roman; b. 1933; French)

Scorsese (Martin; b. 1942; American)
Stroheim (Erich von; 1886–1957; Austrian)
Truffaut (François; 1932–84; French)
Visconti (Luchino; 1906–76; Italian)
Zemeckis (Robert; b. 1952; American)
Zinneman (Fred; 1907–97; American)

9 LETTERS

Almodóvar (Pedro; b. 1951; Spanish)
Antonioni (Michelangelo; b. 1912; Italian)
Greenaway (Peter; b. 1942; English)
Hitchcock (Alfred; 1899–1980; English)
Peckinpah (Sam; 1925–84; American)
Preminger (Otto; 1906–86; American)
Spielberg (Steven; b. 1947; American)
Tarantino (Quentin; b. 1963; American)
Tarkovsky (Andrei; 1932–86; Russian)

10 LETTERS

Bertolucci (Bernardo; b. 1940; Italian)
Cassavetes (John; 1929–89; American)
Cronenberg (David; b. 1943; Canadian)
Eisenstein (Sergei; 1898–1948; Soviet)
Fassbinder (Rainer Werner; 1946–82; German)
Kieslowski (Krzysztof; 1941–96; Polish)
Mankiewicz (Joseph; 1909–93; American)
Rossellini (Roberto; 1906–77; Italian)
Soderbergh (Steven; b. 1963; American)
Zeffirelli (Franco; b. 1923; Italian)

11 LETTERS

Riefenstahl (Leni; 1902–2003; German)
Schlesinger (John; 1926–2003; English)

12 LETTERS

Attenborough (Richard; b. 1923; English)

2 WORDS

de Mille (Cecil B.; 1881–1959; American)
De Palma (Brian; b. 1940; American)
De Sica (Vittorio; 1901–74; Italian)
van Sant (Gus; b. 1953; American)
von Sternberg (Josef; 1894–1969; American)

Inventors and engineers

1 WORD

4 LETTERS

Bell (Alexander Graham; 1847–1922; American inventor, b. in Scotland)
Benz (Karl; 1844–1929; German engineer)
Biró (László; 1899–1985; Hungarian inventor)
Colt (Samuel; 1814–62; American inventor)
Davy (Humphry; 1778–1829; English inventor and chemist)
Howe (Elias; 1819–67; American inventor)
Otis (Elisha; 1811–61; American inventor)
Otto (Nikolaus; 1832–91; German engineer)
Tull (Jethro; 1674–1741; English inventor)
Watt (James; 1736–1819; Scottish engineer)

5 LETTERS

Baird (John Logie; 1888–1946; Scottish inventor)
Braun (Wernher von; 1912–77; American engineer, b. in Germany)
Dewar (James; 1842–1923; Scottish inventor and chemist)
Dyson (James; b. 1947; English inventor)
Gabor (Dennis; 1900–79; British electrical engineer, b. in Hungary)
Morse (Samuel; 1791–1872; American inventor)
Nobel (Alfred; 1833–96; Swedish engineer and chemist)
Tesla (Nikola; 1856–1943; American electrical engineer, b. in Croatia)
Volta (Alessandro; 1745–1827; Italian inventor and physicist)

6 LETTERS

Austin (Herbert; 1866–1941; English engineer and motor manufacturer)
Bramah (Joseph; 1748–1814; English engineer)
Brunel (Isambard Kingdom; 1806–59; English engineer)
Brunel (Marc Isambard; 1769–1849; British engineer, b. in France)
Bunsen (Robert; 1811–99; German inventor and chemist)
Diesel (Rudolf; 1858–1913; German engineer, b. in France)
Dunlop (John; 1840–1921; Scottish inventor)
Edison (Thomas; 1847–1931; American inventor)
Eiffel (Alexandre; 1832–1923; French engineer)
Fokker (Anthony; 1890–1939; American aircraft engineer, b. in the Netherlands)
Fulton (Robert; 1765–1815; American engineer)
Rennie (John; 1761–1821; Scottish civil engineer)
Savery (Thomas; c.1650–1715; English engineer)
Singer (Isaac; 1811–75; American inventor)
Wallis (Barnes; 1887–1979; English inventor)

7 LETTERS

Babbage (Charles; 1792–1871; English inventor and mathematician)
Blériot (Louis; 1872–1936; French aircraft engineer)
Boulton (Matthew; 1728–1809; English engineer)
Curtiss (Glenn; 1878–1930; American aircraft engineer)
Daimler (Gottlieb; 1834–1900; German engineer and motor manufacturer)
Eastman (George; 1854–1932; American inventor)
Fleming (John; 1849–1945; English electrical engineer)
Fresnel (Augustin Jean; 1788–1827; French civil engineer)
Goddard (Robert; 1882–1945; American rocket engineer and physicist)
Lumière (Auguste; 1862–1954; French inventor)

Lumière (Louis; 1864–1948; French inventor)
Marconi (Guglielmo; 1874–1937; Italian electrical engineer)
Nasmyth (James; 1808–90; Scottish engineer)
Parsons (Charles; 1854–1931; English engineer)
Porsche (Ferdinand; 1875–1951; Austrian car designer)
Renault (Louis; 1877–1944; French engineer and motor manufacturer)
Siemens (Charles; 1823–83; British engineer, b. in Germany)
Siemens (Ernst Werner von; 1816–92; German electrical engineer)
Telford (Thomas; 1757–1834; Scottish civil engineer)
Whitney (Eli; 1765–1825; American inventor)
Whittle (Frank; 1907–96; English aircraft engineer)

8 LETTERS

Bessemer (Henry; 1813–98; English engineer and inventor)
Birdseye (Clarence; 1886–1956; American inventor)
Brindley (James; 1716–72; English canal-builder)
Crompton (Samuel; 1753–1827; English inventor)
Daguerre (Louis-Jacques-Mandé; 1789–1851; French inventor)
Ferranti (Sebastian; 1864–1930; English electrical engineer)
Foucault (Jean; 1819–68; French inventor and physicist)
Goldmark (Peter; 1906–77; American inventor, b. in Hungary)
Goodyear (Charles; 1800–60; American inventor)
Guericke (Otto von; 1602–86; German engineer and physicist)
Kennelly (Arthur; 1861–1939; American electrical engineer)
Mitchell (R. J.; 1895–1937; English aircraft engineer)
Newcomen (Thomas; 1663–1729; English engineer)
Shockley (William; 1910–89; American inventor and physicist)
Sikorsky (Igor; 1889–1972; American aircraft engineer, b. in Russia)
Sinclair (Clive; b. 1940; English inventor)

9 LETTERS

Arkwright (Richard; 1732–92; English inventor)
Armstrong (Edwin; 1890–1954; American electrical engineer)
Baekeland (Leo; 1863–1944; Belgian inventor and chemist)
Cockerell (Christopher; 1910–99; English engineer)
Fessenden (Reginald; 1866–1932; American inventor, b. in Canada)
Gutenberg (Johannes; c.1400–68; German inventor)
Heaviside (Oliver; 1850–1925; English electrical engineer and physicist)
Hollerith (Herman; 1860–1929; American engineer)
Kettering (Charles Franklin; 1876–1958; American engineer)
Pickering (William Hayward; 1910–2004; American engineer, born in NZ)

10 LETTERS

Archimedes (c.287–12 BC; Greek inventor)
Cartwright (Edmund; 1743–1823; English inventor)
Hargreaves (James; 1720–78; English inventor)
Lilienthal (Otto; 1848–96; German aircraft engineer)
Stephenson (George; 1781–1848; English engineer)
Stephenson (Robert; 1803–59; English engineer)
Trevithick (Richard; 1771–1833; English engineer)
Wheatstone (Charles; 1802–75; English inventor)

11 LETTERS

Montgolfier (Jacques-Étienne; 1745–99 French inventor)

Montgolfier (Joseph-Michel; 1740–1810 French inventor)
Tsiolkovsky (Konstantin; 1857–1935; Russian aircraft engineer)

12 LETTERS

Westinghouse (George; 1846–1914; American engineer)

13 LETTERS

Messerschmidt (Willy; 1898–1978; German aircraft engineer)

2 WORDS

De Forest (Lee; 1873–1961 American electrical engineer and physicist)

3 WORDS

Leonardo da Vinci (1452–1519; Italian scientist, engineer, and artist)

Lovers (real and fictional)

3 WORDS

Antony and Cleopatra
Bonnie and Clyde
Caesar and Cleopatra
Dante and Beatrice
Daphnis and Chloe
Darby and Joan
David and Bathsheba
Dido and Aeneas
Eros and Psyche
Harlequin and Columbine
Heathcliff and Cathy
Héloïse and Abelard
Hero and Leander
Lancelot and Guinevere
Napoleon and Josephine
Orpheus and Eurydice
Othello and Desdemona
Paolo and Francesca
Paris and Helen
Pelléas and Mélisande
Petrarch and Laura
Porgy and Bess
Pyramus and Thisbe
Romeo and Juliet
Samson and Delilah
Tarzan and Jane
Tristan and Isolde
Troilus and Cressida
Venus and Adonis

4 WORDS

Chopin and George Sand
Lady Chatterley and Mellors
Superman and Lois Lane

5 WORDS

Anna Karenina and Leon Vronski
Byron and Lady Caroline Lamb
Charles II and Nell Gwyn
Edward VIII and Wallis Simpson
Elizabeth Barrett and Robert Browning
Jane Eyre and Edward Rochester
Lord Nelson and Lady Hamilton
Madame Butterfly and Lt Pinkerton
Robin Hood and Maid Marian
Scarlett O'Hara and Rhett Butler

6 WORDS

W. B. Yeats and Maud Gonne

Military leaders

1 WORD

3 LETTERS

Lee (Robert E.; 1807–70; American general)
Ney (Michel; 1768–1815; French marshal)

4 LETTERS

Díaz (Porfirio; 1830–1915; Mexican general/statesman)
Foch (Ferdinand; 1851–71; French general)
Haig (Douglas; 1861–1928; British field marshal)
Tito (1892–1980; Yugoslav marshal/statesman)
Tojo (Hideki; 1884–1948; Japanese military leader/statesman)

5 LETTERS

Clive (Robert; 1725–74; British general/governor)
Dayan (Moshe; 1915–81; Israeli general/statesman)
Drake (Francis; c.1540–96; English sailor)
Grant (Ulysses S.; 1822–85; American general)
Jones (John Paul; 1747–92; American admiral)
Monck (George; 1608–70; English general)
Moore (John; 1761–1809; British general)
Murat (Joachim; c.1767–1815; French general/king of Naples)
Rabin (Yitzhak; 1922–95; Israeli statesman/military leader)
Shaka (c.1787–1828; Zulu military leader)
Smuts (Jan; 1870–1950; South African general/statesman)
Sulla (138–78 BC; Roman general/dictator)
Villa (Pancho; 1878–1923; Mexican revolutionary)
Wolfe (James; 1727–59; British general)

6 LETTERS

Antony (Mark; c.83–30 BC; Roman general/statesman)
Attila (406–53; King of the Huns)
Beatty (David; 1871–1936; British admiral)
Caesar (Julius; 100–44 BC; Roman general/statesman)
Castro (Fidel; b. 1927; Cuban statesman/revolutionary leader)
Custer (George; 1839–76; American cavalry general)
Fabius (Quintus; d. 203 BC; Roman general/statesman)
Franco (Francisco; 1892–1975; Spanish general/statesman)
Gordon (Charles George; 1833–85; British general)
Grivas (George; 1898–1974; Greek Cypriot guerrilla leader)
Harris (Arthur; 1892–1984; British Marshal of the RAF)
Jervis (John; 1735–1823; British admiral)
Joffre (Joseph; 1852–1931; French marshal)
Kruger (Paul; 1825–1904; South African soldier/statesman)
Marius (Gaius; c.157–86 BC; Roman general/politician)
Nelson (Horatio; 1758–1805; British admiral)
Patton (George; 1885–1945; American general)
Pétain (Philippe; 1856–1951; French general/statesman)
Rommel (Erwin; 1891–1944; German Field Marshal)
Rupert (Prince; 1619–82; English general)
Zapata (Emiliano; 1879–1919; Mexican revolutionary)
Zhukov (Georgi; 1896–1974; Soviet military leader)

7 LETTERS

Agrippa (Marcus; 63–12 BC; Roman general)
Allenby (Edmund; 1861–1936; British Field Marshal)
Atatürk (Kemal; 1881–1938; Turkish general/statesman)
Batista (Fulgencio; 1901–73; Cuban soldier/statesman)

Bolívar (Simón; 1738–1830; Venezuelan patriot/statesman)
Cassius (Gaius; d. 42 BC; Roman general)
Dowding (Hugh; 1882–1970; British Marshal of the RAF)
Fairfax (Thomas; 1612–71; English general)
Guevara (Che; 1928–67; Argentinian revolutionary/guerrilla leader)
Jackson (Andrew; 1767–1845; American general/statesman)
Jackson (Thomas; 1824–63; American general)
Roberts (Frederick; 1832–1914; British Field Marshal)
Saladin (c.1137–93; sultan of Egypt and Syria)
Sherman (William; 1820–91; American general)

8 LETTERS

Cromwell (Oliver; 1599–1658; English general/statesman)
Galtieri (Leopoldo; 1926–2003; Argentinian general/statesman)
Geronimo (1829–1909; Apache chief)
Hannibal (247–182 BC; Carthaginian general)
Jellicoe (John; 1859–1935; British admiral)
Lysander (d. 396 BC; Spartan general)
Montcalm (Louis Joseph de; 1712–59; French general)
Montfort (Simon de; c.1208–65; English rebel leader)
Montrose (James; 1612–50; Scottish general)
O'Higgins (Bernardo; c.1778–1842; Chilean revolutionary/statesman)
Pericles (c.495–429 BC; Athenian general/statesman)
Pinochet (Augusto; b. 1915; Chilean general/statesman)
Xenophon (c.430–354 BC; Greek military leader/historian)
Yamamoto (Isoroku; 1884–1943; Japanese admiral)

9 LETTERS

Cetshwayo (c.1826–84; Zulu military leader/ruler)
Garibaldi (Giuseppe; 1807–82; Italian military leader)
Kitchener (Herbert; 1850–1916; British soldier/statesman)
Lafayette (Marie Joseph; 1757–1834; French soldier/statesman)
MacArthur (Douglas; 1880–1964; American general)
Trenchard (Hugh; 1873–1956; British Marshal of the RAF)

10 LETTERS

Clausewitz (Karl von; 1780–1831; Prussian general/military theorist)
Cumberland (Duke of; 1721–65; English military commander)
Eisenhower (Dwight; 1890–1970; American general/statesman)
Hindenburg (Paul; 1847–1934; German Field Marshal/statesman)
Ludendorff (Erich; 1865–1937; German general)
Montgomery (Viscount; 1887–1976; British Field Marshal)
Washington (George; 1732–99; American general/statesman)
Wellington (Duke of; 1769–1852; British Field Marshal/statesman)

11 LETTERS

Albuquerque (Alfonso de; 1453–1515; Portuguese naval commander/statesman)
Marlborough (Duke of; 1650–1722; British general)
Mountbatten (Louis; 1900–79; British admiral/statesman)

2 WORDS

Crazy Horse (c.1849–77; Sioux chief)
de Gaulle (Charles; 1890–1970; French general/statesman)
El Cid (c.1043–99; Spanish military/political leader)
Enver Pasha (1881–1922; Turkish military/political leader)

Genghis Khan (1162–1227; Mongol commander)
Napoleon Bonaparte (1769–1821; French general/emperor)
Scipio Africanus (c.185–129 BC; Roman general/politician)
Sitting Bull (c.1831–90; Sioux chief)

3 WORDS

Alexander the Great (356–323 BC; military commander/king of Macedon)
Chiang Kai-shek (1887–1975; Chinese soldier/statesman)
Pompey the Great (106–48 BC; Roman general/statesman)
Primo de Rivera (1870–1930; Spanish general/statesman)

Musicians, opera singers, and conductors

1 WORD

4 LETTERS

Hess (Myra; 1890–1965; English pianist)
Lind (Jenny; 1820–87; Swedish soprano)
Peña (Paco; b. 1942; Spanish guitarist)
Wood (Henry; 1869–1944; English conductor)

5 LETTERS

Arrau (Claudio; 1903–91; Chilean pianist)
Baker (Janet; b. 1933; English mezzo-soprano)
Boult (Adrian; 1889–1983; English conductor)
Bream (Julian; b. 1933; English guitarist)
Davis (Colin; b. 1927; English conductor)
Gigli (Beniamino; 1890–1957; Italian tenor)
Gobbi (Tito; 1913–84; Italian baritone)
Gould (Glenn; 1932–82; Canadian pianist)
Hallé (Charles; 1819–95; British conductor, b. in Germany)
Mehta (Zubin; b. 1936; Indian conductor)
Melba (Nellie; 1861–1931; Australian soprano)
Ogdon (John; 1937–89; English pianist)
Pears (Peter; 1910–86; English tenor)
Solti (Georg; 1912–97; British conductor, b. in Hungary)
Stern (Isaac; 1920–2001; American violinist, b. in Russia)

6 LETTERS

Boulez (Pierre; b. 1925; French conductor and composer)
Callas (Maria; 1923–77; American soprano)
Caruso (Enrico; 1873–1921; Italian tenor)
Casals (Pablo; 1876–1973; Spanish cellist)
Galway (James; b. 1939; Northern Irish flautist)
Mutter (Anne-Sophie; b. 1963; German violinist)
Norman (Jessye; b. 1945; American soprano)
Previn (André; b. 1929; American conductor, b. in Germany)
Rattle (Simon; b. 1955; English conductor)
Terfel (Bryn; b. 1965; Welsh bass-baritone)

7 LETTERS

Beecham (Thomas; 1879–1961; English conductor)
Brendel (Alfred; b. 1931; Czech pianist)
Caballé (Montserrat; b. 1933; Spanish soprano)
Domingo (Plácido; b. 1941; Spanish tenor)
Ferrier (Kathleen; 1912–53; English contralto)
Garrett (Lesley; b. 1955; English soprano)
Haitink (Bernard; b. 1929; Dutch conductor)
Hammond (Joan; 1912–96; Australian soprano, b. in New Zealand)
Heifetz (Jascha; 1901–87; American violinist, b. in Lithuania)
Karajan (Herbert von; 1908–1989; Austrian conductor)
Kennedy (Nigel; b. 1956; English violinist)
Lympany (Moura; 1915–2005; English pianist)
Menuhin (Yehudi; 1916–99; British violinist, b. in America)

Nilsson (Birgit; b. 1918; Swedish soprano)
Perahia (Murray; b. 1947; American pianist)
Perlman (Itzhak; b. 1945; Israeli violinist)
Sargent (Malcolm; 1895–1967; English conductor and composer)
Segovia (Andrés; 1893–1987; Spanish guitarist)
Shankar (Ravi; b. 1920; Indian sitar player)

8 LETTERS

Carreras (José; b. 1946; Spanish tenor)
Flagstad (Kirsten; 1895–1962; Norwegian soprano)
Goossens (Eugene; 1893–1962; English conductor and composer)
Horowitz (Vladimir; 1904–89; Russian pianist)
Kreisler (Fritz; 1875–1962; American violinist, b. in Austria)
Oistrakh (David; 1908–74; Russian violinist)
Oistrakh (Igor; b. 1931; Ukrainian violinist)
Paganini (Niccolò; 1782–1840; Italian violinist)
Williams (John; b. 1941; Australian guitarist)

9 LETTERS

Ashkenazy (Vladimir; b. 1937; Icelandic pianist and conductor, b. in Russia)
Barenboim (Daniel; b. 1942; Israeli conductor and pianist)
Bernstein (Leonard; 1918–90; American conductor and composer)
Chaliapin (Fyodor; 1873–1938; Russian bass)
Klemperer (Otto; 1885–1973; American conductor and composer, b. in Germany)
McCormack (John; 1884–1945; Irish tenor)
Pavarotti (Luciano; b. 1935; Italian tenor)
Tortelier (Paul; 1914–90; French cellist)
Toscanini (Arturo; 1867–1957; Italian conductor)

10 LETTERS

Barbirolli (John; 1899–1970, English conductor)
Rubinstein (Artur; 1888–1982; American pianist, b. in Poland)
Sutherland (Joan; b. 1926; Australian soprano)

11 LETTERS

Furtwängler (Wilhelm; 1886–1954; German conductor)
Schwarzkopf (Elisabeth; b. 1915; German soprano)

12 LETTERS

Rostropovich (Mstislav; b. 1927; Russian cellist and conductor)

2 WORDS

du Pré (Jacqueline; 1945–87; English cellist)
Fischer-Dieskau (Dietrich; b. 1925; German baritone)
Te Kanawa (Kiri; b. 1944; New Zealand soprano)

3 WORDS

de los Angeles (Victoria; 1923–2005; Spanish soprano)

Photographers

1 WORD

Adams (Ansel; 1902–84; American)
Arbus (Diane; 1923–71; American)
Bailey (David; b. 1938; English)
Beaton (Cecil; 1904–80; English)
Brandt (Bill; 1904–83; British)
Cameron (Julia Margaret; 1815–79; British)
Capa (Robert; 1913–54; Hungarian)
Daguerre (Louis-Jacques-Mandé; 1789–1851; French)
Doisneau (Robert; 1912–94; French)

Karsh (Yousuf; 1908–2002; Turkish)
Leibovitz (Annie; b. 1950; American)
Lichfield (Patrick; 1939–2005; English)
Mapplethorpe (Robert; 1946–89; American)
Muybridge (Eadweard; 1830–1904; English)
Ray (Man; 1890–1976; American)
Snowdon (Earl of; b. 1930; English)
Stieglitz (Alfred; 1864–1946; American)
Talbot (William Fox; 1800–77; English)

2 WORDS

Bourke-White (Margaret; 1906–71; American)
Cartier-Bresson (Henri; 1908–2004; French)
Moholy-Nagy (László; 1895–1946; American)

Poets

1 WORD

3 LETTERS

Paz (Octavio; 1914–98; Mexican)

4 LETTERS

Gray (Thomas; 1716–71; English)
Gunn (Thom; 1929–2004; English)
Hogg (James; 1770–1835; Scottish)
Hood (Thomas; 1799–1845; English)
Hugo (Victor; 1802–85; French)
Lear (Edward; 1812–88; English)
Muir (Edwin; 1887–1959; Scottish)
Nash (Ogden; 1902–71; American)
Ovid (BC 43 –c.17 AD; Roman)
Owen (Wilfred; 1893–1918; English)
Pope (Alexander; 1688–1744; English)

5 LETTERS

Auden (W. H.; 1907–73; American)
Blake (William; 1757–1827; English)
Burns (Robert; 1759–96; Scottish)
Byron (Lord; 1788–1824, English)
Clare (John; 1793–1864; English)
Crane (Hart; 1899–1932; American)
Dante (1265–1321; Italian)
Donne (John; 1572–1631; English)
Eliot (T. S.; 1888–1965; British, b. in America)
Frost (Robert; 1874–1963; American)
Hardy (Thomas; 1840–1928; English)
Heine (Heinrich; 1797–1856; German)
Homer (8th century BC; Greek)
Keats (John; 1795–1821; English)
Lorca (Federico Garcia; 1898–1936; Spanish)
Lucan (39–65; Roman)
Moore (Marianne; 1887–1972; American)
Moore (Thomas; 1779–1852; Irish)
Plath (Sylvia; 1932–63; American)
Pound (Ezra; 1885–1972; American)
Raine (Craig; b. 1944; British)
Rilke (Rainer Maria; 1875–1926; German, b. in Czechoslovakia)
Smith (Stevie; 1902–71; English)
Tasso (Torquato; 1544–95; Italian)
Yeats (W. B.; 1865–1939; Irish)

6 LETTERS

Adcock (Fleur; b. 1934; New Zealand)
Arnold (Matthew; 1822–88; English)
Belloc (Hilaire; 1870–1953; British, b. in France)
Borges (Jorge; 1899–1986; Argentinian)
Breton (André; 1896–1966; French)
Brooke (Rupert; 1887–1915; English)
Butler (Samuel; 1612–80; English)
Cavafy (Constantine; 1863–1933; Greek)
Clough (Arthur Hugh; 1819–61; English)
Cowper (William; 1731–1800; English)
Crabbe (George; 1754–1832; English)
Dryden (John; 1631–1700; English)
Dunbar (William; c.1456–c.1513; Scottish)
Éluard (Paul; 1895–1952; French)
Empson (William; 1906–84; English)
Ennius (239–169 BC; Roman)
Goethe (Johann Wolfgang von; 1749–1832; German)

Graves (Robert; 1895–1985; English)
Gurney (Ivor; 1890–1937; English)
Heaney (Seamus; b. 1939; Irish)
Hesiod (8th century BC; Greek)
Horace (65–8 BC; Roman)
Hughes (Ted; 1930–98; English)
Jonson (Ben; 1572–1637; English)
Landor (Walter Savage; 1775–1864; English)
Larkin (Philip; 1922–85; English)
Lowell (Amy; 1874–1925; American)
Lowell (Robert; 1917–77; American)
Milton (John; 1608–74; English)
Motion (Andrew; b. 1952; English)
Neruda (Pablo; 1904–73; Chilean)
Pindar (c.518–c.438 BC; Greek)
Porter (Peter; b. 1929; British, b. in Australia)
Sappho (c.610–c.580 BC; Greek)
Sidney (Philip; 1554–86; English)
Tagore (Rabindranath; 1861–1941; Indian)
Thomas (Dylan; 1914–53; Welsh)
Thomas (Edward; 1878–1917; English)
Valéry (Paul; 1871–1945; French)
Virgil (70–19 BC; Roman)
Warren (Robert Penn; 1905–89; American)

7 LETTERS

Alcaeus (c.620–c.580 BC; Greek)
Angelou (Maya; b. 1928; American)
Ariosto (Ludovico; 1474–1533; Italian)
Blunden (Edmund; 1896–1974; English)
Bridges (Robert; 1844–1930; English)
Brodsky (Joseph; 1940–96; American, b. in Russia)
Bunting (Basil; 1900–85; English)
Caedmon (7th century AD; Anglo-Saxon)
Chapman (George; c.1560–1634; English)
Chaucer (Geoffrey; c.1342–1400; English)
Emerson (Ralph Waldo; 1803–82; American)
Flecker (James Elroy; 1884–1915; English)
Herbert (George; 1593–1633; English)
Herrick (Robert; 1591–1674; English)
Hopkins (Gerard Manley; 1844–89; English)
Housman (A. E.; 1859–1936; English)
Martial (c.40–c.104; Roman)
Marvell (Andrew; 1621–78; English)
Patmore (Coventry; 1823–96; English)
Pushkin (Aleksandr; 1799–1837; Russian)
Rimbaud (Arthur; 1854–91; French)
Russell (George; 1867–1935; Irish)
Sassoon (Siegfried; 1886–1967; English)
Shelley (Percy Bysshe; 1792–1822; English)
Sitwell (Edith; 1887–1964; English)
Skelton (John; c.1460–1529; English)
Southey (Robert; 1774–1843; English)
Spender (Stephen; 1909–95; English)
Spenser (Edmund; c.1552–99; English)
Stevens (Wallace; 1879–1955; American)
Vaughan (Henry; 1621–95; Welsh)
Walcott (Derek; b. 1930; St Lucian)
Whitman (Walt; 1819–92; American)

8 LETTERS

Anacreon (c.570–478 BC; Greek)
Betjeman (John; 1906–84; English)
Browning (Elizabeth Barrett; 1806–61; English)
Browning (Robert; 1812–89; English)
Campbell (Roy; 1901–57; South African)
Catullus (c.84–c.54 BC; Roman)
cummings (e. e.; 1894–1962; American)
Ginsberg (Allen; 1926–97; American)
Harrison (Tony; b. 1937; English)
Langland (William; c.1330–c.1400; English)
Lawrence (D. H.; 1885–1930; English)
Lovelace (Richard; 1618–57; English)
MacNeice (Louis; 1907–63; Northern Irish)
Malherbe (François de; 1555–1628; French)
Mallarmé (Stéphane; 1842–98; French)
Meleager (fl. 1st century BC; Greek)
Petrarch (1304–74; Italian)
Rossetti (Christina; 1830–94; English)
Rossetti (Dante Gabriel; 1828–82; English)
Schiller (Friedrich von; 1759–1805; German)
Taliesin (6th century; Welsh)
Tennyson (Alfred Lord; 1809–92; English)
Traherne (Thomas; 1637–74; English)
Verlaine (Paul; 1844–96; French)
Williams (William Carlos; 1883–1963; American)

9 LETTERS

Akhmatova (Anna; 1889–1966; Russian)
Coleridge (Samuel Taylor; 1772–1834; English)
D'Annunzio (Gabriele; 1863–1938; Italian)
Dickinson (Emily; 1830–86; American)
Doolittle (Hilda; 1886–1961; American)

Hölderlin (Friedrich; 1770–1843; German)
Lamartine (Alphonse de; 1790–1869; French)
Lucretius (c.95–c.55 BC; Roman)
Marinetti (Filippo; 1876–1944; Italian)
Masefield (John; 1878–1967; English)
Pasternak (Boris; 1890–1960; Russian)
Quasimodo (Salvatore; 1901–68; Italian)
Rochester (Earl of; 1647–80; English)
Swinburne (Algernon Charles; 1837–1909; English)

10 LETTERS

Baudelaire (Charles; 1821–67; French)
Chatterton (Thomas; 1752–70; English)
FitzGerald (Edward; 1809–83; English)
Longfellow (Henry Wadsworth; 1807–82; American)
Macdiarmid (Hugh; Christopher Grieve; 1892–1978; Scottish)
Mandelstam (Osip; 1891–1938; Russian, b. in Poland)
Mayakovsky (Vladimir; 1893–1930; Russian)
Propertius (Sextus; c.50–c.16 BC; Roman)
Tannhäuser (c.1200–c.70; German)
Theocritus (c.310–250 BC; Greek)
Wordsworth (William; 1770–1850; English)

11 LETTERS

Apollinaire (Guillaume; Wilhelm de Kostrowitzki; 1880–1918; French)
Shakespeare (William; 1569–1616; English)
Yevtushenko (Yevgenii; b. 1933; Russian)

12 LETTERS

Ferlinghetti (Lawrence; b. 1919; American)
Hofmannsthal (Hugo von; 1874–1929; Austrian)

2 WORDS

Day Lewis (C.; 1904–72; English)
La Fontaine (Jean de; 1621–95; French)
Omar Khayyám (c.1048–c.1122; Persian)

3 WORDS

Chrétien de Troyes (12th century; French)
de la Mare (Walter; 1873–1956; English)
Leconte de Lisle (Charles; 1818–94; French)

Popes from 1600 (with dates in office)

Clement VIII (1592–1605)
Leo XI (1605)
Paul V (1605–21)
Gregory XV (1621–3)
Urban VIII (1623–44)
Innocent X (1644–55)
Alexander VII (1655–67)
Clement IX (1667–9)
Clement X (1670–6)
Innocent XI (1676–89)
Alexander VIII (1689–91)
Innocent XII (1691–1700)
Clement XI (1700–21)
Innocent XIII (1721–4)
Benedict XIII (1724–30)
Clement XII (1730–40)
Benedict XIV (1740–58)
Clement XIII (1758–69)
Pius VI (1775–99)
Pius VII (1800–23)
Leo XII (1823–9)
Pius VIII (1829–30)
Gregory XVI (1831–46)
Pius IX (1846–78)
Leo XIII (1878–1903)
Pius X (1903–14)
Benedict XV (1914–22)
Pius XI (1922–39)
Pius XII (1939–58)
John XXIII (1958–63)
Paul VI (1963–78)
John Paul I (1978)

John Paul II (1978–2005)
Benedict XVI (since April 2005)

Popular music and jazz: artists and groups

1 WORD

2 LETTERS

U2 (Irish rock band)

3 LETTERS

Lee (Peggy; 1920–2002; American singer)
Jam (English rock band)
REM (American rock band)
Who (English rock band)
Yes (English rock band)

4 LETTERS

Abba (Swedish pop group)
AC/DC (Australian rock band)
Baez (Joan; b. 1941; American singer)
Blur (English rock band)
Bush (Kate; b. 1958; English singer)
Cash (Johnny; 1932–2003; American singer)
Cher (b. 1946; American singer)
Cole (Nat King; 1919–65; American singer)
Como (Perry; 1912–2001; American singer)
Getz (Stan; 1927–91; American jazz saxophonist)
Crow (Sheryl; b. 1962; American singer)
Cure (English rock band)
Dido (b. 1971; English singer)
Dion (Celine; b. 1968; French-Canadian singer)
Dury (Ian; 1942–2000; English singer)
Free (English rock band)
Gaye (Marvin; 1939–84 American singer)
Joel (Billy; b. 1949; American singer)
John (Elton; b. 1947; English singer)
King (B. B.; b. 1925; American guitarist)
King (Carole; b. 1942; American singer)
Last (James; b. 1929; German bandleader)
Lynn (Loretta; b. 1935; American singer)
Monk (Thelonius; 1917–82; American pianist)
Paul (Les; b. 1915; American guitarist)
Pine (Courtney; b. 1964; English saxophonist)
Pulp (English pop group)
Reed (Lou; b. 1942; American singer)
Rich (Buddy; 1917–87; American drummer)
Ross (Diana; b. 1944; American singer)
Shaw (Artie; 1910–2004; American clarinettist)
Shaw (Sandie; b. 1947; English singer)
UB40 (English rock band)
Wham (English pop duo)

5 LETTERS

Adams (Bryan; b. 1959; Canadian singer)
Baker (Chet; 1929–88; American trumpeter/singer)
Basie (Count; 1904–84; American pianist/bandleader)
Berry (Chuck; b. 1931; American singer)
Björk (b. 1965; Icelandic singer)
Bolan (Marc; 1947–77; English singer)
Bowie (David; b. 1947; English singer)
Brown (James; b. 1928; American singer)
Carey (Mariah; b. 1970; American singer)
Clash (English punk band)
Cline (Patsy; 1932–53: American singer)
Cohen (Leonard; b. 1934; Canadian singer)
Corea (Chick; b. 1941; American pianist)
Corrs (Irish pop group)
Cream (English rock band)
Davis (Miles; 1926–91; American trumpeter)
Doors (American rock band)
Dylan (Bob; b. 1941; American singer)
Evans (Gil; 1912–88; Canadian pianist)
Ferry (Bryan; b. 1945; English singer)
Green (Al; b. 1946; American singer)
Haley (Bill; 1925–81; American singer)
Holly (Buddy; 1936–59; American singer)
Jones (Tom; b. 1940; Welsh singer)
Kinks (English rock band)
Laine (Cleo; b. 1927; English singer)
Lewis (Jerry Lee; b. 1935; American singer)
Lopez (Jennifer; b. 1969; American singer)

Oasis (English rock band)
Queen (English rock band)
Scott (Ronnie; 1927–96; English saxophonist)
Simon (Carly; b. 1945; American singer)
Simon (Paul; b. 1941; American singer)
Slade (English rock band)
Smith (Bessie; 1894–1937; American jazz singer)
Starr (Ringo; b. 1940; English drummer)
Sting (b. 1951; English singer)
Tatum (Art; 1910–56; American pianist)
Twain (Shania; b. 1965; Canadian singer)
Waits (Tom; b. 1949; American singer)
White (Barry; 1944–2003; American singer)
Young (Neil; b. 1945; Canadian singer)
Zappa (Frank; 1940–93; American singer)

6 LETTERS

Bassey (Shirley; b. 1937; Welsh singer)
Blakey (Art; 1919–90; American drummer)
Bolton (Michael; b. 1954; American singer)
Brooks (Garth; b. 1962; American singer)
Cobain (Kurt; 1967–94; American singer)
Cocker (Joe; b. 1944; English singer)
Cooder (Ry; b. 1947; American guitarist)
Crosby (Bing; 1904–77; American singer)
Denver (John; 1943–97; American singer)
Domino (Fats; b. 1928; American pianist/singer)
Eagles (American rock band)
Eminem (b. 1972; American singer)
Harris (Emmylou; b. 1947; American singer)
Jagger (Mick; b; 1943; English singer)
Joplin (Janis; 1943–70; American singer)
Kenton (Stan; 1911–79; American bandleader)
Knight (Gladys; b. 1944; American singer)
Lennon (John; 1940–80; English singer)
Marley (Bob; 1945–81: Jamaican singer)
Martin (Dean; 1917–95; American singer)
Mathis (Johnny; b. 1935; American singer)
McLean (Don; b. 1945; American singer)
Miller (Glenn; 1904–44; American trombonist/ bandleader)
Mingus (Charlie; 1922–79; American bassist)
Morton (Jelly Roll; 1885–1941; American pianist)
Nelson (Willie; b. 1933; American singer)
Parker (Charlie; 1920–55; American saxophonist)
Parton (Dolly; b. 1946; American singer)
Pitney (Gene; b. 1941; American singer)
Police (English rock band)
Prince (b. 1958; American singer)
Reeves (Jim; 1923–64; American singer)
Richie (Lionel; b. 1949; American singer)
Rogers (Kenny; b. 1938; American singer)
Sedaka (Neil; b. 1939; American singer)
Simone (Nina; 1933–2003; American singer)
Smiths (English rock band)
Spears (Britney; b. 1981; American singer)
Summer (Donna; b. 1948; American singer)
Taylor (James; b. 1948; American singer)
Turner (Tina; b. 1939; American singer)
Waller (Fats; 1904–43; American pianist)
Waters (Muddy; 1915–83; American guitarist)
Weller (Paul; b. 1958; English singer)
Wonder (Stevie; b. 1950; American singer)

7 LETTERS

Beatles (English pop/rock band)
Blondie (American rock band)
Boyzone (Irish pop group)
Brubeck (Dave; b. 1920; American pianist)
Charles (Ray; 1930–2004; American singer)
Clapton (Eric; b. 1945; English guitarist)
Cochran (Eddie; 1938–60; American singer)
Coleman (Ornette; b. 1930; American saxophonist)
Collins (Phil; b. 1951; English singer)
Diamond (Neil; b. 1941; American singer)
Diddley (Bo; b. 1928; American singer)
Donegan (Lonnie; 1931–2002; Scottish musician)
Genesis (English rock band)
Glitter (Gary; b. 1944; English singer)
Goodman (Benny; 1909–86; American clarinettist/bandleader)
Guthrie (Woody; 1912–67; American singer)
Hancock (Herbie; b. 1940; American pianist)
Hawkins (Coleman; 1904–69; American saxophonist)
Holiday (Billie; 1915–59; American singer)
Hendrix (Jimi; 1942–70; American singer)
Houston (Whitney; b. 1963; American singer)
Jackson (Janet; b. 1966; American singer)
Jackson (Michael; b. 1958; American singer)
Madness (English rock band)

Madonna (b. 1958; American singer)
Manilow (Barry; b. 1943; American singer)
Michael (George; b. 1963; English singer)
Minogue (Kylie; b. 1968; Australian singer)
Monkees (American pop group)
Nirvana (American grunge band)
Orbison (Roy; 1936–88; American singer)
Presley (Elvis; 1935–77; American singer)
Ramones (American punk band)
Redding (Otis; 1941–67; American singer)
Richard (Cliff; b. 1940; English singer)
Santana (American rock band)
Shadows (English pop group)
Sinatra (Frank; 1915–98; American singer)
Sinatra (Nancy; b. 1940; American singer)
Stewart (Rod; b. 1945; English singer)
Vaughan (Sarah; 1924–90; American singer)
Warwick (Dionne; b. 1940; American singer)
Wynette (Tammy; 1942–98; American singer)

8 LETTERS

Aguilera (Christina; b. 1980; American singer)
Calloway (Cab; 1907–94; American singer/bandleader)
Campbell (Glen; b. 1936; American singer)
Coldplay (English rock band)
Coltrane (John; 1926–67; American saxophonist)
Costello (Elvis; b. 1954; English singer)
Drifters (American pop group)
Franklin (Aretha; b. 1942; American singer)
Harrison (George; 1943–2001; English guitarist)
Marsalis (Wynton; b. 1961; American trumpeter)
Mitchell (Joni; b. 1943; Canadian singer)
Morrison (Jim; 1943–71; American singer)
Morrison (Van; b. 1945; Northern Irish singer)
Oldfield (Mike; b. 1953; English musician)
Peterson (Oscar; b. 1925; Canadian pianist)
Robinson (Smokey; b. 1940; American singer)
Supremes (American pop group)
Vandross (Luther; 1951–2005; American singer)
Westlife (Irish pop group)
Williams (Andy; b. 1927; American singer)
Williams (Hank; 1923–53; American singer)
Williams (Robbie; b. 1974; English singer)

9 LETTERS

Armstrong (Louis; 1900–71; American trumpeter/singer)
Dankworth (John; b. 1927; English saxophonist)
Ellington (Duke; 1899–1974; American bandleader/pianist)
Garfunkel (Art; b. 1941; American singer)
Gillespie (Dizzy; 1917–93; American trumpeter/bandleader)
Grappelli (Stephane; 1908–97; French violinist)
Lyttelton (Humphrey; b. 1921; English trumpeter)
McCartney (Paul; b. 1942; English singer)
Metallica (American heavy metal band)
Motorhead (English rock band)
Mouskouri (Nana; b. 1934; Greek singer)
Radiohead (English rock band)
Reinhardt (Django; 1910–53; Belgian guitarist)
Streisand (Barbra; b. 1942; American singer)

10 LETTERS

Carmichael (Hoagy; 1899–1981; American pianist/singer)
Carpenters (American pop duo)
Commodores (American soul/funk group)
Eurythmics (English rock duo)
Fitzgerald (Ella; 1918–96; American singer)
Pretenders (English rock band)
Timberlake (Justin; b. 1981; American singer)

11 LETTERS

Beiderbecke (Bix; 1903–31; American cornetist/pianist)
Humperdinck (Engelbert; b. 1936; British singer)
Springfield (Dusty; 1939–1999; English singer)
Springsteen (Bruce; b. 1949; American singer)

2 WORDS

All Saints (English pop group)

Alice Cooper (American rock band)
Beach Boys (American pop group)
Bee Gees (English pop group)
Black Sabbath (English heavy metal band)
Bon Jovi (American rock band)
Boy George (b. 1961; English singer/DJ)
Culture Club (English pop group)
Deep Purple (English rock band)
Dire Straits (English rock band)
Duran Duran (English pop/rock band)
Everly Brothers (American pop duo)
Fleetwood Mac (British/American rock band)
Four Tops (American pop group)
Iggy Pop (b. 1947; American singer)
Iron Maiden (English rock band)
Isley Brothers (American soul group)
Jackson Five (American pop group)
Led Zeppelin (English rock band)
Little Richard (b. 1932; American singer)
Massive Attack (English band)
Meat Loaf (b. 1947; American singer)
Moody Blues (English rock band)
New Order (English rock band)
Newton-John (Olivia; b. 1948; Australian singer)
New Order (English rock band)
Pink Floyd (English rock band)
Public Enemy (American hip-hop band)
Righteous Brothers (American pop duo)
Rolling Stones (English rock band)
Roxy Music (English rock band)
Sex Pistols (English punk band)
Simply Red (English pop group)
Snoop Dogg (b. 1971; American singer)
Spandau Ballet (English pop group)
Spice Girls (English pop group)
Status Quo (English rock band)
Stone Roses (English rock band)
Talking Heads (American rock band)
Take That (English pop group)
T Rex (English rock band)
Velvet Underground (American rock band)

3 WORDS

Guns n' Roses (American rock band)
Manic Street Preachers (Welsh rock band)
Simon and Garfunkel (American pop duo)
Wet Wet Wet (Scottish pop group)

4 WORDS

Mammas and the Papas (American pop group)

Presidents of the USA (with dates in office)

Washington (George; 1789–97)
Adams (John; 1797–1801)
Jefferson (Thomas; 1801–9)
Madison (James; 1809–17)
Monroe (James; 1817–25)
Adams (John Quincy; 1825–9)
Jackson (Andrew; 1829–37)
Van Buren (Martin; 1837–41)
Harrison (William H.; 1841)
Tyler (John; 1841–5)
Polk (James K.; 1845–9)
Taylor (Zachary; 1849–50)
Fillmore (Millard; 1850–3)
Pierce (Franklin; 1853–7)
Buchanan (James; 1857–61)
Lincoln (Abraham; 1861–5)
Johnson (Andrew; 1865–9)
Grant (Ulysses S.; 1869–77)
Hayes (Rutherford; 1877–81)
Garfield (James; 1881)
Arthur (Chester; 1881–5)
Cleveland (Grover; 1885–9)
Harrison (Benjamin; 1889–93)
Cleveland (Grover; 1893–7)
McKinley (William; 1897–1901)
Roosevelt (Theodore; 1901–9)

Taft (William; 1909–13)
Wilson (Woodrow; 1913–21)
Harding (Warren; 1921–3)
Coolidge (Calvin; 1923–9)
Hoover (Herbert; 1929–33)
Roosevelt (Franklin D.; 1933–45)
Truman (Harry S.; 1945–53)
Eisenhower (Dwight D.; 1953–61)
Kennedy (John F.; 1961–3)
Johnson (Lyndon; 1963–9)
Nixon (Richard; 1969–74)
Ford (Gerald; 1974–7)
Carter (James; 1977–81)
Reagan (Ronald; 1981–9)
Bush (George; 1989–93)
Clinton (Bill; 1993–2001)
Bush (George W.; since 2001)

Prime ministers of Great Britain/UK

Walpole (Sir Robert; 1721–42)
Wilmington (Earl of; 1742–3)
Pelham (Henry; 1743–54)
Newcastle (Duke of; 1754–6)
Devonshire (Duke of; 1756–7)
Newcastle (Duke of; 1757–62)
Bute (Earl of; 1762–3)
Grenville (George; 1763–5)
Rockingham (Marquess of; 1765–6)
Pitt the Elder (William; 1766–8)
Grafton (Duke of; 1768–70)
North (Lord; 1770–82)
Rockingham (Marquess of; 1782)
Shelburne (Earl of; 1782–3)
Portland (Duke of; 1783)
Pitt the Younger (William; 1783–1801)
Addington (Henry; 1801–4)
Pitt the Younger (William; 1804–6)
Grenville (Lord WIlliam; 1806–7)
Portland (Duke of; 1807–9)
Perceval (Spencer; 1809–12)
Liverpool (Earl of; 1812–27)
Canning (George; 1827)
Goderich (Viscount; 1827–8)
Wellington (Duke of; 1828–30)
Grey (Earl; 1830–4)
Melbourne (Viscount; 1834)
Wellington (Duke of; 1834)
Peel (Sir Robert; 1834–5)
Melbourne (Viscount; 1835–41)
Peel (Sir Robert; 1841–6)
Russell (Lord John; 1846–52)
Derby (Earl of; 1852)
Aberdeen (Earl of; 1852–5)
Palmerston (Viscount; 1855–8)
Derby (Earl of; 1858–9)
Palmerston (Viscount; 1859–65)
Russell (Earl; 1865–6)
Derby (Earl of; 1866–8)
Disraeli (Benjamin; 1868)
Gladstone (William Ewart; 1868–74)
Disraeli (Benjamin; 1874–80)
Gladstone (William Ewart; 1880–5)
Salisbury (Marquess of; 1885–6)
Gladstone (William Ewart; 1886)
Salisbury (Marquess of; 1886–92)
Gladstone (William Ewart; 1892–4)
Rosebery (Earl of; 1894–5)
Salisbury (Marquess of; 1895–1902)
Balfour (Arthur; 1902–5)
Campbell-Bannerman (Henry; 1905–8)
Asquith (Herbert; 1908–16)
Lloyd George (David; 1916–22)
Law (Andrew Bonar; 1922–3)
Baldwin (Stanley; 1923–4)
MacDonald (James Ramsay; 1924)
Baldwin (Stanley; 1924–9)
MacDonald (James Ramsay; 1929–35)
Baldwin (Stanley; 1935–7)
Chamberlain (Neville; 1937–40)
Churchill (Winston; 1940–5)
Attlee (Clement; 1945–51)
Churchill (Sir WInston; 1951–5)
Eden (Sir Anthony; 1955–7)
Macmillan (Harold; 1957–63)
Douglas-Home (Sir Alec; 1963–4)

Wilson (Harold; 1964–70)
Heath (Edward; 1970–4)
Wilson (Harold; 1974–6)
Callaghan (James; 1976–9)
Thatcher (Margaret; 1979–90)
Major (John; 1990–7)
Blair (Tony; since 1997)

Roman emperors (with dates of reign)

Augustus (27 BC–AD 14)
Tiberius (14–37)
Caligula (37–41)
Claudius (41–54)
Nero (54–68)
Galba (68–9)
Otho (69)
Vitellius (69–70)
Vespasian (69–79)
Titus (79–81)
Domitian (81–96)
Nerva (96–8)
Trajan (98–117)
Hadrian (117–38)
Antoninus Pius (138–61)
Marcus Aurelius (161–80)
Lucius Verus (161–9; with Marcus Aurelius)
Commodus (180–92)
Pertinax (193)
Didius Julianus (193)
Septimius Severus (193–211)
Clodius Albinus (193–7)
Pescennius Niger (193–4)
Caracalla (211–17)
Geta (211–12)
Macrinus (217–18)
Heliogabalus ((Elagabalus); 218–22)
Alexander Severus (222–35)
Maximinus (Thrax) (235–8)
Pupienus (238)
Balbinus (238)
Gordian I (238)
Gordian II (238)
Gordian III (238–44)
Philip (244–9)
Decius (249–51)
Hostilian (250–1)
Gallus (251–3)
Aemilian (253)
Valerian (253–60)
Gallienus (253–68)
Claudius II (Gothicus) (268–70)
Quintillus (270)
Aurelian (270–5)
Tacitus (275–6)
Florian (276)
Probus (276–82)
Carus (282–3)
Carinus (283–5)
Numerian (283–4)
Diocletian (284–305)
Maximian (286–305; 307–8)
Constantius I (305–6)
Galerius (305–11)
Severus (306–7)
Maxentius (307–12)
Licinius (308–24)
Maximin (310–3)
Constantine I (the Great) (306–37)
Constantine II (337–40)
Constantius II (337–61)
Magnentius (350–1)
Julian (360–3)
Jovian (363–4)
Valentinian I (364–75)
Valens (364–78)
Procopius (365–6)
Gratian (375–83)
Valentinian II (375–92)
Theodosius I (379–95)
Arcadius (395–408)
Honorius (395–423)
Theodosius II (408–50)
Constantius III (421–3)
Valentinian III (423–55)
Marcian (450–7)

Petronius Maximus (455)
Avitus (455–6)
Leo I (457–74)
Majorian (457–61)
Libius Severus (461–7)
Anthemius (467–72)
Olybrius (472–3)
Julius Nepos (474–5)
Leo II (474)
Zeno (474–91)
Romulus Augustulus (475–6)

Rulers of England (with dates of reign)

Edwy (Eadwig) (955–7)
Edgar (959–75)
Edward the Martyr, St (975–8)
Ethelred the Unready (978–1013)
Sweyn Forkbeard (1013–14)
Ethelred the Unready (1014–16)
Edmund II (Ironside) (1016)
Canute (1017–35)
Harold I (Harefoot) (1037–40)
Hardecanute (1040–42)
Edward the Confessor, St (1042–66)
Harold II (1066)
William I (the Conqueror) (1066–87)
William II (Rufus) (1087–1100)
Henry I (1100–35)
Stephen (1135–54)
Henry II (1154–89)
Richard I (1189–99)
John (1199–1216)
Henry III (1216–72)
Edward I (1272–1307)
Edward II (1307–27)
Edward III (1327–77)
Richard II (1377–99)
Henry IV (1399–1413)
Henry V (1413–22)
Henry VI (1422–61, 1470–1)
Edward IV (1461–83)
Edward V (1483)
Richard III (1483–85)
Henry VII (1485–1509)
Henry VIII (1509–47)
Edward VI (1547–53)
Mary I (1553–58)
Elizabeth I (1558–1603)
James I (1603–25)
Charles I (1625–49)
Oliver Cromwell (Lord Protector; 1653–58)
Richard Cromwell (1658–59)
Charles II (1660–85)
James II (1685–88)
William III and Mary II (1689–94)
William III (1694–1702)
Anne (1702–14)
George I (1714–27)
George II (1727–60)
George III (1760–1820)
George IV (1820–30)
William IV (1830–37)
Victoria (1837–1901)
Edward VII (1901–10)
George V (1910–36)
Edward VIII (1936)
George VI (1936–52)
Elizabeth II (since 1952)

Rulers of Scotland (with dates of reign)

Kenneth I (MacAlpin) (c.844–58)
Donald I (858–62)
Constantine I (862–77)
Aedh (877–78)
Eocha, Girac (878–89)
Donald II (889–900)
Constantine II (900–43)
Malcolm I (943–54)
Indolphus (Indolf) (954–62)
Duff (962–66)
Colin (966–71)
Kenneth II (971–95)
Constantine III (995–97)
Kenneth III (997–1005)
Malcolm II (1005–34)
Duncan I (1034–40)
Macbeth (1040–57)
Malcolm III (1057–93)
Donald III (1093–94)
Duncan II (1094)
Donald III (1094–97)
Edgar (1097–1107)
Alexander I (1107–24)
David I (1124–53)
Malcolm IV (1153–65)
William the Lion (1165–1214)
Alexander II (1214–49)
Alexander III (1249–86)
Margaret, Maid of Norway (1286–90)
John Balliol (1292–96)
Edward I of England (1296–1306)
Robert I (the Bruce) (1306–29)
David II (1329–32)
Edward Balliol (1332–56)
David II (restored; 1356–71)
Robert II (1371–90)
Robert III (1390–1406)
James I (1406–37)
James II (1437–60)
James III (1460–88)
James IV (1488–1513)
James V (1513–42)
Mary, Queen of Scots (Mary Stuart) (1542–67)
James VI (1567–1625; King of England (as James I) 1603–25)

Saints

1 WORD

3 LETTERS

Leo

4 LETTERS

Anne
Bede
Elmo
John
Jude
Luke
Mark
Mary
Paul

5 LETTERS

Agnes
Aidan
Alban
Basil
Bruno
Clare
Cyril
David
Denis
Hilda
James
Louis
Peter
Simon
Titus
Vitus

6 LETTERS

Agatha
Andrew
Anselm
Edmund
Edward
George
Helena
Hilary
Jerome
Joseph
Justin

Martin
Monica
Ninian
Oswald
Philip
Teresa
Thomas
Ursula

7 LETTERS

Ambrose
Anthony
Bernard
Brendan
Bridget
Cecilia
Clement
Columba
Crispin
Dominic
Dunstan
Francis
Gregory
Joachim
Matthew
Michael
Patrick
Stephen
Swithin
Timothy

8 LETTERS

Barnabas
Benedict
Boniface
Cuthbert
Laurence
Margaret
Matthias
Nicholas
Veronica
Vladimir

9 LETTERS

Augustine
Catherine
Elizabeth
Hildegard
Sebastian
Valentine
Wenceslas

10 LETTERS

Athanasius
Bernadette
Stanislaus

11 LETTERS

Bartholomew
Bonaventura
Christopher

2 WORDS

Albertus Magnus
Alexander Nevsky
Edmund Campion
Francis Xavier
Ignatius Loyola
John Chrysostom
Mary Magdalene
Simeon Stylites
Thomas Aquinas
Thomas More

3 WORDS

Francis of Assisi
Joan of Arc
John the Baptist
Thomas à Becket
Vincent de Paul

4 WORDS

John of the Cross

Scientists and mathematicians

1 WORD

3 LETTERS

Ohm (Georg; 1787–1854; German physicist)

4 LETTERS

Airy (George; 1801–92; English astronomer)
Best (Charles; 1899–1978; Canadian physiologist)
Bohr (Niels; 1885–1962; Danish physicist)
Born (Max; 1882–1970; German theoretical physicist)
Bose (Satyendra Nath; 1894–1974; Indian physicist)
Davy (Humphry; 1778–1829; English chemist)
Funk (Casimir; 1884–1967; American biochemist, b. in Poland)
Hahn (Otto; 1879–1968; German chemist)
Jung (Carl; 1875–1961; Swiss psychologist)
Koch (Robert; 1843–1910; German bacteriologist)
Mach (Ernst; 1838–1916; Austrian physicist)

5 LETTERS

Adler (Alfred; 1870–1937; Austrian psychologist/psychiatrist)
Boyle (Robert; 1627–91; Irish physicist/chemist)
Braun (Karl; 1850–1918; German physicist)
Chain (Ernst; 1906–79; British biochemist, b. in Germany)
Crick (Francis; 1916–2004; English biophysicist)
Curie (Marie; 1867–1934; French physicist, b. in Poland)
Curie (Pierre; 1859–1906; French physicist)
Dewar (James; 1842–1923; Scottish chemist/physicist)
Dirac (Paul; 1902–84; English theoretical physicist)
Ellis (Havelock; 1859–1939; English psychologist)
Euler (Leonhard; 1707–83; Swiss mathematician)
Fermi (Enrico; 1901–54; American physicist)
Frege (Gottlob; 1848–1925; German mathematician/physicist)
Freud (Anna; 1895–1982; British psychoanalyst)
Freud (Sigmund; 1856–1939; Austrian psychotherapist)
Gamow (George; 1904–68; American physicist, b. in Russia)
Gauss (Karl; 1777–1855; German mathematician)
Haber (Fritz; 1868–1934; German chemist)
Hertz (Heinrich; 1857–94; German physicist)
Hooke (Robert; 1635–1703; English physicist)
Hoyle (Fred; 1915–2001; English astrophysicist)
Jones (Steve; b. 1944; English geneticist)
Joule (James; 1818–89; English physicist)
Klein (Melanie; 1882–1960; Austrian psychoanalyst)
Lacan (Jacques; 1901–81; French psychoanalyst)
Laing (R. D.; 1927–89; Scottish psychiatrist)
Nobel (Alfred; 1833–96; Swedish chemist)
Pauli (Wolfgang; 1900–58; American physicist, b. in Austria)
Raman (Chandrasekhara; 1888–1970; Indian physicist)
Sagan (Carl; 1934–96; American astronomer)
Soddy (Frederick; 1877–1956; English physicist)
Volta (Alessandro; 1745–1827; Italian physicist)
White (Gilbert; 1720–93; English naturalist)

6 LETTERS

Agnesi (Maria; 1718–99; Italian mathematician)
Ampère (André-Marie; 1775–1836; French physicist/mathematician)
Bunsen (Robert; 1811–99; German chemist)
Carson (Rachel; 1907–64; American naturalist)
Cuvier (Georges; 1769–1832; French naturalist)
Dalton (John; 1766–1844; English chemist)
Darwin (Charles; 1809–82; English naturalist)
Euclid (c.300 BC; Greek mathematician)
Fermat (Pierre de; 1601–65; French mathematician)
Florey (Howard; 1898–1968; Australian pathologist)
Geiger (Hans; 1882–1945; German physicist)
Halley (Edmond; 1656–1742; English astronomer)
Hubble (Edwin; 1889–1953; American astronomer)
Huxley (Julian; 1887–1975; English biologist)
Huxley (T. H.; 1825–95; English biologist)
Kelvin (William; 1824–1907; British physicist)
Kepler (Johannes; 1571–1630; German astronomer)
Kinsey (Alfred; 1894–1956; American zoologist)
Mendel (Gregor; 1822–84; Moravian pioneer of genetics)
Morley (Edward Williams; 1838–1923; American physicist)
Napier (John; 1550–1617; Scottish mathematician)
Newton (Isaac; 1642–1727; English physicist/mathematician)
Pascal (Blaise; 1623–62; French mathematician/physicist)
Pavlov (Ivan; 1849–1936; Russian physiologist)

Perrin (Jean Baptiste; 1870–1942; French chemist)
Piaget (Jean; 1896–1980; Swiss psychologist)
Planck (Max; 1858–1947; German physicist)
Ramsay (William; 1852–1916; Scottish chemist)
Teller (Edward; 1908–2003; American physicist, b. in Hungary)
Turing (Alan; 1912–54; English mathematician)
Walton (E. T. S.; 1903–95; Irish physicist)
Watson (James; b. 1928; American biologist)
Watson (John; 1878–1958; American psychologist)

7 LETTERS

Alvarez (Luis; 1911–88; American physicist)
Babbage (Charles; 1791–1871; English mathematician)
Bateson (William; 1861–1926; English geneticist)
Compton (Arthur; 1892–1962; American physicist)
Dawkins (Richard; b. 1941; English biologist)
Doppler (Christian; 1803–53; Austrian physicist)
Ehrlich (Paul; 1854–1915; German medical scientist)
Eysenck (Hans; 1916–97; British psychologist, b. in Germany)
Faraday (Michael; 1791–1867; English chemist/physicist)
Feynman (Richard; 1918–88; American physicist)
Fleming (Alexander; 1881–1955; Scottish bacteriologist)
Fourier (Jean-Baptiste; 1768–1830; French mathematician)
Haldane (J. B. S.; 1892–1964; Scottish biologist)
Hawking (Stephen; b. 1942; English theoretical physicist)
Hodgkin (Dorothy; 1910–94; British biochemist, b. in Egypt)
Huygens (Christiaan; 1629–95; Dutch physicist/mathematician)
Lamarck (Jean-Baptiste de; 1744–1829; French)
Maxwell (James Clerk; 1831–79; Scottish physicist)
Medawar (Peter; 1915–87; English immunologist)
Meitner (Lise; 1878–1968; Swedish physicist, b. in Austria)
Pasteur (Louis; 1822–95; French chemist/bacteriologist)
Pauling (Linus; 1901–94; American chemist)
Riemann (Georg; 1826–66; German mathematician)
Röntgen (Wilhelm; 1845–1923; German physicist)
Seaborg (Glenn; 1912–99; American nuclear chemist)
Thomson (Joseph; 1856–1940; English atomic physicist)
Tyndall (John; 1820–93; Irish physicist)
Virchow (Rudolf; 1821–1902; German physician/pathologist)
Wallace (Alfred; 1823–1913; English naturalist)
Warburg (Otto Heinrich; 1883–1970; German biochemist)
Wegener (Alfred; 1880–1930; German meteorologist)
Wilkins (Maurice; 1916–2004; British biochemist, b. in New Zealand)

8 LETTERS

Anderson (Elizabeth; 1836–1917; English physician)
Ångström (Anders; 1814–74; Swedish physicist)
Appleton (Edward; 1892–1965; English physicist)
Avogadro (Amedeo; 1776–1856; Italian physicist/chemist)
Bjerknes (Vilhelm; 1862–1951; Norwegian meteorologist/geophysicist)
Blackett (Patrick M. S.; 1897–1974; English physicist)
Chadwick (James; 1891–1974; English physicist)
Culpeper (Nicholas; 1616–54; English herbalist)
Davisson (Clinton J.; 1881–1958; American physicist)

Einstein (Albert; 1879–1955; American physicist, b. in Germany)
Foucault (Jean; 1819–68; French physicist)
Franklin (Benjamin; 1706–90; American scientist)
Herschel (William; 1738–1822; British astronomer, b. in Germany)
Linnaeus (Carolus; 1707–78; Swedish botanist)
Lovelace (Augusta; 1815–52; English mathematician)
Lovelock (James; b. 1919; English scientist)
Poincaré (Jules; 1854–1912; French mathematician)
Rayleigh (John; 1842–1919; English physicist)
Sakharov (Andrei; 1921–89; Russian nuclear physicist)
Shockley (William; 1910–89; American physicist)
Tombaugh (Clyde; 1906–97; American astronomer)
Weismann (August; 1834–1914; German biologist)

9 LETTERS

Arrhenius (Svante; 1859–1927; Swedish chemist)
Becquerel (Antoine-Henri; 1852–1908; French physicist)
Boltzmann (Ludwig; 1844–1906; Austrian physicist)
Cavendish (Henry; 1731–1810; English physicist/chemist)
Cherenkov (Pavel; 1904–90; Soviet physicist)
Cockcroft (John; 1897–1967; English physicist)
Eddington (Arthur; 1882–1944; English astronomer)
Fibonacci (Leonardo; c.1170–c.1250; Italian mathematician)
Lavoisier (Antoine; 1743–94; French chemist)
Mendeleev (Dmitri; 1834–1907; Russian chemist)
Michelson (A. A.; 1852–1931; American physicist)

10 LETTERS

Archimedes (c.287–212 BC; Greek mathematician)
Copernicus (Nicolaus; 1473–1543; Polish)
Heisenberg (Werner; 1901–76; German physicist)
Mandelbrot (Benoit; b. 1924; French mathematician)
Pythagoras (c.580–500 BC; Greek mathematician)
Rutherford (Ernest; 1871–1937; New Zealand physicist)
Torricelli (Evangelista; 1608–47; Italian physicist/mathematician)

11 LETTERS

Leeuwenhoek (Antoni van; 1632–1723; Dutch naturalist)
Oppenheimer (Robert; 1904–67; American theoretical physicist)
Schrödinger (Erwin; 1887–1961; Austrian theoretical physicist)

2 WORDS

de Broglie (Louis-Victor; 1892–1987; French physicist)
Galileo Galilei (1564–1642; Italian physicist)
Gay-Lussac (Joseph; 1778–1850; French chemist/physicist)
Gell-Mann (Murray; b. 1929; American physicist)
Van Allen (James; b. 1914; American physicist)
Watson-Watt (Robert; 1892–1973; Scottish physicist)

Sportspeople

1 WORD

3 LETTERS

Ali (Muhammad; b. 1942; American boxer)
Coe (Sebastian; b. 1956; English runner)
Els (Ernie; b. 1969; South African golfer)
May (Peter; 1929–1994; English cricketer)

4 LETTERS

Ashe (Arthur; 1943–93; American tennis player)
Best (George; 1946–2005; Northern Irish footballer)
Borg (Björn; b. 1956; Swedish tennis player)
Budd (Zola; b. 1966; South African runner)
Cram (Steve; b. 1960; English runner)
Dean (Christopher; b. 1958; English ice skater)
Figo (Luis; b. 1972; Portuguese footballer)
Graf (Steffi; b. 1969; German tennis player)
Hill (Damon; b. 1962; English motor-racing driver)
Hill (Graham; 1929–75; English motor-racing driver)
Hunt (James; 1947–93; English motor-racing driver)
John (Barry; b. 1945; Welsh rugby player)
Khan (Imran; b. 1952; Pakistani cricketer)
King (Billie Jean; b. 1943; American tennis player)
Lara (Brian; b. 1969; West Indian cricketer)
Lomu (Jonah; b. 1975; NZ rugby player)
Lyle (Sandy; b. 1958; Scottish golfer)
Moss (Stirling; b. 1929; English motor-racing driver)
Owen (Michael; b. 1979; English footballer)
Pelé (b. 1940; Brazilian footballer)
Ruth (Babe; 1895–1948; American baseball player)
Wade (Virginia; b. 1945; English tennis player)
Witt (Katerina; b. 1965; German ice skater)
Zico (b. 1953; Brazilian footballer)
Zoff (Dino; b. 1942; Italian footballer)
Zola (Gianfranco; b. 1966; Italian footballer)

5 LETTERS

Banks (Gordon; b. 1937; English footballer)
Berra (Yogi; b. 1925; American baseball player)
Bruno (Frank; b. 1961; English boxer)
Bubka (Sergei; b. 1963; Ukrainian pole-vaulter)
Budge (Don; 1915–2000; American tennis player)
Bueno (Maria; b. 1939; Brazilian tennis player)
Busby (Matt; 1909–94; Scottish footballer/manager)
Clark (Jim; 1936–68; Scottish motor-racing driver)
Curry (John; 1949–94; English ice skater)
Davis (Fred; 1913–98; English billiards and snooker player)
Davis (Joe; 1901–78; English billiards and snooker player)
Davis (Steve; b. 1957; English snooker player)
Evert (Chris; b. 1954; American tennis player)
Faldo (Nick; b. 1957; English golfer)
Giggs (Ryan; b. 1973; Welsh footballer)
Gooch (Graham; b. 1953; English cricketer)
Gower (David; b. 1957; English cricketer)
Grace (W. G.; 1848–1915; English cricketer)
Henry (Thierry; b. 1977; French footballer)
Hobbs (Jack; 1882–1963; English cricketer)
Hogan (Ben; 1912–97; American golfer)
Hurst (Geoff; b. 1941; English footballer)
Jones (Bobby; 1902–71; American golfer)
Lauda (Niki; b. 1949; Austrian motor-racing driver)
Laver (Rod; b. 1938; Australian tennis player)
Lendl (Ivan; b. 1960; American tennis player)
Lewis (Carl; b. 1961; American athlete)
Lewis (Lennox; b. 1965; English boxer)
Lloyd (Clive; b. 1944; West Indian cricketer)
Louis (Joe; 1941–81; American boxer)
Milla (Roger; b. 1952; Cameroonian footballer)
Moore (Bobby; 1941–93; English footballer)
Moses (Ed; b. 1955; American athlete)
Nepia (George; 1905–86; NZ rugby player)
O'Neal (Shaquille; b. 1972; American basketball player)
Ovett (Steve; b. 1955; English runner)

Owens (Jesse; 1913–80; American athlete)
Perry (Fred; 1909–95; American tennis player)
Prost (Alain; b. 1955; French motor-racing driver)
Seles (Monica; b. 1973; American tennis player)
Senna (Ayrton; 1960–94; Brazilian motor-racing driver)
Smith (Harvey; b. 1938; English showjumper)
Spitz (Mark; b. 1950; American swimmer)
Suker (Davor; b. 1968; Croatian footballer)
Tyson (Mike; b. 1966; American boxer)
Vieri (Christian; b. 1973; Italian footballer)
Viren (Lasse; b. 1949; Finnish runner)
Vogts (Berti; b. 1946; German footballer/manager)
Walsh (Courtney; b. 1962; Jamaican cricketer)
Warne (Shane; b. 1969; Australian cricketer)
Waugh (Steve; b. 1965; Australian cricketer)
Woods (Tiger; b. 1975; American golfer)

6 LETTERS

Agassi (Andre; b. 1970; American tennis player)
Aouita (Saïd; b. 1960; Moroccan runner)
Baggio (Roberto; b. 1967; Italian footballer)
Bailey (Donovan; b. 1967; Canadian athlete)
Beamon (Bob; b. 1946; American long jumper)
Becker (Boris; b. 1967; German tennis player)
Botham (Ian; b. 1955; English cricketer)
Bryant (David; b. 1931; English bowls player)
Carson (Willie; b. 1942; Scottish jockey)
Cawley (Evonne; b. 1951; Australian tennis player)
Clough (Brian; 1935–2004; English footballer/manager)
Cooper (Henry; b. 1934; English boxer)
Cruyff (Johan; b. 1947; Dutch footballer/manager)
Davies (Laura; b. 1963; English golfer)
Decker (Mary; b. 1958; American runner)
Edberg (Stefan; b. 1966; Swedish tennis player)
Eddery (Pat; b. 1952; Irish jockey)
Fangio (Juan Manuel; 1911–95; Argentinian motor-racing driver)
Finney (Tom; b. 1922; English footballer)
Fraser (Dawn; b. 1937; Australian swimmer)
Gehrig (Lou; 1903–41; American baseball player)
Gibson (Althea; 1927–2003; American tennis player)
Greene (Maurice; b. 1974; American athlete)
Gullit (Ruud; b. 1962; Dutch footballer/manager)
Hadlee (Richard; b. 1951; New Zealand cricketer)
Hendry (Stephen; b. 1969; Scottish snooker player)
Henman (Tim; b. 1974; English tennis player)
Hewitt (Lleyton; b. 1981; Australian tennis player)
Hingis (Martina; b. 1980; Czech tennis player)
Hoddle (Glenn; b. 1957; English footballer/manager)
Holmes (Kelly; b. 1970; English runner)
Hutton (Len; 1916–90; English cricketer)
Jordan (Michael; b. 1963; American basketball player)
Joyner (Florence Griffith; 1959–1998; American runner)
Karpov (Anatoly; b.1951; Russian chess player)
Keegan (Kevin; b. 1951; English footballer/manager)
Korbut (Olga; b. 1955; Soviet gymnast)
Lawton (Tommy; 1919–96; English footballer)
Lillee (Dennis; b. 1949; Australian cricketer)
Liston (Sonny; 1932–70; American boxer)
Merckx (Eddy; b. 1945; Belgian cyclist)
Norman (Greg; b. 1955; Australian golfer)
Palmer (Arnold; b. 1929; American golfer)
Phelps (Michael; b. 1985; American swimmer)
Piquet (Nelson; b. 1952; Brazilian motor-racing driver)
Player (Gary; b. 1935; South African golfer)
Puskas (Ferenc; b. 1927; Hungarian footballer)
Ramsey (Alf; 1922–99; English footballer/manager)
Rhodes (Wilfred; 1877–1973; English cricketer)
Robson (Bryan; b. 1957; English footballer/manager)
Rooney (Wayne; b. 1985; English footballer)
Sheene (Barry; 1950–2003; English racing motorcyclist)

Sobers (Gary; b. 1936; West Indian cricketer)
Thorpe (Ian; b. 1982; Australian swimmer)
Walker (John; b. 1952; New Zealand runner)
Wright (Billy; 1924–94; English footballer)
Zidane (Zinedine; b. 1972; French footballer)

7 LETTERS

Beckham (David; b. 1975; English footballer)
Boycott (Geoffrey; b. 1940; English cricketer)
Brabham (Jack; b. 1926; Australian motor-racing driver)
Bradman (Don; 1908–2001; Australian cricketer)
Bristow (Eric; b. 1957; English darts player)
Campese (David; b. 1962; Australian rugby player)
Carling (Will; b. 1965; English rugby player)
Compton (Denis; 1918–97; English cricketer and footballer)
Connors (Jimmy; b. 1952; American tennis player)
Courier (Jim; b. 1970; American tennis player)
Cowdrey (Colin; 1932–2000; English cricketer)
Dempsey (Jack; 1895–1983; American boxer)
Dettori (Frankie; b. 1970; Italian jockey)
Edwards (Gareth; b. 1947; Welsh rugby player)
Edwards (Jonathan; b. 1966; English athlete)
Eusebio (b. 1942; Portuguese footballer)
Federer (Roger; b. 1981; Swiss tennis player)
Fischer (Bobby; b. 1943; American chess player)
Fogarty (Carl; b. 1966; English racing motorcyclist)
Foreman (George; b. 1948; American boxer)
Fosbury (Richard; b. 1947; American high jumper)
Frazier (Joe; b. 1944; American boxer)
Freeman (Cathy; b. 1973; Australian runner)
Gerrard (Steven; b. 1980; English footballer)
Greaves (Jimmy; b. 1940; English footballer)
Gunnell (Sally; b. 1966; English hurdler)
Higgins (Alex; b. 1949; Northern Irish snooker player)
Jacklin (Tony; b. 1944; English golfer)
Jackson (Colin; b. 1967; Welsh hurdler)
Jardine (Douglas; 1900–58; English cricketer)
Johnson (Ben; b. 1961; Canadian runner)
Johnson (Earvin; b. 1959; American basketball player)
Johnson (Jack; 1878–1946; American boxer)
Johnson (Michael; b. 1967; American athlete)
Larwood (Harold; 1904–95; English cricketer)
Lenglen (Suzanne; 1899–1938; French tennis player)
Leonard (Sugar Ray; b. 1956; American boxer)
Liddell (Eric; 1902–45; British athlete)
Lineker (Gary; b. 1960; English footballer)
Maldini (Paolo; b. 1968; Italian footballer)
Mansell (Nigel; b. 1953; English motor-racing driver)
McBride (Willie John; b. 1940; rugby player)
McEnroe (John; b. 1959; American tennis player)
Piggott (Lester; b. 1935; English jockey)
Platini (Michel; b. 1955; French footballer)
Ronaldo (b. 1976; Brazilian footballer)
Sampras (Pete; b. 1971; American tennis player)
Sarazen (Gene; 1902–99; American golfer)
Shankly (Bill; 1919–81; Scottish footballer/ manager)
Shearer (Alan; b. 1970; English footballer)
Shilton (Peter; b. 1949; English footballer)
Souness (Graeme; b. 1953; Scottish footballer)
Spassky (Boris; b. 1937; Russian chess player)
Stewart (Alec; b. 1963; Scottish cricketer)
Stewart (Jackie; b. 1939; Scottish motor-racing driver)
Torvill (Jayne; b. 1957; English ice skater)
Trevino (Lee; b. 1939; American golfer)
Trueman (Fred; b. 1931; English cricketer)
Vaughan (Michael; b. 1974; English cricketer)
Woosnam (Ian; b. 1958; British golfer)
Zatopek (Emil; 1922–2000; Czech runner)

8 LETTERS

Abrahams (Harold; 1899–1978; English athlete)
Agostini (Giacomo; b. 1944; Italian racing motorcyclist)
Alekhine (Alexander; 1892–1946; French chess player)
Andretti (Mario; b. 1940; American motor-racing driver)

Atherton (Michael; b. 1968; English cricketer)
Bergkamp (Dennis; b. 1969; Dutch footballer)
Campbell (Donald; 1921–67; English motor-racing driver)
Campbell (Malcolm; 1885–1948; English motor-racing driver)
Chappell (Greg; b. 1948; Australian cricketer)
Chappell (Ian; b. 1943; Australian cricketer)
Charlton (Bobby; b. 1937; English footballer)
Charlton (Jack; b. 1935; English footballer/manager)
Christie (Linford; b. 1960; British sprinter)
Comaneci (Nadia; b. 1961; American gymnast)
Connolly (Maureen; 1934–69; American tennis player)
Dalglish (Kenny; b. 1951; Scottish footballer/manager)
DiMaggio (Joe; 1914–99; American baseball player)
Eriksson (Sven-Goran; b. 1948; Swedish football manager)
Ferguson (Alex; b. 1941; Scottish football manager)
Flintoff (Andrew; b. 1977; English cricketer)
Francome (John; b. 1952; English jockey)
Hailwood (Mike; 1940–81; English racing motorcyclist)
Häkkinen (Mika; b. 1968; Finnish motor-racing driver)
Indurain (Miguel; b. 1964; Spanish racing cyclist)
Kasparov (Gary; b. 1963; Azerbaijani chess player)
Kluivert (Patrick; b. 1976; Dutch footballer)
Korchnoi (Victor; b. 1931; Russian chess player)
Maradona (Diego; b. 1960; Argentinian footballer)
Marciano (Rocky; 1923–69; American boxer)
Matthews (Stanley; 1915–2000; English footballer)
Mcguigan (Barry; b. 1961; Irish boxer)
Mourinho (José b. 1963; Portuguese football manager)
Newcombe (John; b. 1944; Australian tennis player)
Nicklaus (Jack; b. 1940; American golfer)
Richards (Gordon; 1904–96; English jockey)
Richards (Viv; b. 1952; West Indian cricketer)
Robinson (Sugar Ray; 1920–89; American boxer)
Rosewall (Ken; b. 1934; American tennis player)
Thompson (Daley; b. 1958; English decathlete)
Williams (J. P. R.; b. 1949; Welsh rugby player)
Williams (Serena; b. 1981; American tennis player)
Williams (Venus; b. 1980; American tennis player)

9 LETTERS

Armstrong (Lance, b. 1971; American racing cyclist)
Bannister (Roger; b. 1929; English runner)
Bonington (Chris; b. 1934; English mountaineer)
Dallaglio (Lawrence; b. 1972; English rugby player)
Davenport (Lindsay; b. 1976; American tennis player)
D'Oliveira (Basil; b. 1931; British cricketer)
Gascoigne (Paul; b. 1967; English footballer)
Goolagong (Evonne; b. 1951; Australian tennis player)
Holyfield (Evander; b. 1962; American boxer)
Llewellyn (Harry; 1911–99; Welsh showjumper)
MacArthur (Ellen; b. 1976; English yachtswoman)
O'Sullivan (Ronnie; b. 1975; English snooker player)
Radcliffe (Paula; b. 1973; English runner)
Rivellino (Roberto; b. 1946; Brazilian footballer)
Szewinska (Irena; b. 1946; Polish runner)
Tendulkar (Sachin; b. 1973; Indian cricketer)
Wilkinson (Johnny; b. 1979; English rugby player)

10 LETTERS

Capablanca (José 1888–1942; Cuban chess player)

Fittipaldi (Emerson; b. 1946; Brazilian motor-racing driver)
Ronaldinho (b. 1980; Brazilian footballer)
Schmeichel (Peter; b. 1963; Danish footballer)
Schumacher (Michael; b. 1969; German motor-racing driver)
Villeneuve (Jacques; b. 1971; Canadian motor-racing driver)
Weismuller (Jonny; 1904–84; American swimmer)

11 LETTERS

Ballesteros (Seve; b. 1957; Spanish golfer)
Beckenbauer (Franz; b. 1945; German footballer)
Illingworth (Ray; b. 1932; English cricketer)
Ivanisevich (Goran; b. 1971; Croatian tennis player)
Kristiansen (Ingrid; b. 1956; Norwegian runner)
Montgomerie (Colin; b. 1963; Scottish golfer)
Navratilova (Martina; b. 1956; American tennis player)
Turishcheva (Ludmilla; b. 1952; Soviet gymnast)

12 LETTERS

Gebrselassie (Haile; b. 1973; Ethiopian runner)

2 WORDS

Di Stefano (Alfredo; b. 1926; Argentinian footballer)
el-Guerrouj (Hicham; b. 1974; Moroccan athlete)
Heyhoe-Flint (Rachael; b. 1939; English cricketer)
Kapil Dev (b. 1959; Indian cricketer)
Rui Costa (Manuel; b. 1972; Portuguese footballer)
Van Basten (Marco; b. 1964; Dutch footballer)
Van Nistelrooy (Ruud; b. 1976; Dutch footballer)

UN Secretaries General (with dates in office)

Annan (Kofi; since 1997)
Boutros-Ghali (Boutros; 1992–96)
Hammarskjöld (Dag; 1953–61)
Lie (Trygve; 1946–52)
Pérez de Cuéllar (Javier; 1982–91)
U Thant (1961–71)
Waldheim (Kurt; 1972–81)

Writers

1 WORD

3 LETTERS

Eco (Umberto; b. 1932; Italian)
Lee (Harper; b. 1926; American)
Lee (Laurie; 1914–97; English)
Nin (Anaïs; 1903–77; American)
Paz (Octavio; 1914–98; Mexican)
Poe (Edgar Allan; 1809–49; American)
Pym (Barbara; 1913–80; English)

4 LETTERS

Amis (Kingsley; 1922–95; English)
Amis (Martin; b. 1949; English)
Behn (Aphra; 1640–89; English)
Böll (Heinrich; 1917–85; German)

Cary (Joyce; 1888–1957; English)
Dahl (Roald; 1916–90; English)
Dick (Philip K.; 1928–82; American)
Ford (Ford Madox; 1873–1939; English)
Gide (André; 1869–1951; French)
Hall (Radclyffe; 1883–1943; English)
Hill (Reginald; b. 1936; English)
Hill (Susan; b. 1942; English)
Hugo (Victor; 1802–85; French)
King (Stephen; b. 1947; American)
Levi (Primo; 1919–87; Italian)
Lyly (John; 1554–1606; English)
Mann (Thomas; 1875–1955; German)
Okri (Ben; b. 1959; Nigerian)
Puzo (Mario; 1920–99; American)
Rhys (Jean; 1890–1979; British)
Rice (Anne; b. 1941; American)
Roth (Philip; b. 1933; American)
Sade (Marquis de; 1740–1814; French)
Saki (1870–1916; British)
Sand (George; 1804–76; French)
Seth (Vikram; b. 1952; Indian)
Snow (C. P.; 1905–80; English)
Wain (John; 1925–94; English)
West (Rebecca; 1892–1983; English)
Wood (Mrs Henry; 1814–87; English)
Wren (P. C.; 1885–1941; English)
Zola (Émile; 1840–1902; French)

5 LETTERS

Adams (Douglas; 1952–2001; English)
Aesop (6th century BC; Greek)
Awdry (Reverend W.; 1911–97; English)
Banks (Iain; b. 1958; Scottish)
Barth (John; b. 1930; American)
Bates (H. E.; 1905–74; English)
Bowen (Elizabeth; 1899–1973; British)
Brink (André; b. 1935; South African)
Brown (Dan; b. 1964; American)
Byatt (A. S.; b. 1936; English)
Camus (Albert; 1913–60; French)
Carey (Peter; b. 1943; Australian)
Crane (Stephen; 1871–1900; American)
Defoe (Daniel; c.1660–1731; English)
Doyle (Arthur Conan; 1859–1930; Scottish)
Dumas (Alexandre; 1802–70; French)
Duras (Marguerite; 1914–96; French)
Eliot (George; 1819–80; English)
Frame (Janet; 1924–2004; New Zealand)
Genet (Jean; 1910–86; French)
Gogol (Nikolai; 1809–52; Russian)
Gorky (Maxim; 1868–1936; Russian)
Grass (Günter; b. 1927; German)
Hardy (Thomas; 1840–1928; English)
Henry (O.; 1862–1910; American)
Hesse (Hermann; 1877–1962; Swiss)
Heyer (Georgette; 1902–74; English)
James (Henry; 1843–1916; British)
James (M. R.; 1862–1932; English)
James (P. D.; b. 1920; English)
Joyce (James; 1882–1941; Irish)
Kafka (Franz; 1883–1924; Czech)
Kesey (Ken; 1935–2001; American)
Lewis (C. S.; 1898–1963; English)
Lewis (Sinclair; 1885–1951; American)
Lodge (David; b. 1935; English)
Lowry (Malcolm; 1909–57; English)
Lurie (Alison; b. 1926; American)
Marsh (Ngaio; 1899–1982; New Zealand)
Milne (A. A.; 1882–1956; English)
Moore (George; 1852–1933; Irish)
Munro (Alice; b. 1931; Canadian)
Newby (Eric; b. 1919; English)
Orczy (Baroness; 1865–1947; British, b. in Hungary)
Pater (Walter; 1839–94; English)
Paton (Alan; 1903–88; South African)
Peake (Mervyn; 1911–68; English)
Pepys (Samuel; 1633–1703; English)
Queen (Ellery; 1905–82; American)
Sagan (François; 1935–2004; French)
Scott (Walter; 1771–1832; Scottish)
Shute (Nevil; 1899–1960; English)
Spark (Muriel; b. 1918; Scottish)
Stein (Gertrude; 1874–1946; American)
Stowe (Harriet Beecher; 1811–96; American)
Swift (Jonathan; 1667–1745; Irish)
Twain (Mark; 1835–1910; American)
Tyler (Anne; b. 1941; American)
Verne (Jules; 1828–1905; French)
Vidal (Gore; b. 1925; American)
Waugh (Evelyn; 1903–66; English)
Wells (H. G.; 1866–1946; English)
Welty (Eudora; 1909–2001; American)
White (Patrick; 1912–90; Australian)
White (T. H.; 1906–64; British)

Wolfe (Tom; b. 1931; American)
Woolf (Virginia; 1882–1941; English)

6 LETTERS

Achebe (Chinua; b. 1930; Nigerian)
Alcott (Louisa May; 1832–88; American)
Aldiss (Brian; b. 1925; English)
Asimov (Isaac; 1920–92; American)
Atwood (Margaret; b. 1939; Canadian)
Austen (Jane; 1775–1817; English)
Balzac (Honoré de; 1799–1850; French)
Barnes (Julian; b. 1946; English)
Bawden (Nina; b. 1925; English)
Belloc (Hilaire; 1870–1953; British)
Bellow (Saul; 1915–2005; American)
Binchy (Maeve; b. 1940; Irish)
Borges (Jorge Luis; 1899–1986; Argentinian)
Braine (John; 1922–86; English)
Brontë (Anne; 1820–49; English)
Brontë (Charlotte; 1816–55; English)
Brontë (Emily; 1818–48; English)
Bryson (Bill; b. 1951; American)
Buchan (John; 1875–1940; Scottish)
Bunyan (John; 1628–88; English)
Burney (Fanny; 1752–1840; English)
Butler (Samuel; 1835–1902; English)
Capote (Truman; 1924–84; American)
Carter (Angela; 1940–92; English)
Carver (Raymond; 1938–88; American)
Cather (Willa; 1876–1974; American)
Clancy (Tom; b. 1947; American)
Clarke (Arthur C.; b. 1917; English)
Conrad (Joseph; 1857–1924; British)
Cooper (James Fenimore; 1789–1851; American)
Cronin (A. J.; 1896–1981; Scottish)
Daudet (Alphonse; 1840–97; French)
Davies (Robertson; 1913–95; Canadian)
Dexter (Colin; b.1930; English)
Evelyn (John; 1620–1706; English)
Fowles (John; 1926–2005; English)
France (Anatole; 1844–1924; French)
Gibson (William; b. 1948; American)
Graves (Robert; 1895–1985; English)
Greene (Graham; 1904–91; English)
Hamsun (Knut; 1859–1952; Norwegian)
Heller (Joseph; 1923–99; American)
Holmes (Oliver Wendell; 1809–94; American)
Hornby (Nick; b. 1957; English)
Huxley (Aldous; 1894–1963; English)
Irving (John; b. 1942; American)
Irving (Washington; 1783–1859; American)
Jerome (Jerome K.; 1859–1927; English)
Kadare (Ismail; b. 1936; Albanian)
Laclos (Pierre Choderlos de; 1741–1803; French)
Lesage (Alain-René; 1668–1747; French)
London (Jack; 1876–1916; American)
Ludlum (Robert; 1927–2001; American)
Lytton (Lord; 1803–73; English)
Mailer (Norman; b. 1923; American)
Malory (Thomas; c.1400–71; English)
McEwan (Ian; b. 1948; English)
Miller (Henry; 1891–1980; American)
Nesbit (E.; 1858–1924; English)
O'Brian (Patrick; 1914–2000; Irish)
O'Brien (Edna; b. 1932; Irish)
O'Brien (Flann; Brian O'Nolan; 1911–66; Irish)
Orwell (George; 1903–50; English)
Parker (Dorothy; 1893–1967; American)
Pavese (Cesare; 1908–50; Italian)
Porter (Katherine Anne; 1890–1980; American)
Potter (Beatrix; 1866–1943; English)
Powell (Anthony; 1905–2000; English)
Proust (Marcel; 1871–1922; French)
Rankin (Ian; b. 1960; Scottish)
Runyon (Damon; 1884–1946; American)
Sartre (Jean-Paul; 1905–80; French)
Sayers (Dorothy L.; 1893–1957; English)
Singer (Isaac Bashevis; 1904–91; American, b. in Poland)
Sterne (Laurence; 1713–68; Irish)
Stoker (Bram; 1847–1912; Irish)
Symons (Julian; 1912–94; English)
Trevor (William; b. 1928; Irish)
Updike (John; b. 1932; American)
Walker (Alice; b. 1944; American)
Walton (Izaak; 1593–1683; English)
Warren (Robert Penn; 1905–89; American)
Weldon (Fay; b. 1931; English)
Wesley (Mary; 1912–2002; English)
Wilder (Thornton; 1897–1975; American)
Wilson (Angus; 1913–91; English)
Wilson (Jacqueline; b. 1945; English)

7 LETTERS

Ackroyd (Peter; b. 1949; English)
Addison (Joseph; 1672–1719; English)
Alarcón (Pedro de; 1833–91; Spanish)
Angelou (Maya; b. 1928; American)
Baldwin (James; 1924–87; American)
Ballard (J. G.; b. 1930; British, b. in China)
Bennett (Arnold; 1867–1931; English)
Boswell (James; 1740–95; Scottish)
Burgess (Anthony; 1917–93; English)
Calvino (Italo; 1923–85; Italian)
Canetti (Elias; 1905–94; British)
Carroll (Lewis; 1832–98; English)
Chatwin (Bruce; 1940–89; English)
Cheever (John; 1912–82; American)
Coetzee (J. M.; b. 1940; South African)
Colette (1873–1954; French)
Collins (Wilkie; 1824–89; English)
Cookson (Catherine; 1906–98; English)
Dickens (Charles; 1812–70; English)
Dinesen (Isak; 1885–1962; Danish)
Drabble (Margaret; b. 1939; English)
Durrell (Lawrence; 1912–90; English)
Fleming (Ian; 1908–64; English)
Follett (Ken; b. 1949; English)
Forster (E. M.; 1879–1970; English)
Forsyth (Frederick; b. 1938; English)
Francis (Dick; b. 1920; English)
Fuentes (Carlos; b. 1928; Mexican)
Gaskell (Mrs; 1810–65; English)
Gissing (George; 1857–1903; English)
Golding (William; 1911–93; English)
Grahame (Kenneth; 1859–1932; Scottish)
Grisham (John; b. 1955; American)
Haggard (Rider; 1856–1925; English)
Hammett (Dashiell; 1894–1961; American)
Hartley (L. P.; 1895–1972; English)
Hazlitt (William; 1778–1830; English)
Herriot (James; 1916–95; English)
Hornung (Ernest; 1866–1921; English)
Jansson (Tove; 1914–2001; Finnish)
Kerouac (Jack; 1922–69; American)
Kipling (Rudyard; 1865–1936; British)
Kundera (Milan; b. 1929; Czech)
Leonard (Elmore; b. 1925; American)
Lessing (Doris; b. 1919; English)
Maclean (Alistair; 1922–87; Scottish)
Mahfouz (Naguib; b. 1911; Egyptian)
Malamud (Bernard; 1914–86; American)
Malraux (André; 1901–76; French)
Manning (Olivia; 1911–80; English)
Marryat (Frederick; 1792–1848; English)
Maugham (Somerset; 1874–1965; English)
Mauriac (François; 1885–1970; French)
Mérimée (Prosper; 1803–70; French)
Mishima (Yukio; 1925–70; Japanese)
Mitford (Nancy; 1904–73; English)
Murdoch (Iris; 1919–99; British)
Nabokov (Vladimir; 1899–1977; American)
Naipaul (V. S.; b. 1932; British)
Narayan (R. K.; 1906–2001; Indian)
Peacock (Thomas Love; 1785–1866; English)
Pullman (Philip; b. 1946; English)
Pynchon (Thomas; b. 1937; American)
Ransome (Arthur; 1884–1967; English)
Renault (Mary; 1814–84; British)
Rendell (Ruth; b. 1930; English)
Richler (Mordecai; 1931–2001; Canadian)
Robbins (Harold; 1916–97; American)
Rowling (J. K.; b. 1965; English)
Rushdie (Salman; b. 1947; British, b. in India)
Shelley (Mary; 1797–1851; English)
Simenon (Georges; 1903–89; Belgian)
Sitwell (Edith; 1887–1964; English)
Soyinka (Wole; b. 1934; Nigerian)
Theroux (Paul; b. 1941; American)
Thoreau (Henry; 1817–62; American)
Tolkien (J. R. R.; 1892–1973; British)
Tolstoy (Leo; 1828–1910; Russian)
Wallace (Edgar; 1875–1932; English)
Walpole (Horace; 1717–97; English)
Wharton (Edith; 1862–1937; American)
Wyndham (John; 1903–69; English)

8 LETTERS

Andersen (Hans Christian; 1805–75; Danish)
Beauvoir (Simone de; 1908–86; French)
Beerbohm (Max; 1872–1956; English)
Bradbury (Malcolm; 1932–2000; English)
Bradbury (Ray; b. 1920; American)
Bradford (Barbara Taylor; b. 1933; English)
Brittain (Vera; 1893–1970; English)
Brookner (Anita; b. 1928; English)

Cartland (Barbara; 1901–2000; English)
Chandler (Raymond; 1888–1959; American)
Christie (Agatha; 1890–1976; English)
Cornwell (Patricia; b. 1956; American)
Crompton (Richmal; 1890–1969; English)
Deighton (Len; b. 1929; English)
Doctorow (E. L.; b. 1931; American)
Faulkner (William; 1897–1962; American)
Fielding (Helen; b. 1958; English)
Fielding (Henry; 1707–54; English)
Flaubert (Gustave; 1821–80; French)
Forester (C. S.; 1899–1966; English)
Franklin (Miles; 1879–1954; Australian)
Goncourt (Edmond de; 1822–96; French)
Goncourt (Jules de; 1830–70; French)
Gordimer (Nadine; b. 1923; South African)
Ishiguro (Kazuo; b. 1954; British)
Keneally (Thomas; b. 1935; Australian)
Kingsley (Charles; 1819–75; English)
Koestler (Arthur; 1905–83; British)
Lagerlöf (Selma; 1858–1940; Swedish)
Lawrence (D. H.; 1885–1930; English)
Lawrence (T. E.; 1888–1935; English)
Macaulay (Rose; 1881–1958; English)
McCarthy (Mary; 1912–89; American)
Melville (Herman; 1819–91; American)
Meredith (George; 1828–1909; English)
Mitchell (Margaret; 1900–49; American)
Morrison (Toni; b. 1931; American)
Ondaatje (Michael; b. 1943; Canadian)
Perelman (S. J.; 1904–79; American)
Perrault (Charles; 1628–1703; French)
Plutarch (c.46–c.1207 AD; Greek)
Rabelais (François; c.1494–1553; French)
Salinger (J. D.; b. 1919; American)
Sillitoe (Alan; b. 1928; English)
Smollett (Tobias; 1721–71; Scottish)
Spillane (Mickey; b. 1918, American)
Stendhal (1783–1842; French)
Strachey (Lytton; 1880–1932; English)
Thompson (Flora; 1876–1947; English)
Tremaine (Rose; b. 1943; English)
Trollope (Anthony; 1815–82; English)
Trollope (Joanna; b. 1943; English)
Turgenev (Ivan; 1818–83; Russian)
Voltaire (Francois-Marie Arouet; 1694–1778; French)
Vonnegut (Kurt; b. 1922; American)

9 LETTERS

Blackmore (Richard; 1825–1900; English)
Boccaccio (Giovanni; 1313–75; Italian)
Burroughs (Edgar Rice; 1875–1950; American)
Burroughs (William S.; 1914–97; American)
Cervantes (Miguel de; 1547–1616; Spanish)
Edgeworth (Maria; 1767–1849; Irish)
Goldsmith (Oliver; 1730–74; Irish)
Goncharov (Ivan; 1812–91; Russian)
Hawthorne (Nathaniel; 1804–64; American)
Hemingway (Ernest; 1899–1961; American)
Highsmith (Patricia; 1921–95; American)
Isherwood (Christopher; 1904–86; American)
Lampedusa (Giuseppe Tomasi di; 1896–1957; Italian)
Mackenzie (Compton; 1883–1972; English)
Mansfield (Katherine; 1888–1923; New Zealand)
McCullers (Carson; 1917–67; American)
Monsarrat (Nicholas; 1910–79; English)
Montaigne (Michel de; 1533–92; French)
Pasternak (Boris; 1890–1960; Russian)
Pratchett (Terry; b. 1948; English)
Priestley (J. B.; 1894–1984; English)
Pritchett (V. S.; 1900–97; English)
Radcliffe (Ann; 1764–1823; English)
Steinbeck (John; 1902–68; American)
Stevenson (Robert Louis; 1850–94; Scottish)
Thackeray (William Makepeace; 1811–63; British)
Wodehouse (P. G.; 1881–1975; British)

10 LETTERS

Bainbridge (Beryl; b. 1934; English)
Chesterton (G. K.; 1874–1936; English)
Dostoevsky (Fyodor; 1821–81; Russian)
FitzGerald (F. Scott; 1896–1940; American)
Galsworthy (John; 1867–1933; English)
Maupassant (Guy de; 1850–93; French)
Richardson (Samuel; 1689–1761; English)
Williamson (Henry; 1895–1977; English)

12 LETTERS

Solzhenitsyn (Alexander; b. 1918; Russian)

2 WORDS

Compton-Burnett (Ivy; 1884–1969; English)
de Bernières (Louis; b. 1954; English)
De Quincey (Thomas; 1785–1859; English)
Dos Passos (John; 1896–1970; American)
Du Maurier (Daphne; 1907–89; English)
García Márquez (Gabriel; b. 1928; Colombian)
La Rochefoucauld (1613–80; French)
Le Carré (John; b. 1931; English)
Le Fanu (Sheridan; 1814–73; Irish)
Le Guin (Ursula; b. 1929; American)
Robbe-Grillet (Alain; b. 1922; French)
Sackville-West (Vita; 1892–1962; English)
Saint-Exupéry (Antoine; 1900–44; French)
Vargas Llosa (Mario; b. 1936; Peruvian)

Food and drink

Alcoholic drinks

1 WORD

3 LETTERS

ale
gin
rum
rye

4 LETTERS

arak
Asti
beer
bock
cava
fino
fizz
hock
malt
mead
mild
ouzo
Pils
port
raki
sack
sake
Sekt
wine

5 LETTERS

cider
Gamay
kvass
lager
Médoc
noyau
perry
Rioja
Soave
stout
Syrah
Tavel
Tokay
vodka

6 LETTERS

arrack
Bandol
Barolo
Barsac
Beaune
bitter
brandy
cassis
claret
cognac
fraise
grappa
Graves
kirsch
kümmel
Malbec
Merlot
mescal
muscat
pastis
porter
poteen
Saumur
Scotch
shandy
sherry
Shiraz
whisky

7 LETTERS

alcopop
amoroso
aquavit
Auslese
bourbon
cachaca
catawba
Chablis
Chianti
curaçao
Eiswein
genever
liqueur
Madeira
malmsey
Margaux
Marsala
moscato
Moselle
oloroso
Orvieto
Pilsner
ratafia
retsina
sambuca
scrumpy
tequila
Vouvray
whiskey

8 LETTERS

absinthe
advocaat
amaretto
anisette
Armagnac
burgundy
Calvados
cocktail
Frascati
Grenache
Kabinett
Malvasia
Muscadet
muscatel
Pilsener
Riesling
Sancerre
schnapps
Sémillon
Spätlese
Spumante
Sylvaner
Traminer
Verdelho
vermouth
Viognier

9 LETTERS

applejack
Bardolino
champagne
framboise
Lambrusco
Meursault
Minervois
Sauternes
Sauvignon
slivovitz
Trebbiano
Zinfandel

10 LETTERS

Beaujolais
Chardonnay
chartreuse
manzanilla
maraschino
Montrachet
Piesporter
Sangiovese
Verdicchio

11 LETTERS

aguardiente
amontillado
Monbazillac
Niersteiner

12 LETTERS

Valpolicella

13 LETTERS

Beerenauslese
Liebfraumilch
Montepulciano

2 WORDS

barley wine
brown ale
Bull's Blood
Cabernet Franc
Cabernet Sauvignon
canary wine
cask beer
Chenin Blanc
cherry brandy
cream sherry
draught beer
fine champagne
ginger wine
grain whisky
ice beer
Irish whiskey
keg beer
light ale
malt whisky
milk stout
Müller-Thurgau
pale ale
palm wine
Pinot Blanc
Pinot Grigio
Pinot Noir
Pouilly-Fuissé
Pouilly-Fumé
real ale
Rosé d'Anjou
Saint-Émilion
Scotch whisky
single malt
sloe gin
sour mash
spruce beer
Tia Maria
triple sec
vinho verde

3 WORDS

Blanc de blancs
Côtes du Rhône
crème de cacao
crème de menthe
Entre-deux-Mers
Nuits St George

Bread and bread rolls

1 WORD

3 LETTERS

bap
bun
cob
nan

4 LETTERS

farl
naan
pone
puri
roti

5 LETTERS

bagel
boxty
matzo
pitta

6 LETTERS

damper
hoagie
kaiser
kulcha
muffin
panino

7 LETTERS

bannock
bloomer
brioche
challah
crumpet
paratha
pikelet
stollen

8 LETTERS

baguette
chapatti
ciabatta
focaccia
poppadom

9 LETTERS

barmbrack
cornbread
flatbread
panettone
sourdough
wheatmeal
wholemeal

12 LETTERS

pumpernickel

2 WORDS

bara brith
barm cake
bridge roll
cottage loaf
farmhouse loaf
French stick
fruit loaf
granary bread
malt loaf
milk loaf
multigrain loaf
petit pain
quartern loaf
rye bread
soda bread
split tin

Cakes, biscuits, and desserts

1 WORD

3 LETTERS

bun

4 LETTERS

baba
fool
rusk
tart
whip

5 LETTERS

bombe
brack
crêpe
fancy
halwa
jelly
kulfi
matzo
scone
torte

6 LETTERS

cookie
eclair
gateau
gelato
junket
mousse
muffin
parkin
pashka
sorbet

sponge
sundae
trifle
waffle
yogurt

7 LETTERS

baklava
beignet
bourbon
brownie
cassata
cobbler
compote
crumble
crumpet
cupcake
granita
oatcake
pancake
parfait
pavlova
popover
pretzel
ratafia
saltine
savarin
soufflé
stollen
strudel
tartlet
tartufo

8 LETTERS

Berliner
biscotti
cracknel
doughnut
dumpling
flapjack
flummery
macaroon
marquise
meringue
panforte
sandwich
semolina
streusel
syllabub
tiramisu
turnover

9 LETTERS

charlotte
clafoutis
digestive
garibaldi
madeleine
panettone
shortcake

10 LETTERS

Battenberg
blancmange
cheesecake
crispbread
Florentine
frangipane
mousseline
shortbread
zabaglione

11 LETTERS

gingerbread
profiterole
Sachertorte

12 LETTERS

apfelstrudel
millefeuille

13 LETTERS

croquembouche

2 WORDS

almond cake
angel cake
apple charlotte
apple pie
baked Alaska
Bakewell tart
banana split
Banbury cake
banoffee pie
banoffi pie
Bath bun
Bath Oliver
brandy snap
bread pudding
Brown Betty
butterfly cake
cabinet pudding
charlotte russe
chocolate chip
cream cracker
cream puff
crème brûlée
crème caramel
crêpe Suzette
custard cream
custard pie
custard tart
Danish pastry
drop scone
Dundee cake
Eccles cake
egg custard
Eskimo pie
Eve's pudding
fairy cake
floating island
fortune cookie
fruit cocktail
fruit salad
funnel cake
Genoa cake
ginger nut
ginger snap
hasty pudding
hokey-pokey
ice cream
Knickerbocker Glory
lady's finger
lardy cake
layer cake
Lincoln biscuit
Madeira cake
marble cake
marie biscuit
milk pudding
mince pie
Nice biscuit

peach Melba
petit beurre
petit four
plum duff
plum pudding
pound cake
queen cake
rice pudding
rock cake
roly-poly
sago pudding
Sally Lunn
seed cake
ship's biscuit
simnel cake
singing hinny
sponge pudding
spotted dick
steamed pudding
suet pudding
summer pudding
sweetmeal biscuit
Swiss roll
tarte Tatin
tipsy cake
treacle tart
tutti-frutti
Victoria sponge
water biscuit
water ice
wholemeal biscuit
yule log

3 WORDS

angel food cake
Black Forest gateau
death by chocolate
devil's food cake
hot cross bun
langue de chat
maid of honour
Mississippi mud pie
queen of puddings
shoo-fly pie
upside-down cake

4 WORDS

bread-and-butter pudding

Cheeses

1 WORD

4 LETTERS

Brie
Edam
feta

5 LETTERS

Derby
fetta
Gouda
panir
quark

6 LETTERS

asiago
cantal
chèvre
crowdy
Dunlop
paneer
Romano
Tilsit

7 LETTERS

Boursin
Chaumes
Cheddar
crowdie
fontina
Gruyère
havarti
ricotta
Stilton

8 LETTERS

Cheshire
Emmental
halloumi
Manchego
Parmesan
pecorino
scamorza
taleggio

9 LETTERS

Camembert
Jarlsberg
Leicester
Limburger
provolone
Roquefort

10 LETTERS

Caerphilly
Dolcelatte
Gloucester
Gorgonzola
Lancashire
mascarpone
mozzarella
Neufchâtel

11 LETTERS

Wensleydale

2 WORDS

Bel Paese

blue Brie
blue cheese
blue vinny
cottage cheese
cream cheese
curd cheese
Danish blue
Double Gloucester
fromage blanc
fromage frais
Monterey Jack
Parmigiano Reggiano
Pont l'Évêque
Port Salut
Red Leicester
sage Derby

Cocktails and mixed drinks

1 WORD

Bellini
B52
Bronx
caipirinha
cobbler
cosmopolitan
daiquiri
eggnog
gimlet
grog
highball
Kir
manhattan
margarita
Martini
mojito
negroni
nog
punch
rattlesnake
sangria
screwdriver
sidecar
slammer
snakebite
snowball
sour
spritzer
toddy
zombie

2 WORDS

Black Russian
black velvet
Bloody Mary
blue lagoon
brandy Alexander
Buck's Fizz
champagne cocktail
Cuba libre
egg flip
gin sling
Harvey Wallbanger
Irish coffee
John Collins
Kir Royale
mai tai
mint julep
old-fashioned
pina colada
pink gin
pink lady
planter's punch
prairie oyster
sea breeze
Singapore sling
tequila slammer
tequila sunrise
Tom Collins
whisky mac
whisky sour
White Lady
White Russian

3 WORDS

between the sheets
G and T
rum and black

4 WORDS

Long Island iced tea
sex on the beach

Cooking and drinking containers

1 WORD

3 LETTERS

cup
mug
pan
pot
wok

4 LETTERS

dish
tian

5 LETTERS

billy
dixie
flute
glass
stein
tazza

6 LETTERS

beaker
copita
flagon
frypan
goblet
karahi
pipkin
rummer
teacup

7 LETTERS

balloon
chalice
cocotte
marmite
poacher
ramekin
skillet
snifter
steamer
stewpot
tankard
tumbler

8 LETTERS

billycan
cauldron
pannikin
saucepan
schooner
stockpot

9 LETTERS

casserole
demitasse

2 WORDS

bain-marie
casserole dish
chafing dish
coffee cup
double boiler
drinking horn
Dutch oven
fish kettle
frying pan
loving cup
mess tin
moustache cup
pressure cooker
pudding basin
shot glass
sippy cup
slow cooker
stirrup cup
toby jug

3 WORDS

yard of ale

Dietary habits

1 WORD

cannibal (person/animal that eats flesh of own species)
carnivore (animal that feeds on meat)
folivore (animal that feeds on leaves)
frugivore (animal that feeds on fruit)
fruitarian (person who eats only fruit)
herbivore (animal that feeds on plants)
omnivore (person/animal that eats both plants and meat)

pescatarian (person who eats fish but not meat)
piscivore (animal that feeds on fish)
vegan (person who does not eat/use any animal products)
vegetarian (person who does not eat meat or fish)

2 WORDS

lacto-vegetarian (person who eats only dairy products and vegetables)

Food preparation terms

1 WORD

3 LETTERS

cut
fry
ice

4 LETTERS

bake
bard
beat
boil
bone
chop
coat
dice
lard
pipe
sear
stew
whip

5 LETTERS

baste
broil
brown
carve
curry
glaze
grill
knead
poach
purée
roast
sauté
scald
slice
smoke
steam
sweat
toast

6 LETTERS

blanch
braise
coddle
fillet
flambé
napped
reduce
reheat
simmer

7 LETTERS

deglaze
griddle
parboil
precook

8 LETTERS

barbecue
devilled
macerate
marinate
meunière
scramble
tandoori
truffled

9 LETTERS

casserole
charbroil
fricassée
microwave

10 LETTERS

bordelaise
caramelize
Parmentier
Parmigiana
provençale

2 WORDS

al dente
au gratin
bonne femme
deep-fry
dry-fry
en papillote
oven-roast
pan-fry
pot-roast
pressure-cook
spit-roast
stir-fry

Fruit and nuts

1 WORD

3 LETTERS

cob
fig

4 LETTERS

date
lime
pear
plum
sloe
sorb

5 LETTERS

ackee
apple
gourd
grape
guava
lemon
mango
melon
olive
peach
pecan
piñon

6 LETTERS

almond
banana
Brazil
cashew
cherry
citron
cobnut
damson
durian
feijoa
hognut
jujube
longan
loquat
lychee
mammee
medlar
orange
papaya
pawpaw
peanut
pomelo
quince
tomato
walnut

7 LETTERS

apricot
avocado
bullace
chayote
coconut
currant
filbert
kumquat
pumpkin
satsuma
soursop
tangelo

8 LETTERS

bilberry
chestnut
cowberry
dewberry
earthnut
hazelnut
mandarin
minneola
mulberry
plantain
rambutan
sweetsop
tamarind
tayberry

9 LETTERS

blueberry
butternut
carambola
cherimoya
chincapin
cranberry
greengage
groundnut
jackfruit
macadamia
naseberry
nectarine
ortanique
persimmon
pineapple
pistachio
raspberry
sapodilla
starfruit
tamarillo
tangerine
wineberry

10 LETTERS

blackberry
breadfruit
cantaloupe
clementine
cloudberry
elderberry
gooseberry
granadilla
grapefruit
loganberry
mangosteen
redcurrant
strawberry
watermelon
youngberry

11 LETTERS

boysenberry
huckleberry
pomegranate
salmonberry

12 LETTERS

blackcurrant
checkerberry
serviceberry
thimbleberry
whortleberry

2 WORDS

avocado pear
betel nut
blood orange
Cape gooseberry
cashew apple
cherry plum
Chinese gooseberry
cola nut
crab apple
custard apple
galia melon
honeydew melon
kiwi fruit
monkey nut
musk melon
navel orange
passion fruit
pine nut
prickly pear
sharon fruit
star anise
star apple
sugar apple
sweet chestnut
tiger nut
Ugli fruit
Victoria plum
water chestnut
white currant

Herbs and spices

1 WORD

3 LETTERS

rue

4 LETTERS

dill
mace
mint
sage

5 LETTERS

anise
basil
caper
clary
clove
cumin
sumac
thyme

6 LETTERS

ajowan
balsam
borage
cassia
chilli
chives
fennel
garlic
ginger
hyssop
lovage
nutmeg
pepper
savory
sorrel

7 LETTERS

aniseed
caraway
chervil
chicory
damiana
dittany
ginseng
mustard
oregano
paprika
parsley
pimento
saffron
vanilla

8 LETTERS

allspice
angelica
bergamot
camomile
cardamom
cilantro
cinnamon
feverfew
galangal
jalapeño
lavender
marjoram
rosemary
tarragon
turmeric

9 LETTERS

coriander
echinacea
fenugreek
spearmint

10 LETTERS

asafoetida
peppermint

2 WORDS

bay leaf
black pepper
cayenne pepper
curry powder
dong quai
garam masala
green pepper
juniper berry
lemon balm
lemon grass
lemon mint
milk thistle
star anise
sweet balm
sweet cicely
white pepper

3 WORDS

five-spice powder
grains of Paradise
St John's wort

Meals

1 WORD

banquet
barbecue
barbie
breakfast
brunch
buffet
clambake
cookout
dinner
elevenses
feast
lunch
luncheon
meze
picnic
smorgasbord
supper
takeaway
tapas
tea

2 WORDS

afternoon tea
continental breakfast
cream tea
dinner party
evening meal
finger buffet
harvest supper
high tea
midday meal
packed lunch
safari supper
TV dinner
wedding breakfast

Meat cuts and joints

1 WORD

3 LETTERS

leg
rib

4 LETTERS

chop
hand
hock
loin
neck
rack
rump
shin
side
skirt

5 LETTERS

belly
chine
chuck
flank
gigot
hough
round
shank

6 LETTERS

collar
cutlet
fillet
saddle

7 LETTERS

brisket
knuckle
sirloin
topside

8 LETTERS

escalope
noisette
shoulder
undercut

9 LETTERS

entrecôte
tournedos

10 LETTERS

fricandeau
silverside
tenderloin

13 LETTERS

chateaubriand

2 WORDS

best end
porterhouse steak
spare rib
T-bone

3 WORDS

baron of beef

Meat types and products

1 WORD

3 LETTERS

ham

4 LETTERS

beef
duck
game
lamb
pâté
pork
Spam
veal

5 LETTERS

bacon
brawn
goose
liver
mince
offal
steak
tripe
wurst

6 LETTERS

banger
burger
faggot
gammon
haslet
kidney
lights
mutton
oxtail
rabbit
salami
tongue
turkey
weenie
wiener

7 LETTERS

bologna
chicken
chorizo
merguez
poultry
rissole
sausage
saveloy
venison

8 LETTERS

bresaola
bushmeat
cervelat
kielbasa

9 LETTERS

andouille
boerewors
bratwurst
chipolata
hamburger
pepperoni
saucisson

10 LETTERS

beefburger
knackwurst
mortadella
prosciutto
sweetbread
Weisswurst

11 LETTERS

frankfurter

12 LETTERS

chitterlings

2 WORDS

black pudding
blood pudding
blood sausage
corned beef
Cumberland sausage
lamb's fry
luncheon meat

Parma ham
pig's trotters
salt pork
white pudding

Non-alcoholic drinks

1 WORD

3 LETTERS

tea

4 LETTERS

cola
maté

5 LETTERS

Assam
bohea
cocoa
crush
decaf
lassi
latte
mocha
pekoe

6 LETTERS

coffee
Keemun
oolong
orgeat
pressé
squash
tisane

7 LETTERS

arabica
cordial
limeade
robusta
seltzer
sherbet

8 LETTERS

espresso
horchata
infusion
lemonade
pouchong
smoothie
souchong

9 LETTERS

cherryade
milkshake
orangeade

10 LETTERS

buttermilk
cappuccino
Darjeeling
mochaccino

12 LETTERS

sarsaparilla

2 WORDS

barley water
bitter lemon
black tea
cafe noir
caffè latte
caffè macchiato
camomile tea
carbonated water
Ceylon tea
China tea
citron pressé
club soda
cream soda
decaffeinated coffee
drinking chocolate
Earl Grey
filter coffee
fruit juice
fruit tea
Gaelic coffee
ginger ale
ginger beer
Greek coffee
green tea
gunpowder tea
herbal tea
hot chocolate
iced tea
Indian tea
instant coffee
isotonic drink
jasmine tea
Lapsang Souchong
lemon tea
malted milk
mineral water
mint tea
orange pekoe
peppermint tea
prairie oyster
root beer
rosehip tea
Russian tea
soda water
soya milk
sports drink
spring water
St Clements
tonic water
Turkish coffee
yerba maté

3 WORDS

cafe au lait
dandelion and burdock

Pasta, types of

1 WORD

4 LETTERS

orzo
pipe
ziti

5 LETTERS

penne

6 LETTERS

bigoli
rotini

7 LETTERS

capelli
fusilli
lasagne
lumache
noodles
ravioli
rotelle

8 LETTERS

bucatini
ditalini
farfalle
fedelini
gramigna
linguine
macaroni
rigatoni
tortelli
trenette

9 LETTERS

agnolotti
capellini
manicotti
radiatore
spaghetti

10 LETTERS

cannelloni
casareccie
conchiglie
farfalline
fettuccine
tagliolini
tortellini
tortelloni
vermicelli

11 LETTERS

cappelletti
maltagliati
orecchiette
pappardelle
spaghettini
tagliatelle
tortiglioni

12 LETTERS

strozzapreti

2 WORDS

angel hair

Sauces, dips, and dressings

1 WORD

aioli
gravy
guacamole
harissa
hollandaise
hummus
jus
ketchup
mayonnaise
pesto
ragù
remoulade
salsa
soubise
Tabasco
taramasalata
tzatziki
velouté
vinaigrette

2 WORDS

apple sauce
baba ganoush

barbecue sauce
Béarnaise sauce
béchamel sauce
Bolognese sauce
bordelaise sauce
bread sauce
brown sauce
Caesar dressing
carbonara sauce
chasseur sauce
chaud-froid
cheese sauce
chilli sauce
cranberry sauce
curry sauce
demi-glace
fish sauce
French dressing
hoisin sauce
horseradish sauce
mint sauce
mornay sauce
mousseline sauce
mustard sauce
onion sauce
oyster sauce
parsley sauce
pepper sauce
pizzaiola sauce
puttanesca sauce
ranch dressing
salad cream
salsa verde
satay sauce
soy sauce
tartare sauce
teriyaki sauce
tomato ketchup
tomato sauce
white sauce
Worcester sauce

3 WORDS

black bean sauce
blue cheese dressing
Thousand Island dressing

4 WORDS

sweet-and-sour sauce

Soups and stews

1 WORD

3 LETTERS

pho

5 LETTERS

broth
daube
gruel
gumbo
salmi
shchi

6 LETTERS

bisque
congee
hotpot
menudo
oxtail
potage
ragout
tagine

7 LETTERS

borscht
chowder
goulash
navarin
stifado
tsimmes

8 LETTERS

bouillon
callaloo
consommé
étouffée
feijoada
gazpacho
grillade

9 LETTERS

casserole
cassoulet
fricassée
lobscouse
madrilene

10 LETTERS

avgolemono
carbonnade
minestrone

11 LETTERS

ratatouille
vichyssoise

12 LETTERS

mulligatawny

13 LETTERS

bouillabaisse
stracciatella

2 WORDS

boeuf bourguignon
Cullen skink
Irish stew
Lancashire hotpot

miso soup
mock turtle
olla podrida
osso buco
pepper pot
Scotch broth

3 WORDS

bird's nest soup
chilli con carne
cock-a-leekie
coq au vin
pot-au-feu

Sweets and confectionery, types of

1 WORD

4 LETTERS

chew
mint
rock

5 LETTERS

candy
fudge
halva
jelly
laddu
lolly

6 LETTERS

bonbon
comfit
dragée
humbug
jalebi
jujube
nougat
toffee

7 LETTERS

brittle
caramel
fondant
gumdrop
praline
sherbet
truffle

8 LETTERS

bullseye
cracknel
lollipop
marzipan
pastille

9 LETTERS

chocolate
liquorice

10 LETTERS

candyfloss
gobstopper
peppermint

11 LETTERS

marshmallow

12 LETTERS

butterscotch

2 WORDS

acid drop
aniseed ball
barley sugar
boiled sweet
candy cane
chewing gum
chocolate drop
coconut ice
crystallized fruit
dolly mixtures
Easter egg
fruit drop
fruit gum
fruit pastille
gulab jamun
jelly baby
jelly bean
liquorice allsort
pear drop
peppermint cream
Pontefract cake
sherbet dip
sherbet lemon
sugared almond
toffee apple
Turkish delight
walnut whip
wine gum

3 WORDS

Kendal mint cake

Vegetables

1 WORD

3 LETTERS

pea
yam

4 LETTERS

bean
beet
gobo
kale
leek
okra
taro

5 LETTERS

ackee
chard
cress
gourd
mooli
onion
swede

6 LETTERS

adzuki
carrot
celery
endive
fennel
garlic
greens
jicama
lentil
manioc
marrow
mizuna
orache
pepper
potato
radish
rocket
squash
tannia
tomato
turnip
wasabi
waxpod

7 LETTERS

alfalfa
cabbage
cardoon
cassava
chayote
chervil
chicory
gherkin
lettuce
mustard
parsnip
pumpkin
romaine
salsify
shallot
soybean
spinach
succory

8 LETTERS

beetroot
broccoli
capsicum
celeriac
chickpea
cucumber
drumhead
eggplant
escarole
garbanzo
kohlrabi
mushroom
pimiento
plantain
rutabaga
samphire
scallion
zucchini

9 LETTERS

artichoke
asparagus
aubergine
calabrese
courgette
flageolet
mangetout
radicchio
sweetcorn

10 LETTERS

breadfruit
scorzonera
watercress

11 LETTERS

cauliflower

2 WORDS

acorn squash
aduki bean
bamboo shoots
black bean
borlotti bean
broad bean
Brussels sprout
butter bean
butterhead lettuce
butternut squash
cabbage lettuce
cannellini bean
cavolo nero
Chinese cabbage
Chinese leaves
cos lettuce
curly kale
cush-cush
custard marrow
fava bean
French bean
garden pea

globe artichoke
haricot bean
iceberg lettuce
Jerusalem artichoke
kidney bean
lamb's lettuce
lima bean
Little Gem
lollo rosso
marrowfat pea
mung bean
oak leaf
oyster plant
pak choi
petits pois
pinto bean
puy lentil
red cabbage
runner bean
savoy cabbage
scarlet runner
sea kale
snow pea
spinach beet
spring greens
spring onion
string bean
sugar pea
sweet pepper
sweet potato
tiger nut
vegetable spaghetti
water chestnut

3 WORDS

black-eyed bean
sugar snap pea

4 WORDS

corn on the cob

Wine bottles

Balthazar
jeroboam
magnum
methuselah
Nebuchadnezzar
rehoboam
salmanazar

History, politics, and war

Armour

1 WORD

4 LETTERS

coif
mail

5 LETTERS

nasal
visor

6 LETTERS

beaver
bracer
camail
casque
cuisse
gorget
greave
helmet
morion
poleyn
sallet
tasses

7 LETTERS

basinet
coutere
cuirass
hauberk
jambeau
sabaton
ventail

8 LETTERS

brassard
burgonet
chausses
corselet
gauntlet
pectoral
plastron
pouldron
solleret
vambrace

9 LETTERS

habergeon
nosepiece
rerebrace

10 LETTERS

brigandine

11 LETTERS

breastplate

2 WORDS

chain mail
lance rest
neck guard

Battles (with dates)

1 WORD

4 LETTERS

Mons (1914)
Nile (1798)

5 LETTERS

Boyne (1690)
Bulge (1944–5)
Crécy (1346)
Marne (1914; 1918)
Sedan (1870)
Somme (1916)
Ypres (1914; 1915; 1917)

6 LETTERS

Actium (31 BC)
Arnhem (1944)
Imphal (1944)
Midway (1942)
Mohács (1526)
Naseby (1645)
Verdun (1916)

7 LETTERS

Britain (1940)
Corunna (1809)

Falkirk (1298)
Flodden (1513)
Jutland (1916)
Lepanto (1571)
Megiddo (1918)
Plassey (1757)
Salamis (480 BC)

8 LETTERS

Atlantic (1939–45)
Blenheim (1704)
Borodino (1812)
Bosworth (1485)
Culloden (1746)
Edgehill (1642)
Hastings (1066)
Navarino (1827)
Waterloo (1815)

9 LETTERS

Agincourt (1415)
Balaclava (1854)
Gallipoli (1915–16)
Lexington (1775)
Oudenarde (1708)
Ramillies (1706)
Sedgemoor (1685)
Trafalgar (1805)

10 LETTERS

Austerlitz (1805)
Gettysburg (1863)
Malplaquet (1709)
Stalingrad (1942–3)

11 LETTERS

Bannockburn (1314)
Guadalcanal (1942)
Prestonpans (1745)

12 LETTERS

Nechtansmere (685)
Roncesvalles (778)

13 LETTERS

Passchendaele (1917)

2 WORDS

Aboukir Bay (1798)
Bosworth Field (1485)
Bunker Hill (1775)
El Alamein (1942)
Flodden Field (1513)
Goose Green (1982)
Little Bighorn (1876)
Marston Moor (1644)

3 WORDS

Plains of Abraham (1759)

Empires

1 WORD

4 LETTERS

Inca
Mali

5 LETTERS

Aztec
Greek
Khmer
Mayan
Mogul
Roman

6 LETTERS

French
German
Median
Mongol
Tartar

7 LETTERS

British
Hittite
Islamic
Ottoman
Persian
Russian
Spanish
Turkish

8 LETTERS

Assyrian
Athenian
Austrian
Frankish
Parthian
Seleucid
Venetian

9 LETTERS

Almoravid
Byzantine
Sassanian

10 LETTERS

Babylonian
Macedonian
Phoenician
Portuguese

12 LETTERS

Carthaginian
Eastern (Roman)
Western (Roman)

2 WORDS

Austro-Hungarian
Holy Roman

Heraldic terms

1 WORD

2 LETTERS

or

3 LETTERS

bar
per

4 LETTERS

bend
fess
fret
orle
pale
pall
paly
pile
semé
vair
vert
wavy

5 LETTERS

armed
azure
barry
baton
chief
coney
crest
field
flory
fusil
gules
gyron
party
sable
tenné
torse

6 LETTERS

argent
bezant
billet
blazon
bonnet
canton
charge
couped
device
dexter
ermine
gorged
mascle
moline
mullet
naiant
nebuly
pallet
potent
proper
raguly
rising
sejant
shield
voided
volant
wyvern

7 LETTERS

annulet
armiger
bearing
bendlet
bordure
cadency
chevron
compony
cottise
courant
dormant
impaled
issuant
langued
martlet
nombril
passant
purpure
rampant
roundel
salient
saltire
slipped
statant
tierced

8 LETTERS

couchant
crescent
escallop
guardant
haurient
invected
mantling
naissant
ordinary
reversed
sanguine
sinister
tincture
tressure
trippant

9 LETTERS

displayed
embattled
engrailed
quartered
regardant
supporter

10 LETTERS

cinquefoil
cockatrice
cognizance
diminutive
fimbriated
quartering

11 LETTERS

achievement

compartment
subordinary

2 WORDS

bend sinister
canting arms
Catherine wheel
coat armour
fess point
honour point
mural crown

3 WORDS

coat of arms
fleur-de-lis
sun in splendour

Law-making assemblies

1 WORD

assembly
boule
Bundesrat
Bundestag
chamber
commune
Congress
Diet
divan
Duma
executive
government
house
Knesset
legislature
majlis
parliament
politburo
presidium
Seanad
senate
signory
Storting

2 WORDS

Dáil Éireann
Federal Assembly
Federal Parliament
First Chamber
Lok Sabha
lower chamber
lower house
National Assembly
National Congress
People's Assembly
Rajya Sabha
Second Chamber
States General
Supreme Soviet
upper chamber
upper house

3 WORDS

House of Commons
House of Lords
House of Representatives

Military ranks

1 WORD

Admiral
Aircraftman
Aircraftwoman
Bombardier
Brigadier
Captain
Colonel
Commander
Commodore
Corporal
Ensign
General
Gunner
Lieutenant
Major
Midshipman
Private
Seaman
Sergeant

2 WORDS

Air Commodore
Air Marshal
Brigadier General
Field Marshal
First Lieutenant
Fleet Admiral
Flight Lieutenant
Flight Sergeant
Flying Officer
Group Captain
Lance Bombardier
Lance Corporal
Leading Aircraftman
Lieutenant Colonel
Lieutenant Commander
Lieutenant General
Major General
Petty Officer
Pilot Officer
Rear Admiral
Second Lieutenant
Senior Aircraftman
Squadron Leader
Staff Sergeant
Sub Lieutenant
Vice Admiral
Warrant Officer
Wing Commander

3 WORDS

Acting Pilot Officer
Air Chief Marshal
Air Vice-Marshal
Chief of Staff
Chief Petty Officer
Lieutenant junior grade
Private First Class

4 WORDS

Admiral of the Fleet
Master Chief Petty Officer
Senior Chief Petty Officer

6 WORDS

Marshal of the Royal Air Force

Nobles and rulers

1 WORD

3 LETTERS

aga
bey
don

4 LETTERS

czar
duke
earl
emir
khan
king
raja
rani
shah
tsar

5 LETTERS

baron
begum
boyar
chief
count
Mogul
nawab
Negus
queen
rajah
Tenno
thane

6 LETTERS

caesar
caliph
Führer
Junker
kaiser
knight
mikado
prince
regent
satrap
sheikh

shogun
squire
sultan

7 LETTERS

baronet
duchess
emperor
empress
esquire
grandee
hidalgo
marquis
paladin
pharaoh
viceroy
vicomte

8 LETTERS

archduke
baroness
contessa
countess
governor
maharaja
margrave
marquess
marquise
princess
seigneur
viscount

9 LETTERS

castellan
commander
electress
palsgrave
rangatira
vicereine

10 LETTERS

margravine
vicomtesse

11 LETTERS

marchioness
viscountess

2 WORDS

grand duke
knight commander
life peer
life peeress

Police officers and forces

1 WORD

2 LETTERS

DC
DI
MP
PC

3 LETTERS

CID
DCI
KGB
Met

4 LETTERS

LAPD
NYPD
SOCO

5 LETTERS

cadet
chief
Garda
stasi
super

6 LETTERS

askari
Gardai
redcap
Sûreté

7 LETTERS

captain
marshal
Mountie
officer
special
Sweeney
trooper

8 LETTERS

gendarme
havildar
Homicide
sergeant

9 LETTERS

commander
constable
inspector
policeman
roundsman

10 LETTERS

lieutenant

11 LETTERS

carabiniere
carabinieri
commissaire
gendarmerie
policewoman

12 LETTERS

commissioner
constabulary

2 WORDS

bomb squad
chief constable
chief inspector
chief superintendent
crime squad
desk sergeant
detective constable
detective inspector
detective sergeant
detective superintendent
drug squad
flying squad
fraud squad
investigating officer
military police
military policeman
military policewoman
murder squad
police constable
police department
police officer
port police
provost marshal
Scotland Yard
secret police
security police
snatch squad
special constable
station sergeant
strike force
SWAT team
Texas Ranger
transport police
vice squad

3 WORDS

assistant chief constable
Bow Street Runner
community police officer
deputy chief constable
detective chief inspector
master-at-arms

4 WORDS

Royal Canadian Mounted Police

Political philosophies and systems

1 WORD

6 LETTERS

Maoism

7 LETTERS

diarchy
elitism
fascism
leftism
Marxism
statism
Titoism
tyranny

8 LETTERS

Blairism
gynarchy
Leninism
monarchy
populism
rightism
synarchy

9 LETTERS

anarchism
autocracy
communism
democracy
despotism
dirigisme
heptarchy
monocracy
oligarchy
pluralism
socialism
Sovietism
Stalinism
theocracy
timocracy

10 LETTERS

absolutism
Bolshevism

capitalism
centralism
federalism
hierocracy
liberalism
monarchism
plutocracy
Trotskyism
utopianism

11 LETTERS

bureaucracy
colonialism
imperialism
meritocracy
nationalism
syndicalism
technocracy
Thatcherism

12 LETTERS

collectivism
conservatism
dictatorship

13 LETTERS

Eurocommunism
individualism
republicanism

2 WORDS

laissez-faire
neo-Marxism
social democracy
third way

Soldier, types of

1 WORD

3 LETTERS

NCO

4 LETTERS

kern
SEAL

5 LETTERS

cadet
scout
sepoy

6 LETTERS

archer
bowman
ensign
evzone
gunner
hussar
klepht
knight
lancer
marine
ranger
ranker
redcap
sapper
sentry
yeoman

7 LETTERS

dragoon
hoplite
officer
orderly
recruit
redcoat
regular
sabreur
samurai
trooper

8 LETTERS

cavalier
commando
fencible
fusilier
havildar
partisan
rifleman
sentinel
spearman

9 LETTERS

beefeater
cannoneer
centurion
conscript
freelance
grenadier
guardsman
guerrilla
irregular
janissary
legionary
mercenary
musketeer
pistoleer
reservist
swordsman

10 LETTERS

carabineer
cavalryman
cuirassier
galloglass
halberdier
militiaman

11 LETTERS

infantryman
legionnaire
paratrooper
Territorial

12 LETTERS

artilleryman

2 WORDS

blue helmet
drum major
enlisted man
foot soldier
military policeman
point man

Wars (with dates)

2 WORDS

Balkan Wars (1912–13)
Boer War (1880–1; 1899–1902)
Bosnian War (1992–5)
Chaco War (1932–5)
Chechen Wars (1994–6; 1999 to present)
Crimean War (1853–6)
Falklands War (1982)
Gallic Wars (58–51 BC)
Great War (1914–18)
Gulf War (1980–8; 1991)
June War (1967)
Korean War (1950–3)
Macedonian Wars (3rd and 2nd centuries BC)
Mexican War (1846–8)
Napoleonic Wars (1800–15)
October War (1973)
Opium Wars (1839–42; 1856–60)
Peloponnesian War (431–434 BC)
Peninsular War (1808–14)
Persian Wars (5th century BC)
Punic Wars (264–241 BC; 218–201 BC; 149–146 BC)
Sikh Wars (1845; 1848–9)
Suez crisis (1956)
Vietnam War (1957–75)
Winter War (1939–40)

3 WORDS

American Civil War (1861–5)
English Civil War (1642–9)
First Boer War (1880–1)
First World War (1914–18)
Franco-Prussian War (1870–1)
Great Northern War (1700–21)
Hundred Years War (1337–1453)
Iran-Iraq War (1980–8)
New Zealand Wars (1845–8; 1860–72)
Russian Civil War (1918–21)
Russo-Finnish War (1939–40)
Russo-Japanese War (1904–5)
Second Boer War (1899–1902)
Second World War (1939–45)
Seven Years War (1756–63)
Sino-Japanese Wars (1894–5; 1937–45)
Six Day War (1967)
Spanish-American War (1898)
Spanish Civil War (1936–9)
Thirty Years War (1618–48)
World War I (1914–18)
World War II (1939–45)
Yom Kippur War (1973)
Yugoslavian Civil War (1991–5)

4 WORDS

French Wars of Religion (1562–98)
Greek War of Independence (1821–30)
War of American Independence (1775–83)
War of Jenkins's Ear (1739)
Wars of the Roses (1455–87)

5 WORDS

War of the Austrian Succession (1740–8)
War of the Spanish Succession (1701–14)

Warships

1 WORD

Agamemnon
Alabama
Amethyst
Arizona
Belfast
Belgrano
Bismarck
Bounty
Conqueror
Constitution
Dreadnought
Enterprise
Gloire
Hood
Illustrious
Invincible
Iowa
Kiev
Kuznetsov
Nautilus
Nimitz
Potemkin
Resolution
Tirpitz
Victory
Warrior
Warspite
Yamato

2 WORDS

Ark Royal
Mary Rose
New Jersey
Queen Elizabeth
Royal George
Royal Sovereign

3 WORDS

Admiral Graf Spee
King George V

Weapons, bombs, and missiles

1 WORD

3 LETTERS

axe
gun
Uzi

4 LETTERS

bill
bomb
club
Colt
cosh
dirk
épée
foil
ICBM
kris
mace
pike
Scud
slug

5 LETTERS

baton
blade
fusil
knife
kukri
lance
lathi
Luger
panga
rifle
sabre
shell
skean
spear
staff

stave
stick
sword

6 LETTERS

cannon
cudgel
dagger
Exocet
Mauser
mortar
musket
parang
pellet
petard
pistol
rapier
rocket
Semtex
tracer

7 LETTERS

bayonet
bazooka
carbine
cordite
cutlass
Gatling
grenade
halberd
handgun
harpoon
hatchet
javelin
machete
missile
Polaris
poleaxe
poniard
shotgun
sidearm
sjambok
torpedo
Trident
warhead

8 LETTERS

arquebus
birdshot
bludgeon
Browning
buckshot
catapult
claymore
dynamite
falchion
falconet
firebomb
firelock
howitzer
landmine
revolver
scimitar
stiletto
tomahawk
yataghan

9 LETTERS

artillery
automatic
battleaxe
blackjack
derringer
doodlebug
flintlock
gelignite
grapeshot
guncotton
gunpowder
harquebus
jackknife
matchlock
plastique
truncheon

10 LETTERS

broadsword
cannonball
knobkerrie
misericord
shillelagh
swordstick
Winchester

11 LETTERS

blunderbuss
Kalashnikov
switchblade

12 LETTERS

quarterstaff

13 LETTERS

knuckleduster

2 WORDS

A-bomb
air gun
assault rifle
atom bomb
atomic bomb
ballistic missile
baseball bat
baton round
Bofors gun
bowie knife
brass knuckles
breech-loader
Bren gun
car bomb
case knife
cluster bomb
cruise missile
daisy-cutter
depth charge
dirty bomb
duelling pistol
dumdum bullet
express rifle
flick knife
flying bomb
forty-five
fragmentation bomb
fragmentation grenade

fusion bomb
guided missile
hand grenade
harpoon gun
H-bomb
high explosive
horse pistol
hydrogen bomb
incendiary bomb
incendiary device
Lee-Enfield
letter bomb
Lewis gun
life preserver
limpet mine
machine gun
magnetic mine
mail bomb
Maxim gun
Mills bomb
Molotov cocktail
neutron bomb
nuclear bomb
nulla-nulla
parcel bomb
petrol bomb
plastic bullet
plastic explosive
pom-pom
rubber bullet
semi-automatic
sheath knife
siege gun
six-shooter
skean-dhu
slung shot
small arm
small arms
small sword
smoke bomb
smooth-bore
starting pistol
Sten gun
thirty-eight
time bomb
tommy gun
trench mortar
zip gun

3 WORDS

anti-aircraft gun
pump-action shotgun
sawn-off shotgun
Smith and Wesson
sub-machine gun

Literature and language

Characters in Shakespeare

1 WORD

3 LETTERS

Hal

4 LETTERS

Eros
Hero
Iago
Lear
Peto
Puck

5 LETTERS

Ariel
Celia
Cleon
Edgar
Feste
Henry
Paris
Poins
Regan
Romeo
Timon
Viola

6 LETTERS

Alonso
Antony
Audrey
Banquo
Bianca
Bottom
Brutus
Caesar
Cassio
Dromio
Duncan
Edmond
Emilia
Fabian
Hamlet
Helena
Hermia
Imogen
Jaques
Juliet
Lucius
Oberon
Olivia
Orsino
Oswald
Phoebe
Pistol
Portia
Thaisa
Tybalt

7 LETTERS

Agrippa
Antonio
Caliban
Capulet
Cesario
Claudio
Fleance
Goneril
Gonzalo
Horatio
Hotspur
Jessica
Laertes
Lavinia
Leontes
Lepidus
Lorenzo
Macbeth
Macduff
Malcolm
Mariana
Miranda
Nerissa
Octavia
Ophelia
Orlando
Othello
Perdita
Proteus
Richard
Shylock
Stefano
Theseus
Titania
Troilus

8 LETTERS

Bardolph
Bassanio
Beatrice
Belarius
Benedick
Benvolio
Charmian
Claudius
Cordelia
Cressida
Dogberry

Falstaff
Florizel
Fluellen
Gertrude
Gratiano
Hermione
Isabella
Lucentio
Lysander
Malvolio
Mercutio
Octavius
Pandarus
Parolles
Pericles
Polonius
Prospero
Richmond
Roderigo
Rosalind
Rosaline
Trinculo
Volumnia

9 LETTERS

Antiochus
Brabanzio
Cleopatra
Cornelius
Cymbeline
Demetrius
Desdemona
Donalbain
Elizabeth
Enobarbus
Ferdinand
Guiderius
Helicanus
Hortensio
Katherine
Mamillius
Petruccio
Polixenes
Posthumus
Sebastian

10 LETTERS

Antipholus
Coriolanus
Fortinbras
Gloucester
Touchstone

11 LETTERS

Bolingbroke
Rosencrantz

12 LETTERS

Guildenstern

2 WORDS

Christopher Sly
Corporal Nim
Francis Flute
Friar Laurence
Julius Caesar
Lady Macbeth
Mark Antony
Mistress Quickly
Peter Quince
Titus Andronicus
Tom Snout

3 WORDS

Sir Andrew Aguecheek
Sir Toby Belch

Children's books

1 WORD

Borrowers (Mary Norton)
Heidi (Johanna Spyri)
Hobbit (J R R Tolkien)
Junk (Melvin Burgess)
Matilda (Roald Dahl)
Moonfleet (J Meade Falkner)
Pollyanna (Eleanor H Porter)
Skellig (David Almond)
Snowman (Raymond Briggs)

2 WORDS

Amber Spyglass (Philip Pullman)
Ballet Shoes (Noel Streatfeild)
Black Beauty (Anna Seward)
Carrie's War (Nina Bawden)
Charlotte's Web (E B White)
Coral Island (R M Ballantyne)
Famous Five (Enid Blyton)
Flour Babies (Anne Fine)
Gathering Light (Jennifer Donnelly)
Harry Potter (series; J K Rowling)
Huckleberry Finn (Mark Twain)
Jungle Book (Rudyard Kipling)

Little Prince (Antoine de Saint-Exupéry)
Little Princess (Frances Hodgson Burnett)
Little Women (Louisa M Alcott)
Mary Poppins (P L Travers)
National Velvet (Enid Bagnold)
Northern Lights (Philip Pullman)
Owl Service (Alan Garner)
Peter Pan (J M Barrie)
Pippi Longstocking (Astrid Lindgren)
Railway Children (E Nesbit)
Ruby Holler (Sharon Creech)
Secret Garden (Frances Hodgson Burnett)
Secret Seven (Enid Blyton)
Stuart Little (E B White)
Subtle Knife (Philip Pullman)
Tom Sawyer (Mark Twain)
Treasure Island (Robert Louis Stevenson)
Vicky Angel (Jacqueline Wilson)
Watership Down (Richard Adams)

3 WORDS

Alice in Wonderland (Lewis Carroll)
Chronicles of Narnia (C S Lewis)
Fungus the Bogeyman (Raymond Briggs)
Girls in Love (Jacqueline Wilson)
Goodnight Mister Tom (Michelle Magorian)
Grimm's Fairy Tales (Jacob and Wilhelm Grimm)
His Dark Materials (Philip Pullman)
Just-So Stories (Rudyard Kipling)
Little Lord Fauntleroy (Frances Hodgson Burnett)
Magic Faraway Tree (Enid Blyton)
Stalky and Co. (Rudyard Kipling)
Swallows and Amazons (Arthur Ransome)
Swiss Family Robinson (Johann Wyss)
Tom Brown's Schooldays (Thomas Arnold)
Tom's Midnight Garden (Phillipa Pearce)
What Katy Did (Susan Coolidge)
Winnie-the-Pooh (A A Milne)
Wizard of Earthsea (Ursula K Le Guin)
Wrinkle in Time (Madeleine L'Engle)

4 WORDS

Cat in the Hat (Dr Seuss)
Five Children and It (E Nesbit)
Lord of the Flies (William Golding)
Lord of the Rings (J R R Tolkien)
Series of Unfortunate Events (Lemony Snicket)
Story of Tracy Beaker (Jacqueline Wilson)
Sword in the Stone (T H White)
Tale of Peter Rabbit (Beatrix Potter)
Through the Looking Glass (Lewis Carroll)
What Katy Did Next (Susan Coolidge)
When the Wind Blows (Raymond Briggs)
Wind in the Willows (Kenneth Grahame)
Wonderful Wizard of Oz (L Frank Baum)

5 WORDS

Where the Wild Things Are (Maurice Sendak)

6 WORDS

Lion, the Witch, and the Wardrobe (C S Lewis)

Drama, types and forms of

1 WORD

burlesque
comedy
docudrama
dumbshow
duologue
farce
improvisation
kabuki
masque
melodrama
mime
monodrama
Noh
pantomime
play
romcom
teleplay
tragedy
tragicomedy

2 WORDS

closet drama
closet play
commedia dell'arte
Grand Guignol
Greek drama
miracle play
morality play
mummers' play
mystery play
nativity play
passion play
soap opera
two-hander

3 WORDS

comedy of manners
kitchen-sink drama

Fiction, types and forms of

1 WORD

allegory
antinovel
Bildungsroman
blockbuster
bonkbuster
cliffhanger
comedy
conte
epic
fable
fanfic
fantasy
legend
mystery
myth
noir
novel
novelette
novella
parable
policier
romance
saga
thriller
western
whodunnit

2 WORDS

adventure story
Aga saga
bedtime story
black comedy

bodice-ripper
chick lit
crime story
detective story
dime novel
epistolary novel
fairy story
fairy tale
fan fiction
folk story
folk tale
ghost story
gothic novel
graphic novel
historical novel
horror story
nouveau roman
picaresque novel
police procedural
roman-fleuve
romantic novel
science fiction
sci-fi
short story
spine-chiller
tear-jerker
urban myth

3 WORDS

roman-à-clef
stream of consciousness
sword and sorcery

Fictional characters

1 WORD

3 LETTERS

Gay (Walter; Dombey and Son; Charles Dickens)
Jim (Lord; Lord Jim; Joseph Conrad)
Kim (Kim; Rudyard Kipling)
Oak (Gabriel; Far from the Madding Crowd; Thomas Hardy)
Owl (Winnie-the-Pooh/The House at Pooh Corner; A A Milne)
Pan (Peter; Peter Pan; J M Barrie)
Pip (Great Expectations; Charles Dickens)
Roo (Winnie-the-Pooh/The House at Pooh Corner; A A Milne)

4 LETTERS

Aziz (Dr; A Passage to India; E M Forster)
Bede (Adam; Adam Bede; George Eliot)
Bott (Violet Elizabeth; Richmal Crompton)
Bray (Madeline; Nicholas Nickleby; Charles Dickens)
Cass (Eppie; Silas Marner; George Eliot)
Casy (Reverend Jim; The Grapes of Wrath; John Steinbeck)
Dean (Nelly; Wuthering Heights; Emily Brontë)
Eyre (Jane; Jane Eyre; Charlotte Brontë)
Finn (Huckleberry; The Adventures of Huckleberry Finn; Mark Twain)
Fogg (Phileas; Around the World in Eighty Days; Jules Verne)
Gamp (Mrs; Martin Chuzzlewit; Charles Dickens)
Gray (Dorian; The Picture of Dorian Gray; Oscar Wilde)
Gunn (Ben; Treasure Island; R L Stevenson)
Heep (Uriah; David Copperfield, Charles Dickens)
Hook (Captain; Peter Pan; J M Barrie)
Hyde (Edward; Dr Jekyll and Mr Hyde; R L Stevenson)
Joad (Tom; The Grapes of Wrath; John Steinbeck)
Mole (Mr; Wind in the Willows; Kenneth Grahame)
Nemo (Captain; Twenty Thousand Leagues under the Sea; Jules Verne)
Pooh (Winnie-the-Pooh/The House at Pooh Corner; A A Milne)
Ridd (John; Lorna Doone; R D Blackmore)
Self (John; Money; Martin Amis)
Toad (Mr; Wind in the Willows; Kenneth Grahame)

Took (Peregrine (Pippin); Lord of the Rings; J R R Tolkien)
Troy (Sergeant Francis; Far from the Madding Crowd; Thomas Hardy)
Vyse (Cecil; A Room with a View; E M Forster)

5 LETTERS

Akela (The Jungle Book; Rudyard Kipling)
Alice (Alice's Adventures in Wonderland/ Through the Looking-Glass; Lewis Carroll)
Arwen (Lord of the Rings; J R R Tolkien)
Aslan (The Lion, the Witch, and the Wardrobe; C S Lewis)
Baloo (The Jungle Book; Rudyard Kipling)
Bloom (Leopold; Ulysses; James Joyce)
Bloom (Molly; Ulysses; James Joyce)
Brown (Father; G K Chesterton)
Brown (Tom; Tom Brown's Schooldays; Thomas Hughes)
Brown (William; Richmal Crompton)
Boxer (Animal Farm; George Orwell)
Clare (Ada; Bleak House; Charles Dickens)
Clare (Angel; Tess of the D'Ubervilles; Thomas Hardy)
Crich (Gerald; Women in Love; D H Lawrence)
Darcy (Fitzwilliam; Pride and Prejudice; Jane Austen)
Dixon (James; Lucky Jim; Kingsley Amis)
Doone (Lorna; Lorna Doone; R D Blackmore)
Drood (Edwin; The Mystery of Edwin Drood; Charles Dickens)
Eowyn (Lord of the Rings; J R R Tolkien)
Fagin (Oliver Twist; Charles Dickens)
Finch (Atticus; To Kill a Mockingbird; Harper Lee)
Finch (Scout; To Kill a Mockingbird; Harper Lee)
Flyte (Sebastian; Brideshead Revisited; Evelyn Waugh)
Frost (Detective Inspector; R D Wingfield)
Gimli (Lord of the Rings; J R R Tolkien)
Ghote (Inspector Ganesh; H R F Keating)
Jones (Bridget; Bridget Jones's Diary/Bridget Jones: the Edge of Reason; Helen Fielding)
Jones (Tom; Tom Jones; Henry Fielding)
Kanga (Winnie-the-Pooh; A A Milne)
Kipps (Arthur; Kipps; H G Wells)
Kurtz (Heart of Darkness; Joseph Conrad)
Lewis (Detective Sergeant; Colin Dexter)
March (Amy; Little Women; Louisa M Alcott)
March (Beth; Little Women; Louisa M Alcott)
March (Jo; Little Women; Louisa M Alcott)
March (Meg; Little Women; Louisa M Alcott)
Mason (Perry; Erle Stanley Gardner)
Mitty (Walter; The Secret Life of Walter Mitty; James Thurber)
Morel (Paul; Sons and Lovers; D H Lawrence)
Morse (Detective Inspector; Colin Dexter)
Noddy (Enid Blyton)
O'Hara (Scarlett; Gone with the Wind; Margaret Mitchell)
Nancy (Oliver Twist; Charles Dickens)
Parry (Will; His Dark Materials; Philip Pullman)
Piggy (Lord of the Flies; William Golding)
Polly (Alfred; The History of Mr Polly; H G Wells)
Poole (Grace; Jane Eyre; Charlotte Brontë)
Queen (Ellery; Ellery Queen)
Quilp (Daniel; The Old Curiosity Shop; Charles Dickens)
Ralph (Lord of the Flies; William Golding)
Rebus (Detective Inspector John; Ian Rankin)
Ryder (Charles; Brideshead Revisited; Evelyn Waugh)
Rudge (Barnaby; Barnaby Rudge; Charles Dickens)
Sharp (Becky; Vanity Fair; William Makepeace Thackeray)
Sikes (Bill; Oliver Twist; Charles Dickens)
Smike (Nicholas Nickleby; Charles Dickens)
Smith (Winston; Nineteen-Eighty-Four; George Orwell)
Snape (Severus; Harry Potter series; J K Rowling)
Snowe (Lucy; Villette; Charlotte Brontë)
Tarka (Tarka the Otter; Henry Williamson)
Twist (Oliver; Oliver Twist; Charles Dickens)

6 LETTERS

Asriel (Lord; His Dark Materials; Philip Pullman)

Badger (Wind in the Willows; Kenneth Grahame)
Barkis (David Copperfield; Charles Dickens)
Bennet (Catherine; Pride and Prejudice; Jane Austen)
Bennet (Elizabeth; Pride and Prejudice; Jane Austen)
Bennet (Lydia; Pride and Prejudice; Jane Austen)
Bennet (Mary; Pride and Prejudice; Jane Austen)
Birkin (Rupert; Women in Love; D H Lawrence)
Bovary (Emma; Madame Bovary; Flaubert)
Brooke (Dorothea; Middlemarch; George Eliot)
Bumble (Oliver Twist; Charles Dickens)
Butler (Rhett; Gone with the Wind; Margaret Mitchell)
Carton (Sydney; A Tale of Two Cities; Charles Dickens)
Crusoe (Robinson; Robinson Crusoe; Daniel Defoe)
Darnay (Charles; A Tale of Two Cities; Charles Dickens)
Dombey (Florence; Dombey and Son; Charles Dickens)
Dombey (Paul; Dombey and Son; Charles Dickens)
Dorrit (Amy; Little Dorrit; Charles Dickens)
Eeyore (Winnie-the-Pooh/The House at Pooh Corner; A A Milne)
Elrond (Lord of the Rings; J R R Tolkien)
Fawley (Jude; Jude the Obscure; Thomas Hardy)
Friday (Man; Robinson Crusoe; Daniel Defoe)
Gamgee (Sam; Lord of the Rings; J R R Tolkien)
Gatsby (Jay; The Great Gatsby; F Scott FitzGerald)
Gollum (Lord of the Rings; J R R Tolkien)
Hagrid (Rubeus; Harry Potter series; J K Rowling)
Hannay (Richard; The Thirty-Nine Steps; John Buchan)
Holmes (Sherlock; Sir Arthur Conan Doyle)
Jeeves (P G Wodehouse)
Jekyll (Henry; Dr Jekyll and Mr Hyde; R L Stevenson)
Linton (Edgar; Wuthering Heights; Emily Brontë)
Linton (Isabella; Wuthering Heights; Emily Brontë)
Malfoy (Draco; Harry Potter series; J K Rowling)
Malone (Mary; His Dark Materials; Philip Pullman)
Marley (Jacob; A Christmas Carol; Charles Dickens)
Marner (Silas; Silas Marner; George Eliot)
Marlow (Heart of Darkness; Joseph Conrad)
Marple (Miss Jane; Agatha Christie)
Mowgli (The Jungle Book; Rudyard Kipling)
Newson (Elizabeth-Jane; The Mayor of Casterbridge; Thomas Hardy)
Nutkin (Squirrel; The Tale of Squirrel Nutkin; Beatrix Potter)
Pascoe (Detective Inspector Peter; Reginald Hill)
Piglet (Winnie-the-Pooh/The House at Pooh Corner; A A Milne)
Poirot (Hercule; Agatha Christie)
Potter (Harry; Harry Potter series; J K Rowling)
Rabbit (Peter; The Tale of Peter Rabbit; Beatrix Potter)
Radley (Boo; To Kill a Mockingbird; Harper Lee)
Sauron (Lord of the Rings; J R R Tolkien)
Sawyer (Tom; The Adventures of Tom Sawyer; Mark Twain)
Shandy (Tristram; Tristram Shandy; Laurence Sterne)
Silver (Long John; Treasure Island; R L Stevenson)
Smiley (George; John Le Carré)
Sorrel (Hetty; Adam Bede; George Eliot)
Thorpe (Isabella; Northanger Abbey; Jane Austen)
Tigger (Winnie-the-Pooh/The House at Pooh Corner; A A Milne)
Tilney (Henry; Northanger Abbey; Jane Austen)
Varden (Dolly; Barnaby Rudge; Charles Dickens)
Watson (Dr; Sir Arthur Conan Doyle)
Weller (Sam; Pickwick Papers; Charles Dickens)
Wilcox (Henry; Howard's End; E M Forster)
Wilcox (Paul; Howard's End; E M Forster)

Wilkes (India; Gone with the Wind; Margaret Mitchell)
Wimsey (Lord Peter; Dorothy L Sayers)

7 LETTERS

Aragorn (Lord of the Rings; J R R Tolkien)
Baggins (Bilbo; The Hobbit/Lord of the Rings; J R R Tolkien)
Baggins (Frodo; Lord of the Rings; J R R Tolkien)
Belaqua (Lyra; His Dark Materials; Philip Pullman)
Bingley (Charles; Pride and Prejudice; Jane Austen)
Boromir (Lord of the Rings; J R R Tolkien)
Brandon (Colonel; Sense and Sensibility; Jane Austen)
Cadfael (Brother; Ellis Peters)
Collins (Reverend William; Pride and Prejudice; Jane Austen)
Coulter (Mrs; His Dark Materials; Philip Pullman)
Dalziel (Detective Superintendent Andy; Reginald Hill)
Danvers (Mrs; Rebecca; Daphne Du Maurier)
Darling (Wendy; Peter Pan; J M Barrie)
Dedalus (Simon; A Portrait of the Artist as a Young Man; James Joyce)
Dedlock (Lady; Bleak House; Charles Dickens)
Deronda (Daniel; Daniel Deronda; George Eliot)
Dracula (Count; Dracula; Bram Stoker)
Dursley (Petunia; Harry Potter series; J K Rowling)
Dursley (Vernon; Harry Potter series; J K Rowling)
Emerson (George; A Room with a View; E M Forster)
Estella (Great Expectations; Charles Dickens)
Faramir (Lord of the Rings; J R R Tolkien)
Farfrae (Donald; The Mayor of Casterbridge; Thomas Hardy)
Ferrars (Edward; Sense and Sensibility; Jane Austen)
Forsyte (Fleur; The Forsyte Saga; John Galsworthy)
Forsyte (Irene; The Forsyte Saga; John Galsworthy)
Forsyte (Jolyon; The Forsyte Saga; John Galsworthy)
Forsyte (Soames; The Forsyte Saga; John Galsworthy)
Gandalf (Lord of the Rings; J R R Tolkien)
Granger (Hermione; Harry Potter series; J K Rowling)
Harleth (Gwendolen; Daniel Deronda; George Eliot)
Hawkins (Jim; Treasure Island; R L Stevenson)
Jellyby (Mrs; Bleak House; Charles Dickens)
Lampton (Joe; Room at the Top; John Braine)
Legolas (Lord of the Rings; J R R Tolkien)
Maigret (Inspector Jules; Georges Simenon)
Marlowe (Philip; Raymond Chandler)
Mellors (Oliver; Lady Chatterley's Lover; D H Lawrence)
Morland (Catherine; Northanger Abbey; Jane Austen)
Pekkala (Serafina; His Dark Materials; Philip Pullman)
Quested (Adela; A Passage to India; E M Forster)
Saruman (Lord of the Rings; J R R Tolkien)
Scrooge (Ebenezer; A Christmas Carol; Charles Dickens)
Smollet (Captain; Treasure Island; R L Stevenson)
Squeers (Wackford; Nicholas Nickleby; Charles Dickens)
Theoden (Lord of the Rings; J R R Tolkien)
Weasley (Ginny; Harry Potter series; J K Rowling)
Weasley (Ron; Harry Potter series; J K Rowling)
Wexford (Detective Inspector Reg; Ruth Rendell)
Wooster (Bertie; P G Wodehouse)

8 LETTERS

Angstrom (Harry; Rabbit, Run; John Updike)
Bagheera (The Jungle Book; Rudyard Kipling)
Boldwood (William; Far from the Madding Crowd; Thomas Hardy)
Bombadil (Tom; Lord of the Rings; J R R Tolkien)
Brangwen (Gudrun; The Rainbow/Women in Love; D H Lawrence)
Brangwen (Ursula; The Rainbow/Women in Love; D H Lawrence)

Brownlow (Mr; Oliver Twist; Charles Dickens)
Buchanan (Daisy; The Great Gatsby; F Scott FitzGerald)
Buchanan (Tom; The Great Gatsby; F Scott FitzGerald)
Byrnison (Iorek; His Dark Materials; Philip Pullman)
Carraway (Nick; The Great Gatsby; F Scott FitzGerald)
Casuabon (Reverend Edward; Middlemarch; George Eliot)
Cratchit (Bob; A Christmas Carol; Charles Dickens)
Dashwood (Elinor; Sense and Sensibility; Jane Austen)
Dashwood (Marianne; Sense and Sensibility; Jane Austen)
Earnshaw (Catherine; Wuthering Heights; Emily Brontë)
Earnshaw (Hindley; Wuthering Heights; Emily Brontë)
Everdene (Bathsheba; Far from the Madding Crowd; Thomas Hardy)
Flanders (Moll; Moll Flanders; Daniel Defoe)
Flashman (Tom Brown's Schooldays; Thomas Hughes)
Havisham (Miss; Great Expectations; Charles Dickens)
Henchard (Michael; The Mayor of Casterbridge; Thomas Hardy)
Jarndyce (John; Bleak House; Charles Dickens)
Ladislaw (Will; Middlemarch; George Eliot)
Lestrade (Inspector; Sir Arthur Conan Doyle)
Lockwood (Wuthering Heights; Emily Brontë)
Magwitch (Abel; Great Expectations; Charles Dickens)
Micawber (Wilkins; David Copperfield; Charles Dickens)
Moriarty (Dean; On the Road; Jack Kerouac)
Moriarty (Professor; Sir Arthur Conan Doyle)
Napoleon (Animal Farm; George Orwell)
Nickleby (Nicholas; Nicholas Nickleby; Charles Dickens)
Paradise (Sal; On the Road; Jack Kerouac)
Peggotty (Clara; David Copperfield; Charles Dickens)
Pickwick (Mr; Pickwick Papers; Charles Dickens)
Schlegel (Helen; Howard's End; E M Forster)
Schlegel (Margaret; Howard's End; E M Forster)
Scoresby (Lee; His Dark Materials; Philip Pullman)
Smithson (Charles; The French Lieutenant's Woman; John Fowles)
Snowball (Animal Farm; George Orwell)
Svengali (Trilby; George Du Maurier)
Traddles (Tommy; David Copperfield; Charles Dickens)
Trotwood (Betsy; David Copperfield; Charles Dickens)
Tulliver (Maggie; The Mill on the Floss; George Eliot)
Tulliver (Tom; The Mill on the Floss; George Eliot)
Whittier (Polyanna; Polyanna; Eleanor H Porter)
Woodruff (Sarah; The French Lieutenant's Woman; John Fowles)

9 LETTERS

Bridehead (Sue; Jude the Obscure; Thomas Hardy)
Caulfield (Holden; The Catcher in the Rye; J D Salinger)
Churchill (Frank; Emma; Jane Austen)
Dalgleish (Commander Adam; P D James)
Galadriel (Lord of the Rings; J R R Tolkien)
Gradgrind (Thomas; Hard Times; Charles Dickens)
Knightley (Mr; Emma; Jane Austen)
Marchmain (Lord; Brideshead Revisited; Evelyn Waugh)
Murdstone (Edward; David Copperfield; Charles Dickens)
Pecksniff (Seth; Martin Chuzzlewit; Charles Dickens)
Rochester (Edward; Jane Eyre; Charlotte Brontë)
Scarpetta (Kay; Patricia Cornwell)
Summerson (Esther; Bleak House; Charles Dickens)

Treebeard (Lord of the Rings; J R R Tolkien)
Trelawney (Sibyll; Harry Potter series; J K Rowling)
Voldemort (Lord; Harry Potter series; J K Rowling)
Wickfield (Agnes; David Copperfield; Charles Dickens)
Woodhouse (Emma; Emma; Jane Austen)
Yossarian (Captain John; Catch-22; Joseph Heller)

10 LETTERS

Brandybuck (Meriadoc (Merry); Lord of the Rings; J R R Tolkien)
Chatterley (Lady Constance; Lady Chatterley's Lover; D H Lawrence)
Chuzzlewit (Martin; Martin Chuzzlewit; Charles Dickens)
Dumbeldore (Albus; Harry Potter series; J K Rowling)
Heathcliff (Wuthering Heights; Emily Brontë)
Hornblower (Horatio; C S Forester)
Steerforth (James; David Copperfield; Charles Dickens)
Tweedledee (Through the Looking-Glass; Lewis Carroll)
Tweedledum (Through the Looking-Glass; Lewis Carroll)
Warshawski (V I; Sara Paretsky)
Willoughby (John; Sense and Sensibility; Jane Austen)

11 LETTERS

Copperfield (David; David Copperfield; Charles Dickens)
D'Uberville (Alec; Tess of the D'Ubervilles; Thomas Hardy)
Durbeyfield (Tess; Tess of the D'Ubervilles; Thomas Hardy)
Honeychurch (Lucy; A Room with a View; E M Forster)

12 LETTERS

Brocklehurst (Mr; Jane Eyre; Charlotte Brontë)

2 WORDS

Artful Dodger (Oliver Twist; Charles Dickens)
Big Ears (Enid Blyton)
Black Dog (Treasure Island; R L Stevenson)
Cheshire Cat (Alice's Adventures in Wonderland; Lewis Carroll)
De Bourgh (Lady Catherine; Pride and Prejudice; Jane Austen)
De Winter (Max; Rebecca; Daphne Du Maurier)
Fat Controller (Reverend W Awdry)
Humpty-Dumpty (Through the Looking-Glass; Lewis Carroll)
Little Nell (The Old Curiosity Shop; Charles Dickens)
Mad Hatter (Alice's Adventures in Wonderland; Lewis Carroll)
March Hare (Alice's Adventures in Wonderland; Lewis Carroll)
Red Queen (Through the Looking-Glass; Lewis Carroll)
Shere Khan (The Jungle Book; Rudyard Kipling)
Tinker Bell (Peter Pan; J M Barrie)
Tiny Tim (A Christmas Carol; Charles Dickens)
Water Rat (Wind in the Willows; Kenneth Grahame)

3 WORDS

Winnie-the-Pooh (Winnie-the-Pooh/The House at Pooh Corner; A A Milne)

4 WORDS

Thomas the Tank Engine (Reverend W. Awdry)

Languages

1 WORD

3 LETTERS

Lao
Mon

4 LETTERS

Fula
Manx
Thai
Tupi
Urdu
Zulu

5 LETTERS

Carib
Czech
Dayak
Dutch
Farsi
Greek
Hausa
Hindi
Irish
Karen
Khmer
Ladin
Latin
Malay
Maori
Nguni
Oriya
Shona
Tajik
Tamil
Tatar
Tigre
Uzbek
Welsh
Xhosa
Yupik

6 LETTERS

Arabic
Basque
Berber
Breton
Danish
Fijian
French
Fulani
Gaelic
German
Hebrew
Kazakh
Korean
Kyrgyz
Magyar
Nepali
Nubian
Pashto
Polish
Romany
Samoan
Shelta
Slovak
Telugu
Tongan
Tswana

7 LETTERS

Aramaic
Bengali
Burmese
Catalan
Chechen
Chinese
Cornish
English
Faroese
Finnish
Flemish
Frisian
Goanese
Guarani
Hittite
Iranian
Italian
Khalkha
Kirundi
Konkani
Kurdish
Lappish
Latvian
Lingala
Malinke
Maltese
Marathi
Mordvin
Ndebele
Persian
Punjabi
Quechua
Romansh
Russian
Samoyed
Serbian
Spanish
Swahili
Swedish
Tagalog
Tibetan
Turkish
Turkmen
Yiddish

8 LETTERS

Albanian
Armenian
Assamese
Balinese
Croatian
Dzongkha
Estonian
Galician
Georgian
Gujarati
Gurkhali
Hawaiian
Japanese
Javanese
Kashmiri

Madurese
Malagasy
Mandarin
Manipuri
Romanian
Sanskrit
Setswana
Sumerian
Tahitian

9 LETTERS

Afrikaans
Bulgarian
Cantonese
Congolese
Esperanto
Hungarian
Icelandic
Inuktitut
Kiswahili
Malayalam
Maldivian
Marquesan
Moldavian
Mongolian
Norwegian
Provençal
Sinhalese
Slovenian
Sundanese
Ukrainian

10 LETTERS

Belarusian
Lithuanian
Macedonian
Melanesian
Portuguese
Vietnamese

11 LETTERS

Azerbaijani
Belorussian

2 WORDS

Anglo-Saxon
Irish Gaelic
Old English
Scottish Gaelic

Literary and grammatical terms

1 WORD

3 LETTERS

pun

4 LETTERS

case
mood
noun
root
stem
verb

5 LETTERS

affix
irony
tense
trope
voice

6 LETTERS

adverb
bathos
clause
copula
dative
finite
gender
gerund
neuter
number
object
person
phrase
plural
prefix
simile
suffix
zeugma

7 LETTERS

adjunct
cognate
deictic
euphony
litotes
meiosis
paradox
parsing
pronoun
sarcasm
subject
syncope

8 LETTERS

ablative
allegory
anaphora
chiasmus
ellipsis
euphuism
feminine
genitive
innuendo
locative
metaphor
metonymy
modifier
negative
oxymoron
particle
pleonasm
positive
sentence
singular
vocative

9 LETTERS

adjective
adverbial
assonance
euphemism
expletive
gerundive
hendiadys
hypallage
hyperbole
masculine
partitive
predicate
preterite
prolepsis
qualifier
reflexive
syllepsis
tautology

10 LETTERS

accusative
anastrophe
antecedent
antithesis
apostrophe
apposition
complement
declension
determiner
diminutive
dysphemism
epistrophe
hyperbaton
imperative
indicative
infinitive
inflection
nominative
paralipsis
participle
pluperfect
possessive
synecdoche

11 LETTERS

anacoluthon
antonomasia
attributive
catachresis
comparative
conditional
conjugation
conjunction
intensifier
paronomasia
periphrasis
predicative
preposition
punctuation
qualitative
restrictive
subjunctive
superlative

12 LETTERS

alliteration
interjection
onomatopoeia
postpositive
prosopopoeia

2 WORDS

active voice
agent noun
auxiliary verb
collective noun
common noun
continuous tense
count noun
dangling participle
definite article
demonstrative pronoun
direct object
future tense
hysteron proteron
indefinite article
indirect object
intransitive verb
mass noun
modal verb
objective case
passive voice
past tense
perfect tense
personal pronoun
phrasal verb
present participle
present tense
proper noun
relative clause
relative pronoun
rhetorical question
sentence adverb
transitive verb
word class

3 WORDS

figure of speech
part of speech

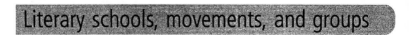

Literary schools, movements, and groups

1 WORD

Acmeism
Augustans
classicism
Dadaism
expressionism
futurism
imagism
minimalism
modernism
naturalism
neoclassicism
Parnassians
postmodernism
primitivism
realism
romanticism
structuralism
surrealism
symbolism
Vorticism

2 WORDS

Aesthetic Movement
beat generation
Bloomsbury Group
Cavalier poets
Georgian poets
Harlem Renaissance
Lake Poets
Liverpool poets
magical realism
magic realism
metaphysical poets
neo-realism
post-structuralism
socialist realism
social realism

3 WORDS

Angry Young Men
Sturm und Drang

Novels

1 WORD

3 LETTERS

Kim (Rudyard Kipling)
She (Rider Haggard)

4 LETTERS

Emma (Jane Austen)
Nana (Émile Zola)

5 LETTERS

Chéri (Colette)
Kipps (H G Wells)
Magus (John Fowles)

6 LETTERS

Herzog (Saul Bellow)
Hobbit (J R R Tolkien)
Lolita (Vladimir Nabokov)
Pamela (Samuel Richardson)
Warden (Anthony Trollope)

7 LETTERS

Dracula (Bram Stoker)
Erewhon (Samuel Butler)
Ivanhoe (Sir Walter Scott)
Orlando (Virginia Woolf)
Rainbow (D H Lawrence)
Rebecca (Daphne Du Maurier)

Shirley (Charlotte Brontë)
Ulysses (James Joyce)

8 LETTERS

Cranford (Mrs Gaskell)
Nostromo (Joseph Conrad)
Villette (Charlotte Brontë)

9 LETTERS

Kidnapped (Robert Louis Stevenson)
Moonstone (Wilkie Collins)

10 LETTERS

Bostonians (Henry James)
Clayhanger (Arnold Bennett)
Goldfinger (Ian Fleming)
Kenilworth (Sir Walter Scott)
Persuasion (Jane Austen)
Possession (A S Byatt)

11 LETTERS

Ambassadors (Henry James)
Gormenghast (Mervyn Peake)
Middlemarch (George Eliot)
Woodlanders (Thomas Hardy)

12 LETTERS

Buddenbrooks (Thomas Mann)
Frankenstein (Mary Shelley)
Silmarillion (J R R Tolkien)

13 LETTERS

Metamorphosis (Franz Kafka)

2 WORDS

Adam Bede (George Eliot)
Alexandria Quartet (Lawrence Durrell)
Animal Farm (George Orwell)
Antic Hay (Aldous Huxley)
Aspern Papers (Henry James)
Barchester Towers (Anthony Trollope)
Barnaby Rudge (Charles Dickens)
Beau Geste (P C Wren)
Big Sleep (Raymond Chandler)
Billy Budd (Herman Melville)
Billy Liar (Keith Waterhouse)
Bleak House (Charles Dickens)
Brideshead Revisited (Evelyn Waugh)
Brighton Rock (Graham Greene)
Brothers Karamazov (Fyodor Dostoevsky)
Cancer Ward (Alexander Solzhenitsyn)
Cannery Row (John Steinbeck)
Casino Royale (Ian Fleming)
Castle Rackrent (Maria Edgeworth)
Christmas Carol (Charles Dickens)
Clarissa Harlowe (Samuel Richardson)
Clockwork Orange (Anthony Burgess)
Confidential Agent (Graham Greene)
Daisy Miller (Henry James)
Daniel Deronda (George Eliot)
David Copperfield (Charles Dickens)
Doctor Zhivago (Boris Pasternak)
Dr No (Ian Fleming)
Earthly Powers (Anthony Burgess)
English Patient (Michael Ondaatje)
Ethan Frome (Edith Wharton)
Eugene Onegin (Aleksandr Pushkin)
Fanny Hill (John Cleland)
Finnegans Wake (James Joyce)
Forsyte Saga (John Galsworthy)
Frenchman's Creek (Daphne Du Maurier)
Go-Between (L P Hartley)
Golden Bowl (Henry James)
Golden Notebook (Doris Lessing)
Gravity's Rainbow (Thomas Pynchon)
Great Expectations (Charles Dickens)
Great Gatsby (F Scott FitzGerald)
Gulliver's Travels (Jonathan Swift)
Hard Times (Charles Dickens)
Honorary Consul (Graham Greene)
Howard's End (E M Forster)
Huckleberry Finn (Mark Twain)
Human Factor (Graham Greene)
Jacob's Room (Virginia Woolf)
Jamaica Inn (Daphne Du Maurier)
Jane Eyre (Charlotte Brontë)
Joseph Andrews (Henry Fielding)
Les Misérables (Victor Hugo)
Little Dorrit (Charles Dickens)
London Fields (Martin Amis)
Long Goodbye (Raymond Chandler)
Lord Jim (Joseph Conrad)
Lorna Doone (R D Blackmore)

Lost World (Arthur Conan Doyle)
Lucky Jim (Kingsley Amis)
Maltese Falcon (Dashiel Hammett)
Mansfield Park (Jane Austen)
Martin Chuzzlewit (Charles Dickens)
Midnight's Children (Salman Rushdie)
Moby Dick (Herman Melville)
Mrs Dalloway (Virginia Woolf)
Naked Lunch (William Burroughs)
Nicholas Nickleby (Charles Dickens)
Northanger Abbey (Jane Austen)
Old Devils (Kingsley Amis)
Oliver Twist (Charles Dickens)
Phineas Finn (Anthony Trollope)
Pickwick Papers (Charles Dickens)
Pilgrim's Progress (John Bunyan)
Pincher Martin (William Golding)
Portnoy's Complaint (Philip Roth)
Quiet American (Graham Greene)
Rachel Papers (Martin Amis)
Raj Quartet (Paul Scott)
Rob Roy (Sir Walter Scott)
Satanic Verses (Salman Rushdie)
Scarlet Letter (Nathaniel Hawthorne)
Scarlet Pimpernel (Baroness Orczy)
Schindler's Ark (Thomas Keneally)
Secret Agent (Joseph Conrad)
Shell Seekers (Rosamunde Pilcher)
Sheltering Sky (Paul Bowles)
Silas Marner (George Eliot)
Slaughterhouse-Five (Kurt Vonnegut)
Smiley's People (John Le Carré)
Suitable Boy (Vikram Seth)
Third Man (Graham Greene)
Thorn Birds (Colleen McCullough)
Time Machine (H G Wells)
Tom Jones (Henry Fielding)
Tom Sawyer (Mark Twain)
Treasure Island (Robert Louis Stevenson)
Tristram Shandy (Laurence Sterne)
Two Towers (J R R Tolkien)
Uncle Silas (Sheridan Le Fanu)
Vanity Fair (William Thackeray)
Vile Bodies (Evelyn Waugh)
Washington Square (Henry James)
Water-Babies (Charles Kingsley)
Watership Down (Richard Adams)
White Fang (Jack London)
Wuthering Heights (Emily Brontë)
Zuleika Dobson (Max Beerbohm)

3 WORDS

Age of Innocence (Edith Wharton)
Alice in Wonderland (Lewis Carroll)
Brave New World (Aldous Huxley)
Bridget Jones's Diary (Helen Fielding)
Captain Corelli's Mandolin (Louis de Bernières)
Carry On Jeeves (P G Wodehouse)
Cider with Rosie (Laurie Lee)
Cold Comfort Farm (Stella Gibbons)
Da Vinci Code (Dan Brown)
Death in Venice (Thomas Mann)
Decline and Fall (Evelyn Waugh)
Dombey and Son (Charles Dickens)
East of Eden (John Steinbeck)
Eyeless in Gaza (Aldous Huxley)
Farewell My Lovely (Raymond Chandler)
Farewell to Arms (Ernest Hemingway)
French Lieutenant's Woman (John Fowles)
Goodbye Mr Chips (James Hilton)
Grapes of Wrath (John Steinbeck)
Handful of Dust (Evelyn Waugh)
Heart of Darkness (Joseph Conrad)
Heart of Midlothian (Sir Walter Scott)
Heat and Dust (Ruth Prawer Jhabvala)
Jude the Obscure (Thomas Hardy)
Kane and Abel (Jeffrey Archer)
King Solomon's Mines (Rider Haggard)
Lady Chatterley's Lover (D H Lawrence)
Master and Margarita (Mikhail Bulgakov)
Mayor of Casterbridge (Thomas Hardy)
Moon and Sixpence (Somerset Maugham)
Mr Midshipman Easy (Frederick Marryat)
Nineteen-Eighty-Four (George Orwell)
North and South (Mrs Gaskell)
Of Human Bondage (Somerset Maugham)
Old Curiosity Shop (Charles Dickens)
On the Beach (Nevil Shute)
On the Road (Jack Kerouac)
Oscar and Lucinda (Peter Carey)

Our Mutual Friend (Charles Dickens)
Passage to India (E M Forster)
Point Counter Point (Aldous Huxley)
Pride and Prejudice (Jane Austen)
Prisoner of Zenda (Anthony Hope)
Sense and Sensibility (Jane Austen)
Sign of Four (Sir Arthur Conan Doyle)
Sons and Lovers (D H Lawrence)
Study in Scarlet (Sir Arthur Conan Doyle)
Sun Also Rises (Ernest Hemingway)
Things Fall Apart (Chinua Achebe)
Thirty-Nine Steps (John Buchan)
To the Lighthouse (Virginia Woolf)
Town Like Alice (Nevil Shute)
Tropic of Cancer (Henry Miller)
Tropic of Capricorn (Henry Miller)
Uncle Tom's Cabin (Harriet Beecher Stowe)
Under the Volcano (Malcolm Lowry)
Under Western Eyes (Joseph Conrad)
Vicar of Wakefield (Oliver Goldsmith)
What Maisie Knew (Henry James)
Woman in White (Wilkie Collins)
Women in Love (D H Lawrence)

4 WORDS

Adventures of Sherlock Holmes (Sir Arthur Conan Doyle)
Call of the Wild (Jack London)
Catcher in the Rye (J D Salinger)
Code of the Woosters (P G Wodehouse)
Count Of Monte Cristo (Alexandre Dumas)
Darling Buds of May (H E Bates)
Day of the Jackal (Frederick Forsyth)
Day of the Triffids (John Wyndham)
Death on the Nile (Agatha Christie)
Diary of a Nobody (George and Weedon Grossmith)
End of the Affair (Graham Greene)
Fellowship of the Ring (J R R Tolkien)
Gone with the Wind (Margaret Mitchell)
Hound of the Baskervilles (Sir Arthur Conan Doyle)
Island of Dr Moreau (H G Wells)
Last of the Mohicans (James Fenimore Cooper)
Lord of the Flies (William Golding)
Lord of the Rings (J R R Tolkien)
Memoirs of Sherlock Holmes (Sir Arthur Conan Doyle)
Mill on the Floss (George Eliot)
Murder of Roger Ackroyd (Agatha Christie)
Mystery of Edwin Drood (Charles Dickens)
Naked and the Dead (Norman Mailer)
Name of the Rose (Umberto Eco)
Of Mice and Men (John Steinbeck)
Our Man in Havana (Graham Greene)
Picture of Dorian Gray (Oscar Wilde)
Portrait of a Lady (Henry James)
Portrait of the Artist (James Joyce)
Power and the Glory (Graham Greene)
Red Badge of Courage (Stephen Crane)
Remains of the Day (Kazuo Ishiguro)
Return of the King (J R R Tolkien)
Return of the Native (Thomas Hardy)
Riddle of the Sands (Erskine Childers)
Room at the Top (John Braine)
Room with a View (E M Forster)
Sound and the Fury (William Faulkner)
Tale of Two Cities (Charles Dickens)
Tenant of Wildfell Hall (Anne Brontë)
Tender is the Night (F Scott FitzGerald)
Tess of the d'Urbervilles (Thomas Hardy)
Through the Looking Glass (Lewis Carroll)
Tinker Tailor Soldier Spy (John Le Carré)
To Kill a Mockingbird (Harper Lee)
Turn of the Screw (Henry James)
Unbearable Lightness of Being (Milan Kundera)
Under the Greenwood Tree (Thomas Hardy)
War of the Worlds (H G Wells)
Way of All Flesh (Samuel Butler)

5 WORDS

Dr Jekyll and Mr Hyde (Robert Louis Stevenson)

Far from the Madding Crowd (Thomas Hardy)
For Whom the Bell Tolls (Ernest Hemingway)
Heart is a Lonely Hunter (Carson McCullers)
Man in the Iron Mask (Alexandre Dumas)
Murder on the Orient Express (Agatha Christie)
Old Man and the Sea (Ernest Hemingway)
One Hundred Years of Solitude (Gabriel Garcia Márquez)
Prime of Miss Jean Brodie (Muriel Spark)
Secret Diary of Adrian Mole (Sue Townsend)
Three Men in a Boat (Jerome K Jerome)

6 WORDS

Dance to the Music of Time (Anthony Powell)

Phonetic alphabet

Alpha
Bravo
Charlie
Delta
Echo
Foxtrot
Golf
Hotel
India
Juliet
Kilo
Lima
Mike
November
Oscar
Papa
Quebec
Romeo
Sierra
Tango
Uniform
Victor
Whisky
X-ray
Yankee
Zulu

Plays

1 WORD

3 LETTERS

Art (Yasmina Reza)

4 LETTERS

Loot (Joe Orton)

5 LETTERS

Brand (Henrik Ibsen)
Equus (Peter Shaffer)
Medea (Euripides)
Miser (Molière)

6 LETTERS

Closer (Patrick Marber)
Phèdre (Jean Racine)
Rivals (Richard Sheridan)

7 LETTERS

Amadeus (Peter Shaffer)
Arcadia (Tom Stoppard)
Bacchae (Euripides)
Electra (Euripides)
Endgame (Samuel Beckett)
Jumpers (Tom Stoppard)
Oleanna (David Mamet)
Seagull (Anton Chekhov)
Volpone (Ben Jonson)

8 LETTERS

Alcestis (Euripides)
Antigone (Jean Anouilh)
Crucible (Arthur Miller)
Oresteia (Aeschylus)
Tartuffe (Molière)

9 LETTERS

Alchemist (Ben Jonson)
Caretaker (Harold Pinter)
Eumenides (Aeschylus)
Mousetrap (Agatha Christie)
Pygmalion (George Bernard Shaw)

10 LETTERS

Changeling (Thomas Middleton and William Rowley)
Homecoming (Harold Pinter)
Lysistrata (Aristophanes)
Travesties (Tom Stoppard)

11 LETTERS

Misanthrope (Molière)
Tamburlaine (Christopher Marlowe)
Wallenstein (Friedrich von Schiller)

12 LETTERS

Translations (Brian Friel)

2 WORDS

Abigail's Party (Mike Leigh)
Admirable Crichton (J M Barrie)
Beaux' Stratagem (George Farquhar)
Birthday Party (Harold Pinter)
Blithe Spirit (Noel Coward)
Blood Wedding (Federico Lorca)
Browning Version (Terence Rattigan)
Charley's Aunt (Brandon Thomas)
Cherry Orchard (Anton Chekhov)
Cocktail Party (T S Eliot)
Country Wife (William Wycherley)
Doll's House (Henrik Ibsen)
Dr Faustus (Christopher Marlowe)
Ghost Sonata (August Strindberg)
Glass Menagerie (Tennessee Williams)
Happy Days (Samuel Beckett)
Hay Fever (Noel Coward)
Heartbreak House (George Bernard Shaw)
Hedda Gabler (Henrik Ibsen)
Iceman Cometh (Eugene O'Neill)
Ideal Husband (Oscar Wilde)
Inspector Calls (J B Priestley)
Le Cid (Pierre Corneille)
Maid's Tragedy (John Fletcher and Francis Beaumont)
Major Barbara (George Bernard Shaw)
Mary Stuart (Friedrich von Schiller)
Master Builder (Henrik Ibsen)
Miss Julie (August Strindberg)
Mother Courage (Bertolt Brecht)
Noises Off (Michael Frayn)
Odd Couple (Neil Simon)
Oedipus Rex (Sophocles)
Peer Gynt (Henrik Ibsen)
Private Lives (Noel Coward)
Prometheus Bound (Aeschylus)
Recruiting Officer (George Farquhar)
Revenger's Tragedy (Thomas Middleton or Cyril Tourneur)
Saint Joan (George Bernard Shaw)
Spanish Tragedy (Thomas Kyd)
Three Sisters (Anton Chekhov)
Ubu Roi (Alfred Jarry)
Uncle Vanya (Anton Chekhov)
Voysey Inheritance (Harley Granville-Barker)
White Devil (John Webster)
Winslow Boy (Terence Rattigan)

3 WORDS

All for Love (John Dryden)
All My Sons (Arthur Miller)
Caucasian Chalk Circle (Bertolt Brecht)
Dancing at Lughnasa (Brian Friel)
Duchess of Malfi (John Webster)
Entertaining Mr Sloane (Joe Orton)
Glengarry Glen Ross (David Mamet)
Jew of Malta (Christopher Marlowe)
Krapp's Last Tape (Samuel Beckett)
Lady Windermere's Fan (Oscar Wilde)
Man and Superman (George Bernard Shaw)
Mourning Becomes Electra (Eugene O'Neill)
Pillars of Society (Henrik Ibsen)
School for Scandal (Richard Sheridan)
Speed-the-Plow (David Mamet)
Streetcar Named Desire (Tennessee Williams)
Under Milk Wood (Dylan Thomas)
Waiting for Godot (Samuel Beckett)
Woman in Black (Susan Hill)

4 WORDS

Death of a Salesman (Arthur Miller)
House of Bernada Alba (Federico Lorca)
Importance of Being Earnest (Oscar Wilde)
Juno and the Peacock (Sean O'Casey)
Lady's not for Burning (Christopher Fry)
Look Back in Anger (John Osborne)
Man for All Seasons (Robert Bolt)
Run for your Wife (Ray Cooney)
She Stoops to Conquer (Oliver Goldsmith)
Way of the World (William Congreve)
What the Butler Saw (Joe Orton)
Woman of No Importance (Oscar Wilde)

5 WORDS

Every Man in His Humour (Ben Jonson)
Long Day's Journey into Night (Eugene O'Neill)
Playboy of the Western World (J M Synge)
Resistable Rise of Arturo Ui (Bertolt Brecht)
Royal Hunt of the Sun (Peter Shaffer)
'Tis Pity She's a Whore (John Ford)
Who's Afraid of Virginia Woolf? (Edward Albee)

Plays of Shakespeare

1 WORD

Coriolanus
Cymbeline
Hamlet
Macbeth
Othello
Pericles
Tempest

2 WORDS

Henry IV
Henry V
Henry VI
Henry VIII
Julius Caesar
King John
King Lear
Richard II
Richard III
Titus Andronicus
Twelfth Night
Winter's Tale

3 WORDS

Antony and Cleopatra
Comedy of Errors
Love's Labours Lost
Measure for Measure
Merchant of Venice
Midsummer Night's Dream
Romeo and Juliet
Timon of Athens
Troilus and Cressida
Two Noble Kinsmen

4 WORDS

A Midsummer Night's Dream
As You Like It
Merry Wives of Windsor
Much Ado About Nothing
Taming of the Shrew
Two Gentlemen of Verona

5 WORDS

All's Well that Ends Well

Poetry terms

1 WORD

3 LETTERS

lay
ode

4 LETTERS

epic
iamb
poem
saga

5 LETTERS

elegy
epode
haiku
idyll
lyric
paeon
verse

6 LETTERS

aubade
ballad
dactyl
iambus
monody
satire
sonnet

7 LETTERS

alcaics
anapest
ballade
bucolic
couplet
dimeter
distich
eclogue
epigram
georgic
iambics
pyrrhic
rondeau
roundel
sestina
spondee
triolet
triplet
trochee
virelay

8 LETTERS

anapaest
clerihew
doggerel
epyllion
Leonines
limerick
palinode
pastoral
sapphics
tribrach
trimeter

9 LETTERS

dactylics
dithyramb
hexameter
trochaics

10 LETTERS

choriambus
disyllable
heptameter
macaronics
pentameter
tetrameter
villanelle

11 LETTERS

alexandrine
trisyllable

12 LETTERS

decasyllabic
epithalamium
prothalamium

2 WORDS

alcaic verse
alexandrine verse
blank verse
dactylic verse
elegiac couplet
free verse
heroic couplet
heroic verse
Horatian ode
iambic pentameter
iambic verse
macaronic verse
nursery rhyme
ottava rima
Petrarchan sonnet
Spenserian stanza
terza rima
trochaic verse

Punctuation marks

1 WORD

accent
apostrophe
asterisk
asterism
backslash
brace
bracket
caret
colon
comma
dagger
dash
ellipsis
hyphen
obelus
parenthesis
period
point
rule
semicolon
solidus
stop
stroke
virgule

2 WORDS

diacritical mark
em dash
en dash
exclamation mark
full stop
inverted comma
question mark
quotation mark
square bracket
swung dash

Writer, types of

1 WORD

3 LETTERS

sub

4 LETTERS

bard
hack
poet

6 LETTERS

author
critic
editor
lyrist
scribe

7 LETTERS

adaptor
amorist
diarist
farceur
gagster
newsman

8 LETTERS

annalist
essayist
fabulist
hackette
humorist
lyricist
novelist
pressman
prosaist
psalmist
recorder
reporter
reviewer
songster

9 LETTERS

columnist
draftsman
dramatist
memoirist
publicist
rhymester
scenarist
sonneteer
subeditor
tragedian
wordsmith

10 LETTERS

biographer
chronicler
copywriter
dramaturge
journalist
obituarist
playwright
programmer
songwriter
troubadour

11 LETTERS

commentator
contributor
ghostwriter
littérateur
memorialist
Minnesinger
necrologist
pamphleteer

12 LETTERS

hagiographer
hymnographer
newspaperman
remembrancer
screenwriter
scriptwriter

13 LETTERS

correspondent
encyclopedist
lexicographer

2 WORDS

agony aunt
best-seller
city editor
co-author
copy editor
crime writer
cub reporter
feature writer
lobby correspondent
Poet Laureate
speech-writer
story editor
war correspondent

3 WORDS

writer-in-residence

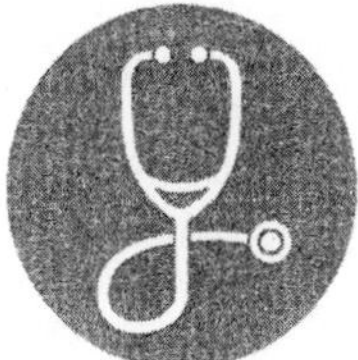

Medicine and the body

Branches of medicine

1 WORD

7 LETTERS

surgery
therapy
urology

8 LETTERS

oncology

9 LETTERS

allopathy
audiology
chiropody
neurology
orthotics
pathology
radiology

10 LETTERS

cardiology
embryology
geriatrics
immunology
nephrology
obstetrics
osteopathy
proctology
psychiatry

11 LETTERS

dermatology
gynaecology
haematology
laryngology
paediatrics
prosthetics
venereology

12 LETTERS

epidemiology
neurosurgery
orthopaedics
parasitology
pharmacology
therapeutics

13 LETTERS

endocrinology
ophthalmology
physiotherapy
psychosurgery

2 WORDS

community medicine
nuclear medicine
plastic surgery
veterinary medicine

Doctors and dentists

1 WORD

2 LETTERS

GP
ME
MO

6 LETTERS

intern

7 LETTERS

dentist
oculist
surgeon

8 LETTERS

houseman

9 LETTERS

allergist
clinician
orthotist
otologist
physician
registrar
urologist

10 LETTERS

consultant
oncologist
podiatrist
specialist

11 LETTERS

audiologist
chiropodist
neurologist
osteologist
pathologist
radiologist

12 LETTERS

anaesthetist
cardiologist
chiropractor
embryologist
geriatrician
immunologist
nephrologist
neurosurgeon
obstetrician
orthodontist
orthopaedist
periodontist
trichologist

13 LETTERS

dermatologist
diagnostician
gerontologist
gynaecologist
haematologist
paediatrician

2 WORDS

brain surgeon
dental surgeon
flying doctor
forensic pathologist
general practitioner
heart surgeon
hospital doctor
house officer
junior doctor
medical examiner
medical officer
plastic surgeon
senior registrar

Hormones

1 WORD

adrenalin
aldosterone
androgen
androsterone
calcitonin
cortisone
endorphin
gastrin
glucagon
gonadotrophin
insulin
melatonin
neurohormone
noradrenaline
oestrogen
oestrone
oxytocin
progesterone
progestogen
prolactin
somatotrophin
testosterone
thromboxane
thyrotropin
thyroxine
vasopressin

2 WORDS

anabolic steroid
antidiuretic hormone
growth hormone
luteinizing hormone

3 WORDS

follicle-stimulating hormone
human growth hormone
thyroid-stimulating hormone

Human bones

1 WORD

3 LETTERS

rib

4 LETTERS

ulna

5 LETTERS

anvil
femur
hyoid
ilium
incus
pubis
skull
spine
talus
tibia
vomer

6 LETTERS

carpal
carpus
cuboid
fibula
hammer
pelvis
rachis
radius
sacrum
stapes
tarsal
tarsus

7 LETTERS

cranium
ethmoid
humerus
ischium
jawbone
kneecap
malleus
maxilla
patella
phalanx
scapula
sternum
stirrup

8 LETTERS

backbone
capitate
clavicle
lacrimal
mandible
scaphoid
sphenoid
vertebra

9 LETTERS

calcaneus
cheekbone

10 LETTERS

astragalus
breastbone
collarbone
metacarpal
metatarsal
triquetral

2 WORDS

ankle bone
cuneiform bone
floating rib
frontal bone
hamate bone
heel bone
innominate bone
lunate bone
navicular bone
occipital bone
palatine bone
parietal bone
pisiform bone
sesamoid bone
shin bone
shoulder blade
spinal column
temporal bone
thigh bone
vertebral column
zygomatic bone

Human glands

1 WORD

liver
ovary
pancreas
testis

2 WORDS

adrenal gland
apocrine gland
corpus luteum
ductless gland
eccrine gland
endocrine gland
exocrine gland
gastric gland
lacrimal gland
mammary gland

parathyroid gland
parotid gland
pineal gland
pituitary gland
prostate gland
salivary gland
sebaceous gland
sublingual gland
submandibular gland
submaxillary gland
sweat gland
thyroid gland

3 WORDS

islets of Langerhans

Human tooth, types of

1 WORD

bicuspid
canine
cuspid
incisor
molar
premolar
tricuspid

2 WORDS

eye tooth
milk tooth
permanent tooth
primary tooth
wisdom tooth

Medication, types and forms of

1 WORD

3 LETTERS

rub

4 LETTERS

drip
pill

5 LETTERS

cream
drops
enema
salve
spray
tonic

6 LETTERS

balsam
cachet
caplet
emetic
gargle
lotion
powder
tablet

7 LETTERS

anodyne
antacid
booster
capsule
dilator
draught
linctus
lozenge
nervine
pessary
placebo
steroid

8 LETTERS

antidote
aperient
curative
diuretic
evacuant
inhalant
laxative
narcotic
ointment
pastille
poultice
relaxant
sedative

9 LETTERS

analeptic
analgesic
anovulant
antiviral

calmative
digestive
febrifuge
fungicide
germicide
mercurial
nebulizer
nootropic
soporific
stimulant
sudorific
vermifuge

10 LETTERS

antibiotic
antiseptic
anxiolytic
convulsant
depressant
euphoriant
hypodermic
injectable
painkiller
palliative
preventive

11 LETTERS

anaesthetic
antipyretic
antitussive
aphrodisiac
carminative
diaphoretic
expectorant
neuroleptic
restorative
suppository
suppressant
vasodilator

12 LETTERS

anthelmintic
antipruritic
decongestant
prophylactic
psychotropic
stupefacient

13 LETTERS

abortifacient
anaphrodisiac
antibacterial
anticoagulant
antihistamine
antipsychotic
antiscorbutic
antispasmodic
contraceptive
tranquillizer

2 WORDS

alpha blocker
anti-emetic
anti-infective
anti-inflammatory
beta blocker
cure-all
ear drops
eye drops
muscle relaxant
nasal spray
sleeping pill

Major human muscles

1 WORD

5 LETTERS

psoas
teres

6 LETTERS

biceps
flexor
rectus
soleus

7 LETTERS

agonist
deltoid
dilator
gluteus
levator
rotator
triceps

8 LETTERS

abductor
adductor
detrusor
elevator
extensor
masseter
pectoral
pronator
scalenus
skeletal
splenius

9 LETTERS

depressor
digastric
obturator
sartorius
sphincter
supinator
trapezius

10 LETTERS

antagonist
buccinator
latissimus
quadriceps
temporalis

11 LETTERS

constrictor
intercostal
rhomboideus

13 LETTERS

gastrocnemius

2 WORDS

gluteus maximus
opponent muscle
peroneal muscle

Nervous system

1 WORD

brain
neuron
neurone
trigeminal

2 WORDS

abducens nerve
accessory nerve
cranial nerve
femoral nerve
glossopharyngeal nerve
hypoglossal nerve
motor nerve
nerve cell
oculomotor nerve
olfactory nerve
optic nerve
peroneal nerve
radial nerve
sciatic nerve
sensory nerve
solar plexus
spinal cord
spinal nerve
tibial nerve
trifacial nerve
trochlear nerve
ulnar nerve
vestibulocochlear nerve

3 WORDS

autonomic nervous system
central nervous system
peripheral nervous system
sympathetic nervous system

Nurses

1 WORD

accoucheur
matron
midwife
sister

2 WORDS

auxiliary nurse
charge nurse
dental nurse
district nurse
geriatric nurse

health visitor
hospital nurse
night nurse
nurse practitioner
nursing officer
scrub nurse
sick nurse
staff nurse
theatre nurse
veterinary nurse

3 WORDS

senior nursing officer
State Enrolled Nurse
State Registered Nurse

Organs of the body

anus
appendix
bladder
brain
breasts
colon
duodenum
ears
eyes
gall bladder
genitals
heart
ileum
intestines
jejunum
kidneys
larynx
liver
lungs
mouth
nose
oesophagus
ovaries
pancreas
penis
rectum
skeleton
spinal cord
spleen
stomach
testicles
tongue
tonsils
trachea
uterus
vagina

Parts of the digestive system

1 WORD

anus
colon
duodenum
ileum
intestine
jejunum
liver
mouth
oesophagus
pancreas
rectum
stomach
teeth
tongue

2 WORDS

alimentary canal
gall bladder
salivary glands

Parts of the ear

1 WORD

anvil
auricle
cochlea
eardrum
hammer
incus
pinna
stapes
stirrup
vestibule

2 WORDS

auditory canal
auditory nerve
Eustachian tube
hair cell

inner ear
middle ear
outer ear
tympanic membrane

3 WORDS

organ of Corti

Parts of the eye

1 WORD

choroid
cone
conjunctiva
cornea
eyeball
eyelash
eyelid
fovea
iris
lens
limbus
orbit
pupil
retina
rod
sclera
socket

2 WORDS

aqueous humour
blind spot
dilator muscle
eye socket
lacrimal glands
optic nerve
tear glands
vitreous humour

Parts of the heart

1 WORD

atrium
epicardium
myocardium
pericardium
ventricle

2 WORDS

aortic valve
mitral valve
pulmonary artery
pulmonary vein
semilunar valve
tricuspid valve
upper chamber
vena cava

Phobias

9 LETTERS

apiphobia (bees)
atephobia (ruin)
neophobia (new things)
zoophobia (animals)

10 LETTERS

acrophobia (sharpness)
aerophobia (air travel)
algophobia (pain)
aurophobia (gold)
autophobia (loneliness)
batophobia (high buildings)
cibophobia (food)
cryophobia (ice)
cymophobia (waves)
cynophobia (dogs)
demophobia (crowds)
dikephobia (justice)
doraphobia (fur)
eosophobia (dawn)
ergophobia (work)
gynophobia (women)
hadephobia (hell)
hodophobia (travel)
homophobia (homosexuals)
ideophobia (ideas)
kenophobia (voids)
kopophobia (fatigue)
lalophobia (stuttering)
logophobia (words)
maniphobia (insanity)
musophobia (mice)
mysophobia (dirt)
nelophobia (glass)
nosophobia (illness)
ochophobia (vehicles)
oikophobia (home)
osmophobia (smell)
panophobia (everything)
papaphobia (Pope)
potophobia (drink)
pyrophobia (fire)
sciophobia (shadows)
selaphobia (flesh)
Sinophobia (Chinese people and things)
sitophobia (food)
theophobia (God)
tocophobia (childbirth)
topophobia (places)
toxiphobia (poison)
xenophobia (foreigners)

11 LETTERS

acarophobia (mites)
acerophobia (sourness)
agoraphobia (open places)
androphobia (men)
anemophobia (wind)
Anglophobia (English people and things)
anthophobia (flowers)
antlophobia (floods)
atelophobia (imperfection)
bathophobia (depth)
clinophobia (bed)
cnidophobia (insect stings)
coitophobia (coitus)
coprophobia (faeces)
cyberphobia (computers)
emetophobia (vomiting)
enetophobia (pins)
eremophobia (solitude)
erotophobia (sex)
febriphobia (fever)
Gallophobia (French people and things)
gymnophobia (nudity)
haemophobia (blood)
hagiophobia (saints)
haptophobia (touch)
heliophobia (sun)
hierophobia (priests)
hippophobia (horses)
hormephobia (shock)
hydrophobia (water)
hygrophobia (dampness)
hypnophobia (sleep)
hypsophobia (high places)
iconophobia (religious works of art)

Italophobia (Italian people and things)
koniophobia (dust)
laliophobia (stuttering)
leprophobia (leprosy)
limnophobia (lakes)
lyssophobia (insanity)
microphobia (small things)
necrophobia (corpses)
nephophobia (clouds)
nyctophobia (night)
ochlophobia (mobs)
paedophobia (children)
pantophobia (everything)
pathophobia (disease)
peniaphobia (poverty)
phagophobia (swallowing)
phobophobia (fear)
phonophobia (speech)
photophobia (light)
poinephobia (punishment)
Russophobia (Russian people and things)
scotophobia (darkness)
Scotophobia (Scottish people and things)
stasophobia (standing)
tachophobia (speed)
taphephobia (being buried alive)
Teutophobia (German people and things)
uranophobia (heaven)

12 LETTERS

ailurophobia (cats)
anginophobia (narrowness)
apeirophobia (infinity)
belonephobia (needles)
blennophobia (slime)
brontophobia (thunder)
cardiophobia (heart disease)
cheimaphobia (cold)
chionophobia (snow)
chromophobia (colour)
chronophobia (time)
chrysophobia (gold)
cometophobia (comets)
cremnophobia (precipices)
entomophobia (insects)
ermitophobia (loneliness)
Francophobia (French people and things)
gametophobia (marriage)
glossophobia (speech)
graphophobia (writing)
hedonophobia (pleasure)
kinetophobia (motion)
kleptophobia (stealing)
linonophobia (string)
musicophobia (music)
odontophobia (teeth)
ommetaphobia (eyes)
oneirophobia (dreams)
phasmophobia (ghosts)
pinaciphobia (lists)
pogonophobia (beards)
potamophobia (rivers)
rhabdophobia (magic)
Satanophobia (Satan)
scabiophobia (scabies)
siderophobia (stars)
spermophobia (germs)
stygiophobia (hell)
technophobia (technology)
teratophobia (giving birth to monsters)
thassophobia (idleness)
thermophobia (heat)
trichophobia (hair)

13 LETTERS

Americophobia (American people and things)
arachnophobia (spiders)
asthenophobia (weakness)
astrapophobia (lightning)
bacillophobia (microbes)
carcinophobia (cancer)
electrophobia (electricity)
erythrophobia (blushing)
gephyrophobia (bridges)
Germanophobia (German people and things)
geumatophobia (taste)
hamartophobia (sin)
harpaxophobia (robbers)
hypegiaphobia (responsibility)
ichthyophobia (fish)
keraunophobia (thunder)
mastigophobia (beating)
mechanophobia (machinery)
metallophobia (metal)
olfactophobia (smell)
onomatophobia (names)

ophidiophobia (snakes)
ornithophobia (birds)
patroiophobia (heredity)
philosophobia (philosophy)
pnigerophobia (smothering)
pteronophobia (feathers)
syphilophobia (venereal disease)
thanatophobia (death)
tonitrophobia (thunder)
trypanophobia (inoculation)
tyrannophobia (tyrants)
vaccinophobia (inoculation)

Physical illnesses

1 WORD

3 LETTERS

flu

4 LETTERS

acne
ague
Aids
cold
flux
gout
rash
SARS
yaws

5 LETTERS

bends
chill
colic
cough
croup
Ebola
fever
hives
lupus
mumps
virus

6 LETTERS

angina
asthma
ataxia
cancer
chorea
cowpox
dengue
eczema
goitre
hernia
herpes
oedema
plague
quinsy
rabies
scurvy
sepsis
thrush
typhus

7 LETTERS

anaemia
anthrax
cholera
colitis
disease
hypoxia
ketosis
leprosy
malaria
measles
pyaemia
pyrexia
rickets
rubella
sarcoma
scabies
sunburn
tetanus
typhoid

8 LETTERS

alopecia
beriberi
botulism
bursitis
cachexia
cataract
cyanosis
cystitis
diabetes
epilepsy
ergotism
gangrene
glaucoma
hepatoma
hookworm
impetigo
jaundice
listeria
lymphoma
mastitis
pellagra
pleurisy
pruritus
rhinitis
ringworm
sciatica
scrofula
shingles
smallpox
syndrome
syphilis
toxaemia
viraemia
vitiligo

9 LETTERS

ankylosis
arthritis
bilharzia
cirrhosis
diarrhoea
dysentery
eclampsia
emphysema
enteritis
gastritis
gigantism
glycaemia
hepatitis
influenza
ischaemia
leukaemia
nephritis
pertussis
phlebitis
pneumonia
porphyria
psoriasis
retinitis
scleritis
sclerosis
silicosis
sinusitis
sunstroke
urticaria

10 LETTERS

asbestosis
bronchitis
chickenpox
dermatitis
dermatosis
diphtheria
erysipelas
fibrositis
filariasis
gingivitis
gonorrhoea
laryngitis
legionella
meningitis
narcolepsy
ophthalmia
rheumatism
salmonella
strabismus
tendinitis
thrombosis
urethritis
vaginismus

11 LETTERS

consumption
haemophilia
hydrophobia
hypothermia
kwashiorkor
listeriosis
paratyphoid
peritonitis
psittacosis
retinopathy
scleroderma
septicaemia
spondylosis
tonsillitis
trichinosis

12 LETTERS

appendicitis
encephalitis
endocarditis
endometritis
hypertension
osteoporosis
pancreatitis
pericarditis
toxocariasis
tuberculosis

13 LETTERS

elephantiasis
endometriosis
hydrocephalus
hypoglycaemia
leishmaniasis
leptospirosis
osteomyelitis
poliomyelitis
schizophrenia
tenosynovitis
toxoplasmosis

2 WORDS

altitude sickness
Alzheimer's disease
ankylosing spondylitis
arc eye
athlete's foot
avian flu
Bell's palsy
bird flu
blackwater fever
blood poisoning
bubonic plague
cerebral palsy
coeliac disease
common cold
Crohn's disease
cystic fibrosis
decompression sickness
deficiency disease
diabetes insipidus
diabetes mellitus
diverticular disease
double pneumonia
Down's syndrome
food poisoning
frozen shoulder
gastric flu
gastro-enteritis
German measles
glandular fever
glue ear
Hansen's disease
hay fever
heat stroke
herpes simplex
Hodgkin's disease
Huntington's disease
infantile paralysis
Kaposi's sarcoma
Lassa fever
lead poisoning

legionnaires' disease
lupus vulgaris
Lyme disease
molluscum contagiosum
morning sickness
mountain sickness
multiple sclerosis
muscular dystrophy
myalgic encephalomyelitis
nappy rash
necrotizing fasciitis
Parkinson's disease
pernicious anaemia
prickly heat
puerperal fever
pulmonary emphysema
radiation sickness
rheumatic fever
rheumatoid arthritis
scarlet fever
sleeping sickness
Spanish flu
spina bifida
Sydenham's chorea
Tourette's syndrome
trench foot
undulant fever
venereal disease
Weil's disease
whooping cough
yellow fever

3 WORDS

carpal tunnel syndrome
chronic fatigue syndrome
coronary heart disease
Creutzfeldt-Jakob disease
deep-vein thrombosis
economy-class syndrome
fetal alcohol syndrome
Gulf War syndrome
irritable bowel syndrome
motor neuron disease
non-Hodgkin's lymphoma
non-specific urethritis
pelvic inflammatory disease
repetitive strain injury
seasonal affective disorder
sexually transmitted disease
sick building syndrome
sickle-cell anaemia
St Vitus's dance
toxic shock syndrome

4 WORDS

sudden infant death syndrome

Poisonous substances and gases

1 WORD

ammonia
antifreeze
arsenic
atropine
bleach
bromine
chlorine
curare
cyanide
cyanogen
digoxin
dioxin
endrin
fluorine
formaldehyde
iodine
lindane
methanol
paraquat
phenol
phosgene
quinine
ricin
sarin
strychnine
turpentine
vitriol
warfarin

2 WORDS

Agent Orange
carbon monoxide
caustic soda
cyanic acid
hydrocyanic acid
hydrogen cyanide
hydrogen sulphide
nerve gas
nitric acid
nitrogen dioxide
oxalic acid
Prussic acid
rat poison
sulphur dioxide
sulphuric acid
white spirit

Psychological illnesses

1 WORD

autism
catatonia
dementia
dysphoria
dysthymia
erotomania
hebephrenia
hyperactivity
hyperkinesis
hypomania
megalomania
paramnesia
paranoia
paraphilia
pica
psychosis
schizophrenia

2 WORDS

anorexia nervosa
Asperger's syndrome
bulimia nervosa
clinical depression
combat fatigue
eating disorder
gender dysphoria
manic depression
Munchausen's syndrome
shell shock

3 WORDS

body dysmorphic disorder
de Clerambault's syndrome
false memory syndrome
post-natal depression
seasonal affective disorder

4 WORDS

Munchausen's syndrome by proxy

Surgical instruments

bistoury
bougie
burr
cannula
colposcope
curette
depressor
dilator
forceps
gouge
guillotine
haemostat
lancet
laparoscope
osteotome
probe
retractor
scalpel
scarificator
scoop
sigmoidoscope
snare
speculum
tenaculum
trepan
trephine
trocar

Surgical operations

8 LETTERS

lobotomy
tenotomy
vagotomy

9 LETTERS

Caesarean
colectomy
colostomy
cystotomy
lithotomy
lobectomy
neurotomy
osteotomy
otoplasty
vasectomy

10 LETTERS

craniotomy
cystectomy
episiotomy
keratotomy
laparotomy
lumpectomy
mastectomy
phlebotomy
rhinoplasty
splenectomy
tracheotomy

11 LETTERS

angioplasty
embolectomy
enterostomy
gastrectomy
laminectomy
laryngotomy
ovariectomy

12 LETTERS

appendectomy
hysterectomy
oophorectomy
orchidectomy
phalloplasty
tracheostomy

13 LETTERS

pneumonectomy
prostatectomy
salpingectomy
salpingostomy
tonsillectomy

Therapies

1 WORD

acupressure
acupuncture
aromatherapy
Ayurveda
bioenergetics
biofeedback
brachytherapy
chemotherapy
chiropractic
cupping
eurhythmics
herbalism
homeopathy

hydropathy
hydrotherapy
hypnotherapy
immunotherapy
moxibustion
naturopathy
osteopathy
physiotherapy
psychotherapy
radionics
radiotherapy
rebirthing
reflexology
reiki
Rolfing
shiatsu
therapy

2 WORDS

Alexander technique
art therapy
autogenic training
aversion therapy
Bates method
behavioural therapy
behaviour therapy
bush medicine
cognitive therapy
colour therapy
combination therapy
craniosacral therapy
crystal healing
drama therapy
faith healing
family therapy
gene therapy
gestalt therapy
group therapy
heat treatment
McTimoney chiropractic
music therapy
neurolinguistic programming
occupational therapy
radiation therapy
recreational therapy
sex therapy
shock therapy
shock treatment
speech therapy
spiritual healing
zone therapy

3 WORDS

hormone replacement therapy

Veins, arteries, and the blood

1 WORD

antibody
aorta
bloodstream
capillary
circulation
corpuscle
erythrocyte
globulin
haematoma
haemoglobin
leucocyte
lymph
lymphocyte
plasma
platelet
serum

2 WORDS

basilic vein
blood clot
blood count
blood group
blood pressure
blood vessel
brachial artery
brachial vein
carotid artery
cephalic vein
coronary artery
femoral artery
femoral vein
hepatic artery
iliac artery
innominate artery
innominate vein
jugular vein
portal vein
pulmonary artery
pulmonary vein
radial artery
renal artery
renal vein
subclavian artery
subclavian vein
suprarenal vein
tibial artery
ulnar artery
ulnar vein
vena cava

3 WORDS

hepatic portal vein
inferior vena cava
red blood cell
superior vena cava
white blood cell

Vitamins

1 WORD

bioflavonoid
biotin
calciferol
inositol
menaquinone
niacin
phylloquinone
pyridoxine
retinol
riboflavin
thiamine
tocopherol

2 WORDS

ascorbic acid
folic acid
nicotinic acid
pantothenic acid

Miscellaneous

Birthstones

amethyst (February)
bloodstone (March)
diamond (April)
emerald (May)
garnet (January)
opal (October)
pearl (June)
ruby (July)
sapphire (September)
sardonyx (August)
topaz (November)
turquoise (December)

Boys' names

2 LETTERS

Al
Ed

3 LETTERS

Abe
Alf
Ali
Art
Bas
Baz
Ben
Bez
Bob
Bud
Cai
Cal
Dai
Dan
Del
Den
Des
Don
Dud
Eli
Ern
Gaz
Gus
Guy
Hal
Huw
Ian
Ike
Ira
Ivo
Jan
Jay
Jed
Jem
Jim
Job
Joe
Jon
Kay
Ken
Kim
Kit
Lee
Len
Leo
Les
Lew
Lex
Lou
Lyn
Mat
Max
Mel
Nat
Ned
Nik
Nye
Pat
Pip
Rab
Ray
Reg
Rex
Rik
Rob
Rod
Ron
Roy
Sam
Seb
Sid
Sol
Stu

Syd
Tam
Ted
Tel
Tex
Tim
Tom
Vic
Vin
Wat
Win
Zak

4 LETTERS

Abel
Adam
Ajay
Alan
Aldo
Alec
Aled
Alex
Algy
Alun
Amos
Andy
Arty
Axel
Bart
Beau
Bert
Bill
Bing
Boyd
Brad
Bram
Bret
Bryn
Burt
Carl
Cary
Ceri
Chad
Chas
Chay
Clem
Clym
Colm
Conn
Curt
Dale
Dave
Davy
Dean
Dewi
Dick
Dion
Dirk
Doug
Drew
Duke
Earl
Eddy
Emil
Eric
Erik
Erle
Esau
Evan
Ewan
Ewen
Ezra
Fred
Gary
Gene
Glen
Glyn
Greg
Gwyn
Hank
Hans
Herb
Huey
Hugh
Hugo
Iain
Ifor
Igor
Ivan
Ivor
Jack
Jago
Jake
Jeff
Jess
Jock
Joel
Joey
John
José
Josh
Juan
Judd
Jude
Kane
Karl
Keir
Kent
King
Kirk
Kris
Kurt
Kyle
Lars
Leon
Levi
Liam
Ludo
Luis
Luke
Lyle
Marc
Mark
Matt
Merv
Mick
Mike
Milo
Mort
Moss
Muir
Neal
Neil
Nick
Noah
Noam
Noel
Norm
Olaf
Olav
Omar
Ossy
Otho
Otis

Otto
Owen
Paul
Pete
Phil
Piet
Rafe
René
Rhys
Rich
Rick
Rolf
Roly
Rory
Ross
Rudi
Rudy
Russ
Ryan
Saul
Sean
Seth
Shaw
Shem
Stan
Stew
Syed
Theo
Toby
Todd
Tony
Trev
Troy
Vere
Vick
Walt
Ward
Wilf
Will
Wynn
Yves
Zack
Zane
Zeke

5 LETTERS

Aaron
Abdul
Abner
Abram
Adair
Adolf
Ahmad
Ahmed
Aidan
Alain
Alban
Alden
Aldus
Alfie
Algie
Alick
Allan
Allen
Alvar
Alvin
André
Angel
Angus
Ansel
Anton
Anwar
Archy
Armin
Arnie
Artie
Asher
Assim
Athol
Barry
Basil
Benet
Benji
Benny
Berny
Bevis
Billy
Bjorn
Blair
Blake
Blane
Blase
Bobby
Boris
Boyce
Brent
Brett
Brian
Brice
Bruce
Bruno
Bryan
Bryce
Byron
Caius
Caleb
Calum
Carey
Carlo
Casey
Cecil
Chris
Chuck
Clark
Claud
Cliff
Clint
Clive
Clyde
Colin
Colum
Conan
Conor
Cosmo
Craig
Cyril
Cyrus
Damon
Danny
Darby
Darcy
Dario
Daryl
David
Denis
Denny
Denys
Derek
Derry
Deryk
Dicky
Diego
Digby
Donal

Donny
Doran
Duane
Dylan
Eamon
Eddie
Edgar
Edwin
Edwyn
Eldon
Elias
Elihu
Eliot
Ellis
Elmer
Elton
Elvin
Elvis
Elwyn
Emery
Emile
Emlyn
Emrys
Enoch
Erich
Ernie
Errol
Ethan
Felix
Fidel
Floyd
Frank
Franz
Garry
Garth
Gavin
Geoff
Gerry
Giles
Glenn
Grant
Guido
Gyles
Harry
Harun
Heath
Henri
Henry
Hiram
Homer
Honor
Howel
Humph
Hyman
Hymie
Hywel
Idris
Imran
Inigo
Irvin
Irwin
Isaac
Izaak
Jabez
Jacky
Jacob
James
Jamie
Jared
Jason
Javed
Jemmy
Jerry
Jesse
Jesus
Jimmy
Jonah
Jonas
Jools
Judah
Judas
Jules
Julio
Kamal
Keith
Kenny
Kevin
Lance
Larry
Lauri
Leigh
Leroi
Leroy
Lewis
Lloyd
Loren
Lorin
Lorne
Louie
Louis
Lucas
Luigi
Madoc
Manny
Manus
Marco
Mario
Marty
Maxim
Micah
Micky
Miles
Mitch
Monte
Monty
Moses
Moshe
Mungo
Myles
Myron
Neddy
Neill
Nevil
Niall
Nicky
Nicol
Nigel
Niles
Nolan
Olave
Ollie
Oscar
Ossie
Oswin
Owain
Ozzie
Pablo
Paddy
Paolo
Parry
Pedro
Perce
Percy
Perry

Peter
Piers
Piran
Quinn
Rajiv
Ralph
Ramon
Randy
Raoul
Ricki
Ricky
Rikki
Roald
Robin
Roddy
Roger
Roily
Rollo
Rolph
Rowan
Royal
Rufus
Sacha
Sammy
Saxon
Scott
Selby
Serge
Shane
Shaun
Shawn
Silas
Simon
Solly
Steve
Sunil
Taffy
Talal
Tariq
Teddy
Terri
Terry
Timmy
Titus
Tommy
Tudor
Ulric
Uriah
Vijay
Vince
Vitus
Waldo
Wally
Wayne
Willy
Woody
Wyatt
Wynne
Yusuf
Zoran

6 LETTERS

Adolph
Adrian
Aeneas
Albert
Aldous
Aldred
Aldwin
Aldwyn
Alexis
Alfred
Alonzo
Alured
Andrei
Andrew
Angelo
Ansell
Anselm
Antony
Archie
Armand
Arnaud
Arnold
Arthur
Arturo
Ashley
Aubert
Aubrey
Austen
Austin
Barney
Barrie
Benito
Bennet
Bernie
Bertie
Bethel
Billie
Blaine
Blaise
Bobbie
Botolf
Botulf
Buster
Caesar
Callum
Calvin
Carlos
Carter
Caspar
Cassim
Cedric
Cerdic
Cesare
Ciaran
Claude
Connor
Conrad
Cormac
Cosimo
Curtis
Dafydd
Damian
Damien
Daniel
Darrel
Darren
Darryl
Declan
Delroy
Dennis
Denzil
Dermot
Deryck
Dexter
Dickie
Dickon
Dillon
Donald
Dorian
Dougal
Dougie
Dudley

Dugald
Duggie
Duncan
Durand
Dustin
Dwayne
Dwight
Eamonn
Edmond
Edmund
Edward
Egbert
Eldred
Elijah
Ellery
Elliot
Eoghan
Ernest
Esmond
Eugene
Evelyn
Fabian
Fergal
Fergie
Fergus
Finlay
Franco
Fraser
Frazer
Freddy
Gareth
Garret
Gawain
George
Gerald
Gerard
Gerwyn
Gethin
Gideon
Gilroy
Godwin
Gordon
Graeme
Graham
Gregor
Gussie
Gustaf
Gustav
Gwilym
Gwylim
Hamish
Hamlet
Hamlyn
Harley
Harold
Haroun
Harvey
Hashim
Hassan
Hayden
Haydon
Hector
Hedley
Herbie
Herman
Hervey
Hilary
Hobart
Holden
Horace
Howard
Howell
Hubert
Hughie
Husain
Ingram
Irvine
Irving
Isaiah
Israel
Itzhak
Jackie
Japhet
Jarred
Jarrod
Jarvis
Jasper
Jeremy
Jerome
Jethro
Johnny
Jolyon
Jordan
Joseph
Joshua
Josiah
Josias
Julian
Julius
Junior
Justin
Kelvin
Kendal
Kenelm
Kenred
Kenton
Khaled
Khalid
Kieran
Kilroy
Launce
Lauren
Laurie
Lawrie
Layton
Lemuel
Lennox
Leslie
Lester
Lionel
Lonnie
Lorcan
Lovell
Lowell
Lucian
Lucien
Lucius
Luther
Lyndon
Magnus
Malise
Malvin
Manley
Mansel
Mansur
Manuel
Marcel
Marcus
Marius
Martin
Martyn
Marvin
Marvyn
Melvin

Melvyn
Merlin
Mervin
Mervyn
Michel
Mickey
Milton
Morgan
Morris
Murray
Nathan
Neddie
Nelson
Newton
Ninian
Norman
Norris
Norton
Nowell
Oberon
Oliver
Osbert
Osborn
Osmond
Osmund
Oswald
Pascal
Philip
Pierre
Prince
Quincy
Rabbie
Rafael
Ramsay
Ramsey
Ranald
Randal
Rashid
Reggie
Reuben
Richie
Robbie
Robert
Rodger
Rodney
Roland
Ronald
Ronnie
Rudolf
Rupert
Russel
Salman
Samson
Samuel
Seamus
Sefton
Selwyn
Sergei
Sergio
Seumas
Sextus
Shamus
Sidney
Simeon
Steven
Stevie
Stuart
Sydney
Talbot
Taylor
Teddie
Thomas
Tobias
Travis
Trefor
Trevor
Tyrone
Valery
Vaughn
Vernon
Victor
Vinnie
Virgil
Wallis
Walter
Warner
Warren
Werner
Wesley
Wilbur
Willie
Willis
Wilmer
Wilmot
Winnie
Wybert
Wystan
Xavier
Yehudi
Yossef

7 LETTERS

Abraham
Adolphe
Ainsley
Ainslie
Alberto
Alfonso
Ambrose
Anatoly
Andreas
Aneirin
Aneurin
Anthony
Antonio
Armando
Auberon
Barnaby
Barnard
Bastian
Bernard
Bertram
Botolph
Bradley
Brandan
Brandon
Brendan
Cameron
Caradoc
Caradog
Carlton
Cedrych
Charles
Charley
Charlie
Chester
Christy
Clayton
Cledwyn
Clement
Clifton
Clinton
Crispin
Cyprian

Darrell
Delbert
Denholm
Derrick
Desmond
Diarmid
Diggory
Dominic
Donovan
Douglas
Dunstan
Earnest
Eleazar
Emanuel
Ephraim
Erasmus
Erskine
Eustace
Evander
Everard
Ezekiel
Feargal
Feargus
Fitzroy
Florian
Francis
Frankie
Frasier
Freddie
Fredric
Gabriel
Garrick
Gaylord
Geordie
Georgie
Geraint
Gerrard
Gervais
Gervase
Gilbert
Godfrey
Grahame
Gregory
Gunther
Gustave
Gwynfor
Hadrian
Hammond
Hartley
Herbert
Hermann
Hillary
Horatio
Hussein
Ibrahim
Ichabod
Isidore
Jacques
Jeffery
Jeffrey
Joachim
Joaquim
Joaquin
Jocelyn
Johnnie
Kendall
Kenneth
Kenrick
Lachlan
Lambert
Leander
Leofric
Leonard
Leopold
Lincoln
Lindsay
Lorenzo
Ludovic
Malachi
Malachy
Malcolm
Manfred
Matthew
Maurice
Maxwell
Maynard
Meirion
Melford
Merrion
Michael
Mikhail
Milburn
Montagu
Mostafa
Murdoch
Murtagh
Neville
Nicolas
Nikolai
Norbert
Obadiah
Olivier
Orlando
Orville
Padraig
Patrick
Phillip
Phineas
Preston
Quentin
Quintin
Randall
Raphael
Raymond
Raymund
Reynard
Reynold
Richard
Rodolph
Rodrigo
Rowland
Royston
Rudolph
Russell
Sampson
Sergius
Seymour
Shannon
Sheldon
Shelley
Sigmund
Sitaram
Solomon
Spencer
Stanley
Stephen
Stewart
Tarquin
Terence
Timothy
Travers
Tristan
Ulysses
Vaughan

Vincent
Wallace
Warwick
Wendell
Wilbert
Wilfred
Wilfrid
Willard
William
Windsor
Winfred
Winfrid
Winston
Woodrow
Wyndham
Wynford
Zachary

8 LETTERS

Abdullah
Adolphus
Alasdair
Alastair
Algernon
Alistair
Allister
Aloysius
Alphonse
Alphonso
Augustin
Augustus
Barnabas
Benedick
Benedict
Benjamin
Berkeley
Bernardo
Bernhard
Berthold
Bertrand
Beverley
Campbell
Carleton
Chandler
Charlton
Christie
Clarence
Claudius
Clifford
Constant
Courtney
Crispian
Cuthbert
Diarmait
Diarmuid
Dominick
Ebenezer
Emmanuel
Farquhar
Fernando
Fletcher
Franklin
Frederic
Fredrick
Garfield
Geoffrey
Giovanni
Giuseppe
Griffith
Hamilton
Hannibal
Harrison
Hercules
Hereward
Humphrey
Ignatius
Iorwerth
Jahangir
Jeremiah
Jeremias
Jermaine
Johannes
Jonathan
Joscelin
Kimberly
Kingsley
Krishnan
Lancelot
Laurence
Lawrence
Leighton
Llewelyn
Marshall
Matthias
Melville
Meredith
Mitchell
Mohammed
Montague
Mordecai
Mortimer
Muhammad
Napoleon
Nehemiah
Nicholas
Perceval
Percival
Philemon
Phinehas
Prescott
Randolph
Reginald
Riccardo
Roderick
Salvador
Septimus
Sheridan
Sinclair
Stafford
Stanford
Stirling
Sylvanus
Taliesin
Terrence
Thaddeus
Theobald
Theodore
Thornton
Tristram
Vladimir
Winthrop
Zedekiah

9 LETTERS

Alexander
Alexandre
Allistair
Alphonsus
Archibald
Augustine
Balthasar
Balthazar
Broderick
Christian

Christmas
Cornelius
Courtenay
Ethelbert
Ferdinand
Francesco
Francisco
Frederick
Friedrich
Granville
Grenville
Jefferson
Kimberley
Launcelot
Llewellyn
Marcellus
Marmaduke
Nathanael
Nathaniel
Nicodemus
Peregrine
Philibert
Salvatore
Sebastian
Siegfried
Sigismund
Silvester
Sylvester
Theodoric
Valentine
Zachariah
Zacharias
Zechariah
Zephaniah

10 LETTERS

Alessandro
Caractacus
Hieronymus
Maximilian
Montgomery
Stanislaus
Theophilus
Washington
Willoughby

11 LETTERS

Bartholomew
Cadwallader
Christopher
Constantine

Chinese zodiac

dog
dragon
horse
monkey
ox
pig
rabbit
rat
rooster
sheep
snake
tiger

Colours

1 WORD

3 LETTERS

bay
dun
jet
red
tan

4 LETTERS

aqua
blue
buff
cyan
dove
drab
ecru
fawn
gold
grey
iris
jade
opal
pink
plum
puce
rose
ruby
rust
sand
teak
teal
wine

5 LETTERS

amber
azure
beige
black
blush
brown
camel
cocoa
coral
cream

ebony
flame
flesh
green
hazel
henna
honey
ivory
khaki
lemon
lilac
mauve
mocha
ochre
olive
pansy
peach
pearl
poppy
raven
sable
sepia
slate
stone
straw
tawny
topaz
umber
white

6 LETTERS

almond
auburn
bisque
blonde
bronze
carrot
cerise
cherry
citron
claret
coffee
copper
damask
damson
ginger
greige
indigo
maroon
nutmeg
orange
pewter
purple
russet
salmon
sienna
silver
sorrel
Titian
violet
walnut
yellow

7 LETTERS

apricot
avocado
biscuit
caramel
carmine
crimson
emerald
fuchsia
gentian
heather
jasmine
magenta
mustard
oatmeal
oxblood
saffron
scarlet

8 LETTERS

amaranth
amethyst
burgundy
charcoal
chestnut
cinnamon
cyclamen
daffodil
eggshell
gunmetal
lavender
magnolia
mahogany
mulberry
mushroom
palomino
platinum
primrose
sapphire
viridian

9 LETTERS

aubergine
champagne
chocolate
grenadine
raspberry
tangerine
turquoise
vermilion

10 LETTERS

anthracite
aquamarine
heliotrope
periwinkle
strawberry
terracotta

11 LETTERS

ultramarine

13 LETTERS

tortoiseshell

2 WORDS

apple green
ash blonde
baby blue
blood-red
bottle green
bubblegum pink
burnt ochre
burnt sienna
burnt umber
cadmium yellow
Cambridge blue
canary yellow
cardinal red

cobalt blue
cornflower blue
electric blue
ice blue
iron grey
kingfisher blue
lapis lazuli
leaf green
lily white
lime green
Lincoln green
lovat green
midnight blue
navy blue
nut-brown
off-white
old gold
Oxford blue
oyster white
peacock blue
pea green
petrol blue
pine green
powder blue
royal blue
royal purple
sea green
shell pink
sky blue
snow-white
steel blue
steel grey
strawberry blonde
Wedgwood blue

3 WORDS

cafe au lait
duck-egg blue
eau de Nil

Criminals

1 WORD

4 LETTERS

capo
pyro

5 LETTERS

felon
fence

6 LETTERS

bagman
coiner
gunman
gunsel
klepht
pirate
rapist
runner
tsotsi

7 LETTERS

burglar
clocker
convict
cracker
firebug
flasher
footpad
goombah
handler
hoodlum
wrecker

8 LETTERS

abductor
gangster
homicide
intruder
knifeman
picklock
receiver
smuggler
wheelman

9 LETTERS

accessory
assailant
desperado
fraudster
godfather
gunrunner
racketeer
transport

10 LETTERS

accomplice
bushranger
delinquent
highbinder
incendiary
trespasser

11 LETTERS

blackmailer
confederate
mosstrooper

12 LETTERS

bodysnatcher
housebreaker

13 LETTERS

counterfeiter

2 WORDS

baby-snatcher
cut-throat
date rapist
fire-raiser
first offender

history-sheeter
hit man
juvenile offender
public enemy
resurrection man
serial killer
sex offender
young offender

Currency units, with countries

2 LETTERS

xu (Vietnam)

3 LETTERS

ban (Romania)
fen (China)
jun (North Korea)
kip (Laos)
lat (Latvia)
lek (Albania)
leu (Romania)
lev (Bulgaria)
øre (Denmark; Norway)
öre (Sweden)
pul (Afghanistan)
pya (Burma)
sen (Cambodia; Brunei; Indonesia; Malaysia)
sol (Peru)
won (North Korea; South Korea)
yen (Japan)

4 LETTERS

baht (Thailand)
birr (Ethiopia)
cedi (Ghana)
cent (US; various other countries)
dong (Vietnam)
dram (Armenia)
euro (some EU member countries)
fils (Iraq; Bahrain; Jordan; Kuwait; Yemen)
jeon (South Korea)
jiao (China)
kobo (Nigeria)
kuna (Croatia)
kyat (Burma)
lari (Maldives)
lipa (Croatia)
lira (Italy, until introduction of euro)
loti (Lesotho)
luma (Armenia)
lwei (Angola)
mark (Germany, until introduction of euro)
peso (several Latin American countries; the Philippines)
punt (Republic of Ireland, until introduction of euro)
rand (South Africa)
real (Brazil)
rial (Saudi Arabia; Iran; Oman; Qatar; Yemen)
riel (Cambodia)
sent (Estonia)
taka (Bangladesh)
yuan (China)

5 LETTERS

agora (Israel)
baiza (Oman)
denar (Macedonia)
dinar (Bosnia; Union of Serbia and Montenegro; some Middle Eastern/North African countries)
eyrir (Iceland)
franc (Switzerland and various other countries)
grosz (Poland)
haler (Czech Republic)
kopek (Russia and several other former USSR countries)
krona (Sweden)
krone (Denmark; Norway)
kroon (Estonia)
kurus (Turkey)
leone (Sierra Leone)
litas (Lithuania)
mongo (Mongolia)
naira (Nigeria)

nakfa (Eritrea)
ngwee (Zambia)
paisa (India; Pakistan; Nepal)
penni (Finland, until introduction of euro)
penny (UK)
pound (UK; Cyprus; various Middle Eastern countries)
qursh (Saudi Arabia)
riyal (Saudi Arabia; Qatar; Yemen; Iran; Oman)
rupee (India; Pakistan; Sri Lanka; Nepal; various other countries)
sente (Lesotho)
sucre (Ecuador)
tolar (Slovenia)
zloty (Poland)

6 LETTERS

balboa (Panama)
centas (Lithuania)
dollar (US; various other countries)
escudo (Portugal, until introduction of euro)
filler (Hungary)
florin (Aruba; former British coin)
forint (Hungary)
halala (Saudi Arabia)
halier (Slovakia)
hryvna (Ukraine)
koruna (Czech Republic; Slovakia)
kwacha (Zambia; Malawi)
kwanza (Angola)
markka (Finland, until introduction of euro)
peseta (Spain, until introduction of euro)
pesewa (Ghana)
poisha (Bangladesh)
qintar (Albania)
rappen (German-speaking cantons of Switzerland and Liechtenstein)
rouble (Russia and several other former USSR countries)
santim (Latvia)
shekel (Israel)
stotin (Slovenia)
tugrik (Mongolia)

7 LETTERS

afghani (Afghanistan)
bolivar (Venezuela)
centavo (Mexico; Brazil; some other countries)
centime (France, Belgium, and Luxembourg, until introduction of euro)
centimo (various Latin American countries)
drachma (Greece, until introduction of euro)
guarani (Paraguay)
guilder (Netherlands, until introduction of euro)
lempira (Honduras)
pfennig (Germany, until introduction of euro)
piastre (some Middle Eastern countries)
ringgit (Malaysia)
rufiyaa (Maldives)
tambala (Malawi)

8 LETTERS

groschen (Austria, until introduction of euro)
renminbi (China)
shilling (Kenya; Tanzania; Uganda; former British coin)
stotinka (Bulgaria)

9 LETTERS

boliviano (Bolivia)
centésimo (Uruguay; Panama)
schilling (Austria, until introduction of euro)

11 LETTERS

Deutschmark (Germany, until introduction of euro)

French Republican calendar (1793–1805)

Vendemiare (22 September to 21 October)
Brumaire (22 October to 20 November)
Frimaire (21 November to 20 December)
Nivose (21 December to 19 January)
Pluviose (20 January to 18 February)
Ventose (19 February to 20 March)
Germinal (21 March to 19 April)
Floréal (20 April to 19 May)
Prairial (20 May to 18 June)
Messidor (19 June to 18 July)
Thermidor (19 July to 17 August)
Fructidor (18 August to 16 September)

Girls' names

2 LETTERS

Di
Em
Jo
Mo
Vi

3 LETTERS

Ada
Ali
Amy
Ann
Ava
Bab
Bea
Bel
Cat
Cis
Deb
Dee
Dot
Eda
Ena
Eva
Eve
Fay
Flo
Gay
Ida
Ivy
Jan
Jay
Jen
Joy
Kay
Kim
Kit
Lea
Les
Lil
Liz
Lou
Lyn
Mae
May
Meg
Mel
Mia
Nan
Pam
Pat
Peg
Pen
Pia
Rae
Ros
Sal
Sam
Sue
Una
Val
Viv
Win
Zoë

4 LETTERS

Abby
Alex
Alix
Ally
Alma
Alva
Anna
Anne
Anya
Babs
Bebe
Bell
Bess
Beth
Cara
Cass
Cath
Ceri
Cher
Ciss
Clem
Cleo
Cora
Dana
Dani
Dawn
Dina
Dora
Eden
Edie
Edna

Eira
Ella
Elle
Elma
Elsa
Emma
Enid
Erin
Esme
Etta
Etty
Evie
Faye
Fern
Fifi
Fran
Gabi
Gaby
Gail
Gale
Gaye
Gill
Gina
Gwen
Gwyn
Hebe
Hedy
Hope
Ilma
Ilse
Iman
Inez
Iona
Iris
Irma
Isla
Jade
Jael
Jane
Jean
Jill
Joan
Jodi
Jody
Joni
Joss
Judi
Judy
June
Kara
Kate
Kath
Katy
Keri
Lana
Leah
Lela
Lena
Lila
Lili
Lily
Lina
Lisa
Lise
Liza
Lois
Lola
Lora
Lori
Lorn
Luce
Lucy
Lulu
Lynn
Mara
Mary
Maud
Maya
Mimi
Mina
Mira
Moll
Mona
Myra
Nell
Nina
Nita
Nola
Nora
Olga
Oona
Opal
Peta
Phil
Poll
Prue
Rena
Rene
Rhea
Rita
Rona
Rosa
Rose
Ruby
Ruth
Sara
Shaz
Sian
Suzy
Tara
Tess
Thea
Tina
Toni
Trix
Vera
Vita
Xena
Zana
Zara
Zena
Zita
Zora

5 LETTERS

Abbie
Adela
Adele
Adina
Aggie
Agnes
Ailsa
Aimee
Aisha
Alana
Alexa
Alice
Aline
Allie
Amber
Anaïs
Andie
Angie
Anita

Annie
Annis
April
Avril
Beata
Becky
Bella
Belle
Berny
Berta
Beryl
Bessy
Betsy
Bette
Betty
Biddy
Bonny
Bride
Brita
Britt
Candy
Carey
Carla
Carly
Carol
Caryl
Casey
Cathy
Celia
Cerys
Chloe
Chris
Ciara
Cilia
Cindy
Cissy
Clara
Clare
Coral
Daisy
Darcy
Debra
Delia
Della
Diana
Diane
Dilys
Dinah
Dione
Dodie
Dolly
Donna
Doris
Edina
Edith
Effie
Elain
Elena
Elise
Eliza
Ellen
Ellie
Elsie
Emily
Emmie
Erica
Erika
Ethel
Ethne
Ettie
Evita
Faith
Fanny
Farah
Faron
Fiona
Fleur
Flora
Freda
Freya
Gabby
Gayle
Gemma
Gerda
Gerry
Gilda
Ginny
Golda
Grace
Greta
Hatty
Hazel
Hedda
Heidi
Helen
Helga
Hetty
Hilda
Holly
Hylda
Imani
Irene
Ismay
Jacky
Janet
Janey
Janie
Janis
Jayne
Jemma
Jenna
Jenny
Jewel
Jinny
Jodie
Jonti
Josie
Joyce
Julia
Julie
Karen
Karin
Kathy
Katie
Kelda
Kelly
Keren
Kerri
Kerry
Kitty
Kylie
Lalla
Laura
Lauri
Leigh
Leila
Lenny
Leona
Lesli
Letty
Liana
Libby
Liddy
Linda

Lindy
Lizzy
Loren
Lorna
Lotty
Lucia
Lucie
Lydia
Lynda
Lynne
Lynzi
Mabel
Mable
Maddy
Madge
Maeve
Magda
Maire
Mamie
Mandy
Marcy
Marge
Margo
Maria
Marie
Marni
Marta
Marti
Marty
Matty
Maude
Maura
Mavis
Meave
Megan
Meggy
Mercy
Merle
Merry
Meryl
Milly
Minna
Minty
Mitzi
Moira
Molly
Morag
Morna
Moyna
Moyra
Myrna
Nadia
Nahum
Nance
Nancy
Nanny
Naomi
Nawal
Nelly
Nerys
Nessa
Nesta
Netta
Nicky
Nikki
Noele
Norah
Norma
Nyree
Odile
Olive
Ollie
Olwen
Olwyn
Owena
Pansy
Patsy
Patti
Patty
Paula
Peace
Pearl
Peggy
Penny
Petra
Phebe
Pippa
Polly
Poppy
Raina
Raine
Reine
Renée
Renie
Rhian
Rhoda
Rhona
Robyn
Ronna
Rosie
Rowan
Sadie
Sally
Sammy
Sandy
Sarah
Seana
Selma
Shani
Sheba
Shena
Shirl
Shona
Sibby
Sibyl
Sissy
Sonia
Sonja
Sonya
Stacy
Sukey
Susan
Susie
Sybil
Tamar
Tammy
Tania
Tansy
Tanya
Terri
Terry
Tessa
Thora
Tibby
Tilda
Tilly
Tisha
Tonia
Tonya
Topsy
Tracy
Trina
Trudi
Trudy

Unity
Valda
Velda
Velma
Venus
Verna
Vicki
Vicky
Vikki
Vilma
Vinny
Viola
Wanda
Wendy
Willa
Wilma
Wynne
Xenia
Zelda
Zelma
Zohra
Zorah

6 LETTERS

Agatha
Agneta
Aileen
Alanna
Aletta
Alexia
Alexis
Alicia
Alison
Althea
Alvina
Amalia
Amalie
Amanda
Amelia
Andrea
Andrée
Angela
Annika
Anthea
Ariane
Arlene
Arline
Armina
Ashley
Astrid
Athena
Athene
Audrey
Auriel
Aurora
Averil
Ayesha
Barbie
Barbra
Beatty
Benita
Bernie
Bertha
Bessie
Bethan
Bethia
Beulah
Bianca
Billie
Birdie
Birgit
Blanch
Blodyn
Blythe
Bobbie
Bonita
Bonnie
Brenda
Bridie
Brigid
Brigit
Briony
Bryony
Canice
Carina
Carita
Carlyn
Carmel
Carmen
Carola
Carole
Carrie
Cassie
Catrin
Cecile
Cecily
Celina
Celine
Cherie
Cherry
Cheryl
Cicely
Cissie
Claire
Colina
Connie
Dagmar
Daphne
Davida
Davina
Deanna
Deanne
Debbie
Denise
Dervla
Dianne
Dionne
Dorcas
Doreen
Dorice
Dorita
Dorrie
Dottie
Dulcie
Dympna
Eartha
Edwina
Eileen
Eilwen
Eirian
Elaine
Elinor
Elisha
Elissa
Eloisa
Eloise
Elspie
Elvira
Emilia
Esther
Eunice
Evelyn
Evonne
Fatima

Ffyona
Flavia
Flower
Franny
Frieda
Gabbie
Gaenor
Garnet
Gaynor
Gertie
Gisela
Gladys
Glenda
Glenis
Glenna
Glenys
Glinys
Gloria
Glynis
Goldie
Gracie
Gretel
Gwenda
Hannah
Hattie
Hayley
Helena
Helene
Hester
Hilary
Honora
Huldah
Imelda
Imogen
Indira
Ingrid
Isabel
Iseult
Ishbel
Isobel
Isolde
Jackie
Jacqui
Jancis
Janice
Janine
Jansis
Jeanie
Jeanne
Jemima
Jennie
Jessie
Joanna
Joanne
Joleen
Jolene
Judith
Juliet
Karina
Keeley
Kellie
Kerrie
Kerris
Kirsty
Laurel
Lauren
Laurie
Lavena
Lavina
Leanne
Leilah
Lennie
Lenore
Leonie
Lesley
Leslie
Lettie
Lianne
Liesel
Lilian
Lilias
Lilith
Lillie
Lizzie
Lolita
Loreen
Lottie
Louisa
Louise
Lucina
Luella
Maddie
Maggie
Mahala
Maidie
Maisie
Marcia
Marcie
Margie
Margot
Mariam
Marian
Mariel
Marika
Marina
Marion
Marisa
Marita
Marlin
Marlyn
Marnie
Marsha
Martha
Martie
Mattie
Maudie
Maxine
Meggie
Meghan
Melody
Mercia
Meriel
Millie
Minnie
Miriam
Miryam
Monica
Muriel
Myrtle
Nadine
Nellie
Nerina
Nessie
Nettie
Nicola
Nicole
Noelle
Noreen
Odette
Odilia
Olivia
Oonagh
Oriana
Pamela

Pattie
Pepita
Petula
Phoebe
Portia
Queeny
Rachel
Raiyah
Ramona
Raquel
Regina
Renata
Rhonda
Robina
Rosina
Rosita
Roslyn
Rowena
Roxana
Roxane
Ruthie
Sabina
Sabine
Salena
Salina
Salome
Sandie
Sandra
Sarina
Sarita
Selena
Selina
Serena
Sharon
Shauna
Sheena
Sheila
Shelly
Sherri
Sherry
Sheryl
Silvia
Simona
Simone
Sinead
Sisley
Sophia
Sophie
Stacey
Stella
Stevie
Sylvia
Sylvie
Tamara
Tamsin
Tanith
Tegwen
Teresa
Tessie
Thelma
Thirsa
Thirza
Tracey
Tricia
Trisha
Trixie
Trudie
Ulrica
Ulrika
Ursula
Vashti
Verena
Verity
Verona
Violet
Vivian
Vivien
Wallis
Winnie
Xanthe
Yasmin
Yvette
Yvonne
Zandra
Zarina

7 LETTERS

Abigail
Adeline
Adriana
Agnetha
Ainsley
Ainslie
Aisling
Aislinn
Alannah
Alberta
Aldreda
Aledwen
Alethea
Alfreda
Allegra
Allison
Aloysia
Annabel
Annette
Anouska
Anselma
Anstice
Antoine
Antonia
Anyetta
Ariadne
Arianna
Arietta
Augusta
Aurelia
Aureole
Aveline
Babette
Barbara
Beatrix
Beattie
Belinda
Bernice
Bethany
Bettina
Beverly
Blanche
Blodwen
Blossom
Branwen
Bridget
Brighid
Bronwen
Bronwyn
Caitlin
Cameron
Camilla
Camille
Candace
Candice
Candida
Caprice

Carleen
Carlene
Carmela
Carolyn
Catrina
Cecilia
Cecilie
Ceinwen
Celeste
Charity
Charley
Charlie
Chrissy
Christa
Christy
Clarice
Claudia
Clodagh
Colette
Colleen
Coralie
Corinna
Corinne
Crystal
Cynthia
Danette
Darlene
Davinia
Deborah
Deirdre
Delilah
Delores
Demelza
Desiree
Dolores
Dorette
Dorinda
Dorothy
Dymphna
Eiluned
Eldreda
Eleanor
Elfreda
Elfrida
Elspeth
Emeline
Emerald
Estella
Estelle
Eugenia
Eugenie
Eulalia
Eulalie
Evelina
Eveline
Fabiana
Felicia
Fenella
Fidelia
Flossie
Fortune
Frances
Francie
Frankie
Frannie
Genevra
Georgia
Georgie
Gillian
Ginette
Ginevra
Giselle
Grainne
Gwynedd
Gwyneth
Harriet
Heather
Héloïse
Heulwen
Hillary
Honoria
Horatia
Isadora
Jacinta
Janetta
Janette
Jasmine
Jayleen
Jeannie
Jenifer
Jessica
Jillian
Jocasta
Jocelyn
Johanna
Josepha
Josette
Juanita
Juliana
Julitta
Justina
Justine
Kathryn
Katrina
Katrine
Khaleda
Kirsten
Kristen
Kristin
Larissa
Laureen
Laurina
Laverne
Lavinia
Leonora
Letitia
Lettice
Lillian
Lindsay
Lindsey
Linette
Lisbeth
Lisette
Lizanne
Lizbeth
Loraine
Loretta
Lorette
Lorinda
Louella
Lucasta
Lucetta
Lucette
Luciana
Lucille
Lucinda
Lucrece
Lynette
Mabelle
Madonna
Mahalah
Mahalia
Malvina
Manuela

Marilyn
Marissa
Marjory
Marlene
Martina
Martine
Matilda
Maureen
Mehalah
Mehalia
Meirion
Melania
Melanie
Melinda
Melissa
Melodie
Melvina
Merilyn
Merrion
Michele
Mildred
Minerva
Mirabel
Miranda
Modesty
Monique
Myfanwy
Nanette
Natalia
Natalie
Natasha
Nerissa
Nichola
Ninette
Noeleen
Noeline
Octavia
Olympia
Ophelia
Ottilia
Ottilie
Pamelia
Pandora
Pascale
Pauline
Perdita
Petrina
Phyllis
Queenie
Rachael
Rafaela
Rebecca
Rebekah
Rhonwen
Ricarda
Roberta
Romaine
Ronalda
Rosabel
Rosalia
Rosalie
Rosalyn
Rosanna
Rosanne
Roseann
Roselyn
Rosetta
Roxanna
Roxanne
Sabrina
Saffron
Sanchia
Saranna
Scarlet
Shannon
Sharron
Sheilah
Shelagh
Shelley
Shirley
Sibella
Sibilla
Sibylla
Silvana
Siobhan
Susanna
Susanne
Suzanna
Suzanne
Suzette
Sybella
Sybilla
Tabitha
Talitha
Tatiana
Theresa
Thérèse
Tiffany
Trissie
Valerie
Vanessa
Venetia
Viviana
Yolanda
Zoulika
Zuleika

8 LETTERS

Adelaide
Adrianne
Adrienne
Angelica
Angelina
Angeline
Angharad
Annalisa
Antonina
Appolina
Arabella
Araminta
Beatrice
Berenice
Beverley
Birgitta
Brigitta
Brigitte
Brunetta
Carlotta
Carolina
Caroline
Cathleen
Ceridwen
Charissa
Charlene
Charmian
Cherelle
Chrissie
Christie
Clarabel
Claribel
Clarinda
Clarissa
Claudine
Clemence

Clemency
Clotilda
Concepta
Concetta
Cordelia
Cornelia
Courtney
Cressida
Daniella
Danielle
Delphine
Dionysia
Dominica
Dorothea
Eleanora
Eleonora
Emanuela
Emmeline
Euphemia
Eustacia
Felicity
Florence
Floretta
Francine
Fredrica
Fredrika
Georgina
Germaine
Gertrude
Gretchen
Griselda
Gwynneth
Hadassah
Hepzibah
Hermione
Hortense
Hyacinth
Ingeborg
Iolanthe
Isabella
Isabelle
Jacintha
Jeanette
Jeannine
Jennifer
Joscelin
Julianne
Julienne
Juliette
Kathleen
Kimberly
Kristina
Kristine
Laetitia
Larraine
Lauraine
Lauretta
Laurette
Laurinda
Lorraine
Lucretia
Lucrezia
Lynnette
Madelina
Madeline
Magdalen
Magnolia
Marcella
Marcelle
Margaret
Marianne
Marietta
Mariette
Marigold
Marjorie
Melicent
Melloney
Mercedes
Meredith
Merrilyn
Michaela
Michelle
Morwenna
Myrtilla
Nathalie
Patience
Patricia
Paulette
Penelope
Perpetua
Philippa
Phillida
Phillipa
Phyllida
Primrose
Prudence
Prunella
Raphaela
Rhiannon
Rochelle
Ronnette
Rosaleen
Rosalind
Rosaline
Rosamond
Rosamund
Roseanna
Roseanne
Roseline
Rosemary
Samantha
Scarlett
Sheelagh
Stefanie
Susannah
Tallulah
Tamasine
Theodora
Theresia
Timothea
Veronica
Victoria
Violetta
Violette
Virginia
Vivienne
Wilfreda
Wilfrida
Winefred
Winifred

9 LETTERS

Albertina
Albertine
Alexandra
Amaryllis
Anastasia
Angelique
Annabella
Annabelle
Anneliese
Apollonia
Aramintha
Artemisia

Augustina
Bathsheba
Bernadina
Carmelita
Cassandra
Catharine
Catherine
Celestina
Celestine
Charlotte
Charmaine
Charmanay
Christina
Christine
Claudette
Clementia
Cleopatra
Columbina
Columbine
Constance
Constancy
Courtenay
Courteney
Desdemona
Dominique
Elisabeth
Elizabeth
Emmanuela
Ernestine
Esmeralda
Fionnuala
Francesca
Francisca
Frederica
Frederika
Gabriella
Gabrielle
Genevieve
Georgette
Georgiana
Geraldine
Ghislaine
Guendolen
Guinevere
Gwendolen
Gwendolyn
Harriette
Henrietta
Henriette
Hildegard
Hippolyta
Hortensia
Jacquelyn
Jacquetta
Jeannette
Jessamine
Josephine
Katharine
Katherine
Kimberley
Laurencia
Laurentia
Madeleine
Magdalena
Magdalene
Margareta
Margarita
Margarite
Mélisande
Millicent
Mirabella
Mirabelle
Nicolette
Phillippa
Philomena
Pollyanna
Priscilla
Rosabella
Rosabelle
Rosalinda
Rosemarie
Seraphina
Stephanie
Thomasina
Thomasine
Valentina
Valentine
Véronique
Victorine
Winnifred

10 LETTERS

Alexandria
Alphonsina
Antoinette
Bernadette
Bernardina
Christabel
Christiana
Cinderella
Clementina
Clementine
Constantia
Ermintrude
Ermyntrude
Evangelina
Evangeline
Gilbertine
Gwendoline
Hildegarde
Jacqueline
Margaretta
Marguerita
Marguerite
Mariabella
Petronella
Petronilla
Temperance
Theophania
Wilhelmina

11 LETTERS

Alexandrina
Christiania

Gregorian calendar

January
February
March
April
May
June
July
August
September
October
November
December

Hairstyles

1 WORD

3 LETTERS

bob
bun
'fro

4 LETTERS

Afro
crop
perm
roll
shag

5 LETTERS

bangs
plait
quiff

6 LETTERS

braids
dreads
fringe
Mohawk
mullet

7 LETTERS

beehive
bunches
chignon
Mohican
pageboy
pigtail
shingle
tonsure
topknot

8 LETTERS

bouffant
cornrows
ponytail
ringlets

9 LETTERS

pompadour

10 LETTERS

dreadlocks

2 WORDS

big hair
body wave
buzz cut
comb-over
crew cut
Eton crop
feather-cut
flat-top
French plait
French pleat
marcel wave
number one
number two
rat's tails
razor cut
widow's peak

4 WORDS

short back and sides

Home, types of

1 WORD

3 LETTERS

hut

4 LETTERS

flat
gîte
riad
semi
tent
yurt

5 LETTERS

adobe
cabin
condo
dacha
hotel
house
hovel
igloo
lodge
manor
manse
motel
ranch
shack
tepee
villa
whare

6 LETTERS

bedsit
castle
chalet
duplex
grange
hostel
jhuggi
manoir
palace
prefab
priory
shanty
wigwam

7 LETTERS

caravan
chateau
cottage
deanery
flatlet
floatel
mansion
rancher
rectory
terrace
trailer

8 LETTERS

barracks
bungalow
hacienda
rondavel
tenement
vicarage

9 LETTERS

apartment
bedsitter
farmhouse
hermitage
homestead
houseboat
longhouse
parsonage
penthouse

10 LETTERS

blockhouse
maisonette
presbytery

11 LETTERS

condominium

2 WORDS

A-frame
country house
detached house
frame house
lake dwelling
log cabin
mobile home
mud hut
park home
pile dwelling
rest home
stately home
studio flat
terraced house
town house
tree house

3 WORDS

back-to-back
bed-sitting room
pied-à-terre
semi-detached house

4 WORDS

two-up two-down

Islamic calendar

Muharram
Safar
Rabi I
Rabi II
Jumada I
Jumada II
Rajab
Shaban
Ramadan
Shawwal
Dhu al-Qadah
Dhu al-Hijjah

Jewish calendar

Nisan
Iyyar
Sivan
Thammuz
Ab
Elul
Tishri
Hesvan
Kislev
Tebet
Sebat
Adar
First Adar

Knot, types of

1 WORD

bend
bow
bowline
clinch
hitch
prusik
sheepshank

2 WORDS

blood knot
carrick bend
clinch knot
clove hitch
fisherman's bend
fisherman's knot
granny knot
half hitch
overhand knot
reef knot
rolling hitch
running knot
sheet bend
slip knot
square knot
surgeon's knot
timber hitch
Turk's head
wale knot
wall knot
weaver's knot
Windsor knot

3 WORDS

true-love knot

Letters

1 WORD

circular
email
encyclical
mailshot
memo
memorandum
newsletter
note
notelet
pastoral
postcard
reference
reminder
reply

2 WORDS

air letter
begging letter
billet-doux
business letter
chain letter
covering letter
cover letter
dead letter
fan mail
form letter
junk mail
letter-card
love letter
mash note
open letter
rejection slip
sick note

3 WORDS

Dear John letter
letter of introduction
letter of recommendation
poison pen letter
thank-you letter

4 WORDS

bread-and-butter letter

Lucky charms

1 WORD

amulet
ankh
churinga
crucifix
fetish
horseshoe
juju
mascot
medallion
mojo
pentacle
scarab
shamrock
talisman
totem

2 WORDS

gris-gris
rabbit's foot

3 WORDS

four-leaf clover
St Christopher medal

Patterns

1 WORD

anthemion
argyle
banding
check
chequers
clock
counterchange
crackle
diaper
fret
herringbone
honeycomb
houndstooth
meander
microcheck
millefleurs
mottle
overcheck
paisley
pinstripe
plaid
spiral
starburst
sunburst
swirl
tartan
veining
waffle
woodgrain

2 WORDS

basket weave
bird's-eye
bow tie
chalk-stripe
dog-tooth
Greek key
log cabin
polka dot
shepherd's plaid

Places of education

1 WORD

cheder
college
comprehensive
convent
faculty
kindergarten
madrasa
school
seminary
university
yeshiva

2 WORDS

boarding school
choir school
church school
city academy
community college
comprehensive school
convent school
day school
elementary school
finishing school
first school
grammar school
high school
infant school
junior school
lower school
magnet school
maintained school
middle school
night school
nursery school
Open College
prep school
primary school
private school
public school
residential school
secondary modern
secondary school
special school
staff college
state school
Sunday school
Talmud Torah
technical college
training college
upper school
voluntary school

3 WORDS

City Technology College
college of education
grant-maintained school
sixth-form college

4 WORDS

college of further education
college of higher education

Punishments

1 WORD

3 LETTERS

rod

4 LETTERS

belt
cane
fine
flog
lash
rope

5 LETTERS

birch
knout
lines
lynch
noose
spank
strap
tawse
wheel

6 LETTERS

branks
gating
gibbet
hiding
paddle
stocks

7 LETTERS

boycott
drawing
ducking
gallows
hanging
jankers
kneecap
penance
torture

8 LETTERS

demotion
fatigues
flogging
gauntlet
keelhaul
lynching
sanction
scaffold
spanking
whipping

9 LETTERS

attainder
bastinado
blackball
blacklist
damnation
debagging
detention
execution
grounding
ostracism
perdition
scourging
strappado

10 LETTERS

banishment
decimation
quartering

11 LETTERS

crucifixion
endorsement
keelhauling
kneecapping
mastheading
rustication

12 LETTERS

blackballing
blacklisting
confiscation
flagellation

13 LETTERS

sequestration

2 WORDS

capital punishment
corporal punishment
cucking stool
death penalty
ducking stool
firing squad
hard labour
internal exile
lethal injection
life sentence
order mark
pack drill
penal servitude
penalty point
solitary confinement
spud-bashing
suspended sentence

3 WORDS

auto-da-fé
run the gauntlet
send to Coventry
tarring and feathering

4 WORDS

peine forte et dure
six of the best

Relatives

1 WORD

3 LETTERS

son

4 LETTERS

aunt
twin
wife

5 LETTERS

niece
uncle
widow

6 LETTERS

cousin
father
mother
nephew
parent
sister
spouse

7 LETTERS

brother
husband
partner
sibling
stepson
widower

8 LETTERS

daughter
grandson

9 LETTERS

stepchild

10 LETTERS

babyfather
babymother
grandchild
stepfather
stepmother
stepsister

11 LETTERS

grandfather
grandmother
grandparent
stepbrother

12 LETTERS

stepdaughter

13 LETTERS

granddaughter

2 WORDS

adoptive father
adoptive mother
adoptive parent
birth mother
birth parent
co-parent
cross-cousin
first cousin
foster-father
foster-mother
foster-parent
great-aunt
great-grandchild
great-granddaughter
great-grandfather
great-grandmother
great-grandparent
great-grandson
great-nephew
great-niece
great-uncle
half-brother
half-sister
in-law
kissing cousin
parallel cousin
second cousin
step-parent
surrogate mother
third cousin

3 WORDS

brother-in-law
daughter-in-law
father-in-law
mother-in-law
sister-in-law
son-in-law

Rooms

1 WORD

3 LETTERS

den
loo

4 LETTERS

cell
hall
loft
snug
ward

5 LETTERS

attic
foyer
lobby
salon
study

6 LETTERS

atrium
bedsit
carrel
cellar
garret
larder
loggia
lounge
office
pantry
saloon
studio
toilet

7 LETTERS

bedroom
boudoir
buttery
dinette
gallery
gunroom
kitchen
landing
library
nursery
parlour
sickbay
tambour
taproom

8 LETTERS

anteroom
ballroom
basement
bathroom
darkroom
lavatory
playroom
restroom
sacristy
scullery
sickroom
solarium
vestiary
workroom

9 LETTERS

boardroom
classroom
cloakroom
dormitory
gatehouse
guardroom
oubliette
stateroom
stockroom
storeroom
vestibule

10 LETTERS

bedchamber
sanatorium
schoolroom

11 LETTERS

kitchenette
scriptorium

12 LETTERS

conservatory

2 WORDS

assembly room
boiler room
box room
breakfast room
card room
changing room
common room
conference room
consulting room
cutting room
day room
dining hall
dining room
drawing room
dressing room
edit suite
engine room
family room
fitting room
front room
green room
guest room
lecture room
living room
locker room
lumber room
meeting room
morning room
orderly room
pump room
reception room
recreation room
robing room
rumpus room
sitting room
smoking room
spare room
still room

study-bedroom
sun lounge
tack room
utility room
waiting room
winter garden

3 WORDS

bed-sitting room
chill-out room

Wedding anniversaries

paper (first)
cotton (second)
leather (third)
flowers (or fruit) (fourth)
wood (fifth)
iron (sixth)
wool (or copper) (seventh)
bronze (or pottery) (eighth)
pottery (or willow) (ninth)
tin (or aluminium) (tenth)
steel (eleventh)
silk (or linen) (twelfth)
lace (thirteenth)
ivory (fourteenth)
crystal (fifteenth)
china (twentieth)
silver (twenty-fifth)
pearl (thirtieth)
coral (thirty-fifth)
ruby (fortieth)
sapphire (forty-fifth)
gold (fiftieth)
emerald (fifty-fifth)
diamond (sixtieth)

Writing implements

1 WORD

ballpoint
biro
crayon
highlighter
marker
pen
pencil
quill
rollerball
stylograph
stylus

2 WORDS

chinagraph pencil
dip pen
fibre tip
fountain pen
lead pencil
mapping pen
propelling pencil

3 WORDS

felt-tip pen

Zodiac

Aquarius (20 January to 18 February)
Aries (21 March to 19 April)
Cancer (22 June to 22 July)
Capricorn (22 December to 19 January)
Gemini (21 May to 21 June)
Leo (23 July to 22 August)
Libra (23 September to 23 October)
Pisces (19 February to 20 March)
Sagittarius (22 November to 21 December)
Scorpio (24 October to 21 November)
Taurus (20 April to 20 May)
Virgo (23 August to 22 September)

Places and peoples

African peoples

3 LETTERS

Edo
Ewe
Fon
Ibo
San
Twa
Twi

4 LETTERS

Afar
Akan
Efik
Fang
Hutu
Igbo
Issa
Kung
Moor
Nama
Nuer
Zulu

5 LETTERS

Bemba
Dinka
Fante
Galla
Hausa
Kamba
Kongo
Mande
Masai
Mbuti
Mende
Ngoni
Nguni
Oromo
Pygmy
Shona
Sotho
Swazi
Tembu
Temne
Tonga
Tutsi
Venda
Wolof
Xhosa
Zande

6 LETTERS

Berber
Damara
Fulani
Herero
Kabyle
Kikuyu
Nubian
Nyanja
Ovambo
Somali
Tsonga
Tswana
Tuareg
Watusi
Welamo
Yoruba

7 LETTERS

Ashanti
Baganda
Bambara
Basotho
Bushman
Danakil
Khoikoi
Khoisan
Makonde
Malinke
Ndebele
Samburu
Songhai
Swahili
Turkana

8 LETTERS

Mandingo
Mandinka
Matabele
Negrillo

American Indian peoples

1 WORD

3 LETTERS

Ute

4 LETTERS

Cree
Crow
Dene
Hopi
Inca
Maya
Pima
Tewa
Tiwa
Zuni

5 LETTERS

Aztec
Creek
Haida
Huron
Omaha
Osage
Sioux

6 LETTERS

Abnaki
Apache
Cayuga
Cayuse
Dakota
Dogrib
Lakota
Mandan
Micmac
Mixtec
Mohawk
Mojave
Navajo
Nootka
Ojibwa
Oneida
Paiute
Papago
Pawnee
Peigan
Pequot
Pueblo
Salish
Seneca
Slavey
Toltec

7 LETTERS

Anasazi
Arapaho
Chinook
Choctaw
Chumash
Klamath
Mahican
Mohegan
Mohican
Palouse
Shawnee
Tlingit
Zapotec

8 LETTERS

Cherokee
Cheyenne
Chippewa
Comanche
Delaware
Iroquois
Kickapoo
Kwakiutl
Muskogee
Onondaga
Powhatan
Seminole
Shoshone

9 LETTERS

Algonquin
Blackfoot
Chichimec
Chickasaw
Menominee
Tsimshian
Tuscarora
Wampanoag
Winnebago

10 LETTERS

Athabaskan
Montagnais
Potawatomi

12 LETTERS

Narragansett

2 WORDS

Nez Percé

Ancient and medieval peoples

1 WORD

3 LETTERS

Hun

4 LETTERS

Celt
Copt
Gaul
Goth
Inca
Jute
Pict

5 LETTERS

Angle
Aryan
Frank
Roman

6 LETTERS

Briton
Dorian
Hebrew
Ionian
Khazar
Minoan
Norman
Sabine
Tartar
Trojan
Vandal
Viking

7 LETTERS

Achaean
Edomite
Hittite
Lombard
Mercian
Moabite
Persian
Saracen
Spartan

8 LETTERS

Akkadian
Aramaean
Assyrian
Athenian
Chaldean
Ephesian
Etruscan
Galatian
Illyrian
Norseman
Parthian
Phrygian
Scythian
Thracian
Visigoth

9 LETTERS

Canaanite
Mycenaean
Samaritan

10 LETTERS

Babylonian
Corinthian
Philistine
Phoenician

12 LETTERS

Carthaginian
Mesopotamian

2 WORDS

Ancient Greek
Anglo-Saxon

Australian states and territories

Australian Capital Territory (Canberra)
Jervis Bay Territory
New South Wales (Sydney)
Northern Territory (Darwin)
Queensland (Brisbane)
South Australia (Adelaide)
Tasmania (Hobart)
Victoria (Melbourne)
Western Australia (Perth)

Bridges

2 WORDS

Angostura Bridge (Venezuela)
Bendorf Bridge (Germany)
Bosporus Bridge (Turkey)
Brooklyn Bridge (USA)
Forth Bridge (Scotland)
Gladesville Bridge (Australia)
Humber Bridge (England)
Jamuna Bridge (Bangladesh)
Millau Viaduct (France)
Öland Bridge (Sweden)
Penang Bridge (Malaysia)
Pont Neuf (France)
Severn Bridge (England,Wales)
Tatara Bridge (Japan)
Tower Bridge (England)
Tyne Bridge (England)
Williamsburg Bridge (USA)

3 WORDS

Bridge of Sighs (Italy)
Forth Road Bridge (Scotland)
George Washington Bridge (USA)
Golden Gate Bridge (USA)
Hooghly River Bridge (India)
Huang Ho Bridge (China)
London Milennium Bridge (England)
Menai Suspension Bridge (Wales)
Rio Niteroi Bridge (Brazil)
Second Narrows Bridge (Canada)
Seven Mile Bridge (USA)
Sunshine Skyway Bridge (USA)
Sydney Harbour Bridge (Australia)
Tagus River Bridge (Portugal)
Yokohama Bay Bridge (Japan)

4 WORDS

Mahatma Gandhi Setu Bridge (India)
Zarate-Brazo Largo Bridge (Argentina)

Buildings and monuments

1 WORD

Acropolis (Athens)
Alhambra (Granada, Spain)
Bastille (Paris)
Colosseum (Rome)
Erechtheum (Athens)
Fernsehturm (Berlin)
Hermitage (St Petersburg)
Louvre (Paris)
Pantheon (Rome)
Parthenon (Athens)
Pentagon (Virginia, USA)
Pyramids (Egypt)
Reichstag (Berlin)
Sphinx (Egypt)
Versailles (Paris)

2 WORDS

Big Ben (London)
Blue Mosque (Istanbul)
Brandenburg Gate (Berlin)
BT Tower (London)
Buckingham Palace (London)
Canary Wharf (London)
Casa Milá (Barcelona)
Chartres Cathedral (Chartres, France)
Chrysler Building (New York)

CN Tower (Toronto)
Coit Tower (San Francisco)
Cologne Cathedral (Cologne, Germany)
Crystal Palace (London)
Doges' Palace (Venice)
Edinburgh Castle (Edinburgh)
Eiffel Tower (Paris)
Flatiron Building (New York)
Golden Temple (Amritsar, India)
Guggenheim Museum (New York; Bilbao)
Hampton Court (Richmond-upon-Thames, London)
Horyu-ji (Nara, Japan)
Jefferson Memorial (Washington DC)
Lincoln Centre (New York)
Marble Arch (London)
Millennium Dome (London)
Nelson's Column (London)
Notre-Dame (Paris)
Petronas Towers (Kuala Lumpur)
Pompidou Centre (Paris)
Reims Cathedral (Reims, France)
Royal Pavilion (Brighton)
Sagrada Familia (Barcelona)
Sainte-Chapelle (Paris)
Sears Tower (Chicago)
St Peter's (Rome)
St Sophia (Istanbul)
Taj Mahal (Agra, India)
US Capitol (Washington DC)
Westminster Abbey (London)
White House (Washington DC)
Windsor Castle (Windsor)

3 WORDS

Arc de Triomphe (Paris)
Empire State Building (New York)
Houses of Parliament (London)
John Hancock Center (Chicago)
King's College Chapel (Cambridge, England)
Statue of Liberty (New York)
St Basil's Cathedral (Moscow)
St Mark's Cathedral (Venice)
St Patrick's Cathedral (New York)
St Paul's Cathedral (London)
Sydney Opera House (Sydney)
Tower of London (London)
World Trade Center (New York)

4 WORDS

Dome of the Rock (Jerusalem)
Galleria Vittorio Emanuele II (Milan)
Hall of Supreme Harmony (Beijing)
J. Paul Getty Museum (Malibu, California)
Leaning Tower of Pisa (Pisa, Italy)
30 St Mary Axe ('the Gherkin', London)

Canadian provinces and territories

Alberta (Edmonton)
British Columbia (Victoria)
Manitoba (Winnipeg)
New Brunswick (Fredericton)
Newfoundland and Labrador (St John's)
Northwest Territories (Yellowknife)
Nova Scotia (Halifax)
Nunavut (Iqaluit)
Ontario (Toronto)
Prince Edward Island (Charlottetown)
Quebec (Quebec City)
Saskatchewan (Regina)
Yukon Territory (Whitehorse)

Cities and towns

1 WORD

3 LETTERS

Ayr
Ely
Rio
Spa
Ulm

4 LETTERS

Acre
Aden
Akko
Bath
Bonn
Caen
Cork
Doha
Edam
Elat
Faro
Gaya
Gent
Giza
Graz
Hove
Hull
Jena
Kiel
Kiev
Kobe
León
Lima
Łódź
Metz
Mons
Nice
Oban
Oslo
Pisa
Reno
Riga
Rome
Sian
Suva
Xian
York

5 LETTERS

Accra
Amman
Arles
Arras
Ascot
Aspen
Baden
Bahia
Basle
Basra
Berne
Bondi
Brest
Cadiz
Cairo
Cowes
Crewe
Cuzco
Dakar
Delft
Delhi
Derby
Dhaka
Dijon
Dover
Dubai
Eilat
Epsom
Essen
Fiume
Genoa
Ghent
Gorky
Gotha
Gouda
Hague
Haifa
Hanoi
Hsian
Ibiza
Izmir
Jaffa
Jammu
Jerez
Joppa
Kabul
Kabwe
Kandy
Kyoto
Lagos
Leeds
Lewes
Lhasa
Liège
Lille
Limón
Lucca
Luton
Luxor
Lyons
Mahon
Mainz
Mecca
Medan
Miami
Milan
Minsk
Mosul
Najaf
Namur
Nancy
Natal
Navan
Neath
Newry
Nîmes
Okara
Omaha
Osaka
Padua
Palma
Paris
Parma

Patna
Perth
Petra
Poole
Poona
Porto
Quito
Rabat
Reims
Rouen
Rugby
Salem
Sana'a
Scone
Semei
Seoul
Siena
Simla
Sligo
Sofia
Split
Sucre
Tokyo
Tours
Trier
Troon
Truro
Tulsa
Tunis
Turin
Vaduz
Vichy
Wigan
Worms
Ypres

6 LETTERS

Aachen
Albany
Amiens
Angers
Angora
Ankara
Antrim
Aquila
Armagh
Arnhem
Assisi
Athens
Attica
Austin
Beirut
Bergen
Berlin
Bhopal
Bilbao
Bissau
Bodrum
Bogotá
Bolton
Bombay
Boston
Bremen
Bruges
Calais
Cannes
Canton
Chania
Cracow
Cuenca
Dallas
Danzig
Darwin
Denver
Dieppe
Dublin
Dudley
Dundee
Durban
Durham
Exeter
Fátima
Foggia
Forfar
Fresno
Galway
Gdańsk
Geneva
Grasse
Grozny
Gstaad
Gujrat
Harare
Harlow
Havana
Havant
Hebron
Helena
Hobart
Hohhot
Ibadan
Jaipur
Jalapa
Jarrow
Jiddah
Joburg
Kassel
Kendal
Kirkuk
Kraków
Lahore
Leiden
Leuven
Lisbon
London
Lübeck
Lusaka
Madras
Madrid
Malaga
Malibu
Manaus
Manila
Mantua
Maputo
Medina
Modena
Moscow
Mostar
Mumbai
Munich
Murcia
Muscat
Mysore
Nantes
Napier
Naples
Nassau
Nelson
Nevers
Newark
Niamey
Odense
Odessa

Oldham
Oporto
Orange
Ostend
Ottawa
Oviedo
Oxford
Padang
Palmas
Peking
Penang
Phuket
Pilsen
Prague
Quebec
Regina
Rennes
Rhodes
Rijeka
Rimini
Riyadh
Rostov
Saigon
Samara
Santos
Sardis
Schwyz
Shiraz
Skopje
Slough
Smyrna
Sousse
Soweto
Sparta
Stalin
Sydney
Tehran
Thebes
Tirana
Toledo
Toulon
Tralee
Troyes
Venice
Verona
Vienna
Warsaw
Weimar
Whitby
Widnes
Woking
Zagreb
Zurich

7 LETTERS

Abidjan
Aintree
Algiers
Almería
Antibes
Antigua
Antwerp
Assyria
Atlanta
Avignon
Babylon
Baghdad
Bandung
Bangkok
Bedford
Beijing
Belfast
Bologna
Breslau
Bristol
Buffalo
Calgary
Caracas
Cardiff
Carrara
Cayenne
Chennai
Chester
Chicago
Cologne
Colombo
Concord
Cordoba
Corinth
Corunna
Cotonou
Cremona
Cwmbran
Detroit
Douglas
Dresden
Dunedin
Dunkirk
Ephesus
Estoril
Falkirk
Ferrara
Glasgow
Granada
Grimsby
Haarlem
Halifax
Hamburg
Hampton
Hanover
Harlech
Harwich
Houston
Ipswich
Jackson
Jakarta
Jericho
Jodhpur
Kampala
Karachi
Keswick
Leipzig
Limoges
Lincoln
Locarno
Lourdes
Lucknow
Madison
Managua
Meissen
Memphis
Messina
Mombasa
Morpeth
Mülheim
Münster
Mycenae
Nairobi
Nanjing
Nanking
Newport
Nicosia
Nineveh
Norwich

Oakland
Olympia
Orlando
Orleans
Orvieto
Paisley
Palermo
Perugia
Phoenix
Piraeus
Pompeii
Potsdam
Preston
Raleigh
Rangoon
Reading
Rostock
Salerno
Salford
Samaria
Sapporo
Seattle
Segovia
Seville
Stanley
Swansea
Swindon
Tangier
Taunton
Telford
Tianjin
Tilbury
Toronto
Torquay
Trieste
Tripoli
Utrecht
Vicenza
Walsall
Warwick
Watford
Wexford
Wichita
Wicklow
Windsor
Wrexham
Zermatt

8 LETTERS

Aberdeen
Acapulco
Adelaide
Alicante
Amritsar
Auckland
Barnsley
Basildon
Bathurst
Bayreuth
Belgrade
Bergerac
Berkeley
Biarritz
Bismarck
Bordeaux
Boulogne
Bradford
Brasilia
Brighton
Brisbane
Brussels
Budapest
Calcutta
Canberra
Carlisle
Carthage
Chartres
Chişinău
Columbia
Columbus
Coventry
Damascus
Dortmund
Dumfries
Edmonton
Elsinore
Florence
Flushing
Freetown
Freiburg
Grasmere
Grenoble
Guernica
Hamilton
Hartford
Helsinki
Hereford
Hertford
Holyhead
Honolulu
Iráklion
Istanbul
Kandahar
Kawasaki
Khartoum
Kilkenny
Kingston
Kinshasa
Klosters
Lausanne
Limerick
Longford
Mafeking
Mandalay
Mannheim
Marbella
Monterey
Montreal
Montreux
Nagasaki
Nazareth
Nuneaton
Paignton
Pamplona
Pasadena
Pembroke
Penzance
Peshawar
Philippi
Plymouth
Poitiers
Portland
Pretoria
Pyinmana
Redditch
Richmond
Rosslare
Salonica
Salvador
Salzburg
Santiago
Sarajevo
Savannah

Shanghai
Smolensk
Solihull
Sorrento
Stafford
Stirling
Syracuse
Tamworth
Tashkent
Tientsin
Timbuktu
Tintagel
Toulouse
Tyneside
Valencia
Veracruz
Victoria
Weymouth
Winnipeg
Worthing
Würzburg
Yokohama

9 LETTERS

Aldershot
Algeciras
Allahabad
Amsterdam
Anchorage
Angostura
Annapolis
Arlington
Astrakhan
Aylesbury
Baltimore
Bangalore
Barcelona
Bethlehem
Blackburn
Blackpool
Brunswick
Bucharest
Byzantium
Cambridge
Cartagena
Castlebar
Charlotte
Cherbourg
Chernobyl
Chiangmai
Chongqing
Chungking
Cleveland
Constanţa
Dartmouth
Doncaster
Dubrovnik
Edinburgh
Frankfurt
Fremantle
Galveston
Gateshead
Göttingen
Guangzhou
Guayaquil
Guildford
Halesowen
Heilbronn
Heraklion
Hiroshima
Hyderabad
Innsbruck
Inverness
Islamabad
Jalalabad
Jamestown
Jerusalem
Karlsruhe
Kathmandu
Killarney
Kimberley
Kingstown
Kirkcaldy
Kitchener
Knoxville
Kwangchow
Lancaster
Leicester
Leningrad
Lexington
Liverpool
Ljubljana
Llandudno
Lockerbie
Lowestoft
Magdeburg
Maidstone
Marrakesh
Melbourne
Milwaukee
Mogadishu
Monterrey
Nashville
Newcastle
Newmarket
Nuremberg
Perpignan
Prestwick
Reykjavik
Rochester
Roscommon
Rotherham
Rotterdam
Salamanca
Salisbury
Samarkand
Santander
Saragossa
Sheffield
Southport
Stevenage
Stockholm
Stockport
Stornoway
Stranraer
Stuttgart
Trondheim
Vancouver
Volgograd
Wakefield
Waterford
Wiesbaden
Woodstock
Worcester
Wuppertal
Zeebrugge

10 LETTERS

Alexandria
Birkenhead
Birmingham
Bratislava
Bridgetown
Burlington

Caernarfon
Canterbury
Carmarthen
Casablanca
Charleston
Chelmsford
Cheltenham
Chichester
Cincinnati
Colchester
Copenhagen
Darjeeling
Darlington
Dorchester
Düsseldorf
Eastbourne
Felixstowe
Folkestone
Georgetown
Gillingham
Gloucester
Gothenburg
Harrisburg
Hartlepool
Heidelberg
Huntingdon
Interlaken
Kilmarnock
Launceston
Leverkusen
Libreville
Louisville
Luxembourg
Maastricht
Maidenhead
Manchester
Marseilles
Montevideo
Montgomery
Montpelier
Nottingham
Oranjestad
Pittsburgh
Portsmouth
Providence
Sacramento
Scunthorpe
Sebastopol
Shrewsbury
Srebrenica
Strasbourg
Sunderland
Trowbridge
Valladolid
Warrington
Washington
Wellington
Whitehorse
Winchester

11 LETTERS

Albuquerque
Aldermaston
Bournemouth
Brazzaville
Carcassonne
Cirencester
Constantine
Cumbernauld
Dunfermline
Enniskillen
Farnborough
Fredericton
Glastonbury
Helsingborg
Herculaneum
Kaliningrad
Londonderry
Minneapolis
Montpellier
Northampton
Rockhampton
Saarbrücken
Scarborough
Southampton
Springfield
Tegucigalpa
Vladivostok
Yellowknife

12 LETTERS

Buenaventura
Chesterfield
Christchurch
Huddersfield
Jacksonville
Johannesburg
Loughborough
Ludwigshafen
Oberammergau
Peterborough
Philadelphia
Thessaloníki
Williamsburg

13 LETTERS

Berchtesgaden
Charlottetown
Kidderminster
Kirkcudbright
Middlesbrough
Wolverhampton

2 WORDS

Abu Dhabi
Addis Ababa
Aghios Nikolaos
Alice Springs
Baden-Baden
Belize City
Beverly Hills
Buenos Aires
Cape Town
Des Moines
Dodge City
East London
El Paso
Fort William
Fort Worth
Fray Bentos
George Town
Gretna Green
Guatemala City
Hemel Hempstead
Iowa City
Jersey City
Kansas City
Key West
Kuala Lumpur
Kuwait City
La Paz
La Rochelle

Las Palmas
Las Vegas
Leamington Spa
Le Havre
Le Mans
Long Beach
Los Alamos
Los Angeles
Machu Picchu
Merthyr Tydfil
Mexico City
Milton Keynes
Monte Carlo
Montego Bay
New Delhi
New Orleans
New York
Niagara Falls
Oklahoma City
Palm Beach
Palm Springs
Palo Alto
Panama City
Pearl Harbor
Phnom Penh
Port Louis
Port Mahon
Porto Novo
Port Said
Port Stanley
Port Sudan
Quebec City
Saint-Denis
Saint John
San Antonio
San Diego
San Francisco
San José
San Juan
San Salvador
San Sebastián
Santa Barbara
Santa Cruz
Santa Fe
Santa Monica
Santo Domingo
São Paulo
Spanish Town
St Albans
St Andrews
St David's
St Émilion
St George's
St Helens
St Louis
St Malo
St Moritz
St-Nazaire
St Petersburg
St-Tropez
Sutton Coldfield
Tel Aviv
Thunder Bay
Tunbridge Wells
Ulan Bator
Washington DC

3 WORDS

Aix-en-Provence
Aix-la-Chapelle
Berwick-upon-Tweed
Burton-upon-Trent
Dar es Salaam
Hook of Holland
Kingston upon Hull
Port-au-Prince
Port-of-Spain
Rio de Janeiro
Royal Leamington Spa
Royal Tunbridge Wells
Salt Lake City
Southend-on-Sea
Stockton-on-Tees
Stoke-on-Trent
Stratford-upon-Avon
Welwyn Garden City
Weston-super-Mare

4 WORDS

Ho Chi Minh City
Santa Fé de Bogotá

Continents and regions of the world

1 WORD

Africa
Antarctica
Arctic
Asia
Australasia
Australia
Balkans
Caribbean
Eurasia
Europe
Indochina
Melanesia
Micronesia
Occident
Oceania
Orient
Polynesia
Scandinavia

2 WORDS

Baltic States
Central America
East Africa
East Indies
Far East
Indian subcontinent
Latin America
Meso-America

Middle East
Near East
New World
North Africa
North America
South America
Southeast Asia
Sub-Saharan Africa
West Africa
West Indies

Counties and county boroughs of Wales

1 WORD

Breconshire (former county)
Bridgend (Bridgend)
Caerphilly (Hengoed)
Cardiff (unitary authority)
Cardiganshire (former county)
Carmarthenshire (Carmarthen)
Ceredigion (Aberaeron)
Clwyd (former county)
Conwy (Conwy)
Denbighshire (Ruthin)
Dyfed (former county)
Flintshire (Mold)
Glamorgan (former county)
Gwent (former county)
Gwynedd (Caernarfon)
Monmouthshire (Cwmbran)
Newport (Newport)
Pembrokeshire (Haverfordwest)
Powys (Llandrindod Wells)
Radnorshire (former county)
Swansea (Swansea)
Torfaen (Pontypool)
Wrexham (Wrexham)

2 WORDS

Blaenau Gwent (Ebbw Vale)
East Glamorgan (former county)
Merthyr Tydfil (Merthyr Tydfil)
Mid Glamorgan (former county)
South Glamorgan (former county)
West Glamorgan (former county)

3 WORDS

Isle of Anglesey (Llangefni)
Neath Port Talbot (Port Talbot)
Rhondda Cynon Taff (Tonypandy)
Vale of Glamorgan (Barry)

Countries, with capitals

1 WORD

2 LETTERS

UK (London)

3 LETTERS

USA (Washington DC)

4 LETTERS

Chad (N'Djamena)
Cuba (Havana)
Fiji (Suva)
Iran (Tehran)
Iraq (Baghdad)
Laos (Vientiane)
Mali (Bamako)
Oman (Muscat)
Peru (Lima)
Togo (Lomé)

5 LETTERS

Benin (Porto Novo)
Burma (Pyinmana)
Chile (Santiago)
China (Beijing)
Congo (Brazzaville)
Egypt (Cairo)
Gabon (Libreville)
Ghana (Accra)
Haiti (Port-au-Prince)
India (New Delhi)
Italy (Rome)
Japan (Tokyo)
Kenya (Nairobi)
Libya (Tripoli)
Malta (Valletta)
Nepal (Kathmandu)
Niger (Niamey)
Qatar (Doha)
Samoa (Apia)
Spain (Madrid)
Sudan (Khartoum)
Syria (Damascus)
Tonga (Nuku'alofa)
Wales (Cardiff)
Yemen (Sana'a)
Zaire (Kinshasa)

6 LETTERS

Angola (Luanda)
Belize (Belmopan)
Bhutan (Thimphu)
Brazil (Brasilia)
Brunei (Bandar Seri Begawan)
Canada (Ottawa)
Cyprus (Nicosia)
France (Paris)
Gambia (Banjul)
Greece (Athens)
Guinea (Conakry)
Guyana (Georgetown)
Israel (Jerusalem)
Jordan (Amman)
Kuwait (Kuwait City)
Latvia (Riga)
Malawi (Lilongwe)
Mexico (Mexico City)
Monaco
Norway (Oslo)
Panama (Panama City)
Poland (Warsaw)
Russia (Moscow)
Rwanda (Kigali)
Sweden (Stockholm)
Taiwan (Taipei)
Turkey (Ankara)
Tuvalu (Funafuti)
Uganda (Kampala)
Zambia (Lusaka)

7 LETTERS

Albania (Tirana)
Algeria (Algiers)
Andorra (Andorra la Vella)
Armenia (Yerevan)
Austria (Vienna)
Bahamas (Nassau)
Bahrain (Manama)
Belarus (Minsk)
Belgium (Brussels)
Bermuda (Hamilton)
Bolivia (La Paz)
Britain
Burundi (Bujumbura)
Croatia (Zagreb)
Denmark (Copenhagen)
Ecuador (Quito)
England (London)
Eritrea (Asmara)
Estonia (Tallinn)
Finland (Helsinki)
Georgia (Tbilisi)
Germany (Berlin)
Grenada (St George's)
Holland (Amsterdam)
Hungary (Budapest)
Iceland (Reykjavik)
Jamaica (Kingston)
Lebanon (Beirut)
Lesotho (Maseru)
Liberia (Monrovia)
Moldova (Chisinau)
Morocco (Rabat)
Namibia (Windhoek)
Nigeria (Abuja)
Romania (Bucharest)
Senegal (Dakar)
Somalia (Mogadishu)
Tunisia (Tunis)
Ukraine (Kiev)
Uruguay (Montevideo)
Vanuatu (Vila)
Vietnam (Hanoi)

8 LETTERS

Barbados (Bridgetown)
Botswana (Gaborone)
Bulgaria (Sofia)
Cambodia (Phnom Penh)
Cameroon (Yaoundé)
Colombia (Bogotá)

Djibouti (Djibouti)
Dominica (Roseau)
Ethiopia (Addis Ababa)
Honduras (Tegucigalpa)
Malaysia (Kuala Lumpur)
Maldives (Male)
Mongolia (Ulan Bator)
Pakistan (Islamabad)
Paraguay (Asunción)
Portugal (Lisbon)
Scotland (Edinburgh)
Slovakia (Bratislava)
Slovenia (Ljubljana)
Suriname (Paramaribo)
Tanzania (Dodoma)
Thailand (Bangkok)
Zimbabwe (Harare)

9 LETTERS

Argentina (Buenos Aires)
Australia (Canberra)
Guatemala (Guatemala City)
Indonesia (Jakarta)
Lithuania (Vilnius)
Macedonia (Skopje)
Mauritius (Port Louis)
Nicaragua (Managua)
Singapore (Singapore City)
Swaziland (Mbabane)
Venezuela (Caracas)

10 LETTERS

Azerbaijan (Baku)
Bangladesh (Dhaka)
Kazakhstan (Astana)
Kyrgyzstan (Bishkek)
Luxembourg (Luxembourg)
Madagascar (Antananarivo)
Mauritania (Nouakchott)
Mozambique (Maputo)
Seychelles (Victoria)
Tajikistan (Dushanbe)
Uzbekistan (Tashkent)

11 LETTERS

Afghanistan (Kabul)
Netherlands (Amsterdam)
Philippines (Manila)
Switzerland (Berne)

12 LETTERS

Turkmenistan (Ashgabat)

13 LETTERS

Liechtenstein (Vaduz)

2 WORDS

Bosnia-Herzegovina (Sarajevo)
Burkina Faso (Ouagadougou)
Costa Rica (San José)
Czech Republic (Prague)
Dominican Republic (Santo Domingo)
El Salvador (San Salvador)
Equatorial Guinea (Malabo)
Guinea-Bissau (Bissau)
Ivory Coast (Yamoussoukro)
Marshall Islands (Majuro)
New Zealand (Wellington)
Northern Ireland (Belfast)
North Korea (Pyongyang)
Saudi Arabia (Riyadh)
Sierra Leone (Freetown)
Solomon Islands (Honiara)
South Africa (Pretoria)
South Korea (Seoul)
Sri Lanka (Colombo)
St Lucia (Castries)
United Kingdom (London)
Vatican City

3 WORDS

Cape Verde Islands (Praia)
Papua New Guinea (Port Moresby)
Republic of Ireland (Dublin)
Trinidad and Tobago (Port-of-Spain)
United Arab Emirates (Abu Dhabi)

4 WORDS

United States of America (Washington DC)

5 WORDS

Union of Serbia and Montenegro (Belgrade)

Deserts

2 WORDS

Arabian Desert (Egypt)
Atacama Desert (Chile)
Colorado Desert (USA)
Death Valley (USA)
Gibson Desert (Australia)
Gobi Desert (Mongolia, China)
Kalahari Desert (Botswana, Namibia, South Africa, Zimbabwe)
Kara Kum (Turkmenistan)
Kyzyl Kum (Kazakhstan, Uzbekistan)
Libyan Desert (Libya)
Mojave Desert (USA)
Namib Desert (Namibia)
Negev Desert (Israel)
Nubian Desert (Sudan)
Painted Desert (USA)
Patagonian Desert (Argentina)
Sahara Desert (North Africa)
Simpson Desert (Australia)
Sonora Desert (USA, Mexico)
Sturt Desert (Australia)
Syrian Desert (Syria, Iraq, Jordan, Saudi Arabia)
Taklimakan Desert (China)
Thar Desert (India, Pakistan)

3 WORDS

Great Basin Desert (USA)
Great Indian Desert (India, Pakistan)
Great Sandy Desert (Australia)
Great Victoria Desert (Australia)
Rub' al Khali (Saudi Arabia, Oman, Yemen, United Arab Emirates)

English counties, with county towns

1 WORD

4 LETTERS

Avon (former county)
Kent (Maidstone)

5 LETTERS

Devon (Exeter)
Essex (Chelmsford)

6 LETTERS

Dorset (Dorchester)
Durham (Durham)
Surrey (Kingston-upon-Thames)
Sussex (former county)

7 LETTERS

Cumbria (Carlisle)
Norfolk (Norwich)
Rutland (Oakham)
Suffolk (Ipswich)

8 LETTERS

Cheshire (Chester)
Cornwall (Truro)
Somerset (Taunton)

9 LETTERS

Berkshire (former county)
Cleveland (former county)
Hampshire (Winchester)
Middlesex (former county)
Wiltshire (Trowbridge)
Yorkshire (former county)

10 LETTERS

Cumberland (former county)
Derbyshire (Matlock)
Humberside (former county)
Lancashire (Preston)
Merseyside (former county)
Shropshire (Shrewsbury)

11 LETTERS

Oxfordshire (Oxford)
Westmorland (former county)

12 LETTERS

Bedfordshire (Bedford)
Lincolnshire (Lincoln)
Warwickshire (Warwick)

13 LETTERS

Herefordshire (Hereford)
Hertfordshire (Hertford)
Staffordshire (Stafford)

2 WORDS

County Durham (Durham)
East Sussex (Lewes)
Greater London (metropolitan area)
Greater Manchester (metropolitan county)
North Yorkshire (Northallerton)
South Yorkshire (former metropolitan county)
West Midlands (metropolitan county)
West Sussex (Chichester)
West Yorkshire (former metropolitan county)

3 WORDS

Isle of Ely (former county)
Isle of Wight (Newport)
Tyne and Wear (former metropolitan county)

French regions, with chief towns

Alsace (Strasbourg)
Aquitaine (Bordeaux)
Auvergne (Clermont-Ferrand)
Basse-Normandie (Caen)
Brittany (Rennes)
Burgundy (Dijon)
Centre (Orleans)
Champagne-Ardenne (Rheims)
Corsica (Ajaccio)
Franche-Comté (Besançon)
Haute-Normandie (Rouen)
Île-de-France (Paris)
Languedoc-Roussillon (Montpellier)
Limousin (Limoges)
Lorraine (Nancy)
Midi-Pyrénées (Toulouse)
Nord-Pas-de-Calais (Lille)
Pays de la Loire (Nantes)
Picardie (Amiens)
Poitou-Charentes (Poitiers)
Provence-Alpes-Côte d'Azur (Marseilles)
Rhône-Alpes (Lyons)

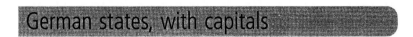

German states, with capitals

Baden-Württemberg (Stuttgart)
Bavaria (Munich)
Berlin
Brandenburg (Potsdam)
Bremen (Bremen)
Hamburg (Hamburg)
Hessen (Wiesbaden)
Lower Saxony (Hanover)
Mecklenburg-West Pomerania (Schwerin)
North Rhine-Westphalia (Düsseldorf)
Rhineland-Palatinate (Mainz)
Saarland (Saarbrücken)
Saxony (Dresden)
Saxony-Anhalt (Magdeburg)
Schleswig-Holstein (Kiel)
Thuringia (Erfurt)

International airports

Arlanda (Stockholm, Sweden)
Atatürk (Istanbul, Turkey)
Barajas (Madrid, Spain)
Beijing Capital (Beijing, China)
Benito Juárez (Mexico City, Mexico)
Changi (Singapore)
Charleroi (Brussels, Belgium)
Charles de Gaulle (Paris, France)
Cointrin (Geneva, Switzerland)
Dallas-Fort Worth (Dallas, USA)
Domodedovo (Moscow, Russia)
Eleftherios Venizelos (Athens, Greece)
Franz Josef Strauss (Munich, Germany)
Gatwick (London, UK)
Guarulhos (São Paulo, Brazil)
Haneda (Tokyo, Japan)
Hartsfield-Jackson Atlanta (Atlanta, USA)
Heathrow (London, UK)
John F Kennedy (New York, USA)
Keflavik (Iceland)
Kingsford Smith (Sydney, Australia)
LaGuardia (New York, USA)
Leonardo da Vinci (Rome, Italy)
Linate (Milan, Italy)
McCarran (Las Vegas, USA)
Narita (Tokyo, Japan)
O'Hare (Chicago, USA)
Orly (Paris, France)
Schiphol (Amsterdam, Netherlands)
Shannon (Limerick, Republic of Ireland)
Sheremetyevo (Moscow, Russia)
Stansted (London, UK)
Tegel (Berlin, Germany)
Toronto Pearson (Toronto, Canada)
Washington Dulles (Washington DC, USA)

Islands and island groups

1 WORD

3 LETTERS

Kos
Rum

4 LETTERS

Bali
Cebu
Cuba
Eigg
Elba
Fiji
Gozo
Guam
Herm
Iona
Java
Jura
Lido
Mull
Oahu
Rhum
Sark
Skye

5 LETTERS

Arran
Capri
Corfu
Crete
Delos
Ibiza
Islay
Lundy
Luzon
Malta
Melos
Naxos
Nevis
Paros
Samoa
Samos
Sumba
Timor
Tonga
Zante

6 LETTERS

Azores
Banaba
Bikini
Borneo
Cyprus
Faroes
Gomera
Hainan
Hawaii
Honshu
Ischia
Ithaca
Jersey
Kyushu
Lesbos
Límnos
Negros
Orkney
Patmos
Penang
Phuket
Rhodes
Sicily
Staffa
Tahiti
Tarawa
Tobago

7 LETTERS

Antigua
Bahamas
Barbuda
Bermuda
Bonaire
Caymans
Corsica
Curaçao
Gotland
Grenada
Iceland
Ireland
Jamaica
Madeira
Majorca
Minorca
Mykonos
Okinawa
Orkneys
Réunion
Rockall
Shikoku
Sumatra
Tokelau
Tortola
Zealand

8 LETTERS

Alcatraz
Alderney
Anglesey
Anguilla
Antilles
Barbados
Canaries
Cyclades
Dominica
Guernsey
Hebrides
Hokkaido
Krakatoa
Mainland
Maldives
Malvinas
Marianas
Mindanao
Moluccas
Mustique
Sardinia
Scillies
Shetland
Skiathos
Solomons
Sporades

Sulawesi
Tasmania
Tenerife
Trinidad
Zanzibar

9 LETTERS

Aleutians
Balearics
Carolines
Falklands
Greenland
Lanzarote
Manhattan
Mauritius
Nantucket
Santorini
Shetlands
Singapore
Zakinthos

10 LETTERS

Cephalonia
Dodecanese
Formentera
Grenadines
Guadeloupe
Hispaniola
Madagascar
Martinique
Mascarenes
Montserrat
Seychelles

11 LETTERS

Guadalcanal
Lindisfarne
Philippines
Spitsbergen

12 LETTERS

Bougainville
Newfoundland

2 WORDS

Aegean Islands
Aleutian Islands
American Samoa
Aran Islands
Ascension Island
Baffin Island
Balearic Islands
Basse-Terre
Bora-Bora
British Isles
Canary Islands
Caroline Islands
Cayman Islands
Channel Islands
Chappaquiddick Island
Christmas Island
Cocos Islands
Cook Islands
Devil's Island
Diego Garcia
Easter Island
Ellesmere Island
Ellis Island
Fair Isle
Falkland Islands
Farne Islands
Faroe Islands
Fiji Islands
Florida Keys
French Polynesia
Friendly Islands
Frisian Islands
Galapagos Islands
Gambier Islands
Gilbert Islands
Gran Canaria
Grande Comore
Great Britain
Greater Antilles
Grenadine Islands
Holy Island
Inner Hebrides
Ionian Islands
Keeling Islands
Key Largo
La Palma
Leeward Islands
Lesser Antilles
Line Islands
Lipari Islands
Long Island
Malay Archipelago
Mariana Islands
Marquesas Islands
Martha's Vineyard
Mascarene Islands
Midway Islands
Molucca Islands
Netherlands Antilles
New Caledonia
New Georgia
New Guinea
Nicobar Islands
Norfolk Island
North Island
Ocean Island
Orkney Islands
Outer Hebrides
Phoenix Islands
Pitcairn Islands
Puerto Rico
Robben Island
Ryukyu Islands
Sandwich Islands
Scilly Isles
Shetland Islands
Society Islands
Solomon Islands
South Georgia
South Island
Spice Islands
Sri Lanka
Staten Island
St Croix
Stewart Island
St Helena
St John
St Kilda
St Kitts
St Thomas
St Vincent
Sunda Islands
Truk Islands
Tubuai Islands
Vancouver Island
Virgin Islands
Viti Levu

Western Isles
West Indies
Windward Islands

3 WORDS

British Virgin Islands
Cape Breton Island
Hong Kong Island
Isle of Man
Isle of Wight
Isles of Scilly
Lewis and Harris
Lewis with Harris
Mont St Michel
Prince Edward Island
Queen Charlotte Islands
Three Mile Island
Tierra del Fuego
Tristan da Cunha

4 WORDS

Andaman and Nicobar Islands
Prince of Wales Island
Turks and Caicos Islands

Italian regions, with capitals

Abruzzo (L'Aquila)
Basilicata (Potenza)
Calabria (Catanzaro)
Campania (Naples)
Emilia-Romagna (Bologna)
Friuli-Venezia Giulia (Trieste)
Lazio (Rome)
Liguria (Genoa)
Lombardy (Milan)
Marche (Ancona)
Molise (Campobasso)
Piedmont (Turin)
Puglia (Bari)
Sardinia (Cagliari)
Sicily (Palermo)
Trentino-Alto Adige (Bolzano)
Tuscany (Florence)
Umbria (Perugia)
Valle d'Aosta (Aosta)
Veneto (Venice)

Major lakes

1 WORD

3 LETTERS

Van

4 LETTERS

Chad
Como
Erie
Eyre

5 LETTERS

Garda
Huron
Nyasa
Onega
Taupo

6 LETTERS

Albert
Baikal
Geneva
Kariba
Ladoga
Malawi
Nasser

7 LETTERS

Balaton
Balqash
Hemkund
Lucerne
Ontario

8 LETTERS

Balkhash
Kinneret
Maggiore
Michigan
Superior
Titicaca
Victoria
Winnipeg

9 LETTERS

Constance
Maracaibo
Neuchâtel
Nicaragua

10 LETTERS

Okeechobee
Tanganyika
Windermere

2 WORDS

Dead Sea
Loch Lomond
Loch Ness
Lough Neagh

3 WORDS

Great Bear Lake
Great Salt Lake
Great Slave Lake
Sea of Galilee

Mountains and mountain ranges

1 WORD

4 LETTERS

Alps (France, Italy, Switzerland, Liechtenstein, Austria)
Cook (New Zealand)
Etna (Italy)
Fuji (Japan)
Jura (France, Switzerland)
K2 (Pakistan, China)

5 LETTERS

Andes (South America)
Eiger (Switzerland)
Ghats (India)
Kenya (Kenya)
Logan (Canada)
Pelée (Martinique)
Urals (Russia)

6 LETTERS

Ararat (Turkey)
Carmel (Israel)
Denali (USA)
Egmont (New Zealand)
Elbert (USA)
Elbrus (Russia, Georgia)
Erebus (Antarctica)
Ozarks (USA)
Pamirs (Asia)
Tatras (Poland, Slovakia)
Vosges (France)

7 LETTERS

Balkans (Bulgaria)
Brocken (Germany)
Dapsang (Pakistan, China)
Everest (Nepal, Tibet)
Olympus (Greece; Cyprus)
Rockies (North America)
Snowdon (Wales)
Stanley (central Africa)

8 LETTERS

Cévennes (France)
Cotopaxi (Ecuador)
Jungfrau (Switzerland)
Kinabalu (Borneo)
McKinley (USA)
Mulhacén (Spain)
Pennines (England)
Pinatubo (Philippines)
Pyrenees (France, Spain)
Rushmore (USA)

Taranaki (New Zealand)
Vesuvius (Italy)

9 LETTERS

Aconcagua (Chile, Argentina)
Annapurna (Nepal)
Apennines (Italy)
Dolomites (Italy)
Grampians (Scotland)
Himalayas (southern Asia)
Karakoram (central Asia)
Kosciusko (Australia)
Parnassus (Greece)
Tongariro (New Zealand)

10 LETTERS

Cairngorms (Scotland)
Chimborazo (Ecuador)
Matterhorn (Switzerland, Italy)

11 LETTERS

Adirondacks (USA)
Carpathians (Poland, Slovakia, Romania)
Kilimanjaro (Tanzania)

12 LETTERS

Appalachians (Canada, USA)
Kanchenjunga (Nepal, Sikkim)
Popocatépetl (Mexico)

2 WORDS

Adirondack Mountains (USA)
Altai Mountains (central Asia)
Appalachian Mountains (Canada, USA)
Atlas Mountains (North Africa)
Balkan Mountains (Bulgaria)
Ben Nevis (Scotland)
Cairngorm Mountains (Scotland)
Carpathian Mountains (Poland, Slovakia, Romania)
Continental Divide (North America)
Dolomite Mountains (Italy)
Drakensberg Mountains (southern Africa)
Eastern Ghats (India)
Godwin-Austen (Pakistan, China)
Grampian Mountains (Scotland)
Great Divide (North America; Australia)
Harz Mountains (Germany)
Hindu Kush (Pakistan, Afghanistan)
Mauna Kea (Hawaii)
Mauna Loa (Hawaii)
Mont Blanc (France, Italy)
Mourne Mountains (Northern Ireland)
Ozark Mountains (USA)
Pamir Mountains (Asia)
Pennine Hills (England)
Pindus Mountains (Greece)
Rocky Mountains (North America)
Scafell Pike (England)
Sierra Madre (Mexico)
Sierra Nevada (Spain; USA)
Southern Alps (New Zealand)
St Helens (USA)
Table Mountain (South Africa)
Tatra Mountains (Poland, Slovakia)
Taurus Mountains (Turkey)
Tirich Mir (Pakistan)
Ural Mountains (Russia)
Vinson Massif (Antarctica)
Western Ghats (India)
Yr Wyddfa (Wales)

3 WORDS

Aoraki-Mount Cook (New Zealand)
Great Dividing Range (Australia)
Ismail Samani Peak (Tajikistan)

Ocean currents

Agulhas Current
Benguela Current
California Current
Canaries Current
Gulf Stream
Humboldt Current
Japan Current
Japanese Current
Kuroshio
Labrador Current
North Atlantic Drift
North Equatorial Current
Peruvian Current
South Equatorial Current

Republic of Ireland provinces and counties

Carlow (Carlow)
Cavan (Cavan)
Clare (Ennis)
Connacht (province)
Cork (Cork)
Donegal (Lifford)
Dublin (Dublin)
Galway (Galway)
Kerry (Tralee)
Kildare (Naas)
Kilkenny (Kilkenny)
Laois (Port Laois)
Leinster (province)
Leitrim (Carrick-on-Shannon)
Limerick (Limerick)
Longford (Longford)
Louth (Dundalk)
Mayo (Castlebar)
Meath (Navan)
Monaghan (Monaghan)
Munster (province)
Offaly (Tullamore)
Roscommon (Roscommon)
Sligo (Sligo)
Tipperary (Clonmel)
Ulster (former province)
Waterford (Waterford)
Westmeath (Mullingar)
Wexford (Wexford)
Wicklow (Wicklow)

Provinces of South Africa

Eastern Cape (Bisho)
Free State (Bloemfontein)
Gauteng (Johannesburg)
KwaZulu-Natal (Pietermaritzburg)
Limpopo (Polokwane)
Mpumalanga (Nelspruit)
Northern Cape (Kimberley)
North West (Mafikeng)
Western Cape (Cape Town)

Regions of Spain

Andalucia (Seville)
Aragon (Zaragoza)
Asturias (Oviedo)
Balearic Islands (Palma de Mallorca)
Basque Provinces (Vitoria)
Canary Islands (Santa Cruz; Las Palmas)
Cantabria (Santander)
Castilla la Mancha (Toledo)
Castilla-León (Valladolid)
Catalonia (Barcelona)
Comunidad de Madrid (Madrid)
Extremadura (Mérida)
Galicia (Santiago de Compostela)
La Rioja (Logroño)
Murcia (Murcia)
Navarre (Pamplona)
Valencia (Valencia)

Rivers and canals

1 WORD

2 LETTERS

Ob
Po

3 LETTERS

Dee
Don
Lot
Tay
Wye

4 LETTERS

Amur
Arno
Avon
Cher
Ebro
Elbe
Lena
Main
Nile
Oder
Ouse
Oxus
Saar
Spey
Tarn
Tees
Tyne

5 LETTERS

Clyde
Congo
Douro
Forth
Indus
Jumna
Loire
Marne
Meuse
Mosel
Niger
Plate
Rhine
Rhône
Saône
Seine
Somme
Stour
Tagus
Tamar
Tiber
Tisza
Trent
Tweed
Volga
Volta
Yukon

6 LETTERS

Amazon
Danube
Donets
Ganges
Hudson
Humber
Iguaçu
Irtysh
Jordan
Kolyma
Liffey
Mekong
Mersey
Murray
Neckar
Neisse
Paraná
Severn
Swanee
Thames
Tigris
Vltava
Yamuna

7 LETTERS

Darling
Dnieper
Garonne
Limpopo
Niagara
Orinoco
Potomac
Shannon
Vistula
Waikato
Yangtze
Yenisei
Zambezi

8 LETTERS

Charente
Colorado
Columbia
Delaware
Dniester
Dordogne
Mahaweli
Missouri
Suwannee
Tunguska

9 LETTERS

Euphrates
Irrawaddy
Mackenzie
Macquarie
Tennessee

11 LETTERS

Brahmaputra
Mississippi

12 LETTERS

Guadalquivir
Murrumbidgee

2 WORDS

Albert Nile
Amu Darya
Blue Nile
Caledonian Canal
Chang Jiang
Chao Phraya
Corinth Canal
Grand Canal
Great Ouse
Huang He
Huang Ho
Hudson River
Kiel Canal
Krishna River
Little Ouse
Mittelland Canal
Moscow Canal
Orange River
Panama Canal
Pearl River
Red River
Rio Grande
Snake River
St Lawrence
Suez Canal
Victoria Nile
White Nile
Yellow River
Yuan Jiang

3 WORDS

Canal du Midi
Grand Union Canal
Indira Ghandi Canal
Manchester Ship Canal
Shatt al-Arab
St Lawrence Seaway
Welland Ship Canal

Scottish council areas

1 WORD

Aberdeenshire (Aberdeen)
Angus (Forfar)
Argyllshire (former county)
Ayrshire (former county)
Banffshire (former county)
Berwickshire (former county)
Bute (former county)
Caithness (former county)
Clackmannanshire (Alloa)
Dumfriesshire (former county)
Dunbartonshire (former county)
Falkirk (Falkirk)
Fife (Glenrothes)
Highland (Inverness)
Kincardineshire (former county)
Kirkcudbrightshire (former county)
Lanarkshire (former county)
Midlothian (Dalkeith)
Moray (Elgin)
Nairnshire (former county)
Peeblesshire (former county)
Perthshire (former county)
Renfrewshire (Paisley)
Roxburghshire (former county)

Selkirkshire (former county)
Stirling (Stirling)
Stirlingshire (former county)
Sutherland (former county)
Wigtownshire (former county)

2 WORDS

East Ayrshire (Kilmarnock)
East Dunbartonshire (Kirkintilloch)
East Lothian (Haddington)
East Renfrewshire (Giffnock)
Inverness-shire (former county)
Kinross-shire (former county)
North Ayrshire (Irvine)
North Lanarkshire (Motherwell)
Orkney Islands (Kirkwall)
Scottish Borders (Melrose)
Shetland Islands (Lerwick)
South Ayrshire (Ayr)
South Lanarkshire (Hamilton)
West Dunbartonshire (Dumbarton)
Western Isles (Stornoway)
West Lothian (Livingston)

3 WORDS

Argyle and Bute (Lochgilphead)
Dumfries and Galloway (Dumfries)
Perth and Kinross (Perth)
Ross and Cromarty (former county)

Seas and oceans

2 WORDS

Adriatic Sea
Aegean Sea
Antarctic Ocean
Arabian Sea
Aral Sea
Arctic Ocean
Atlantic Ocean
Baltic Sea
Banda Sea
Barents Sea
Beaufort Sea
Bering Sea
Black Sea
Caribbean Sea
Caspian Sea
China Sea
Coral Sea
Dead Sea
Greenland Sea
Huang Hai
Indian Ocean
Ionian Sea
Irish Sea
Java Sea
Ligurian Sea
Mediterranean Sea
North Sea
Pacific Ocean
Red Sea
Ross Sea
Sargasso Sea
Southern Ocean
Sulu Sea
Tasman Sea
Timor Sea
Tyrrhenian Sea
Weddell Sea
White Sea
Yellow Sea

3 WORDS

East China Sea
Sea of Azov
Sea of Japan
Sea of Marmara
South China Sea

Seven wonders of the world

Colossus (Rhodes, Greece)
Hanging Gardens (Babylon, present-day Iraq)
Mausoleum of Halicarnassus (present-day Turkey)
Pharos (Alexandria, Egypt)
Pyramids (Egypt)
Statue of Zeus (Olympia, Greece)
Temple of Artemis (Ephesus, present-day Turkey)

Six Counties of Northern Ireland

Antrim (Belfast)
Armagh (Armagh)
Down (Downpatrick)
Fermanagh (Enniskillen)
Londonderry (Londonderry)
Tyrone (Omagh)

States and union territories of India

1 WORD

Assam (Dispur)
Bihar (Patna)
Goa (Panaji)
Gujarat (Gandhinagar)
Haryana (Chandigarh)
Jharkand (Ranchi)
Karnataka (Bangalore)
Kerala (Trivandrum)
Lakshadweep (Kavaratti)
Maharashtra (Mumbai)
Manipur (Imphal)
Meghalaya (Shillong)
Mizoram (Aizawl)
Nagaland (Kohima)
Orissa (Bhubaneswar)
Pondicherry (Pondicherry)
Punjab (Chandigarh)
Rajasthan (Jaipur)
Sikkim (Gangtok)
Tripura (Agartala)
Uttaranchal (Dehra Dun)

2 WORDS

Andhra Pradesh (Hyderabad)
Arunachal Pradesh (Itanagar)
Himachal Pradesh (Simla)
Madhya Pradesh (Bhopal)
Tamil Nadu (Chennai)
Uttar Pradesh (Lucknow)
West Bengal (Kolkata)

3 WORDS

Jammu and Kashmir (Srinagar (summer); Jammu (winter))

4 WORDS

Andaman and Nicobar Islands (Port Blair)

5 WORDS

National Capital Territory of Delhi

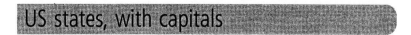

US states, with capitals

1 WORD

4 LETTERS

Iowa (Des Moines)
Ohio (Columbus)
Utah (Salt Lake City)

5 LETTERS

Idaho (Boise)
Maine (Augusta)
Texas (Austin)

6 LETTERS

Alaska (Juneau)
Hawaii (Honolulu)
Kansas (Topeka)
Nevada (Carson City)
Oregon (Salem)

7 LETTERS

Alabama (Montgomery)
Arizona (Phoenix)
Florida (Tallhassee)
Georgia (Atlanta)
Indiana (Indianapolis)
Montana (Helena)
Vermont (Montpelier)
Wyoming (Cheyenne)

8 LETTERS

Arkansas (Little Rock)
Colorado (Denver)
Delaware (Dover)
Illinois (Springfield)
Kentucky (Frankfort)
Maryland (Annapolis)
Michigan (Lansing)
Missouri (Jefferson City)
Nebraska (Lincoln)
Oklahoma (Oklahoma City)
Virginia (Richmond)

9 LETTERS

Louisiana (Baton Rouge)
Minnesota (St Paul)
Tennessee (Nashville)
Wisconsin (Madison)

10 LETTERS

California (Sacramento)
Washington (Olympia)

11 LETTERS

Connecticut (Hartford)
Mississippi (Jackson)

12 LETTERS

Pennsylvania (Harrisburg)

13 LETTERS

Massachusetts (Boston)

2 WORDS

New Hampshire (Concord)
New Jersey (Trenton)
New Mexico (Santa Fe)
New York (Albany)
North Carolina (Raleigh)
North Dakota (Bismarck)
Rhode Island (Providence)
South Carolina (Columbia)
South Dakota (Pierre)
West Virginia (Charleston)

3 WORDS

District of Columbia (-)

Volcanoes

1 WORD

4 LETTERS

Etna (Italy)
Fuji (Japan)
Laki (Iceland)
Taal (Philippines)

5 LETTERS

Hekla (Iceland)
Mayon (Philippines)
Pelée (Martinique)
Thera (Greece)
Unzen (Japan)

6 LETTERS

Ararat (Turkey)
Colima (Mexico)
Erebus (Antarctica)
Hudson (Chile)
Katmai (Alaska)
Merapi (Java)
Pacaya (Guatemala)

7 LETTERS

Jurullo (Mexico)
Kilauea (Hawaii)
Rainier (USA)
Ruapehu (New Zealand)
Surtsey (Iceland)
Tambora (Indonesia)
Vulcano (Italy)

8 LETTERS

Cotopaxi (Ecuador)
Krakatoa (Indonesia)
Pinatubo (Philippines)
Tarawera (New Zealand)
Vesuvius (Italy)

9 LETTERS

Aconcagua (Argentina/Chile)
Coseguina (Nicaragua)
Helgafell (Iceland)
Lamington (Papua New Guinea)
Paricutín (Mexico)
Santorini (Greece)
Soufrière (St Vincent)
Stromboli (Italy)

10 LETTERS

Bezymyanny (Russia)
Galunggung (Java)

11 LETTERS

Kilimanjaro (Tanzania)
Nyamuragira (Democratic Republic of Congo)

12 LETTERS

Klyuchevskoy (Russia)
Llullaillaco (Argentina/Chile)
Popocatépetl (Mexico)

2 WORDS

Cerro Negro (Nicaragua)
El Chichón (Mexico)
Lassen Peak (USA)
Mauna Loa (Hawaii)
Soufrière Hills (Montserrat)
St Helens (USA)

Waterfalls

2 WORDS

Angel Falls (Venezuela)
Augrabies Falls (South Africa)
Boyoma Falls (Congo)
Cauvery Falls (India)
Cuquenán Falls (Venezuela)
Della Falls (Canada)
Gersoppa Falls (India)
Glomach Falls (Scotland)
Grande Cascade (France)
Huangguoshu Falls (China)
Iguaçu Falls (Argentina/Brazil)
Jog Falls (India)
Kabalega Falls (Uganda)
Kaieteur Falls (Guyana)
Kalambo Falls (Tanzania/Zambia)
Kapachira Falls (Malawi)
Kegon Falls (Japan)
Khone Falls (Laos)
Krimmler Falls (Austria)
Livingstone Falls (Congo)
Mardalsfossen Falls (Norway)
Marmore Falls (Italy)
Niagara Falls (Canada/USA)
Reichenbach Falls (Switzerland)
Ribbon Falls (USA)
Ruacana Falls (Angola)
Sutherland Falls (New Zealand)
Takakkaw Falls (Canada)
Tisisat Falls (Ethiopia)
Tugela Falls (South Africa)
Victoria Falls (Zimbabwe/Zambia)
Wallaman Falls (Australia)
Yosemite Falls (USA)

3 WORDS

Kota Tinggi Falls (Malaysia)
Paulo Afonso Falls (Brazil)

4 WORDS

Eas Coul Aulin Falls (Scotland)

Religion and mythology

Apostles of Jesus

Andrew
Bartholomew
James (son of Alphaeus)
James (son of Zebedee)
John
Judas (son of James)
Judas Iscariot
Matthew
Matthias (replaced Judas)
Peter
Philip
Simon
Thaddaeus (other name for Judas, son of James)
Thomas

Books of the Bible (including the Apocrypha)

1 WORD

3 LETTERS

Job

4 LETTERS

Acts
Amos
Ezra
Joel
John
Jude
Luke
Mark
Ruth

5 LETTERS

Hosea
James
Jonah
Kings
Micah
Nahum
Peter
Titus
Tobit

6 LETTERS

Baruch
Daniel
Esdras
Esther
Exodus
Haggai
Isaiah
Joshua
Judges
Judith
Psalms
Romans
Samuel

7 LETTERS

Ezekiel
Genesis
Hebrews
Malachi
Matthew
Numbers
Obadiah
Susanna
Timothy

8 LETTERS

Habakkuk
Jeremiah
Nehemiah
Philemon
Proverbs

9 LETTERS

Ephesians
Galatians
Leviticus
Maccabees
Zechariah
Zephaniah

10 LETTERS

Chronicles
Colossians
Revelation

11 LETTERS

Corinthians
Deuteronomy
Philippians

12 LETTERS

Ecclesiastes
Lamentations

13 LETTERS

Thessalonians

3 WORDS

Letter of Jeremiah
Prayer of Manasses
Song of Solomon
Wisdom of Solomon

4 WORDS

Bel and the Dragon

6 WORDS

Song of the Three Holy Children

Characters from Arthurian legend

Agravain
Arthur
Bedivere
Bors
Ector
Elaine
Galahad
Gareth
Gawain
Green Knight
Guinevere
Igraine
Iseult
Isolde
Kay
Lady of the Lake
Lancelot
Lot
Merlin
Mordred
Morgan le Fay
Morgause
Nimue
Owain
Parsival
Perceval
Tristram
Uther Pendragon

Christian religious orders

1 WORD

Augustinian
Benedictine
Capuchin
Carmelite
Carthusian
Cistercian
Cluniac
Conventual
Dominican
Franciscan
Hospitaller
Jesuit
Marist
Norbertine
Salesian
Servite
Sulpician
Trappist
Ursuline

2 WORDS

Black Friar
Black Monk
Canon Regular
Grey Friar
Knight Hospitaller
Knight Templar
Poor Clare

The Fates

Atropos (cuts the thread of life)
Clotho (spins the thread of life)
Lachesis (assigns a person's destiny)

Gods and goddesses

GREEK

Aeolus (god of winds)
Aphrodite (goddess of beauty and sexual love)
Apollo (god of sun, music, prophecy, etc.)
Ares (god of war)
Artemis (goddess of the moon and hunting)
Asclepius (god of healing)
Athena (goddess of wisdom)
Bacchus (another name for Dionysus)
Cronus (supreme god before Zeus)
Cybele (a mother goddess)
Demeter (goddess of agriculture)
Dionysus (god of wine; inspires creativity)
Eos (goddess of the dawn)
Eros (god of love)
Gaia (the Earth personified as a goddess)
Hades (another name for Pluto)
Hebe (daughter of Zeus, cup-bearer of the gods)
Hecate (goddess of dark places)
Helios (the sun personified as a god)
Hephaestus (god of fire and craftsmen)
Hera (queen of the gods)
Hermes (messenger of the gods)
Hestia (goddess of the hearth)
Hypnos (god of sleep)
Iris (goddess of the rainbow)
Nemesis (goddess who punished wrongdoing or arrogance)
Nereus (a sea god)
Nike (goddess of victory)
Pan (god of flocks and herds)
Persephone (goddess of the underworld)
Pluto (god of the underworld)
Pallas (another name for Athena)
Poseidon (god of the sea)
Priapus (god of fertility)
Rhea (a Titan, mother of Zeus)
Selene (goddess of the moon)
Uranus (first ruler of the universe)
Zeus (the supreme god)

ROMAN

Aesculapius (god of healing)
Aurora (goddess of the dawn)
Bacchus (god of wine)
Ceres (goddess of agriculture)
Cupid (god of love)
Diana (goddess of the moon and hunting)
Janus (god of doorways and gates)
Juno (queen of the gods)
Jupiter (the supreme god)
Mars (god of war)
Mercury (messenger of the gods)
Minerva (goddess of wisdom)
Morpheus (god of dreams and sleep)
Neptune (god of the sea)
Pluto (god of the underworld)
Proserpina (goddess of the underworld)
Saturn (god of agriculture)
Sol (the sun personified as a god)
Somnus (god of sleep)
Venus (goddess of love)
Vesta (goddess of the hearth)
Vulcan (god of fire)

NORSE

Aegir (god of the sea)
Balder (god of the summer sun)
Bragi (god of poetry)
Eir (goddess of healing)
Frey (god of fertility)
Freya (goddess of love and of the night)
Frigga (goddess of married love)
Heimdall (guardian of Asgard)
Hel (goddess of the underworld)
Hődur (god of night)
Idun (goddess of youth)
Loki (god of mischief)
Norns (the three goddesses of destiny)
Odin (the supreme god)
Thor (god of thunder, the weather, etc.)
Tyr (god of battle)
Valkyries (the twelve handmaids of Odin)
Vidar (god of silence and revenge)

EGYPTIAN

Amun (a supreme god)
Anubis (god of the underworld)
Apis (god of fertility and strength in war)
Aten (the sun personified as a god)
Bastet (a goddess, protector of the pharaoh)
Bes (god who dispelled evil spirits)
Hathor (a sky goddess)
Horus (a god, protector of the monarchy)
Isis (goddess of fertility)
Khonsu (a moon god)
Maat (goddess of truth and justice)
Mut (wife of Amun)
Nut (the goddess of the sky)
Osiris (a god of fertility)
Ptah (creator of the universe)
Ra (the god of the sun)
Sekhmet (wife of Ptah)
Seth (god of evil)
Thoth (god of wisdom, justice, and writing)

HINDU

Aditi (goddess of the sky)
Agni (god of fire)
Brahma (creator god)
Devi (the supreme goddess)
Durga (wife of Shiva)
Ganesh (god of learning)
Hanuman (a semi-divine monkey-like being)
Indra (god of war and storm)
Kali (goddess of destruction)
Kama (god of love)
Kartikeya (god of war and masculinity)
Krishna (the eighth incarnation of Vishnu)
Lakshmi (goddess of prosperity)
Parvati (a benevolent goddess)
Radha (mistress of Krishna)
Rama (seventh incarnation of Vishnu)
Sakti (female principle of divine energy)
Shiva/Siva (a god associated with reproduction and destruction)
Skanda (god of war)
Surya (god of the sun)
Varuna (god of the waters)
Vishnu (the supreme god and saviour)
Yama (guardian and ruler of the dead)

Labours of Hercules

Augean stables (cleaning the stables of King Augeas)
cattle of Geryon (capturing the cattle of the giant Geryon)
Cerberus (taking the dog from the underworld)
Cretan bull (capturing the bull from the island of Crete)
girdle of Hippolyte (taking the magic girdle of the queen of the Amazons)
golden apples of Hesperides (taking the apples from the garden)
hind of Ceryneia (capturing the hind from Mount Ceryneia)
horses of Diomedes (stealing the horses of King Diomedes)
Lernaean hydra (killing the monster that lived in Lake Lerna)
Nemean lion (killing the lion that lived in Nemea)
Stymphalian birds (killing the birds that lived by Lake Stymphalus)
wild boar of Erymanthus (capturing the boar from Mount Erymanthus)

The Muses

Calliope (epic poetry)
Clio (history)
Erato (lyric poetry)
Euterpe (flute playing)
Melpomene (tragedy)
Polyhymnia (mime)
Terpsichore (dance)
Thalia (comedy)
Urania (astronomy)

Mythical creatures

1 WORD

3 LETTERS

elf
orc
roc

4 LETTERS

Fury
jinn
ogre
peri
yeti

5 LETTERS

demon
devil
dryad
fairy
fiend
genie
giant
gnome
harpy
Hydra
lamia
naiad
nymph
oread
pixie
pooka
siren
sylph
troll

6 LETTERS

afreet
bunyip
dragon
dybbuk
goblin
gorgon
hobbit
kelpie
kobold
kraken
Lilith
Medusa
merman
Nereid
ogress

Scylla
selkie
simurg
sphinx
sprite
undine
wyvern
zombie

7 LETTERS

banshee
Bigfoot
bugbear
centaur
chimera
gremlin
Grendel
griffin
gryphon
mermaid
Oceanid
Pegasus
phoenix
taniwha
unicorn
vampire
windigo

8 LETTERS

basilisk
Cerberus
giantess
Godzilla
Minotaur
werewolf

9 LETTERS

Charybdis
firedrake
hamadryad
hellhound
hobgoblin
leviathan
manticore
Sasquatch
tokoloshe

10 LETTERS

cockatrice
hippogriff
leprechaun

11 LETTERS

amphisbaena
lycanthrope

2 WORDS

Abominable Snowman
erl-king
Frankenstein's monster
King Kong
Midgard's serpent
sea serpent

3 WORDS

Loch Ness monster

Mythical places

1 WORD

Acheron
Asgard
Atlantis
Avalon
Camelot
Castalia
Charybdis
Eden
Elysium
Gehenna
Hades
Heaven
Hell
Jotunheim
Lethe
Midgard
Niflheim
Olympus
Purgatory
Sheol
Styx
Tartarus
Valhalla
Yggdrasil

2 WORDS

El Dorado
Fiddler's Green
Shangri-La

3 WORDS

Garden of Eden
Tir-na-nog

4 WORDS

Islands of the Blessed

Names for God

1 WORD

Adonai
Allah
Almighty
Creator
Deity
Divine
Elohim
Eternal
Father
Godhead
Jah
Jehovah
Lord
Maker
Trinity
Yahweh

2 WORDS

Almighty God
Divine Being
First Cause
Holy Ghost
Holy Spirit
Holy Trinity
Our Father
Prime Mover
Supreme Being

3 WORDS

Alpha and Omega
Ancient of Days
God the Father
King of Kings
Lord of Lords

Names for the Devil

Abaddon
Apollyon
Arch-enemy
Arch-fiend
Beelzebub
Belial
Evil One
Lord of the Flies
Lucifer
Mephisto
Mephistopheles
Old Nick
Prince of Darkness
Satan
Shaitan
Tempter

Orders of angels

angels
archangels
cherubim
dominations
powers
principalities
seraphim
thrones
virtues

People in the Bible

1 WORD

3 LETTERS

Dan
Eli
Eve
Gad
Ham
Job
Lot

4 LETTERS

Abel
Adam
Amos
Anne
Cain
Esau
Jehu
John
Jude
Levi
Luke
Magi
Mark
Mary
Noah
Paul
Saul
Shem

5 LETTERS

Aaron
David
Enoch
Hagar
Hosea
Isaac
Jacob
James
Jesse
Jesus
Jonah
Judah
Judas
Micah
Moses
Nahum
Peter
Sarah
Simon
Uriah

6 LETTERS

Andrew
Caspar
Daniel
Elijah
Elisha
Esther
Gideon
Haggai
Isaiah
Joseph
Joshua
Judith
Martha
Philip
Reuben
Salome
Samson
Samuel
Simeon
Thomas

7 LETTERS

Abraham
Ananias
Deborah
Delilah
Ezekiel
Gabriel
Goliath
Ishmael
Japheth
Jezebel
Matthew
Obadiah
Raphael
Solomon
Susanna

8 LETTERS

Benjamin
Emmanuel
Habakkuk
Issachar
Jephthah
Jeremiah
Jonathan
Manasseh
Matthias
Melchior
Nehemiah
Potiphar
Rehoboam
Zedekiah

9 LETTERS

Balthasar
Bathsheba
Thaddaeus
Zechariah
Zephaniah

10 LETTERS

Holofernes
Methuselah

11 LETTERS

Jehoshaphat

2 WORDS

Doubting Thomas
Jesus Christ
Judas Iscariot
Judas Maccabaeus
Mary Magdalene
Virgin Mary

3 WORDS

James the Great
James the Less
Jesus of Nazareth
John the Baptist
John the Divine
John the Evangelist
Simon the Zealot
Three Wise Men

Places of worship

1 WORD

3 LETTERS

wat

4 LETTERS

kirk
shul

5 LETTERS

abbey
duomo
stupa

6 LETTERS

chapel
church
mosque
pagoda
shrine
temple

7 LETTERS

chantry
chorten
martyry
minster
oratory

8 LETTERS

basilica
gurdwara
marabout
pantheon
peculiar
teocalli

9 LETTERS

baptistry
cathedral
nymphaeum
sacrarium
sanctuary
synagogue

10 LETTERS

baptistery
tabernacle

2 WORDS

collegiate church
Lady chapel
meeting house
sanctum sanctorum

3 WORDS

chapel of ease
holy of holies
house of God

Religions, sects, and dominations

1 WORD

3 LETTERS

Zen

5 LETTERS

Amish
Islam
Shias
Wicca

6 LETTERS

Babism
Druzes
Sufism
Sunnis
Taoism
Voodoo

7 LETTERS

animism
Judaism
Lamaism
Macumba
Mahdism
Myalism
Parsees
Quakers
Shakers
Sikhism
Umbanda
Zionism

8 LETTERS

Baptists
Buddhism
Druidism
Falashas
Hasidism
Ismailis
Kabbalah
Mahayana
Nichiren
Paganism
Tantrism
Totemism

9 LETTERS

Adventism
Candomblé
Digambara
Huguenots
Maronites
Methodism
Pocomania
Shamanism
Theosophy
Theravada
Vishnuism
Wahhabism

10 LETTERS

Brahmanism
Hutterites
Mennonites
Puritanism
Svetambara

11 LETTERS

Anabaptists
Catholicism
Neopaganism
Scientology
Wesleyanism

12 LETTERS

Christianity
Salvationism
Spiritualism
Unitarianism

13 LETTERS

Protestantism

14 LETTERS

Rosicrucianism

15 LETTERS

Presbyterianism

2 WORDS

Anglo-Catholicism
cargo cult
Christian Science
Conservative Judaism
Episcopal Church
Evangelical Church
Falun Gong
Jehovah's Witness
Lutheran Church
Malabar Christian
neo-Confucianism
Orthodox Church
Orthodox Judaism
Pentecostal Church
Plymouth Brethren
Reform Judaism
Roman Catholicism
Tibetan Buddhism
Uniate Church
Unification Church
Zen Buddhism

3 WORDS

Church of England
Church of Scotland
Eastern Orthodox Church
Greek Orthodox Church
Russian Orthodox Church
Seventh-Day Adventism
Society of Friends
Southern Baptist Church
United Reformed Church

Religious festivals and holy days

1 WORD

Annunciation (Christian: 25 March)
Beltane (Pagan: May Day)
Candlemas (Christian: 2 February)
Christmas (Christian: 25 December)
Diwali (Hindu: October and November)
Dussehra (Hindu: October)
Easter (Christian: March/April)
Epiphany (Christian: 6 January)
Hanukkah (Jewish: December)
Holi (Hindu: spring)
Mawlid (Islamic)
Muharram (Islamic)
Navaratri (Hindu: October)
Passover (Jewish: spring)
Pentecost (Christian/Jewish: May/June)
Pesach (Jewish: spring)
Purim (Jewish: spring)
Samhain (Pagan: 1 November)
Shavuoth (Jewish: May/June)
Succoth (Jewish: autumn)
Vesak (Buddhist: May/June)

2 WORDS

Ascension Day (Christian: 40 days after Easter)
Ash Wednesday (Christian: February/March)
Good Friday (Christian: March/April)
Greater Bairam (Islamic: November/December/January)
Kumbh Mela (Hindu: every 12 years)
Lag b'Omer (Jewish; between Pesach and Shavuoth)
Lesser Bairam (Islamic: October/November)
Maundy Thursday (Christian: March/April)
New Year (various religions and dates)
Palm Sunday (Christian: March/April)
Raksha Bandhan (Hindu: August)
Rosh Hashana (Jewish: September/October)
Shrove Tuesday (Christian: February/March)
Whit Sunday (Christian: May/June)
Yom Kippur (Jewish: September/October)

3 WORDS

All Saints' Day (Christian: 1 November)
Day of Atonement (Jewish: September/October)
Eid ul-Adha (Islamic: November/December/January)
Eid ul-Fitr (Islamic: October/November)

Religious offices and officials

1 WORD

3 LETTERS

nun

4 LETTERS

dean
guru
imam
lama
monk
pope

5 LETTERS

abbot
augur
canon
cohen
dayan
Druid
elder
fakir
friar
kohen
magus
mambo
padre
panda
prior
rabbi

rebbe
rishi
vicar

6 LETTERS

abbess
beadle
bishop
caliph
cantor
cleric
curate
dastur
deacon
Maggid
mahant
mullah
oracle
pandit
priest
pujari
rector
sexton
sheikh
sister
verger

7 LETTERS

acolyte
almoner
Brahman
brother
houngan
muezzin
prelate
primate
santero

8 LETTERS

canoness
cardinal
chaplain
haruspex
hierarch
minister
pontifex
preacher
prioress
talapoin
thurifer

9 LETTERS

anchoress
anchorite
ayatollah
confessor
deaconess
mendicant
Monsignor
patriarch
precentor
presbyter
priestess
rebbetzin
sacristan

10 LETTERS

archbishop
archdeacon
hierophant
seminarian
seminarist

12 LETTERS

churchwarden

13 LETTERS

archimandrite

2 WORDS

area dean
chief rabbi
Dalai Lama
high priest
lay brother
lay sister
mother superior
Panchen Lama
rural dean
witch doctor

Seven deadly sins

anger
covetousness
envy
gluttony
lust
pride
sloth

Seven virtues

charity
faith
fortitude
hope
justice
prudence
temperance

Twelve tribes of Israel

Asher
Benjamin
Dan
Gad
Issachar
Judah
Levi
Manasseh
Naphtali
Reuben
Simeon
Zebulun

Science and technology

Alloys

1 WORD

billon
brass
bronze
constantan
electrum
eureka
gunmetal
magnox
nitinol
ormolu
permalloy
pewter
pinchbeck
platinoid
solder
spiegeleisen
steel
terne
tin

2 WORDS

aluminium bronze
babbitt metal
bell metal
Britannia metal
cupro-nickel
Dutch metal
German silver
misch metal
mosaic gold
nickel brass
phosphor bronze
red gold
speculum metal
stainless steel
type metal
white gold
white metal

Branches of engineering

1 WORD

aerodynamics
astronautics
cosmonautics
ergonomics
geotechnics
hydraulics

2 WORDS

aeronautical engineering
aerospace engineering
agricultural engineering
automotive engineering
chemical engineering
civil engineering
electrical engineering
electronics engineering
environmental engineering
fluid dynamics
mechanical engineering
mining engineering
naval engineering
nuclear engineering
production engineering
structural engineering

Branches of geography

1 WORD

biogeography
cartography
climatology
demography
geology
geomorphology
geopolitics
glaciology
hydrology
hypsography
meteorology
oceanography
oceanology
orography
seismology
topography
volcanology

2 WORDS

cultural geography
economic geography
historical geography
human geography
physical geography
political geography
social geography

Branches of science

1 WORD

6 LETTERS

botany
optics

7 LETTERS

anatomy
biology
ecology
geology
physics
zoology
zymurgy

8 LETTERS

cytology
dynamics
ethology
genetics
medicine
mycology
oncology
pedology
robotics
taxonomy
virology

9 LETTERS

acoustics
astronomy
chemistry
cosmology
economics
ethnology
forensics
geography
histology
hydrology
limnology
mechanics
neurology
pathology
petrology
phytology
radiology
sociology
tectonics

10 LETTERS

conchology
cryogenics
dendrology
entomology
exobiology
geophysics
glaciology
holography
immunology
metallurgy
mineralogy
palynology
physiology
psychiatry
psychology
seismology
statistics
toxicology

11 LETTERS

agriscience
climatology
cybernetics
electronics
engineering
haematology
herpetology
ichthyology
linguistics
mathematics
meteorology
ornithology
volcanology
vulcanology

12 LETTERS

aerodynamics
anthropology
astrophysics
bacteriology
biochemistry
epidemiology
geochemistry
hydrostatics
microbiology
neuroscience
oceanography
palaeobotany
parasitology
pharmacology
physiography
sociobiology
spectroscopy
stratigraphy
zoogeography

13 LETTERS

endocrinology
geochronology
geomorphology
hydrodynamics
ophthalmology
palaeontology

2 WORDS

behavioural science
computer science
earth science
electrical engineering
fluid mechanics
genetic engineering
information technology
marine biology
molecular biology
natural history
nuclear chemistry
nuclear physics
particle physics
quantum mechanics
soil science
veterinary medicine

Chemical elements

3 LETTERS

tin (Sn)

4 LETTERS

gold (Au)
iron (Fe)
lead (Pb)
neon (Ne)
zinc (Zn)

5 LETTERS

argon (Ar)
boron (B)
radon (Rn)
xenon (Xe)

6 LETTERS

barium (Ba)
carbon (C)
cerium (Ce)
cobalt (Co)
copper (Cu)
curium (Cm)
erbium (Er)
helium (He)
indium (In)
iodine (I)
nickel (Ni)
osmium (Os)
oxygen (O)
radium (Ra)
silver (Ag)
sodium (Na)

7 LETTERS

arsenic (As)
bismuth (Bi)
bohrium (Bh)
bromine (Br)
cadmium (Cd)
caesium (Cs)
calcium (Ca)
dubnium (Db)
fermium (Fm)
gallium (Ga)
hafnium (Hf)
hassium (Hs)
holmium (Ho)
iridium (Ir)
krypton (Kr)
lithium (Li)
mercury (Hg)
niobium (Nb)
rhenium (Re)
rhodium (Rh)
silicon (Si)
sulphur (S)
terbium (Tb)
thorium (Th)
thulium (Tm)
uranium (U)
yttrium (Y)

8 LETTERS

actinium (Ac)
antimony (Sb)
astatine (At)
chlorine (Cl)
chromium (Cr)
europium (Eu)
fluorine (F)
francium (Fr)
hydrogen (H)
lutetium (Lu)

nitrogen (N)
nobelium (No)
platinum (Pt)
polonium (Po)
rubidium (Rb)
samarium (Sm)
scandium (Sc)
selenium (Se)
tantalum (Ta)
thallium (Tl)
titanium (Ti)
tungsten (W)
vanadium (V)

9 LETTERS

aluminium (Al)
americium (Am)
berkelium (Bk)
beryllium (Be)
germanium (Ge)
lanthanum (La)
magnesium (Mg)
manganese (Mn)
neodymium (Nd)
neptunium (Np)
palladium (Pd)
plutonium (Pu)
potassium (K)
ruthenium (Ru)
strontium (Sr)
tellurium (Te)
ytterbium (Yb)
zirconium (Zr)

10 LETTERS

dysprosium (Dy)
gadolinium (Gd)
lawrencium (Lr)
meitnerium (Mt)
molybdenum (Mo)
phosphorus (P)
promethium (Pm)
seaborgium (Sg)
technetium (Tc)

11 LETTERS

californium (Cf)
einsteinium (Es)
mendelevium (Md)
roentgenium (Rg)

12 LETTERS

darmstadtium (Ds)
praseodymium (Pr)
protactinium (Pa)

13 LETTERS

rutherfordium (Rf)

Chemicals

1 WORD

4 LETTERS

alum
salt
soda

5 LETTERS

borax
ether
sugar

6 LETTERS

baryta
gypsum
lithia
potash
silica
xylene

7 LETTERS

acetone
alcohol
alumina
calomel
cyanide
vitriol

8 LETTERS

cinnabar
corundum
firedamp
magnesia
peroxide
strontia
zirconia

9 LETTERS

acetylene
glycerine
quicklime
saltpetre
verdigris

10 LETTERS

chloroform

11 LETTERS

carborundum

12 LETTERS

formaldehyde

2 WORDS

acetic acid
baking soda
boracic acid
carbolic acid
carbon tetrachloride
caustic potash
caustic soda
chrome yellow
common salt
dry ice

Epsom salts
ethyl alcohol
folic acid
formic acid
hydrochloric acid
jeweller's rouge
laughing gas
marsh gas
nitric oxide
prussic acid
red lead
slaked lime
washing soda
white arsenic

3 WORDS

bicarbonate of soda
cream of tartar
plaster of Paris

Clocks and watches

1 WORD

chronograph
chronometer
clepsydra
clock
hourglass
sandglass
stopwatch
sundial
wristwatch

2 WORDS

alarm clock
atomic clock
caesium clock
carriage clock
clock radio
cuckoo clock
egg-timer
fob watch
grandfather clock
grandmother clock
half-hunter
lever watch
pendulum clock
pocket watch
quartz clock
quartz watch
stem-winder
tabernacle clock
travel clock
water clock

3 WORDS

long-case clock

Computing and the Internet

1 WORD

2 LETTERS

PC

3 LETTERS

bit
bot
bug
bus
CPU
DOS
DVD
FAQ
FTP
GIF
ISP
Net
PDA
PDF
RAM
ROM
URL
VDU
Web
XML
zip

4 LETTERS

baud
BIOS
blog
boot
byte
card
chip
code
data
disk
file
host
HTML
HTTP
icon
JPEG

loop
menu
port
spam
surf
tool
wiki
worm

5 LETTERS

agent
alias
BASIC
board
cache
click
crash
drive
email
input
macro
micro
modem
mouse
virus

6 LETTERS

applet
backup
bitmap
buffer
client
cursor
daemon
domain
editor
filter
format
hacker
keypad
laptop
mailer
memory
online
output
parser
portal
script
server
spider
telnet
toggle
upload
webcam
weblog

7 LETTERS

blogger
browser
console
crawler
desktop
dialler
digital
display
gateway
gigabit
malware
manager
monitor
network
offline
palmtop
podcast
printer
program
routine
scanner
servlet
sniffer
spyware
toolbar
utility
vaccine
website

8 LETTERS

bookmark
computer
debugger
diskette
download
emoticon
Ethernet
filename
firewall
firmware
freeware
hardware
Internet
intranet
joystick
keyboard
kilobyte
megabyte
notebook
phishing
printout
register
software
terminal

9 LETTERS

assembler
digitizer
groupware
hyperlink
hypertext
interface
megapixel
microchip
navigator
newsgroup
processor
sequencer
shareware
talkboard
trackball
wallpaper

10 LETTERS

rollerball
transistor
viewscreen

11 LETTERS

application
coprocessor
interactive
motherboard
spreadsheet
workstation

12 LETTERS

minicomputer
spellchecker

13 LETTERS

microcomputer

2 WORDS

acoustic coupler
bubblejet printer
bulletin board
cache memory
CD-R
CD-ROM
CD-RW
chat room
compact disc
control unit
database management system
dialog box
disk drive
domain name
DVD-R
DVD-ROM
DVD-RW
e-tailer
expansion card
expert system
fax modem
flash memory
floppy disk
games console
graphics card
hard disk
hard drive
home page
in-box
information technology
inkjet printer
laser printer
light pen
line printer
log in
log out
mouse mat
optical disk
plug-in
pop-up
printed circuit
screen saver
search engine
serial port
shell program
silicon chip
sound card
text editor
touch pad
touch screen
Trojan Horse
user interface
video card
virtual reality
web page
word processor
zip file

3 WORDS

bar-code reader
central processing unit
dot-matrix printer
Internet service provider
printed circuit board
random-access memory
read-only memory
visual display unit
World Wide Web

Constellations

1 WORD

3 LETTERS

Leo

4 LETTERS

Apus
Crux
Grus
Lynx
Lyra
Pavo
Vela

5 LETTERS

Aries
Cetus
Draco
Hydra
Indus
Lepus
Libra
Lupus
Mensa
Musca
Norma
Orion
Pyxis
Virgo

6 LETTERS

Antlia
Aquila
Auriga
Boötes
Caelum
Cancer
Carina
Corvus
Crater
Cygnus

Dorado
Fornax
Gemini
Hydrus
Octans
Pictor
Pisces
Puppis
Scutum
Taurus
Tucana
Volans

7 LETTERS

Cepheus
Columba
Lacerta
Pegasus
Perseus
Phoenix
Sagitta
Serpens
Sextans

8 LETTERS

Aquarius
Circinus
Equuleus
Eridanus
Hercules
Scorpius
Sculptor

9 LETTERS

Andromeda
Centaurus
Delphinus
Monoceros
Ophiuchus
Reticulum
Vulpecula

10 LETTERS

Cassiopeia
Chamaeleon
Horologium
Triangulum

11 LETTERS

Capricornus
Sagittarius
Telescopium

12 LETTERS

Microscopium

2 WORDS

Canes Venatici
Canis Major
Canis Minor
Coma Berenices
Corona Australis
Corona Borealis
Leo Minor
Piscis Austrinus
Triangulum Australe
Ursa Major
Ursa Minor

Energy and fuels

1 WORD

acetylene
anthracite
avgas
benzol
biofuel
biogas
briquette
butane
coal
coke
derv
diesel
firewood
gas
gasoline
heat
hydrogen
kerosene
light
lignite
methane
oil
paraffin
peat
petrol
petroleum
propane
turf
wood

2 WORDS

atomic power
bio-diesel
Calor gas
chemical energy
coal gas
electrical power
electromagnetic energy
fossil fuel
fuel oil
fusion energy
geothermal energy
hydroelectric power
leaded petrol
natural gas
nuclear power
renewable energy
solar energy
steam power
tidal power
unleaded petrol
water power
wave power
wind power

Engines

1 WORD

dynamo
generator
inboard
magneto
outboard
ramjet
scramjet
thruster
turbine
turbofan
turbojet
turboprop
turboshaft

2 WORDS

aero engine
beam engine
diesel engine
donkey engine
electric motor
four-stroke
gas turbine
heat engine
jet engine
linear motor
oil engine
petrol engine
piston engine
prop jet
pulse jet
radial engine
rocket engine
rotary engine
steam engine
steam turbine
turbo diesel
two-stroke

3 WORDS

external-combustion engine
flat-four engine
internal-combustion engine
twin-cam engine

Factories and workshops

1 WORD

3 LETTERS

fab

4 LETTERS

mill
mint
shop

5 LETTERS

forge
hydro

6 LETTERS

bakery
smithy
studio
winery

7 LETTERS

armoury
atelier
bindery
brewery
cannery
foundry
pottery
saltern
sawmill
tannery

8 LETTERS

bloomery
boatyard
creamery
gasworks
printery
refinery
shipyard
smithery
windmill

9 LETTERS

bakehouse
brewhouse
brickyard
gristmill
ironworks
malthouse
sweatshop

10 LETTERS

brickworks
distillery
printworks
steelworks

11 LETTERS

maquiladora
workstation

12 LETTERS

microbrewery

2 WORDS

assembly line
assembly shop
body shop
fitting shop
oil mill
paint shop
paper mill
pattern room
power station
printing works
private press
rolling mill
sail loft
salt works
sewage farm
shop floor
stamp mill
strip mill

Galaxies

2 WORDS

Andromeda Galaxy
Cartwheel Galaxy
Helix Galaxy
Magellanic Cloud
Pinwheel Galaxy
Sombrero Galaxy
Spindle Galaxy
Sunflower Galaxy
Triangulum Galaxy
Whirlpool Galaxy

3 WORDS

Black-eye Galaxy
Large Magellanic Cloud
Milky Way Galaxy
Small Magellanic Cloud

Gases

1 WORD

3 LETTERS

CFC

4 LETTERS

neon

5 LETTERS

argon
halon
ozone
radon
sarin
steam
xenon

6 LETTERS

arsine
biogas
butane
ethane
helium
ketene
oxygen
silane

7 LETTERS

ammonia
krypton
methane
propane

8 LETTERS

chlorine
cyanogen
ethylene
fluorine
hydrogen
lewisite
nitrogen
phosgene

9 LETTERS

acetylene
afterdamp
phosphine
propylene

12 LETTERS

formaldehyde

2 WORDS

blister gas
Calor gas
carbon dioxide
carbon monoxide
coal gas
CS gas
greenhouse gas
laughing gas
marsh gas
mustard gas
natural gas
nerve gas
nitrogen dioxide
nitrous oxide

oil gas
producer gas
sulphur dioxide
tear gas
town gas
water gas

Gems

1 WORD

4 LETTERS

jade
onyx
opal
ruby

5 LETTERS

agate
amber
beryl
pearl
topaz

6 LETTERS

garnet
jasper
pyrope
zircon

7 LETTERS

citrine
diamond
emerald
girasol
jacinth

8 LETTERS

amethyst
sapphire
sardonyx
sunstone

9 LETTERS

almandine
cairngorm
carbuncle
carnelian
cornelian
marcasite
moonstone
turquoise

10 LETTERS

aquamarine
bloodstone
chalcedony
chrysolite
greenstone
tourmaline

11 LETTERS

alexandrite
chrysoprase

2 WORDS

balas ruby
cat's-eye
fire opal
lapis lazuli
moss agate
smoky quartz

Geological ages

Archaean period
Azoic period
Cambrian period
Carboniferous period
Cenozoic era
Cretaceous period
Devonian period
Eocene epoch
Holocene epoch
Jurassic period
Mesozoic era
Miocene epoch
Oligocene epoch
Ordovician period
Palaeocene epoch
Palaeozoic era
Permian period
Phanerozoic aeon
Pleistocene epoch
Pliocene epoch
Precambrian era
Proterozoic aeon
Quaternary period
Silurian period
Tertiary period
Triassic period

Geometric shapes

1 WORD

4 LETTERS

kite

5 LETTERS

ovoid

6 LETTERS

circle
oblong
square

7 LETTERS

annulus
decagon
diamond
ellipse
hexagon
lozenge
nonagon
octagon
polygon
rhombus

8 LETTERS

heptagon
pentagon
quadrant
rhomboid
tetragon
triangle

9 LETTERS

dodecagon
pentagram
pentangle
rectangle
trapezium
trapezoid
undecagon

10 LETTERS

hendecagon
quadrangle
semicircle

13 LETTERS

parallelogram
quadrilateral

2 WORDS

equilateral triangle
isosceles triangle
scalene triangle

Laboratory equipment

1 WORD

alembic
aspirator
autoclave
balance
beaker
burette
centrifuge
condenser
crucible
flask
funnel
microscope
pipette
precipitator
retort
slide
spatula
thermometer
tripod

2 WORDS

bell jar
Bunsen burner
capillary tube
conical flask
evaporating dish
filter funnel
gas jar
graduated flask
measuring cylinder
Petri dish
sand bath
test tube
U-tube
watch glass

3 WORDS

pestle and mortar

Lamps and lights

1 WORD

anglepoise
candle
chandelier
downlighter
flambeau
flare
flashgun
flashlight
floodlight
footlight
gaslight
headlamp
headlight
indicator
klieg
lamp
lantern
light
luminaire
pendant
penlight
safelight
searchlight
sidelight
spotlight
strobe
stroboscope
sunlamp
torch
uplighter

2 WORDS

Aldis lamp
arc lamp
brake light
Chinese lantern
courtesy light
Davy lamp
desk lamp
fairy lights
flash lamp
floor lamp
fluorescent light
fog lamp
halogen light
hazard lights
hurricane lamp
lava lamp
navigation lights
neon light
night light
oil lamp
pilot light
reversing light
running lights
safety lamp
spirit lamp
standard lamp
stop light
storm lantern
street light
strip light
table lamp
tail light
tilley lamp
track lighting
traffic lights
Very light

3 WORDS

jack-o'-lantern
sodium-vapour lamp

Mathematical terms

1 WORD

3 LETTERS

set
sum

4 LETTERS

base
cube
mean
mode
node
plot
rank
ring
root
sine
surd

5 LETTERS

array
chain
digit
field
group
limit
locus
power
proof
ratio
unity

6 LETTERS

cosine
factor
googol

matrix
median
origin
random
sample
scalar
secant
series
square
subset
tensor
vector

7 LETTERS

abelian
algebra
average
divisor
formula
fractal
geodesy
integer
inverse
modulus
product
scatter
stratum
tangent
unknown

8 LETTERS

abscissa
addition
analysis
binomial
calculus
cosecant
dividend
division
equation
exponent
fraction
function
geometry
gradient
identity
multiple
operator
quotient
rotation
solution
subgroup
topology
variable

9 LETTERS

algorithm
asymptote
conjugate
cotangent
expansion
factorial
integrand
intercept
iteration
logarithm
mechanics
numerator
parameter
recursion
remainder
transform
trinomial

10 LETTERS

arithmetic
covariance
derivative
difference
eigenvalue
googolplex
inequality
multiplier
polynomial
quaternion
reciprocal
statistics

11 LETTERS

coefficient
denominator
determinant
eigenvector
integration
permutation
subtraction

12 LETTERS

multiplicand
substitution
trigonometry

13 LETTERS

antilogarithm
combinatorics
eigenfunction
extrapolation
interpolation

2 WORDS

applied mathematics
arithmetic mean
arithmetic progression
bell curve
binomial theorem
Boolean algebra
cardinal number
Cartesian coordinates
catastrophe theory
chaos theory
common denominator
complex number
cube root
decimal point
differential calculus
differential equation
Euclidean geometry
exponential function
Fibonacci numbers
Fibonacci series
Fourier series
fuzzy set
game theory
geometric mean
geometric progression
imaginary number
infinitesimal calculus
integral calculus
irrational number
Klein bottle

linear equation
long division
magic square
Mandelbrot set
Möbius strip
natural logarithm
natural numbers
numerical analysis
ordinal number
Pascal's triangle
perfect number
perfect square
polar coordinates
prime number
probability theory
proper fraction
pure mathematics
Pythagoras' theorem
rational number
real number
recurring decimal
set theory
significant figure
simultaneous equations
square number
square root
transfinite number
Venn diagram
vulgar fraction
whole number

3 WORDS

Fermat's last theorem
highest common factor
lowest common denominator
lowest common multiple

Measurement, types of

8 LETTERS

oximetry

9 LETTERS

altimetry
barometry
dosimetry
optometry
perimetry
pyrometry

10 LETTERS

acidimetry
anemometry
astrometry
audiometry
bathymetry
eudiometry
goniometry
gravimetry
hydrometry
hygrometry
micrometry
photometry
planimetry
radiometry
spirometry
viscometry

11 LETTERS

calorimetry
chronometry
colorimetry
craniometry
fluorometry
morphometry
polarimetry
stereometry
thermometry
velocimetry

12 LETTERS

densitometry
magnetometry
olfactometry
psychrometry
spectrometry
turbidimetry

13 LETTERS

anthropometry
potentiometry
refractometry
stoichiometry

Metals

1 WORD

3 LETTERS

tin

4 LETTERS

gold
iron
lead
zinc

5 LETTERS

alloy

6 LETTERS

barium
cobalt
copper
nickel
silver
sodium

7 LETTERS

amalgam
bismuth
cadmium
calcium
lithium
mercury
niobium
thorium
uranium
wolfram

8 LETTERS

actinide
antimony
chromium
platinum
tantalum
thallium
titanium
tungsten
vanadium

9 LETTERS

aluminium
beryllium
magnesium
manganese
potassium
strontium
zirconium

10 LETTERS

lanthanide
molybdenum

2 WORDS

alkali metal
alkaline earth
base metal
heavy metal
noble metal
precious metal
rare earth
transition metal

Minerals

1 WORD

4 LETTERS

mica
onyx
opal
talc

5 LETTERS

agate
beryl
borax
emery
topaz

6 LETTERS

baryte
galena
garnet
gypsum
jasper
natron
quartz
spinel
zircon

7 LETTERS

calcite
diamond
jacinth
jadeite
olivine
peridot
pyrites
zeolite

8 LETTERS

asbestos
chromite
cinnabar
corundum
cryolite
dolomite

feldspar
fluorite
graphite
nephrite
orpiment
steatite

9 LETTERS

alabaster
cairngorm
fluorspar
haematite
magnetite
malachite
manganite
marcasite
muscovite

10 LETTERS

bloodstone
chalcedony
hornblende
serpentine
tourmaline

11 LETTERS

pitchblende
vermiculite

2 WORDS

Blue John
fool's gold
rock salt
smoky quartz

Planets (in order from the sun)

Mercury
Venus
Earth
Mars
Jupiter
Saturn
Uranus
Neptune
Pluto

Rocks

1 WORD

3 LETTERS

rag

4 LETTERS

coal
lava
marl
tuff

5 LETTERS

chalk
chert
flint
shale
slate

6 LETTERS

basalt
gabbro
gneiss
marble
oolite
pumice
schist

7 LETTERS

breccia
cipolin
diorite
granite

8 LETTERS

dolerite
dolomite
hornfels
mudstone
obsidian
porphyry
rhyolite

9 LETTERS

ironstone
limestone
pegmatite
quartzite
sandstone

10 LETTERS

greenstone
peridotite

11 LETTERS

phosphorite

12 LETTERS

conglomerate

2 WORDS

lapis lazuli
mica schist
oil shale

Star types

1 WORD

cepheid
collapsar
giant
lodestar
nova
polar
pulsar
quasar
supergiant
supernova

2 WORDS

brown dwarf
dark star
double star
dwarf star
eclipsing binary
flare star
neutron star
polar star
red dwarf
red giant
white dwarf

Subatomic particles

1 WORD

antiparticle
antiproton
antiquark
axion
baryon
boson
electron
fermion
gluon
hadron
hyperon
kaon
lepton
meson
muon
neutrino
neutron
nucleon
photon
pion
positron
proton
quark
WIMP

2 WORDS

Higgs boson
Higgs particle
lambda particle
tau particle

Ten brightest stars, with constellations

Sirius (Canis Major)
Canopus (Carina)
Alpha Centauri (Centaurus)
Arcturus (Boötes)
Vega (Lyra)
Capella (Auriga)
Rigel (Orion)
Procyon (Canis Minor)
Achernar (Eridanus)
Betelgeuse (Orion)

Tools

1 WORD

3 LETTERS

awl
axe
hob
hoe
ram
saw

4 LETTERS

adze
burr
file
fork
froe
hack
jack
pick
rake
rasp
rule
vice

5 LETTERS

auger
bevel
borer
brace
burin
clamp
cramp
drill
flail
float
jemmy
knife
lathe
lever
plane
punch
shave
spade
swage
wedge

6 LETTERS

beetle
bodkin
bowsaw
chisel
cutter
dibber
dibble
former
fuller
gimlet
graver
hammer
jigsaw
mallet
nailer
needle
padsaw
pestle
plexor
pliers
priest
reamer
riddle
ripsaw
roller
router
sander
scribe
scythe
shears
shovel
sickle
square
trowel
wrench

7 LETTERS

bandsaw
bradawl
chopper
cleaver
crowbar
fretsaw
grinder
grouter
hacksaw
hatchet
jointer
loppers
mattock
nippers
pickaxe
pincers
riffler
scraper
slasher
spanner
swingle
trimmer
whipsaw

8 LETTERS

billhook
blowlamp
chainsaw
diestock
roulette
sawbench
strickle
tinsnips
tweezers

9 LETTERS

blowtorch
burnisher
lawnmower
pitchfork
sandpaper
scarifier
secateurs

10 LETTERS

cultivator
dovetailer
jackhammer

perforator
spokeshave
woodcarver

11 LETTERS

marlinspike
screwdriver

12 LETTERS

sledgehammer

2 WORDS

air gun
Allen key
capstan lathe
centre bit
centre punch
circular saw
claw hammer
compass saw
coping saw
cross peen
edge tool
edging shears
edging tool
frame saw
glass cutter
hammer drill
hedge clipper
hole saw
keyhole saw
mortar board
nail punch
paint gun
panel saw
peen hammer
pein hammer
pruning hook
screw tap
scroll saw
snarling iron
socket wrench
soldering iron
staple gun
steam hammer
tenon saw
tilt hammer
torque wrench
trip hammer
wheel brace
wire cutter
wire stripper

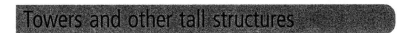

Towers and other tall structures

1 WORD

barbican
bastion
belfry
belvedere
broch
campanile
column
donjon
keep
lighthouse
mast
minaret
mirador
nuragh
pagoda
peel
pele
pylon
pyramid
silo
skyscraper
spire
steeple
turret
watchtower
ziggurat

2 WORDS

bell tower
church tower
clock tower
control tower
cooling tower
gate tower
Martello tower
shot tower
tower block
water tower

Units of measurement

1 WORD

2 LETTERS

cl
cm
ft
in.
kg
km
lb
mg
ml
mm
oz
pt
yd

3 LETTERS

age
bar
bel
bit
cup
day
ell
erg
gal
lux
mil
ohm
rad
rem
rod
tog
ton

4 LETTERS

acre
bale
baud
byte
cord
dyne
foot
gill
gram
gray
hand
hour
inch
knot
line
link
mile
mole
peck
pica
pint
pipe
pole
rood
span
volt
watt
week
yard
year

5 LETTERS

cable
carat
chain
cubit
curie
cycle
epoch
farad
gauss
grain
henry
hertz
joule
litre
lumen
metre
minim
month
ounce
perch
point
poise
pound
quart
stone
tesla
therm
tonne
weber

6 LETTERS

ampere
barrel
bushel
cupful
decade
degree
denier
drachm
fathom
firkin
gallon
kelvin
league
micron
minute
newton
noggin
parsec
pascal
period
radian
second
square

7 LETTERS

calorie
candela
century
coulomb
decibel
dioptre
furlong

gigabit
hectare
kiloton
maxwell
megaton
quarter
quintal
scruple
siemens
sievert

8 LETTERS

angstrom
gigabyte
gigaflop
gigawatt
hogshead
kilobyte
kilogram
kilovolt
kilowatt
megabyte
megaflop
megavolt
megawatt
millibar
roentgen
teaspoon
terabyte
teraflop

9 LETTERS

becquerel
centigram
decalitre
decametre
decilitre
decimetre
gigahertz
kilohertz
kilojoule
kilolitre
kilometre
megahertz
microgram
milligram
nanometre
steradian

10 LETTERS

atmosphere
centilitre
centimetre
horsepower
microlitre
micrometre
millennium
millilitre
millimetre
nanosecond
tablespoon

11 LETTERS

kilocalorie
microsecond
millisecond
pennyweight

12 LETTERS

dessertspoon
electronvolt

13 LETTERS

hundredweight

2 WORDS

air mile
astronomical unit
brake horsepower
fluid drachm
fluid ounce
kilowatt-hour
light year
Mach number
metric ton
nautical mile
quantum bit
troy ounce

3 WORDS

atomic mass unit
British thermal unit

Weather terms

1 WORD

3 LETTERS

fog
ice
low
sun

4 LETTERS

föhn
gale
hail
high
mist
rain
smog
snow
wind

5 LETTERS

cloud
front
frost
ridge
sleet
wrack

6 LETTERS

cirrus
ghibli
haboob
isobar
nimbus
shower
simoom
squall
trough

7 LETTERS

chinook
climate
cumulus
cyclone
drizzle
drought
khamsin
meltemi
mistral
monsoon
rainbow
sirocco
stratus
thermal
thunder
tornado
typhoon

8 LETTERS

blizzard
easterly
heatwave
isotherm
raindrop
rainfall
snowfall
westerly
williwaw

9 LETTERS

hailstone
harmattan
hurricane
lightning
northerly
occlusion
rainstorm
snowstorm
southerly
whirlwind

10 LETTERS

depression
tramontana
turbulence

11 LETTERS

altocumulus
altostratus
anticyclone
meteorology
thunderbolt
thunderclap
thunderhead

12 LETTERS

cirrocumulus
cirrostratus
cumulonimbus
nimbostratus
stratocirrus
thundercloud
thunderstorm

13 LETTERS

cumulostratus
precipitation
stratocumulus

2 WORDS

air frost
anvil cloud
Beaufort scale
cold front
deep depression
El Niño
forked lightning
frontal system
funnel cloud
global warming
greenhouse effect
ground frost
high pressure
hoar frost
Indian summer
jet stream
low pressure
mackerel sky
mare's tails
noctilucent cloud
occluded front
pressure system
prevailing wind
rain cloud
sea breeze
shallow depression
sheet lightning
storm cloud
temperature inversion
trade wind
warm front
warm sector
white-out

Sports and games

American baseball teams

1 WORD

Angels (Anaheim)
Astros (Houston)
Athletics (Oaklands)
Braves (Atlanta)
Brewers (Milwaukee)
Cardinals (St Louis)
Cubs (Chicago)
Diamondbacks (Arizona)
Dodgers (Los Angeles)
Expos (Montreal)
Giants (San Francisco)
Indians (Cleveland)
Mariners (Seattle)
Marlins (Florida)
Mets (New York)
Orioles (Baltimore)
Padres (San Diego)
Phillies (Philadelphia)
Pirates (Pittsburgh)
Rangers (Texas)
Reds (Cincinnati)
Rockies (Colorado)
Royals (Kansas City)
Tigers (Detroit)
Twins (Minnesota)
Yankees (New York)

2 WORDS

Blue Jays (Toronto)
Devil Rays (Tampa Bay)
Red Sox (Boston)
White Sox (Chicago)

American Football teams

1 WORD

Bears (Chicago)
Bengals (Cincinnati)
Broncos (Denver)
Browns (Cleveland)
Buccaneers (Tampa Bay)
Cardinals (Arizona)
Chargers (San Diego)
Chiefs (Kansas City)
Colts (Indianapolis)
Cowboys (Dallas)
Dolphins (Miami)
Eagles (Philadelphia)
Falcons (Atlanta)
Giants (New York)
Jaguars (Jacksonville)
Jets (New York)
Lions (Detroit)
Packers (Green Bay)
Panthers (Carolina)
Patriots (New England)
Raiders (Oakland)
Rams (St Louis)

Ravens (Baltimore)
Redskins (Washington)
Saints (New Orleans)
Seahawks (Seattle)
Steelers (Pittsburgh)
Titans (Tennessee)
Vikings (Minnesota)

2 WORDS

Buffalo Bills (Buffalo)

Athletics events

1 WORD

biathlon
decathlon
discus
hammer
heptathlon
hurdles
javelin
marathon
mile
pentathlon
race
sprint
steeplechase
tetrathlon
triathlon
walking

2 WORDS

cross-country
field event
half-marathon
high jump
long jump
pole vault
relay race
shot-put
track event
triple jump

3 WORDS

cross-country running
long-distance race
middle-distance race
tug of war

Ball games

1 WORD

4 LETTERS

golf
polo
pool

5 LETTERS

boule
bowls
fives
rugby

6 LETTERS

boules
hockey
shinty
soccer
squash
tennis

7 LETTERS

bowling
cricket
croquet
hurling
netball
rackets
snooker

8 LETTERS

baseball
football
handball
lacrosse
ninepins
pétanque
rounders
skittles
softball

9 LETTERS

billiards

10 LETTERS

basketball
volleyball

2 WORDS

American Football
Association Football
beach volleyball
Eton fives
French cricket
Gaelic football
lawn tennis
mini rugby
real tennis
rugby league
rugby union
table tennis
tenpin bowling
water polo

3 WORDS

Australian Rules football
crown-green bowls

4 WORDS

five-a-side football

Boxing weight divisions

1 WORD

bantamweight
cruiserweight
featherweight
flyweight
heavyweight
lightweight
middleweight
welterweight

2 WORDS

junior lightweight
junior middleweight
junior welterweight
light flyweight
light heavyweight
light middleweight
light welterweight

Card games

1 WORD

baccarat
bezique
blackjack
Boston
brag
bridge
canasta
cheat
cribbage
écarté
euchre
faro
loo
monte
nap
Newmarket
ombre
patience
pinochle
piquet
poker
pontoon
rummy
skat
snap
solitaire
whist

2 WORDS

Black Maria
duplicate bridge
fan-tan
gin rummy
happy families
old maid
solo whist
strip poker
stud poker
twenty-one

3 WORDS

beggar-my-neighbour
chemin de fer
vingt-et-un

Cricket roles and positions

1 WORD

bat
batsman
batswoman
bowler
cover
fielder
fieldsman
gully
keeper
midwicket
nightwatchman
opener
paceman
point
runner
seamer
slip
spinner
striker
wicketkeeper

2 WORDS

all-rounder
cover point
deep midwicket
extra cover
last man
leg slip
leg-spinner
long leg
long off
long on
mid-off
off spinner
opening batsman
pace bowler
seam bowler
short leg
short midwicket
silly point
spin bowler
square leg
tail-ender
third man
twelfth man

3 WORDS

silly mid-off
silly mid-on

English and Welsh football clubs

1 WORD

3 LETTERS

QPR

4 LETTERS

Bury

6 LETTERS

Barnet
Bolton
Fulham

7 LETTERS

Arsenal
Burnley
Chelsea
Everton
Norwich
Preston
Reading
Walsall
Watford
Wrexham

8 LETTERS

Barnsley
Charlton
Millwall
Rochdale

9 LETTERS

Blackpool
Brentford
Doncaster
Liverpool
Stockport
Tottenham

10 LETTERS

Darlington
Gillingham
Portsmouth
Sunderland

11 LETTERS

Bournemouth
Southampton

12 LETTERS

Chesterfield

13 LETTERS

Middlesbrough

2 WORDS

Aston Villa
Birmingham City
Blackburn Rovers
Bolton Wanderers
Boston United
Bradford City
Bristol City
Bristol Rovers
Cardiff City
Carlisle United
Charlton Athletic
Cheltenham Town
Chester City
Colchester United
Coventry City
Crewe Alexandra
Crystal Palace
Derby County
Doncaster Rovers
Grimsby Town
Hartlepool United
Huddersfield Town
Hull City
Ipswich Town
Leeds United
Leicester City
Leyton Orient
Lincoln City
Luton Town
Macclesfield Town
Manchester City
Manchester United
Mansfield Town
MK Dons
Newcastle United
Northampton Town
Norwich City
Nottingham Forest
Oldham Athletic
Oxford United
Peterborough United
Plymouth Argyle
Port Vale
Rotherham United
Scunthorpe United
Sheffield United
Sheffield Wednesday
Southend United
Stockport County
Stoke City
Swansea City
Swindon Town
Torquay United
Tottenham Hotspur
Tranmere Rovers
West Brom
West Ham
Wigan Athletic
Wolverhampton Wanderers
Wycombe Wanderers
Yeovil Town

3 WORDS

Milton Keynes Dons
Preston North End
Queen's Park Rangers
Rushden & Diamonds
West Bromwich Albion
West Ham United

4 WORDS

Brighton and Hove Albion

European football clubs

1 WORD

Ajax (Netherlands)
Anderlecht (Belgium)
Barcelona (Spain)
Benfica (Portugal)
Besiktas (Turkey)
Boavista (Portugal)
Fiorentina (Italy)
Galatasaray (Turkey)
Juventus (Italy)
Lazio (Italy)
Lille (France)
Monaco (France)
Olympiakos (Greece)
Panathinaikos (Greece)

Roma (Italy)
Sampdoria (Italy)
Sevilla (Spain)

2 WORDS

AC Milan (Italy)
AEK Athens (Greece)
AJ Auxerre (France)
Athletic Bilbao (Spain)
Atletico Madrid (Spain)
Austria Vienna (Austria)
Bayer Leverkusen (Germany)
Bayern Munich (Germany)
Borussia Dortmund (Germany)
Dinamo Kiev (Ukraine)
Dinamo Moscow (Russia)
Dinamo Tbilisi (Georgia)
Dinamo Zagreb (Croatia)
FC Porto (Portugal)
Feyenoord Rotterdam (Netherlands)
FK Partizan (Union of Serbia and Montenegro)
Hertha Berlin (Germany)
Inter Milan (Italy)
PSV Eindhoven (Netherlands)
Racing Santander (Spain)
Rapid Vienna (Austria)
RCD Espanyol (Spain)
Real Betis (Spain)
Real Madrid (Spain)
Real Sociedad (Spain)
Real Zaragoza (Spain)
Spartak Moscow (Russia)
Sparta Prague (Czech Republic)
Sporting Lisbon (Portugal)
Standard Liege (Belgium)
St Etienne (France)
VfB Stuttgart (Germany)
Werder Bremen (Germany)

3 WORDS

Deportivo La Coruna (Spain)
FC Schalke 04 (Germany)
Olympique de Marseille (France)
Paris St Germain (France)

Fencing terms

1 WORD

3 LETTERS

cut

4 LETTERS

épée
foil
mask
pass

5 LETTERS

blade
botte
feint
forte
guard
lunge
parry
prime
quart
sabre
sixte
volte

6 LETTERS

disarm
engage
foible
octave
quinte
rapier
remise
salute
tierce
touché

7 LETTERS

riposte
seconde
septime

8 LETTERS

plastron

9 LETTERS

disengage

2 WORDS

en garde
single stick

3 WORDS

tac-au-tac

Football roles and positions

1 WORD

attacker
clogger
finisher
goalhanger
goalie
goalkeeper
halfback
keeper
libero
marker
midfield
midfielder
stopper
striker
sweeper
winger
wingman

2 WORDS

centre back
centre forward
centre half
left back
left wing
left-winger
right back
right wing
right-winger
target man
wing back
wing forward

Games

1 WORD

2 LETTERS

go

3 LETTERS

nim
tag
tig

4 LETTERS

dice
ludo
pool

5 LETTERS

bingo
cards
catch
chess
craps
darts
halma
jacks
lotto

6 LETTERS

Cluedo
hoopla
quoits

7 LETTERS

chicken
conkers
frisbee
hangman
kabaddi
marbles
pinball
snooker

8 LETTERS

charades
checkers
dominoes
draughts
forfeits
leapfrog
Monopoly
peekaboo
roulette
sardines
Scrabble
Subbuteo

9 LETTERS

bagatelle
billiards
hopscotch
paintball
solitaire

10 LETTERS

backgammon
fivestones
jackstraws
kriegspiel
Poohsticks
spillikins
thimblerig

11 LETTERS

battleships
shovelboard
tiddlywinks

12 LETTERS

consequences

2 WORDS

Aunt Sally
bar billiards
cat's cradle
Chinese chequers
Chinese whispers
computer game
deck quoits
fantasy football
housey-housey
I spy
mah-jong
mah-jongg
musical bumps
musical chairs
Pac-Man
poker dice
postman's knock
prisoner's base
shove-halfpenny
Simon Says
table football
team game
treasure hunt
Trivial Pursuit
word game

3 WORDS

blind man's buff
cops and robbers
ducks and drakes
dungeons and dragons
follow-my-leader
hide-and-seek
hunt the thimble
noughts and crosses
pass the parcel
pat-a-cake
pitch-and-toss
snakes and ladders
spin the bottle
tic-tac-toe
tug of war

4 WORDS

King of the Castle
murder in the dark
piggy in the middle

5 WORDS

ring-a-ring o' roses

Golfing terms

1 WORD

3 LETTERS

ace
bye
cup
cut
dub
lie
par
pin
tee
toe

4 LETTERS

chip
club
duff
fade
fore
heel
hole
hook
iron
loft
putt
sink

sole
trap
wood

5 LETTERS

bogey
carry
divot
dormy
drive
eagle
green
hosel
links
pitch
rough
round
shank
slice
wedge

6 LETTERS

birdie
borrow
bunker
caddie
driver
hazard
honour
jigger
lofter
mashie
putter
stroke
waggle

7 LETTERS

brassie
fairway
gallery
midiron
niblick
scratch

8 LETTERS

foursome
handicap
mulligan
takeaway

9 LETTERS

albatross
backswing
downswing

10 LETTERS

forecaddie
Stableford

2 WORDS

approach shot
best ball
casual water
dog-leg
double bogey
double eagle
driving iron
driving range
follow-through
leader board
match play
nineteenth hole
pick up
putting green
recovery shot
run-up
sand iron
sand wedge
stroke play

3 WORDS

hole-in-one
pitch and putt

Gymnastic events

artistic gymnastics
asymmetric bars
beam
floor exercises
high bar
parallel bars
pommel horse
rhythmic gymnastics
rings
sports aerobics
uneven bars
vault

Martial arts and combat sports

1 WORD

aikido
boxing
budo
capoeira
fencing
hapkido
jousting
judo
kalaripayattu
karate
kendo
Shotokan
Silat
sumo
wrestling
wushu

2 WORDS

ba gua
ju-jitsu
kick-boxing
Krav Maga
kung fu
pa kua
sumo wrestling
Thai boxing
ultimate fighting
wing chun

3 WORDS

jeet kune do
tae kwon do
t'ai chi chu'an
tang soo do

Motor sports

1 WORD

autocross
enduro
F1
Indy
Indycar
karting
motocross
rallycross
rallying
scrambling
speedway
trials

2 WORDS

cross-country
demolition derby
drag racing
Formula One
go-karting
Grand Prix
hill-climbing
motorcycle racing
off-roading
sidecar racing

3 WORDS

dirt-track racing
stock-car racing

Rugby roles and positions

1 WORD

attacker
backline
breakaway
centre
defender
flanker
forward
fullback
halfback
hooker
jumper
lock
midfield
prop
punter
wing
winger

2 WORDS

back row
dummy half
flank forward
fly half
front row
inside back
inside centre
loose forward
loose head
number eight
outside centre
place-kicker
scrum half
second row
stand-off
three-quarter
tight head
wing forward

3 WORDS

blind-side flanker
loose-head prop
open-side flanker
stand-off half
tight-head prop

Rugby union teams and clubs

All Blacks
Bath
Bristol
British and Irish Lions
Cardiff Blues
Gloucester
Harlequins
Leeds Tykes
Leicester Tigers
Leinster
Lions
Llanelli Scarlets
London Irish
London Welsh
Munster
Neath
Newcastle Falcons
Newport Gwent Dragons
Northampton Saints
Sale Sharks
Saracens
Springboks
Ulster
Wallabies
Wasps
Worcester Warriors

Scottish football clubs

1 WORD

Aberdeen
Arbroath
Celtic
Clyde
Cowdenbeath
Dumbarton
Dundee
Dunfermline
Falkirk
Gretna
Hearts
Hibernian
Kilmarnock
Livingston
Montrose
Morton
Motherwell
Partick
Peterhead
Rangers
Stenhousemuir
Stranraer

2 WORDS

Airdrie United
Albion Rovers
Alloa Athletic
Ayr United
Berwick Rangers
Brechin City
Dundee United
Dunfermline Athletic
East Fife
East Stirlingshire
Elgin City
Forfar Athletic
Glasgow Rangers
Greenock Morton
Hamilton Academical
Partick Thistle
Queen's Park
Raith Rovers
Ross County
Stirling Albion

St Johnstone
St Mirren

3 WORDS

Heart of Midlothian
Inverness Caledonian Thistle

4 WORDS

Queen of the South

Sporting activities

1 WORD

3 LETTERS

BMX

4 LETTERS

golf
luge
polo
pool

5 LETTERS

boule
bowls
darts
fives
skeet

6 LETTERS

boules
boxing
caving
diving
hiking
hockey
pelota
quoits
rowing
shinty
skiing
slalom
soccer
squash
tennis

7 LETTERS

angling
archery
bowling
cricket
croquet
curling
cycling
fencing
fishing
fowling
gliding
hunting
hurling
kabaddi
netball
rackets
rafting
sailing
snooker
surfing
walking

8 LETTERS

aerobics
baseball
beagling
canoeing
climbing
coursing
falconry
football
goalball
gymkhana
handball
kayaking
korfball
lacrosse
langlauf
ninepins
pétanque
rounders
sculling
shooting
skittles
softball
swimming
trotting
yachting

9 LETTERS

athletics
badminton
billiards
canyoning
potholing
skijoring
skydiving
sprinting
wrestling

10 LETTERS

aerobatics
ballooning

basketball
gymnastics
hydrospeed
spelunking
volleyball

11 LETTERS

aquaplaning
freestyling
kitesurfing
parachuting
paragliding
parapenting
parasailing
racquetball
showjumping
snorkelling
tobogganing
waterskiing
wildfowling
windsurfing

12 LETTERS

bobsleighing
bullfighting
kiteboarding
orienteering
parascending
snowboarding
wakeboarding

13 LETTERS

rollerblading
skateboarding
weightlifting

2 WORDS

American football
Association Football
base-jumping
beach volleyball
bungee jumping
caber tossing
Canadian football
clock golf
coarse fishing
cross-country
cycle racing
cyclo-cross
dinghy racing
downhill racing
Eton fives
field hockey
figure-skating
flat racing
fly-fishing
fox-hunting
free skating
French cricket
Gaelic football
game fishing
greyhound racing
hang-gliding
harness racing
heli-skiing
horse racing
ice dancing
ice hockey
ice skating
jai alai
jet-skiing
lawn tennis
match fishing
mountain biking
mountain climbing
pigeon racing
pistol shooting
powerboat racing
real tennis
rock climbing
roller skating
Rugby fives
rugby league
rugby union
scuba-diving
sea fishing
ski jumping
skin-diving
speed skating
synchronized swimming
table tennis
tenpin bowling
trap shooting
water polo

3 WORDS

Australian Rules football
clay-pigeon shooting
cross-country running
crown-green bowls
deep-sea diving
flat-green bowls
point-to-point
three-day eventing
white-water rafting
wild-water racing

4 WORDS

five-a-side football

Swimming strokes, kicks, and dives

1 WORD

backcrawl
backstroke
breaststroke
butterfly
crawl
jackknife
sidestroke
trudgen

2 WORDS

Australian crawl
doggy-paddle
frog kick
front crawl
overarm stroke
recovery stroke
scissors kick
swallow dive
swan dive

Tennis strokes

1 WORD

ace
backhand
dink
drive
forehand
groundstroke
lob
overhead
serve
slice
smash
volley

2 WORDS

cross-court
drop shot
half-volley
passing shot
stop volley

Toys

1 WORD

3 LETTERS

bat
top

4 LETTERS

ally
ball
bear
doll
hoop
jack
kite

5 LETTERS

agate
alley
brick
teddy

6 LETTERS

jigsaw
marble
pegtop
popgun
puppet
puzzle
rattle

7 LETTERS

balloon
beanbag
diabolo
dreidel
frisbee
scooter
tangram

8 LETTERS

catapult
golliwog
teetotum
windmill

9 LETTERS

playhouse
plaything
snowstorm
whirligig

10 LETTERS

marionette

12 LETTERS

kaleidoscope

2 WORDS

action figure
board game
box kite
building block
cuddly toy
doll's house
glove puppet
hobby horse
hula hoop
humming top
jumping bean
jumping jack
model railway
party popper
pea-shooter
pedal car
pogo stick
rag doll
rocking horse
Russian doll
see-saw
skipping rope
spinning top
teddy bear
tin soldier
water gun
water pistol
Wendy house
whipping top
yo-yo

4 WORDS

jack-in-the-box

UK football club nicknames

1 WORD

4 LETTERS

Boro (Middlesborough)
Dons (Milton Keynes Dons; Aberdeen)
Gers (Rangers)
Hibs (Hibernian)
Owls (Sheffield Wednesday)
Pars (Dunfermline Athletic)
Posh (Peterborough United)
Rams (Derby County)
Reds (Liverpool, Nottingham Forest)

5 LETTERS

Blues (Chelsea, Birmingham City, Ipswich Town)
Foxes (Leicester City)
Gills (Gillingham)
Lions (Milwall)
Spurs (Tottenham Hotspur)

6 LETTERS

Blades (Sheffield United)
Eagles (Crystal Palace)
Hearts (Heart of Midlothian)
Killie (Kilmarnock)
Latics (Wigan Athletic)
Pompey (Portsmouth)
Robins (Swindon Town)
Rovers (Blackburn)
Royals (Reading)
Saints (Southampton)
Wolves (Wolverhampton Wanderers)

7 LETTERS

Addicks (Charlton Athletic)
Baggies (West Bromwich Albion)
Bantams (Bradford City)
Clarets (Burnley)
Gunners (Arsenal)
Hammers (West Ham)
Hatters (Luton Town)
Hornets (Watford)
Magpies (Newcastle United)
Millers (Rotherham United)
Potters (Stoke City)
Toffees (Everton)

8 LETTERS

Canaries (Norwich City)
Pilgrims (Plymouth Argyle)
Seagulls (Brighton)
Terriers (Huddersfield Town)
Trotters (Bolton Wanderers)
Villains (Aston Villa)

9 LETTERS

Bluebirds (Cardiff City)
Cottagers (Fulham)
Throstles (West Bromwich Albion)

10 LETTERS

Biscuitmen (Reading)
Lilywhites (Preston North End)
Railwaymen (Crewe Alexandra)

2 WORDS

Black Cats (Sunderland)
Caley Thistle (Inverness Caledonian Thistle)
Dark Blues (Dundee)
Red Devils (Manchester United)
Sky Blues (Coventry City)
Tractor Boys (Ipswich Town)

UK sporting venues

1 WORD

Aintree (horse racing; England)
Anfield (football; Liverpool)
Ascot (horse racing; England)
Belfry (golf; England)
Crucible (snooker; England)
Edgbaston (cricket; Warwickshire)
Gateshead (athletics; rugby league)
Hawthorns (football; West Bromwich Albion)
Headingly (cricket; Yorkshire)
Highbury (football; Arsenal)
Hillsborough (football; Sheffield Wednesday)
Ibrox (football; Rangers)
Lord's (cricket; Middlesex)
Meadowbank (athletics and other sports; Scotland)
Molineux (football; Wolverhampton Wanderers)
Muirfield (golf; Scotland)
Murrayfield (rugby union; Scotland)
Newmarket (horse racing; England)
Oval (cricket; Surrey)
Pittodrie (football; Aberdeen)
Riverside (football; Middlesbrough)
Silverstone (motor racing; England)
Twickenham (rugby union; England)
Valley (football; Charlton Athletic)
Wembley (football and athletics; England)
Wentworth (golf; England)
Wimbledon (tennis; England)

2 WORDS

Boleyn Ground (football; West Ham United)
Bramall Lane (football; Sheffield United)
Brand's Hatch (motor racing; England)
Carrow Road (football; Norwich City)
Celtic Park (football; Celtic)
Craven Cottage (football; Fulham)
Crystal Palace (athletics and other sports; England)
Don Valley (athletics; England)
Easter Road (football; Hibernian)
Elland Road (football; Leeds United)
Epsom Downs (horse racing; England)
Ewood Park (football; Blackburn Rovers)
Fratton Park (football; Portsmouth)
Goodison Park (football; Everton)
Hampden Park (football; Queen's Park)
JJB Stadium (football; Wigan Athletic)
Kenilworth Road (football; Luton Town)
Loftus Road (football; Queens Park Rangers)
Maine Road (football; Manchester City)
Millennium Stadium (rugby union and football; Wales)
Ninian Park (football; Cardiff City)
Old Trafford (cricket; Lancashire)
Old Trafford (football; Manchester United)
Portman Road (football; Ipswich Town)
Pride Park (football; Derby County)
Reebok Stadium (football; Bolton Wanderers)

Royal Birkdale (golf; England)
Stamford Bridge (football; Chelsea)
St Andrews (football; Birmingham City)
Trent Bridge (cricket; Nottinghamshire)
Upton Park (football; West Ham United)
Vicarage Road (football; Watford)
Villa Park (football; Aston Villa)
Walkers Stadium (football; Leicester City)

3 WORDS

Stadium of Light (football; Sunderland)
St Andrews Links (golf; Scotland)
St James' Park (football; Newcastle United)
White Hart Lane (football; Tottenham Hotspur)

5 WORDS

Royal Lytham and St Annes (golf; Lancashire)

Transport and trade

Aircraft, types of

1 WORD

3 LETTERS

jet
tug

5 LETTERS

blimp
drone
jumbo

6 LETTERS

bomber
glider
tanker

7 LETTERS

airship
balloon
biplane
chopper
fighter
gunship
spotter

8 LETTERS

aerostat
airliner
autogiro
jetliner
seaplane
towplane
triplane
turbofan
turbojet
warplane
widebody
Zeppelin

9 LETTERS

dirigible
freighter
gyroplane
minelayer
monoplane
sailplane
turboprop

10 LETTERS

floatplane
gyrocopter
helicopter
hydroplane
microlight
paraglider
spaceplane
whirlybird

11 LETTERS

interceptor

2 WORDS

delta-wing
dive bomber
fighter-bomber
flying boat
hang-glider
jet plane
jumbo jet
jump jet
night fighter
prop jet
ski-plane
stealth bomber
swept-wing
troop carrier
water bomber

3 WORDS

hot-air balloon

Bridge, types of

1 WORD

aqueduct
catwalk
drawbridge
flyover
footbridge
gangway
overbridge
overpass
skyway
underbridge
viaduct

2 WORDS

air bridge
Bailey bridge
bascule bridge
cantilever bridge
catenary bridge
chain bridge
clapper bridge
floating bridge
girder bridge
humpback bridge
pontoon bridge
skew bridge
suspension bridge
swing bridge
toll bridge
transporter bridge

3 WORDS

cable-stayed bridge

Carriages and carts

1 WORD

3 LETTERS

cab
fly
gig

4 LETTERS

dray
trap

5 LETTERS

brake
buggy
coach
coupé
wagon

6 LETTERS

chaise
fiacre
hansom
landau

7 LETTERS

caravan
chariot
droshky
hackney
phaeton
tilbury
trailer
trishaw
tumbril

8 LETTERS

barouche
brougham
carriole
clarence
curricle
handcart
rickshaw
Victoria

9 LETTERS

cabriolet
wagonette

10 LETTERS

postchaise
stagecoach

2 WORDS

breaking cart
covered wagon
dog cart
ox cart

3 WORDS

coach-and-four

Coins

1 WORD

3 LETTERS

sou
yen

4 LETTERS

cent
dime
euro
mark
mite
peso
punt

5 LETTERS

angel
crown
ducat
franc
groat
noble
penny
pound
scudo

6 LETTERS

copper
denier
florin
guinea
nickel
peseta
tanner

7 LETTERS

centime
drachma
guilder
pfennig
quarter
solidus

8 LETTERS

denarius
doubloon
farthing
groschen
napoleon
shilling
sixpence

9 LETTERS

halfpenny
sovereign

10 LETTERS

krugerrand
sestertius

2 WORDS

half-crown
louis d'or
pound coin
threepenny bit

3 WORDS

fifty-pence piece
five-pence piece
ten-pence piece
twenty-pence piece
two-pence piece
two-pound coin

Motor vehicles

1 WORD

3 LETTERS

bus
cab
car
GTi
JCB
van

4 LETTERS

DUKW
Jeep
kart
tank
taxi
tram

5 LETTERS

buggy
coach
coupé
float
lorry
moped
rover
sedan
truck
wagon

6 LETTERS

bowser
camper
digger
estate
4WD
hearse
pickup
ragtop

saloon
tanker
tourer
waggon

7 LETTERS

flatbed
gritter
hardtop
minicab
omnibus
scooter
sidecar
snowcat
taxicab
tractor
trailer
utility
wrecker

8 LETTERS

dragster
dustcart
fastback
horsebox
microcar
roadster
runabout
supercar

9 LETTERS

ambulance
automatic
battlebus
bulldozer
cabriolet
charabanc
hatchback
limousine
minelayer
motorbike
notchback
scrambler
skimobile
sportster
superbike
supermini

10 LETTERS

automobile
bookmobile
juggernaut
motorcycle
roadroller
snowmobile
snowplough
tracklayer
trolleybus

11 LETTERS

caravanette
convertible
steamroller
transporter

12 LETTERS

autorickshaw
pantechnicon

2 WORDS

armoured car
articulated lorry
beach buggy
Black Maria
car transporter
concept car
delivery truck
dirt bike
dumper truck
dune buggy
earth mover
electric car
fire engine
forklift truck
go-kart
golf cart
hackney cab
half-track
hot rod
kit car
low-loader
milk float
motor caravan
off-roader
people carrier
personnel carrier
quad bike
racing car
rally car
recreational vehicle
refrigerated van
removal van
shooting brake
soft top
sports car
station wagon
stock car
stretch limo
three-wheeler
touring car
tow truck
trail bike
troop carrier
tuk-tuk
utility vehicle

3 WORDS

all-terrain vehicle
double-decker bus
four-by-four
four-wheel drive
heavy goods vehicle
large goods vehicle
multi-purpose vehicle
off-road vehicle
passenger-carrying vehicle
public service vehicle
sport utility vehicle

Parts of a bicycle

1 WORD

brake
carrier
chain
chainring
crank
derailleur
dynamo
fork
frame
frameset
freewheel
gear
gearwheel
groupset
handlebars
headset
hub
mudguard
pannier
pedal
reflector
saddle
spokes
sprocket
stabilizers
tyre
wheel

2 WORDS

brake block
brake caliper
chain gear
drop handlebars
inner tube
toe clip
twist-grip

Parts of a car

1 WORD

3 LETTERS

fan

4 LETTERS

axle
boot
dash
gear
horn
seat
sill
sump
trim
tyre
wing

5 LETTERS

brake
crank
hatch
pedal
shaft
stick
valve
wheel

6 LETTERS

bonnet
bumper
clutch
dimmer
engine
fascia
fender
gasket
grille
heater
hooter
hubcap
piston

7 LETTERS

battery
blinker
chassis
cowling
gearbox
muffler
spoiler
starter
sunroof
valance

8 LETTERS

bodywork
camshaft
cylinder
glovebox
headlamp
ignition
odometer
radiator
silencer
subframe
tailgate
wishbone

9 LETTERS

crankcase
dashboard

footbrake
gearstick
generator
handbrake
headlight
indicator
milometer
overdrive
propshaft
reflector
sidelight
transaxle

10 LETTERS

alternator
suspension
switchgear
tachometer
thermostat
underframe
windscreen
windshield

11 LETTERS

accelerator
carburettor
distributor
speedometer

12 LETTERS

transmission
turbocharger

2 WORDS

accelerator pedal
automatic choke
automatic transmission
bench seat
big end
brake disc
brake drum
brake light
brake pad
brake pedal
brake shoe
bucket seat
bull bar
cam belt
catalytic converter
clutch pedal
connecting rod
courtesy light
crumple zone
cylinder head
dip switch
disc brake
door mirror
drum brake
exhaust pipe
fan belt
filler cap
fog lamp
fog light
fuel gauge
fuel tank
gear change
gear lever
ignition key
instrument panel
licence plate
number plate
oil gauge
petrol tank
power brakes
power steering
propeller shaft
quarter-light
radial tyre
radiator grille
registration plate
roll bar
roof light
running board
seat belt
shock absorber
spare tyre
spare wheel
spark plug
starter motor
steering column
steering gear
steering rack
steering wheel
stop light
tail light
tie rod
tow bar
vanity mirror
windscreen washer
windscreen wiper
wing mirror

3 WORDS

anti-lock brake
anti-roll bar
central locking system
four-wheel drive
front-wheel drive
fuel injection pump
hazard warning lights
rack-and-pinion
rear-view mirror
rear-wheel drive

Parts of an aircraft

1 WORD

3 LETTERS

fin
pod
rib

4 LETTERS

flap
hold
nose
prop
skid
skin
tail
wing

5 LETTERS

belly
cabin
float
hatch
pylon
rotor

6 LETTERS

canard
canopy
engine
navaid
rudder
strake

7 LETTERS

aileron
airfoil
cockpit
cowling
fairing
pontoon
spoiler
winglet

8 LETTERS

aerofoil
airframe
airscrew
bulkhead
elevator
flexwing
fuselage
joystick
porthole
throttle
viewport

9 LETTERS

altimeter
astrodome
bombsight
empennage
mainplane
propeller
tailplane

10 LETTERS

stabilizer

13 LETTERS

undercarriage

2 WORDS

air brake
air intake
black box
bomb bay
control column
delta wing
drop tank
ejector seat
escape hatch
flight control
flight deck
flight recorder
fuel tank
heat shield
landing gear
landing lights
nose cone
rotary wing
rotor blade
swept wing
tail boom
tail fin
tail rotor
tail skid
wing tip

Parts of a ship

1 WORD

3 LETTERS

bow
oar

4 LETTERS

brig
head
hold
keel
mast
poop
prow
rail
skeg

5 LETTERS

berth
bilge
board
cabin
cleat
davit
hatch
stack
stern
thole
wheel
winch

6 LETTERS

anchor
bridge
dodger
fo'c'sle
funnel
galley
gunnel
hawser
pintle
rigger
rudder
strake
tiller

7 LETTERS

bollard
capstan
carline
cathead
counter
futtock
gangway
gudgeon
gunwale
keelson
maintop
painter
rowlock
scupper
spanker
transom

8 LETTERS

bulkhead
bullseye
bulwarks
hatchway
mainmast
outboard
planking
porthole
quarters
stringer
trunnion
wardroom
windlass

9 LETTERS

freeboard
gangplank
hawsepipe
mizzentop
outrigger
propeller
stanchion
starboard
stateroom
sternpost
stretcher
waterline

10 LETTERS

figurehead
forecastle
mizzenmast
stabilizer

11 LETTERS

centreboard
daggerboard

12 LETTERS

companionway
weatherboard

2 WORDS

after deck
bilge keel
boat deck
boiler room
chart room
companion ladder
crow's nest
engine room
fin keel
flight deck
guard rail
gun deck
half-deck
hawse hole
orlop deck
paddle wheel
pilot house
Plimsoll line
poop deck
promenade deck
propeller shaft
quarter rail
radio room
riding lamp
round house
weather deck

Roads and streets

1 WORD

3 LETTERS

row

4 LETTERS

drag
hard
lane
loop
pike
road
spur

5 LETTERS

byway
close
drive
route
strip

6 LETTERS

artery
avenue
boreen
bypass
byroad
feeder
parade
radial
street

7 LETTERS

flyover
freeway
highway
orbital
terrace
thruway
viaduct

8 LETTERS

Autobahn
broadway
causeway
clearway
corniche
crescent
driveway
motorway
overpass
ridgeway
speedway
trackway
turnpike

9 LETTERS

autopista
autoroute
boulevard
underpass

10 LETTERS

autostrada
backstreet
bottleneck
expressway
interstate
throughway

12 LETTERS

superhighway
thoroughfare

2 WORDS

approach road
A-road
arterial road
blind alley
B-road
cart track
dead end
drove road
dual carriageway
escape road
high road
high street
main drag
main road
main street
perimeter road
private road
rat run
red route
relief road
ring road
service road
side road
side street
skid road
slip road
through road
toll road
trunk road
unadopted road

3 WORDS

cul-de-sac
no through road
one-way street

Sails

1 WORD

course
foresail
forestaysail
foretopsail
genny
genoa
gunter
headsail
jib
jigger
kite
lugsail
mainsail
maintopsail
mizzen
moonraker
skysail
spanker
spinnaker
spritsail
staysail
studdingsail
topgallant
topsail
trysail

2 WORDS

fore-course
fore-royal
gaff foresail
gaff topsail
lateen sail
main course
royal sail
square sail
storm sail

3 WORDS

fore-topgallant sail

4 WORDS

fore-and-aft sail

Sellers of goods

5 LETTERS

baker (bread)

6 LETTERS

bowyer (archers' bows)
cutler (cutlery)
draper (fabrics)
grocer (food and small household goods)
hatter (hats)
hosier (hosiery)
mercer (fabrics)
pieman (pies)

7 LETTERS

butcher (meat)
florist (flowers)
furrier (furs)
glazier (glass for windows and doors)
milkman (milk and some other products)
woolman (wool)

8 LETTERS

chandler (candles)
clothier (clothes)
dairyman (dairy products)
fishwife (fish)
fletcher (arrows)
gunsmith (firearms)
jeweller (jewellery and jewels)
milliner (hats)
perfumer (perfume)
seedsman (seeds)

9 LETTERS

couturier (designer clothes)
fruiterer (fruit)
furnisher (furniture)
herbalist (medicinal herbs)
newsagent (newspapers, magazines, etc.)
patissier (cakes and pastries)
poulterer (poultry)
stationer (stationery)

10 LETTERS

apothecary (medicines)
fishmonger (fish)
ironmonger (hardware)
victualler (food and other provisions)

11 LETTERS

chocolatier (chocolate)
greengrocer (fruit and vegetables)
haberdasher (sewing items)
tobacconist (cigarettes and tobacco)

12 LETTERS

cheesemonger (cheese)
confectioner (sweets)
costermonger (fruit and vegetables)

Ships and boats

1 WORD

3 LETTERS

gig
tub
tug

4 LETTERS

brig
dhow
dory
junk
pink
pram
proa
punt
raft
scow
yawl

5 LETTERS

barge
butty
canoe
coble
ferry
gulet
jolly
kayak
ketch
liner
oiler
scull
shell
skiff
sloop
smack
xebec
yacht

6 LETTERS

barque
bireme
boatel
caique
coaler
cutter
dinghy
dugout
galley
lateen
launch
lugger
pedalo
rigger
sampan
sealer
slaver
tanker
tender
trader
whaler
wherry

7 LETTERS

airboat
bumboat
caravel
carrack
catboat
clipper
coaster
collier
coracle
cruiser
dredger
drifter
felucca
frigate
galleon
galliot
gondola
gunboat
iceboat
inboard
jetboat
jetfoil
lighter
monitor
pinnace
pirogue
pontoon
shallop
steamer
trawler
trireme
tugboat
warship

8 LETTERS

cockboat
corvette
flagship
flatboat
Indiaman
ironclad
keelboat
lifeboat
longboat
longship
mailboat
monohull
outboard
schooner
showboat
skipjack
trimaran
workboat

9 LETTERS

auxiliary
catamaran
destroyer
freighter
houseboat
hydrofoil
lightship
minelayer
multihull
outrigger
powerboat
privateer
riverboat
speedboat
steamboat
steamship

submarine
troopship
vaporetto
weekender
whaleboat

10 LETTERS

battleship
brigantine
hovercraft
hydroplane
minehunter
narrowboat
windjammer

11 LETTERS

barquentine
bathyscaphe
bathysphere
cockleshell
dreadnought
merchantman
minesweeper
quinquereme
submersible
supertanker

12 LETTERS

sternwheeler

13 LETTERS

battlecruiser

2 WORDS

aircraft carrier
bateau mouche
bulk carrier
cabin cruiser
cable ship
canal boat
capital ship
car ferry
cargo ship
coal ship
container ship
cruise ship
diving bell
double-ender
dragon boat
East Indiaman
E-boat
factory ship
flag boat
full-rigger
helicopter carrier
hermaphrodite brig
hospital ship
ice-breaker
inflatable dinghy
jet ski
landing craft
liberty boat
life raft
merchant ship
motor boat
motor yacht
oil tanker
paddle boat
paddle steamer
passenger ship
pedal boat
pilot boat
pocket battleship
Q-ship
rowing boat
rubber dinghy
safety boat
sailing boat
sailing ship
side-wheeler
single-hander
square-rigger
stake boat
supply ship
tall ship
torpedo boat
training ship
tramp steamer
troop carrier
U-boat
water bus
water taxi

3 WORDS

amphibious assault ship
amphibious landing craft
man-of-war
motor torpedo boat
sloop of war

4 WORDS

roll-on roll-off
ship of the line

Shops and restaurants

1 WORD

4 LETTERS

cafe
mall

5 LETTERS

diner
grill
store

6 LETTERS

arcade
bakery
bistro

bodega
eatery
outlet

7 LETTERS

canteen
cantina
carvery
chemist
grocery
taverna
toyshop

8 LETTERS

boutique
butcher's
crêperie
florist's
galleria
pawnshop
pharmacy
pizzeria
saddlery
takeaway

9 LETTERS

brasserie
cafeteria
chandlery
chophouse
drugstore
gastropub
grillroom
jeweller's
megastore
newsagent
outfitter
perfumery
roadhouse
stationer
trattoria

10 LETTERS

fishmonger
ironmonger
parfumerie
patisserie
rotisserie
steakhouse

11 LETTERS

charcuterie
hypermarket
supermarket
tobacconist

12 LETTERS

delicatessen
greengrocer's
haberdashery

13 LETTERS

confectioner's

2 WORDS

chain store
charity shop
corner shop
department store
discount store
drive-in
factory outlet
factory shop
heel bar
junk shop
milk bar
off-licence
retail outlet
retail park
shopping centre
shopping mall
snack bar
supper club
tea room
transport cafe
tuck shop
wine bar

3 WORDS

fast-food joint
ice-cream parlour

Trains and rolling stock

1 WORD

bogie
boxcar
caboose
car
carriage
coach
couchette
engine
express
flatcar
handcar
hopper
locomotive
maglev
metro
monorail
Pullman
railcar
shunter
sleeper
smokebox
smoker
tender
TGV

2 WORDS

armoured train
brake van
buffet car

bullet train
cable car
diesel-electric
diesel-hydraulic
diesel locomotive
dining car
double-header
electric train
freight train
goods train
goods wagon
guard's van
hospital train
light engine
mail coach
mail train
milk train
motor coach
observation car
pannier tank
passenger train
restaurant car
saddle tank
sleeping car
slow train
steam locomotive
steam train
stopping train
subway train
tank engine
traction unit
underground train
wagon-lit

3 WORDS

diesel multiple unit
high-speed train

Index

- Items in capital letters and **bold** type refer to the main subject headings in the book (e.g. **FAMOUS PEOPLE**).
- Items in small letters and **bold** type refer to subsection headings (e.g. **Mammals**).
- Items in *italics* refer to categories which are not headings in the book, but they act as pointers to a section or subsection in the book (in **bold**) which should give you the information you are looking for (e.g. *Film stars*: see **Actors**)

A

B

C

D

I

J

K

L

M

R

S

T

X Y Z

Lightning Source UK Ltd.
Milton Keynes UK
UKOW051849151112

202285UK00009B/14/P